Anonymus

A Reference Catalogue of Current Literature

Containing the Full Titles of Books Now in Print and on Sale

Anonymus

A Reference Catalogue of Current Literature
Containing the Full Titles of Books Now in Print and on Sale

ISBN/EAN: 9783742868633

Manufactured in Europe, USA, Canada, Australia, Japa

Cover: Foto ©Thomas Meinert / pixelio.de

Manufactured and distributed by brebook publishing software
(www.brebook.com)

Anonymus

A Reference Catalogue of Current Literature

A

REFERENCE CATALOGUE

OF

CURRENT LITERATURE

CONTAINING THE FULL TITLES OF

BOOKS NOW IN PRINT AND ON SALE

WITH THE PRICES AT WHICH THEY MAY BE

OBTAINED OF ALL BOOKSELLERS

London

J. WHITAKER, 12, WARWICK LANE, PATERNOSTER ROW.

Paris : HACHETTE & Co.   Berlin : ASHER & Co.

New York : SCRIBNER, WELFORD & Co.

MDCCCLXXIV.

ADVERTISEMENT.

A LONG Preface to a big book would be inexcusable, but as this volume is not unlikely to be the first of a long series, some introduction is necessary, and the best introduction will be the relation of its history.

In the early part of the present year I received from Mr. Frederick Leypoldt, of New York, a copy of his recently published " Uniform Trade List Annual," a handsome volume of above sixteen hundred pages, containing the catalogues of numerous American publishers, printed specially for the purpose of being inserted in the work. A somewhat similar volume had been previously published by Mr. Howard Challen, of Philadelphia, but that gentleman, like many other original thinkers, does not appear to have been so successful as Mr. Leypoldt, who took up and improved upon the work of his predecessor.

The " Uniform Trade List " was, to me, a work of great interest. I had long been a collector of catalogues, both American and English, but somehow it had been my general experience that just at the moment I had occasion to refer to a particular catalogue, that catalogue was not to be found. And this is the general experience of collectors, whether booksellers or bookbuyers. Here, then, in a convenient form, was a catalogue which, as far as the United States were concerned, saved me all further trouble. Herein was collected the lists of the Appletons, the Harpers, the Lippincotts, the Osgoods, and other well known houses, with the catalogues of publishers whose names had scarcely been heard in this country, and whose publications were entirely unknown. The unobtrusive simplicity of the plan was no inconsiderable merit ; the book required no pushing ; it told its own tale, and its usefulness was apparent to all.

It occurred to me that a similar work would be equally useful in this country, and this opinion was shared by most of the leading publishers, who expressed their willingness to aid in its production, and promised to prepare catalogues for the purpose. As is not unusual where the

co-operation of many persons is required, some are found less diligent than others, and it happened that by the time when all should have completed their quota more than half had failed. This was hardly fair to those publishers who had punctually fulfilled their engagements, although in justice to some of the defaulters, it must be said that the delay rested rather with the printers than the publishers. Patience, united with a little gentle pressure, eventually succeeded, and all the catalogues were at last collected; but between the receipt of the latest and the earliest there was an interval of nearly two months.

Originally the intention was to prefix a few pages indicating the general contents of the volume, and in whose lists books of a particular character were to be found. This would have been a comparatively easy task, and I was pledged to nothing more. On reflection, however, it was clear that a volume of three thousand pages, containing the full titles of perhaps fifty thousand books, required something better than a mere table of contents, and that without a general index it would be deprived of half its value as a Reference Catalogue of Current Literature. I therefore determined to furnish such an Index as should include all the chief books, and all the collections; in some instances under the names of Authors, but generally under the Subjects. This portion of the work has greatly exceeded the contemplated limits, and contains the short titles of no fewer than 14,000 books. Yet, although apparently so copious, regret will be felt that it is not more perfect. Even as it is, its preparation and printing has delayed the issue of the volume a month or six weeks—a delay which, now that the cause has been explained, will, it is hoped, be considered a valid excuse.

J. W.

London, 16th June, 1874.

LIST OF CONTRIBUTORS AND ADVERTISERS.

ALLEN, William H., and Co., 13, Waterloo Place, Pall Mall ... 1
ALLMAN, T. J., 463, Oxford Street 2
ASHER and Co., 13, Bedford Street, Covent Garden 3
BAGSTER, Samuel, and SONS, 15, Paternoster Row 4
BARTHES and LOWELL, 14, Great Marlborough Street ... ... adv.
BEAVIS, Alfred, 16, Paternoster Row ... ... adv.
BELL, George, and SONS, York Street, Covent Garden 5
——— Educational Literature 6
——— Bohn's Libraries 7
BEMROSE and SONS, 10, Paternoster Buildings 8
BENTLEY, Richard, and SON, New Burlington Street 9
BETTS, John, 115, Strand ... ... adv.
BLACK, Adam and Charles, North Bridge, Edinburgh 10
BLACKIE and SONS, 6, Paternoster Buildings, and Glasgow ... 11
BLACKWOOD, James, and Co., 8, Lovell's Court, Paternoster Row 12
BLACKWOOD, William, and SONS, Edinburgh and London... ... 13
BOOK SOCIETY, 28, Paternoster Row ... ... adv.
BRADBURY, AGNEW, and Co., 8, Bouverie Street ... ..: ... 14
BURNS, James, 15, Southampton Row ... ... adv.
BURNS and OATES, 17, Portman Street, and 63, Paternoster Row 15
BUMPUS, Edward, 5, Holborn Bars... ... ... adv.
BUSH, Robert John, 32, Charing Cross ... ... adv.
CAMBRIDGE UNIVERSITY PRESS 16
——— Specimens of Bibles and Prayer Books 17
CAMERON, John, 175, Buchanan Street, Glasgow ... ... adv.
CAMERON and FERGUSON, Glasgow and London 18
CASSELL, PETTER, and GALPIN, London, Paris, and New York ... 19
——— List of Illustrated Works 20
CHAMBERS, W. and R., London and Edinburgh 21
CHAPMAN and HALL, 193, Piccadilly 22
CHATTO and WINDUS, 74, Piccadilly 23
CHURCHILL, J. and A., New Burlington Street 24
CLARENDON PRESS, Oxford 75
CLARK, T. and T., 38, George Street, Edinburgh 25
COCKS, Robert, and Co., New Burlington Street ... ... adv.
COLLINS, William, SONS, & Co., London, Glasgow, and Edinburgh 26
CORNISH Brothers, New Street, Birmingham ... ... adv.

CORNISH, James, and SONS, London, Liverpool, and Dublin ... 27
CORNWALL'S, Dr., Educational Works ... ... *adv.*
CRAMER, J. B., and Co., 201, Regent Street ... ... *adv.*
DEAN and SON, St. Dunstan's Buildings, 160, Fleet Street ... *adv.*
DE LA RUE, Thomas, and Co., 109, Bunhill Row... ... ... *adv.*
DICKINSON and HIGHAM, Farringdon Street 28
DULAU and Co., 37, Soho Square ... ... *adv.*
EDMONSTON and DOUGLAS, 88, Princes Street, Edinburgh ... 29
FELLOWES, Thomas, 3, London House Yard ... ... *adv.*
FORTEY, William S., Monmouth Court, Seven Dials ... ... *adv.*
FROWD and Co., 53, Paternoster Row ... ... *adv.*
GALL and INGLIS, 30, Paternoster Row, and Edinburgh 30
GARDNER, William Wells, 2, Paternoster Buildings ... ... *adv.*
GOODALL and SON, Camden Works, Camden Town ... ... *adv.*
GRIFFIN, J., & Co., 15, Cockspur St., and The Hard, Portsmouth *adv.*
GROOMBRIDGE and SONS, 5, Paternoster Row 31
HACHETTE and Co., 18, King William Street, Strand, and Paris... 32
HADDON, John, and Co., 3, Bouverie Street 33
HAGGER, James, 67, Paternoster Row 34
HALL, J., and SONS, Cambridge 35
HARDWICKE, Robert, 192, Piccadilly 36
HARRISON and SONS, 59, Pall Mall, and 1, St. James's Street ... 37
HATCHARDS, 187, Piccadilly 38
HEYWOOD, Abel, and SON, 56, Oldham Street, Manchester ... 39
HEYWOOD, John, 141, Deansgate, Manchester 40
HODDER and STOUGHTON, 27, Paternoster Row 41
HOULSTON and SONS, 7, Paternoster Square 42
HURST and BLACKETT, 13, Great Marlborough Street 43
ISBISTER, William, and Co., 56, Ludgate Hill 44
JARROLD and SONS, 3, Paternoster Buildings 45
JOHNSTON, William and A. Keith, Edinburgh and London ... 46
KELLAWAY and Co., 10, Warwick Lane 47
KEMPSTER, John, and Co., 9, St. Bride's Avenue, Fleet Street ... *adv.*
KENT, William, and Co., 23, Paternoster Row ... ... *adv.*
KERBY and ENDEAN, 190, Oxford Street ... ... *adv.*
KING, Henry S., and Co., 65, Cornhill, and 12, Paternoster Row... 48
KNIGHT and Co., 90, Fleet Street ... ... *adv.*
LAURIE, Thomas, Cockburn Street, Edinburgh 49
LAYTON, Charles and Edwin, 150, Fleet Street 50
LETTS, SONS, and Co., 8, Royal Exchange... 51
LOCKWOOD and Co., 7, Stationers' Hall Court 52
———— List of Weale's Rudimentary Series 53
———— List of Educational Works... 54
———— List of Popular Works 55
LONGMANS, GREEN, READER, and DYER, 39, Paternoster Row ... 56

MACK, William, 38, Park Street, Bristol ... ... — 57
MacGLASHAN and GILL, 50, Upper Sackville Street, Dublin ... 58
MACINTOSH, William, 24, Paternoster Row ... ... adv.
MACMILLAN and Co., 29, Bedford Street, Strand 59
MacLEOD'S Approved Arithmetical Works ... ... — adv.
MacPHUN, W. R., and SON, Glasgow and London ... — 60
MARR, John S., and SONS, 194, Buchanan Street, Glasgow — 61
MARLBOROUGH, E., & Co., Ave Maria Lane, and 14, Warwick Lane 62
MASTERS, Joseph, and Co., 78, New Bond Street ... ... — 63
MILNER and Co., Paternoster Row, and Halifax ... ... — 64
MORGAN and SCOTT, 12, Paternoster Buildings ... ... — 65
MOZLEY, John and Charles, 6, Paternoster Row ... — ... 66
MULLAN, William, Belfast ... ... — ... ... adv.
MURBY, Thomas, 32, Bouverie Street ... — — ... 67
MURRAY, John, Albemarle Street ... — — — — 68
NELSON, Thomas, and SONS, London, Edinburgh, and New York 69
NICHOLSON, W., and SONS, Wakefield 70
NIMMO, William P., 14, King William Street, and Edinburgh ... 71
NISBET, James, and Co., 21, Berners Street ... — ... 72
NUTT, David, 270, Strand ... — — — ... 73
———— List of Teubner's Greek and Latin Classics ... — 74
OXFORD CLARENDON PRESS ... ... — — 75
PARKER, James, and Co., Oxford, and 377, Strand 76
PARTRIDGE and Co., 9, Paternoster Row 77
PHILIP, George, and SON, 32, Fleet Street, and Liverpool ... 78
PICKERING, Basil Montague, 196, Piccadilly 79
PLATNAUER, J., Aldine Chambers, 13, Paternoster Row ... ... adv.
RAMAGE, John, and Co., 8, Warwick Lane... ... ... adv.
REEVE, Lovell, and Co., 5, Henrietta Street, Covent Garden ... 80
REEVES and TURNER, 196, Strand ... ... adv.
RELIGIOUS TRACT SOCIETY, 56, Paternoster Row 81
RIVERS, George, Aldine Chambers, 13, Paternoster Row... ... adv.
RIVINGTONS, London, Oxford, and Cambridge 82
ROUTLEDGE, George, and SONS, Broadway, Ludgate Hill... ... 83
SANGSTER, James, and Co., 31, Paternoster Row 84
SHAW, John F., and SONS, 48, Paternoster Row 85
SMITH, C., and SON, 63, Charing Cross 86
SMITH, J. Russell, 36, Soho Square... 87
SMITH, ELDER, and Co., 15, Waterloo Place 88
SNOW, John, and Co., 2, Ivy Lane, Paternoster Row 89
SOCIETY FOR PROM. CHRISTIAN KNOWLEDGE, 77, Great Queen St. 90
SOTHERAN, Henry, and Co., Strand, Piccadilly, and Little Tower St. 91
SPON, E. & F. N., 48, Charing Cross, and Broome St., New York 92
STANFORD, Edward, 6, Charing Cross 93
STEVENS and HAYNES, Bell Yard, Temple Bar 94

STEVENSON, Henry, and Co., 65, Paternoster Row ... ... *adv.*
STEVENSON, Thomas G., Antiquarian Bookseller, Edinburgh ... *adv.*
STEWART, Charles J., 11, King William Street, Strand ... ... *adv.*
STOCK, Elliot, 62, Paternoster Row... ... ... *adv.*
STRAHAN, Alexander, 12, Paternoster Row 95
SUNDAY SCHOOL UNION, 56, Old Bailey 96
SUTTABY, Robert and Arthur, 2, Amen Corner, Paternoster Row *adv.*
TEGG, William, Pancras Lane, Cheapside ... ... *adv.*
TINSLEY Brothers, 18, Catherine Street, Strand 97
TINSLEY, Samuel, 10, Southampton Street, Strand... ... ... *adv.*
TRÜBNER and Co., 57, Ludgate Hill 98
TUBBS and BROOK, 11, Market Street, Manchester 99
VAN VOORST, John, 1, Paternoster Row .... *adv.*
VIRTUE, SPALDING, and DALDY, 26, Ivy Lane, Paternoster Row... 100
WALKER, William, and SONS, Otley, Yorkshire 101
WARD, Marcus, and Co., 67, Chandos Street, Strand, and Belfast... 102
WARD, LOCK, and TYLER, Warwick House, Paternoster Row ... 103
———— List of Moxon, Son, and Co.'s Publications 104
WARNE, Frederick, and Co., Bedford Street, Strand 105
WASHBOURNE, R., 18, Paternoster Row 106
WATERLOW and SONS, 65, London Wall ... ... *adv.*
WESLEYAN CONFERENCE OFFICE, 2, Castle Street, City Road ... 107
WHELDON, John, 4, Paternoster Row ... ... *adv.*
WHITAKER, Joseph, 12, Warwick Lane, Paternoster Row... ... *adv.*
WHITTAKER and Co., Ave Maria Lane 108
WILLIAMS and SON, Eton ... ... *adv.*
WILLIAMS and NORGATE, 14, Henrietta Street, and Edinburgh ... 109
WILLOUGHBY, Richard, 29, Paternoster Row ... ... *adv.*
WILSON, Effingham, 11, Royal Exchange 110
YAPP and HAWKINS, 70, Welbeck Street, Cavendish Square ... 111

INDEX

TO THE CHIEF WORKS CONTAINED IN

The Reference Catalogue of Current Literature.

The various Catalogues are arranged in alphabetical order, and the figures indicate the page in each publishers' list, except where, instead of a figure, the letter *a* follows the name: the reference in that case is to the Advertisements at the end of the volume.

The Reader is requested to observe that only the chief books in the different publishers' lists are given; and, as a general rule, the subject rather than the author's name. To index every book was impossible; but every class and every subdivision is carefully noted, and there will be but little difficulty in finding what is required.

Abbeychurch; or, Self Control .. *Mozley* 1
Abbeys and Castles, Timbs...... *Warne* 23
Abbott's August Stories .... *Isbister* 5
—— Histories .... *Allman* 3
—— June Stories .... *Isbister* 23
—— Religious Books............ *Allman* 3
—— Works for the Young.... *Milner* 2
Abbott (Rev. Dr.) Works by .. *Macmillan*.... 1
Abd-el-Kader, A Biography .... *Chapman* 11
Abeokuta .... *Tinsley Bros.* 6
Abercrombie's Essays .... *Edmonston*.. 1
—— (John) Works by .... *Murray* 1
Abingdon, an Account of........ *Parker* 53
Able to Save .... *Isbister* 3
Abolition of the State .... *Trubner* 12
Abominations of Modern Society. *Nickolson* .. 2
Aborigines, Anecdotes of the .... *Partridge* 8
Above Rubies................ *Nelson* 10
Absence of Precision............ *Parker* 6
Absent Man................ *J. Blackwood* 29
Absolution, Power of Priesthood.. *Parker* 3
Abyssinia, Adventures in........ *Isbister* 11
—— Bruce's Travels in........ *Black* 9
—— Blanc .... *Smith & El.* 1
—— British Expedition, Hozier.. *Macmillan*.. 16
—— Expedition, Markham .... *Macmillan*.. 23
—— Geography and Zoology.. *Macmillan*.. 4
—— Nile Tributaries of .... *Macmillan*.. 2
—— Record of Expedition to .. *Harrison*.... 13
—— Three Years in .... *Murray* 25
Acadian Geology, Dawson .... *Macmillan*.. 9
Accepted Addresses .... *Tinsley Bros.* 9
Accidents, First Help in .... *Hardwicke*.. 14
Account Keeping .... *E. Wilson* .. 5
Ackworth Vocabulary .... *Isbister* 3
Acoustics, Light and Heat ...... *Chambers* .. 17
—— Davis .... *Collins* 7
—— Donkin .... *Clar. Press*.. 25
—— Light and Heat .... *J. Heywood* . 61
—— Wonders of .... *Cassell* 8
Across the River Series ...... *Nimmo* 25
—— the Ferry............ *Hodder* 19
—— the Sea .... *S. S. Union.* 3
Acrostics (Double) A. N. E. .... *Mozley* 6
—— Double .... *Lockwood* .. 45
—— by Various Hands.... *Hatchard* .. 11
—— from the Poets .... *Hatchard* .. 13
—— from the Poets .... *Routledge* .. 7
Actors, Representative .... *Warne* 23
Acts of the Apostles .... *Parker* 10
—— of the Apostles, Alexander.. *Nisbet* 3
—— Biscoe on the .... *Clar. Press.* 13
—— Explained to Children .. *Hatchard* .. 2
—— Lessons from .... *Nisbet* 3

Acts, Apocryphal .... *Williams*.... 16
Actuarial Tables, Thomson ...... *Layton*...... 15
Adam and the Adamite.......... *Bentley* 10
Adam's Disobedience .... *Williams*.... 6
Adams' Works on Nat. History.. *Groombridge* 13
Adams (H. C.) Juvenile Books by *Routledge* .. 31
—— (H. C.) School Books ...... *Nutt*...... d
—— (Rev. W.) Works by ...... *Masters* 1
Adams's Sacred Allegories ...... *Rivingtons*.. 17
Adam's Peak .... *Stanford* 63
Addison's (Julia) Juvenile Books *Marlborough* 6
Addison's Works............ *Bohn's Lib.* 11
Addresses to Christ, Young Women *Yapp* 5
—— to Sunday School Teachers.. *Wesleyan* .. 55
Administrations of Gt. Britain.... *Smith & El.* 5
Administration of the Holy Spirit *Parker* 5
Admirals, Lives of .... *Hatchard* .. 24
—— British, Lives of .... *J. Blackwood* 13
Admiralty Charts .... *Stanford* 47
—— Publications .... *Murray* 6
Adrift in a Boat.............. *Warne* 28
Adulterations of Food .... *Isbister* 5
Adventure and Incident Library.. *Warne* 28
Adventures of Allan .... *Smith & El.* 3
—— in the Ice.............. *Virtue & Co* 13
—— in Search of a Religion .... *Washbourne* 3
—— of Dr. Brady .... *Tinsley Bros* 10
—— of Verdant Green .... *J. Blackwood* 18
—— Wonderful .... *Cassell* 8
Advent, Guide for Passing Holily *Parker* 31
—— Readings for .... *Masters* 6
—— Sermons, Alford .... *Hodder* 13
—— Sermons, Tomlin .... *Masters* 16
Advertising, History of.......... *Chatto* 2
Aeronautics (Practical) .... *Spon* 2
Æschyli Eumenides, Drake ...... *Macmillan*.. 1
Æschylus Agamemnon, Davies.. *Williams*.... 1
Æschylus, Orestea, English .... *J. R. Smith* 1
—— Paley .... *Whittaker* .. 1
Æsop (Christian) .... *Burns* 10
Æsop's Fables, by James........ *Murray* 1
—— Fables .... *Routledge* .. 31
—— Fables .... *Warne* 20
—— Griset .... *Cassell* 3
Afar in the Forest .... *Nelson* 15
Afghanistan, Antiq. and Coins of *Williams*.... 10
Affghanistan, Sale's Brigade in .. *Murray* 27
Afflicted, Companion for the .... *Nisbet* 10
Africa (Central) Travels in ...... *Tinsley Bros.* 8
—— Climate of West.......... *Churchill* .. 21
—— East, Wanderings in........ *Hodder* 3
—— Equatorial .... *Murray* 10
—— Life and Adventures ...... *Chatto* 13
—— Livingstone's Travels .... *Murray* 22

Africa, Missionary Labours in　..　Wesleyan..　47
—— Park's Travels in ....　Black ......　15
—— (Savage) ....　Smith & El.　17
—— S. E. Gold Fields of ......　Cassell......　6
—— South, Eleven Years..........　Snow ......　15
—— South (G. Cumming's)......　Murray ....　9
—— South, Missionary Labours..　Snow ......　11
—— South, Zoology of......　Smith & El.　19
—— (Tropical) Flora of ....　Reeve ......　5
—— Walk Across ....　W. Blackw'd　10
—— West, Thomas ....　Marlborough　16
—— West, Wit and Wisdom from　Tinsley Bros.　6
—— (Wilds of) ....　Nelson ......　6
African Cruiser, The ....　King ......　16
—— Desert, Travels in ....　Asher ......　6
—— (E.) Slave Trade, Tale of　Nisbet ......　3
—— Sketch Book ....　Smith & El.　17
—— (South) Affairs ....　Wesleyan ..　42
—— (South) Geography ......　Stanford....　55
—— Travellers, Great ....　Routledge ..　29
After Dark ....　Smith & El.　4
—— Ophir, Lindley ....　Cassell......　5
Against the Stream ....　Ibister ......　3
—— Wind and Tide ....　Smith & El.　13
Agassiz, Works by ....　Trubner ....　1
Age of the Martyrs ....　Parker......　12
—— World, Wallan ....　Smith & El.　21
Agincourt ....　J. R. Smith　1
Agnes of Sorrento ....　Smith & El.　22
Agricultural Com. of Mid. Ages　Williams....　10
—— (Royal) Soc. Journal........　Murray ....　1
—— Calculator ....　Blackie......　11
—— Labourers ....　Hodder ....　0
—— Labourer (The) ....　Chapman ..　19
Agriculture (Ancient and Modern)　Virtue ......　19
—— Cyclopædia of ....　Blackie......　11
—— Encyclopædia ....　Longmans ..　33
—— and Farming ....　Routledge ..　1
—— Johnston ....　W. Blackw'd　30
—— and Prices in England......　Clar. Press..　16
—— Rudimentary Works on .....　Lockwood ..　25
—— Rudimentary Works on ..　W. Blackw'd　53
—— Works on..........　Bradbury ..　9
—— Chemistry ....　Bohn's Lib..　19
—— Chemistry, Morfit ....　Trubner....　20
Agriculturist' Journal ....　Blackie......　11
Aguilar's (Grace) Works ....　Groombridge　3
Ahmedabad, Architecture of....　Murray ....　14
Ahn's Method, Buchheim & Rose　Williams....　1
—— Method of French ....　Nutt ......　22
—— French, Neveu ....　Nutt ......　1
—— of German, Author's own Ed.　Nutt......　11
—— System of Languages ......　Allman ....　3
—— of Foreign Languages......　Trubner ....　1
Aidé (H.) Works of ....　Smith &
Aide-Memoire to Military Science　Lockwood ..　12
Aids to Faith ....　Murray ....　1
—— during Labour ....　Churchill ..　29
—— to Prayer ....　Ibister ......　3
—— to the Spiritual Life ......　Wesleyan ..　42
Ainger (Rev. Alf.) Sermons......　Macmillan..　1
Air and Rain ....　Longmans ..　20
—— and Water, Impurities of....　Hardwicke..　16
Airy (Sir G. B.) Works by ......　Macmillan..　1
Akerman (J. Y.) Works ......　J. R. Smith　1
A. K. H. B., Works by ......　Longmans ..　15
Alaska, Travels in ....　Murray ....　32
Albania (Journey through) ......　Murray ....　1
Albert Memorial (The) ......　Murray ....　1
Albert's (Prince) Speeches ......　Murray ....　5
Albert N'yanza, Basin of the Nile　Macmillan..　2
Album of Pictures ....　Bradbury ..　4
—— Photo-Scrap ....　Remrose ....　9
Albums, Oleographs, &c ....　Ward&Lock　24
Alcoholic Diseases, Macleod....　Churchill....　25
—— Intoxication, Mareet......　Churchill....　25
Alice Stewart ....　S. S. Union.　5
Aldine Poets..........　Bell ......　30
Aldrich's Logic, Mansel ......　Rivingtons ..　7
Alec Devlin ....　Warne ......　30
Alexander (Mrs. E. F.) Works ..　Masters ....　1
—— (Rev. J. A.) Works ......　Nisbet ....　3
—— (Sir W.) Poetical Works ..　Sotheran ....　4
Alford's Greek Testament ......　Rivingtons..　1
—— Greek Testament ....　　　44

Alford's Life ....　Rivingtons..　24
—— New Test English Readers　Rivingtons ..　1
—— Brief Notes on ....　Macmillan..　38
—— Queen's English ....　Hatchard ..　16
—— Works ....　Ibister ......　3
—— Works ....　Hodder ....　3
Alfred (King) Memorials of ..　Russell Smith　2
—— the Great ....　Bohn's Lib..　12
—— Hughes ....　Macmillan ..　35
Algæ, British Marine ....　Van Voorst　2
—— Collector's Handy Book of..　Hardwicke..　2
Algebra, Bryce ....　Black ......　9
—— Elementary..........　J. Heywood.　2
—— Elements of..........　Cassell......　12
—— Elements of, Keiland ......　Black ......　13
—— Elementary Works on......　Laurie ......　2
—— for Junior Classes ......　Stanford....　58
—— for Junior Classes ......　Chambers ..　15
—— and Trigonometry, Griffin ..　Longmans ..　21
—— Introduction to, Young ....　Mozley......　15
Algebraical Errors of Observation　Macmillan..　1
—— Problems, Bland ....　Whittaker ..　13
—— Test Cards ....　Murby ....　6
Algeria in 1871, Herbert ......　Bentley ....　13
Alice de Burgh ....　Virtue ......　8
—— Beresford ....　Masters ....　1
—— Lee ....　Morgan ....　2
—— Middleton ....　S. S. Union.　9
—— Stanley ....　Nelson ......　10
Alice's Adventures in Wonderland　Macmillan..　6
Alison's Europe ....　W. Blackw'd　2
"All about it" Books (Beeton's)　Ward&Lock　6
All but Lost ....　S. S. Union.　7
—— Round the World, Doré's Illus.　Collins ....　2
Allcott (Louisa M.) Novels by....　Routledge ..　42
Allegories, Tales, &c...........　Rivingtons..　17
—— Monro ....　Masters ....　17
Allegories ....　Mozley......　11
Allen and Cornwall's Grammar ..　Cornwall....　0
Allen and Harry ....　Warne ......　29
—— (Rev. R.) Sermons by ......　Nisbet ....　3
Allibone's Dictionary ....　Trubner ....　2
Allingham's Poems..........　Macmillan..　2
—— (W.) Poems ....　Bell ......　35
Allison's (M. A.) England ......　Jarrold ....　3
Alloys (Useful) ....　Chatto ....　30
Almanack, Whitaker's ....　Adult......　0
Almost Faultless..........　Nimmo ....　12
A. L. O. E.'s Series ....　Nelson ......　19
—— Story Books ....　Nelson ......　9
Alone with Jesus..........　Hodder ....　4
—— to the Alone ....　Williams....　4
Alphabets, Ornamental ....　Lockwood ..　15
Alphabet for Unwritten Languages　Williams....　8
Alpha ; or, God in Matter ..　Tubbs ......　2
Alpine Club Maps ....　Longmans ..　38
—— Flowers ....　W. Blackw'd　54
—— for English Gardens ......　Murray ....　21
—— Guides, Ball ....　Longmans ..　38
—— Plants, Wooster ....　Bell ......　17
—— Plants, Rambles in Search of　Macmillan..　22
Alps, Hours of Exercise in the....　Longmans ..　31
—— Scrambles among the......　Murray ....　37
Alsace, Tales from ....　Nisbet ....　34
Altar, Domestic (The) ....　Cassell......　4
—— Service Book ....　Sotheran....　4
Alton Sermons..........　Ibister ....　20
Amadis of Gaul ....　J. R. Smith　2
Amateur Casual, Note Book of the　King ....　10
—— Mechanic's Workshop......　Trubner ....　1
Amazon and Rio Negro ......　Macmillan..　39
—— (River) Naturalists on ......　Murray ....　3
—— on the Banks ....　Nelson ......　6
—— Voyage up ....　Murray ....　10
Amarulu, Religious System of....　Trubner ....　7
America, Autumn Tour in ......　King ......　5
—— and American Church ......　Masley......　2
—— Bancroft's History ......　Routledge ..　21
—— Birds of ....　Morgan ....　2
—— Central, Described ....　Stanford....　50
—— Central, Hardman ......　W. Blackw'd　13
—— Central, Travels in ......　Trubner ....　20
—— before Columbus ....　Nisbet ......　7
—— Cricket in ....　Tinsley Bros.　4
—— Discovery of Great West....　Murray ....　4

America. English Colonization of *Ishister* 32
—— Federal Government........ *Macmillan* .. 11
—— Indian Tribes of .... *Sotheran* .. 25
—— Johnston .... *W. Blackw'd* 17
—— First Impressions of........ *Hodder* 10
—— Impressions of .... *Tinsley Bros.* 7
—— Independence to Secession. *Macmillan* .. 21
—— The Lifted Rocks of ..... *Trubner* 7
—— Mackay's History........ *Virtue* 20
—— Men and Manners....... *W. Blackw'd* 12
—— Methodism in........ *Wesleyan C.* 43
—— My Diary in Midst of War.. *Tinsley Bros.* 7
—— New .... *Hurst* 16
—— New Tracks in North...... *Chapman* .. 11
—— North, Notes on .... *Stanford* .. 42
—— Political History ...... *King* 32
—— Prohibitory Legislation in . *Tinsley Bros.* 8
—— Public Works, in French . *Spon* 32
—— Railroad Manual ...... *Trubner* .. 30
—— Recent Visit to ...... *Wesleyan C.* 43
—— Republican Government.... *Murray* .. 19
—— Schools and Colleges...... *Macmillan* .. 17
—— South, Notes on ...... *Stanford* .. 42
—— Southern States since War.. *Macmillan* .. 33
—— Zincke's Winter, U.S. .... *Murray* .. 32
American Anecdotes .... *Routledge* .. 3
—— Civil War, Fletcher ..... *Bentley* ... 6
—— Clergy, Anecdotes of ..... *Morgan* 2
—— Comic Books .... *Routledge* .. 2
—— Land, Lake, &c., Scenery.. *Virtue* 13
—— Law Works............ *Stevens* ... 19
—— Library .... *Routledge* .. 1
—— Life, Sam Slick ...... *Hurst* 13
—— Nation, the Making of...... *Stanford* .. 60
—— National Preacher....... *Dickinson* .. 10
—— Plantations, 1600 to 1700.. *Chatto* ... 28
—— (S.) Plants, Miers ...... *Williams* .. 9
—— War, Blockade Running ... *Chatto* ... 26
—— War, Cartoons .... *Chatto* 2
—— War, Ross .... *W. Blackw'd* 37
—— War, Von Borcke ..... *W. Blackw'd* 32
Americanisms, De Vere ...... *Trubner* .. 26
—— Dictionary of .... *Trubner* ... 3
Americans at Home .... *Marr* 25
Ammunition, Descrip. Treatise on *Harrison* .. 11
Among My Books, Lowell ... *Macmillan* .. 24
Amusement and Instruction .. *Marr* 12
—— In-door and Out-door .... *Warne* ... 35
Amusing Hours, by Miss Sinclair *Houlston* .. 25
Amy Wilton .... *MacLhun* .. 12
Amye Robsart and Leicester .. *Russell Smith* 2
Anacreon, Illustrated ...... *Chatto* ... 2
Analecta Christiana ...... *Parker* ... 7
Analysis of Hooker ...... *Macintosh* .. 0
Anatomy, Descriptive and Surgical *Longmans* .. 26
—— Elements, Quain ...... *Longmans* .. 26
—— Illustrations of .... *Smith & El.* 6
—— Works on .... *Churchill* ... 0
Anatomical Plates, Quain .. *Smith & El.* 17
—— Remembrancer........ *Churchill* .. 7
Ancient Britain, Religion of .. *Wesleyan C.* 49
—— Britons, by Barber ..... *Russell Smith* 5
—— Classics for English Readers *W. Blackw'd* 42
—— Doctrinal Treatises, &c.... *Parker* .. 7
—— Faiths, Inman .... *Trubner* ... 4
—— History, Chart of ...... *Parker* ... 63
—— History, Lenormant...... *Asher* 5
—— Lights, Kerr .... *Murray* .. 19
—— Nineveh .... *S.S. Union.* 7
—— Pagan and Christ. Symbolism *Trubner* ... 4
—— Rolls of Arms........ *Russell Smith* 2
—— Stone Implements ...... *Longmans* .. 24
—— World, History of ...... *Murray* .. 29
Anderdon (Father) Works by .. *Burns* ... 16
Andersen (Hans) Library .... *Routledge* .. 38
—— (Hans) Fairy Tales ...... *Bell* 22
—— Fairy Tales.......... *Warne* ... 20
—— Stories .... *Routledge* .. 19
Anderson (Rev. Wm.) Life .. *Hodder* .. 24
Andrewes's (Bp.) Man. for Sick *Rivingtons* . 1
Anecdota Literaria ...... *Russell Smith* 2
Anecdote (World of) ...... *Hodder* ... 90
—— Century of .... *Warne* ... 23
—— Series .... *Rel. Tr. Soc.* 2
—— Library.......... *Routledge* .. 3

Anecdotes, Book of 300 ..... *Burns* 3
—— for Family Reading ..... *Kellaway* .. 9
—— Literary and Scientific .. *J. Blackwood* 3
—— in Natural History .... *Partridge* .. 4
—— and Sayings .... *Macmillan* .. 14
—— for the Young ...... *Nicholson* .. 12
Angelo (M.) Drawings at Oxford *Clar. Press.* 17
—— Original Studies ...... *Bell* 7
Angel's Song (The) ...... *Ishister* ... 29
Angels and Heaven ...... *Hodder* .. 25
Angler, Modern Practical.... *Warne* 24
—— (Practical) Trout Fishing .. *Black* 31
—— Walton's) Pocket Ed. .. *Bell* 33
—— and Tourist's Guide to Scot *Black* ... 32
—— The Young .... *Routledge* .. 37
Angler's Manual, Hofland .... *Bohn's Lib.* 9
Anglers, Hints to, Scotland.... *Black* 11
Angling .... *B. Pickering.* 2
Angling .... *Russell Smith* 2
—— Fly Fishing .... *J. Murray* .. 9
—— Fly Fishing ...... *Longmans* .. 43
—— Francis .... *Longmans* .. 41
Angling Songs .... *W. Blackw'd* 7
Anglican Divines, Teaching of . *J. Parker* .. 3
—— Orders .... *J. Parker* .. 3
Anglicans, Difficulties of .... *Burns* 15
Anglo-Catholic Library ..... *Parker* ... 16
Anglo-Saxon .... *Russell Smith* 3
—— Dictionary .... *Clar. Press.* 4
—— Grammar, Rask ...... *Trubner* .. 25
—— Witness for Holy Com... *Rivingtons* .. 5
Anglo-Saxons, History of .... *Bohn's Lib.* 14
Angus (Dr. J.) Works by .... *Rel. Tr. Soc.* 2
Animal Creation, 500 Illustrations *Warne* ... 15
—— Electricity .... *Churchill* .. 30
—— Instinct, Wonders of .... *Cassell* .. 8
—— Kingdom .... *Cassell* ... 12
—— Life, Forms of ...... *Clar. Press.* 27
—— Locomotion .... *King* ... 8
—— Mechanics .... *Longmans* .. 21
—— Physiology, Cleland .... *Collins* .. 8
—— Physiology .... *J. Heywood* 30
—— Physiology .... *Bohn's Lib.* 18
—— Physiology .... *Chambers* .. 17
—— Plagues, Fleming .... *Chapman* .. 18
—— Sagacity, Hall ...... *Partridge* .. 2
—— Sagacity .... *Routledge* .. 31
Animals, Anatomy and Physiology *Longmans* .. 22
—— Anatomy of Domesticated.. *Churchill* .. 20
—— Anecdotes of ...... *Bell* 23
—— and Birds, Wild ...... *Nimmo* ... 15
—— Classification of ...... *Churchill* .. 22
—— Divine Wisdom in Form.. *Nisbet* 5
—— Domestic .... *Ward & Lock* 18
—— Domestic and Wild .... *Stanford* .. 41
—— Grotesque .... *Longmans* .. 25
—— Habits, &c.......... *J. Blackwood* 12
—— Habitations of ...... *Longmans* .. 23
—— Intelligence of ...... *Chapman* .. 20
—— Life, Studies on ...... *Smith & El.* 15
—— Reason in .... *Reeve* ... 13
—— Sketches and Anecdotes.... *Routledge* .. 33
—— Some Talk about .... *Ishister* .. 41
—— Stories about ...... *Cassell* ... 10
—— Stories about ...... *Partridge* .. 14
—— Summary of Extinct...... *Black* 15
—— (Wild) Wolfe ...... *Macmillan* .. 41
—— Wild .... *Ward & Lock* 13
—— Wild .... *Ward & Lock* 8
Anjou (Margaret of) Life & Times *Tinsley Bros.* 6
Anley (C.) Tales by ...... *Hatchard* .. 2
Anna Lee .... *Nelson* ... 14
Annals of Our Time, Irving .. *Macmillan* .. 17
—— of a Quiet Neighbourhood.. *Ishister* ... 27
—— of the Rescued ...... *Nisbet* 2
Anne of Austria, Regency of.. *Tinsley Bros.* 5
Annie Warleigh's Fortunes.. *Smith & El.* 2
Annual Register .... *Rivingtons* .. 26
—— (The) 1842—61 ...... *Sotheran* .. 2
Annuals, Steel Plates ...... *Allman* .. 4
Annuities, Tables of, Farr .... *Harrison* .. 12
Annuity Tables, Chisholm .... *Layton* ... 8
—— Tables, Henry ...... *Layton* ... 10
—— Tables, Lang ...... *Layton* ... 13
Another England .... *Ishister* ... 7

Ante-Nicene Library............ Clark 6
Anthems .... Parker...... 38
Anthology, Sacred............. Trubner ... 8
Anthony Waymouth .... Ward&Lock 8
Anthropology .... Longmans .. 16
Antidote to Fear.............. Nisbet 16
Antipodes and Round the World. Hatchard .. 5
Antiquarian Publications...... Stevenson .. a
Antiquities (Anglo-Saxon) .... Parker..... 51
—— (Northern)............. Parker..... 51
—— Roman and Greek, Rich.. Longmans .. 12
Antitypical Parallels.......... Kellaway ... 6
Aphorisms, Book of .... MacPhun ... 7
Apocalypse, Lect. on Maurice . Macmillan... 24
—— (The) Interpret. Kelly ... Nisbet 20
Apollos ; or the Way of God ... Parker 3
Apologetics .... Clark 10
Apoplexy, Mushet on .... Churchill .. 27
Apostles, The Conflicts of Holy Nutt 5
— of Mediæval Europe..... Macmillan .. 35
Apostles' Prayer (The)........ Morgan 4
—— (The) by Renan......... Trubner ... 25
—— Stories of .... Warne 29
—— Creed .... Rivingtons. 12
—— Creed, Ken (See also Creed) Murray 16
Apostles, Character & Conduct of Murray 29
—— Events in Lives of....... Jarrold 7
—— Preaching to Jews and Gen. Hatchard .. 2
Apostolic Church, History of... Clark 17
—— Epistles .... Hall 4
—— Fathers, Hoole .... Rivingtons.. 12
—— Succession, Conversation on Mozley 10
—— Times and their Lessons... Hatchard .. 24
Apostolical Succession .... Rivingtons. 11
Apparitions, Crosland .... Trubner ... 9
Apple and its Varieties .... Groombridge 8
Approved Educational Works .. M'Leod .... a
Aquarium .... Routledge .. 9
—— Book of................. Groombridge 9
Arabia (Alps of) .... King....... 4
—— A Year's Journey in...... Macmillan .. 27
Arabian Nights .... J. Blackwood 3
—— Nights .... Milner 2
—— Nights .... Burns 21
—— Nights .... Warne 20
—— Entertainments .... Nimmo 6
—— (Family) .... Routledge .. 30
—— (Family) .... Ward&Lock 3
—— Tales.................. Burns 21
—— Tales.................. King....... 31
—— Illustrated .... Cassell 23
—— Sequel to.............. Reeve 15
Arabic Grammar............. Bell Ed. ... 27
—— Grammar and Dictionary.. Trubner ... 28
—— Language .... Allen 33
—— Poets, Ancient .... Trubner ... 1
—— Reading Lessons .... Bagster ... 33
Arabic-English Dictionary .... King....... 7
—— English Lexicon, Lane ... Williams... 8
Arabic Grammar, Wright....... Williams... 16
Arabs in Spain .... Bohn's Lib.. 7
Arbitration .... Smith & El. 10
Arboriculture, Grigor .... Edmonston.. 11
Archæologia Cambrensis .... J. R. Smith 4
—— (The) .... Parker..... 51
Archæology, British .... Reeve 13
—— (Early) British .... Parker..... 51
—— Sacred .... Reeve 12
—— and Science............ Bemrose ... 16
—— Prehistoric .... Bell 12
—— Works on .... Bell 11
Archæological Institute .... J. R. Smith 4
—— Works .... Parker..... 50
Archaia, Dawson .... Hodder..... 12
Archbishops of Canterbury, Hook Bentley ... 4
Archery .... J. R. Smith 4
Arches, Oblique, Hart .... Lockwood .. 4
—— (Table for) .... Spon 2
Archie Armstrong's Banq. of Jests Sotheran .. 5
Archie's old Desk .... S. S. Union. 7
Architect's Legal Handbook .... King....... 6
—— Guide .... Lockwood .. 7
Architects (Young) Hints to .. Lockwood .. 7
Architectural, Eng. &c. Drawing Ward 3
—— Works, French .... Asher 9

Architectural Works, French&Eng. Parker...... 49
—— (Picturesque) Studies .... Spon 12
Architecture Ancient Lights .... Murray ... 19
—— includ. Arts of Construction Black 1
—— Brick and Marble........ Murray ... 31
—— Church Design .... Smith & El. 4
—— Continental............ Blackie.... 7
—— Cottage and Farm....... Warne 10
—— Cottages and Villas ..... Spon 12
—— Country Cottages, Vincent. Hardwicke. 9
—— Country Houses .... Parker.... 54
—— Designs for Cottages, &c. Lockwood .. 7
—— Domestic, Richardson, C. J. Chatto 15
—— Encyclopædia .... Longmans .. 70
—— Fergusson .... Murray ... 12
—— Gentleman's House ...... Murray ... 11
—— Glossary of .... Parker.... 49
—— (Gothic) .... Parker.... 49
—— Gothic, Revival .... Longmans .. 30
—— (Gothic) in Spain .... Murray ... 31
—— Hints on Chapel Building . Snow 4
—— (House) Wheeler .... Murray ... 32
—— Labourers' Cottages ..... Hatchard .. 12
—— Labourers' Cottages...... Stanford .. 50
—— Manual of .... Longmans .. 30
—— Mediæval .... Murray ... 27
—— (Mediæval Domestic) .... Parker.... 49
—— (Military) .... Parker.... 49
—— Modern Parish Churches. King..... 33
—— of Normandy .... Blackie.... 7
—— Old Church .... Edmonston. 5
—— Rudimentary Works...... Lockwood .. 18
—— Secular and Domestic .... Murray ... 27
—— Small Gentleman's House. Murray ... 19
—— Study Book of .... Sotheran .. 17
—— Starforth .... W. Blackw'd 52
—— Villa .... Lockwood .. 7
—— Villa and Cottage .... Blackie.... 7
—— Wonders of............. Cassell 8
—— Works on .... Spon 5
Arctic Discovery .... Cassell 5
—— Explorations .... Nelson 3
—— Hartwig .... Longmans .. 23
—— McClintock............. Murray ... 21
—— Regions, Travels in ...... Asher 6
—— Sea (Chisholm) .... Murray ... 7
Are we Better than our Fathers.. Parker 63
Argyll (Duke) Works by ...... Isbister ... 5
Ariana Antiqua, Wilson ...... Williams .. 16
Aristocracy, Burke's Family Rom. Hurst 14
—— of Three Kingdoms .... Hardwicke. 12
Aristotle's Ethics .... Rivingtons.. 23
—— Nicom. Ethics. Trans. ... Longmans .. 3
—— Politics, Congreve....... Longmans .. 14
—— Rhetoric, Cope .... Macmillan. 8
Aristotle, by Lewes .... Smith & El. 19
—— on Fallacies .... Macmillan.. 2
Arithmetic, Adapted to Standards Collins ... 11
—— Standards .... Cornwell... 11
—— for Beginners .... J. Heywood. 7
—— R. Smith .... Macmillan.. 33
—— Civil Service .... Stanford... 51
—— Civil Service, for Military . Stanford... 51
—— Commercial............ Lockwood .. 30
—— for Colleges and Schools... Bell Ed. .. 15
—— Commercial............ Isbister ... 43
—— of Decimals............ Black 9
—— Dual.................. Spon 15
—— Dual.................. Parker.... 60
—— (Dual) Byrne .... Bell Ed. .. 22
—— Elementary............ Cassell 12
—— Elementary............ Chambers .. 11
—— Elementary............ Philip 35
—— Elements of, De Morgan . Stanford... 53
—— Elements of, Briot....... Hardwicke.. 11
—— Examination Cards ..... J. Heywood. 7
—— Exercises in, Reynolds ... Stanford... 6d
—— French School, Trans..... Hardwicke.. 11
—— Girdlestone .... Rivingtons. 24
—— Graduated .... Murby 4
—— Grammar .... Walker ... 3
—— Grammar .... Whittaker .. 13
—— Helps to .... Macmillan.. 6
—— Horn's Standard .... J. Heywood. 8
—— Jones's Standard .... J. Heywood. 8

Arithmetic (Mental) Willcocke .... *Mozley* 15
—— Mercantile .... *W. Blackw'd* 44
—— Metric System .... *J. Heywood* .. 9
—— Rudimentary Works .... *Lockwood* .. 23
—— Sang .... *W. Blackw'd* 47
—— for Schools . r. .... *Jarrold* 21
—— for Schools .... *Rivingtons* 26
—— for Schools, Young ...... *Mozley* 15
—— for Schools and Families.... *Bell Ed.* 40
—— Sonnenschein .... *Whittaker* .. 13
—— Technical .... *Longmans* .. 21
—— Templar's Gradation .... *J. Heywood* .. 8
—— in Theory and Practice .... *Macmillan* .. 4
—— Walkinghame, Birkin ...... *Mozley* 15
- - - Walkinghame's .... *Nicholson* .. 10
—— Walkinghame's .... *Nicholson* .... a
—— Young Ladies' .... *Whittaker* .. 13
Arithmetical Books and Tables .. *M'Leod* ...... a
—— Tables .... *J. Heywood* .. 9
—— Tables .... *Jarrold* 5
—— Table Book .... *Nicholson* .. 10
—— Table Books .... *Routledge* .. 16
—— Works .... *Fellowes* ...... a
Armadale .... *Smith & El.* .. 4
Armenia, Curzon .... *Murray* 9
Armies, Foreign, Brackenbury .. *Chapman* .. 22
—— Reflections on Formation .. *Stanford* .. 71
Armour (Mediæval) .... *Parker* 50
Arms and Armour .... *Bell* 12
—— and Ammunition ...... *Cassell* 5
Armstrong (F. C.) Novels by .... *Routledge* .. 49
Army, Abolition of Purchase in.. *King* 12
—— British, familiar History of.. *Stanford* .. 69
—— (Brit.) Sketches of Sold. of.. *Stanford* .. 51
—— Drill Books, &c. .... *Harrison* 6
—— History under Fairfax.... *Clar. Press*.. 16
—— Hygiene .... *Churchill* .. 18
—— Lists of Roundheads, &c. .. *Chatto* 2
—— Reserves, Anson .... *King* 12
Arne, Norwegian Peasant Life .. *Isbister* 7
Arnold (Matthew) Works of .... *Smith & El.* .. 1
—— (Matthew) Works by .... *Macmillan* .. 2
—— Lee .... *Warne* 29
Arnold's Gk. & Lat. School Books *Rivingtons* .. 19
—— (Dr.) Works .... *Fellowes* ...... a
—— (Dr. Thos.) Life, Worboise.. *Isbister* 48
Arran, Antiquities of .... *Black* 14
Arrangement with Creditors .... *Waterlow* .. a
Ars, Life of the Curé of ...... *Burns* 21
Artemus Ward................ *Routledge* .. a
—— Works .... *Chatto* 4
Arthur's (Little) History of Eng. *Murray* 1
—— Seat, or Church of the Banned *Macmillan*.. 15
—— Victory .... *S. S. Union.* 6
Arthur (T. S.) Tales by ...... *Nelson* 14
—— (King) La Mort d'Arthur .. *Smith* 4
Arthurian Localities .... *Edmonston* .. 10
Articles, of the Church.......... *Clar. Press*.. 13
—— Thirty-nine .... *Hall* ...... a
Articuli Ecclesia Anglicanæ .... *Parker* 5
Artillery (Bengal) History of .... *King* 11
—— Bengal .... *Allen* ...... a
—— Exercises .... *Harrison* 8
—— Gunner's Pocket Book .... *Spon* 22
—— Macdougall .... *Murray* 21
—— (Modern) Owen .... *Murray* 24
—— Principles and Practice .... *Allen* 17
—— (Royal) History .... *Murray* 10
—— Whitworth .... *Longmans* .. 32
Artist of Collingwood ...... *MacGlashan.* 1
Artistic and Ornamental Works.. *Bell* 3
Artist's Assistant.............. *Philip* 36
Artists, Dictionary of English.... *Longmans* .. 28
Art .... *Clar. Press*.. 30
—— of Amusing .... *Chatto* 3
—— Applied to Industry...... *Parker* 54
—— Catalogue of Books on .... *Chapman*.. 26
—— Christian and Sym. ...... *Smith & El.* 25
—— Dictionary of Terms of .... *Isbister* 14
—— Educational Works........ *Chapman*.. 27
—— Elementary History of...... *Asher* 4
—— Essays on .... *W. Blackw'd* 25
—— and Fashion, Poems...... *Isbister* 42
—— (Fine) Sketch of its History.. *Macmillan* .. 42
—— Gems of English .... *Routledge* .. 27
—— Gems—Lievre .... *Sotheran* .. 17

Art Gift Books for the Young .... *Nelson* 2
—— Gift Books and Prizes ...... *Virtue* 9
—— History of, Lubke ...... *Smith & El.* 14
—— Models and Instruments .. *Chapman* .. 30
—— Relation to Mental Existence *Burns* 27
—— of Teaching, by Fitch ...... *S. S. Union.* 44
—— Essays on, Palgrave........ *Macmillan* .. 28
—— Journal .... *Virtue* 4
—— (The) .... *Virtue* 17
—— Lectures on, Moody's ...... *Bell* 6
—— Lectures on .... *Clar. Press*.. 17
—— Masterpieces of English .... *Bell* 9
—— Papers .... *Virtue* 9
—— Philosophy of, Taine .... *Williams* 14
—— (Pictorial) Handbook .... *Clar. Press*.. 30
—— Pictorial Gallery ...... *Sangster* 6
—— Pictures .... *Routledge* .. 3
—— Rambles at Home .... *Virtue* 9
—— Sacred and Legendary .... *Longmans* .. 29
—— and Song, illustrated .... *Bell* 6
—— Studies from Nature...... *Virtue* 9
—— Thoughts about .... *Macmillan*.. 15
—— Tour to Northern Capitals.. *Macmillan*.. 2
—— Treasures of Germany.... *Hagger* 16
—— Workmanship.......... *Asher* 1
—— Workman .... *Hagger* 13
Arts, Dictionary of, Ure ...... *Longmans* .. 32
—— (Fine) Literature of .... *Murray* 10
—— of the Middle Ages ...... *Chapman* .. 20
—— and Sciences, Eng. Ency... *Bradbury* .. 4
—— (Useful) and Manufactures.. *Soc. P. C. K.* 28
Arundines Cami, Drury ...... *Bell Ed.* 13
Aryan Civilization .... *Parker* 63
—— Languages, Attwell ...... *Williams* 2
—— Nations, Mythology........ *Longmans* .. 5
—— Grammar, Beames........ *Trubner* 4
Ascension, Sermons on ...... *Masters* 29
Ascetical Library, St. Joseph's .. *Burns* 15
Ascham (Roger) The whole Works *J. R. Smith* 4
—— The Schole Master ...... *Bell* 34
Ashantee Campaign .... *W. Blackw'd* 4
Ashanti and the Gold Coast, May *Stanford* 55
Ashford, History of .... *Marlborough* 16
Ashley Down Orphans ...... *Mack* 8
—— Priors .... *Mozley* 1
Asia (Central) Trench ...... *Macmillan* .. 38
—— (Central) Sketches of .... *W. H. Allen* 4
—— (Central) Ker .... *King* 4
—— Empire in .... *Trubner* 20
—— Empires and Cities of .... *Virtue* 8
—— Lennep's Travels ...... *Murray* 20
—— Minor, History of ...... *Clar. Press*.. 17
—— Russians in .... *King* 3
Ask Mamma................ *Bradbury* .. 10
Asked of God, Shipton........ *Morgan* 3
As Pretty as Seven............ *Chatto* 3
Aspronte and Other Poems .... *King* 70
Assam, Travels in .... *Smith & El.* 3
—— and Thibet, Cooper ...... *King* 4
Assayer, Practical .... *Chatto* 29
Assaying, Iron and Steel .... *Chapman* .. 14
—— (Practical) .... *Longmans* .. 32
Assurance, Works on ...... *Layton* 1
Assyria, Rawlinson .... *Murray* 26
Assyrian Dictionary, Norris .... *Williams* 10
—— Grammar, Sayce ...... *Trubner* 26
—— Monuments, Eng. Trans.... *Bagster* 76
Asthma, Salter .... *Churchill* .. 31
—— Thorowgood .... *Churchill* .. 35
Astra Castra, Turnor........ *Chapman* .. 20
Astrology (Horary) Simmonite .. *Walker* 4
—— Introduction to .... *Bohn's Lib.* 10
Astronomy, Descriptive ...... *Clar. Press*.. 27
—— (Dick's) .... *Collins* 4
—— Elementary .... *Jarrold* 23
—— Elementary Lessons........ *Macmillan* .. 23
—— Essays on, Proctor ...... *Longmans* .. 12
—— and Geology .... *Murray* 24
—— Guillemin's, The Heavens.. *Bentley* 17
—— Marvels of Heavens...... *Bentley* 16
—— The Midnight Sky ...... *Rel. Tr. Soc.* 7
—— Orbs of Heaven........ *Routledge* .. 35
—— Pictures of the Heavens .. *Mozley* 9
—— Popular .... *Lockwood* .. 13
—— (Popular) Airy .... *Macmillan* .. 1

Astronomy, Proctor ... King ... 6
— Proctor ... Cassell ... 12
— Proctor ... Chambers ... 17
— Romance of ... Macmillan ... 25
— and Scripture ... Snow ... 11
— Student's Class Book ... J. Heywood ... 40
— The Sun ... Bentley ... 7
— Works on ... Longmans ... 18
— Works on ... Bell Ed. ... 21
Astronomical Diagrams ... Chapman ... 31
— Observations ... Cambridge ... 7
— Observations ... Smith & El. ... 10
— at Greenwich ... Murray ... 2
— and Meteorological Obs. ... Parker ... 62
Athanasian Creed, Origin of ... Rivingtons ... 5
— Creed, Stanley ... Macmillan ... 34
— MacColl ... Rivingtons ... 5
Athanasius, Orations of ... Clar. Press ... 9
At the Back of the North Wind ... Isbister ... 28
At Home in the Wilderness ... Hardwicke ... 6
At Jesus's Feet, Morgan ... Morgan ... 3
At Last, Kingsley ... Macmillan ... 18
At Nightfall and Midnight ... Hodder ... 10
Atheism or Theism ... Houlston ... 35
Athenæ Cantabrigienses ... Bell ... 39
— Cooper ... Macmillan ... 8
Athenians, National Character ... W. Blackw'd ... 26
Athens (Ancient) Dyer ... Bell ... 11
— and Attica ... Murray ... 32
— and the Morea ... Murray ... 6
— to Rome (From) ... Nisbet ... 13
Athletics, Ravenstein ... Trübner ... 25
Athletic Sports ... Routledge ... 18
— Maclaren ... Macmillan ... 21
Atlantic to the Pacific ... Longmans ... 36
Atlas, Ancient, Menke ... Trübner ... 19
— Antiquus, Kiepert ... Williams ... 8
— Antiquus, Spruner ... Nutt ... 10
— Astronomical ... Jarrold ... 11
— (Bible) Clark ... Soc P. C. K. ... 3
— Biblical and Gazetteer ... Rel. Tr. Soc. ... 3
— Blair, Arnold ... Allman ... 4
— of Blank Projections ... C. Smith ... 7
— Cabinet ... Philip ... 2
— Cabinet ... Johnston ... 22
— Chronological School ... Bagster ... 56
— Clark's School ... Allman ... 6
— Classical ... Bell Ed. ... 25
— Classical ... Whittaker ... 3
— Collegiate ... Collins ... 17
— English Travelling ... Chapman ... 19
— Ethnographic ... Bagster ... 56
— Family ... Routledge ... 12
— (General) of the World ... Black ... 3
— of Gt. Britain and Ireland ... Virtue ... 19
— Handy ... Philip ... 6
— Handy Royal ... Johnston ... 40
— (Historical, Hand) Spruner ... Trübner ... 27
— Human Anatomy ... Johnston ... 19
— Imperial ... Philip ... 1
— Imperial ... Blackie ... 7
— International ... Collins ... 17
— Library ... Philip ... 1
— Library ... Collins ... 18
— Political ... Johnston ... 25
— Political, Hist. and Phys. ... Collins ... 18
— Royal ... Johnston ... 39
— (Royal) Companion to ... Johnston ... 48
— of the Stars ... Longmans ... 18
— of the Stars ... Houlston ... 46
— Student's ... Philip ... 7
— University ... Stanford ... 6
— University ... Ward & Lock ... 22
— Wesleyan Methodist ... Bemrose ... 6
Atlases, &c ... Gall ... 12
Atlases ... Black ... 3
Atlases ... Collins ... 16
Atlases ... Warne ... 41
— and Globes ... Betts ... 2
— Geography, &c. ... Jarrold ... 25
— (Harrow) ... Stanford ... 5
— (Harrow) ... Routledge ... 12
— Johnston ... W. Blackw'd ... 17
— and Maps ... Philip ... 1
— and Maps ... J. Heywood ... 12

Atlases and Maps ... Soc. P. C. K. ... 34
— and Maps ... Stanford ... 3
— and Maps ... Chambers ... 11
— and Maps ... J. Blackwood ... 26
— for Schools ... Fellowes ... a
— School ... Johnston Index
— School ... A. Heywood ... 15
— Scripture ... Bagster ... 56
— Special ... Stanford ... 4
— The Public School ... Longmans ... 19
Atmosphere, Experiments in the ... Chapman ... 26
— Reclus ... Chapman ... 6
Atmospheric Vapour ... Soc. P. C. K. ... 8
Atomic Theory ... Clar. Press ... 18
— Weight ... Parker ... 62
Atonement (The) ... Masters ... 2
— Candlish ... Black ... 10
— Catholic Doctrine of ... W. H. Allen ... ?
— of Christ, Barry ... Macmillan ... 3
— Crawford ... W. Blackw'd ... 37
— Doctrine of ... Clark ... 14
— Extent of the ... Snow ... 8
— Love of the ... Masters ... 17
— Martin ... Nisbet ... 26
— Nature of ... Macmillan ... 6
Atterbury, Memoirs, &c. ... W. H. Allen ... 4
Attic Primer, Wright ... Macmillan ... 42
Aubrey's Miscellanies ... Smith ... 28
Auckland Islands ... Lockwood ... 45
Auctioneer's Assistant ... Lockwood ... 16
Auerbach (Bert.) Novels, German ... Nutt ... 11
August Stories (The) ... Isbister ... 5
Aunt Agnes ... Virtue ... 13
— Ailie ... Warne ... 26
— Charlotte's Eng. History ... M. Ward ... 2
— Edith ; or, Love to God ... Nisbet ... 3
— Fanny's Nursery Tales ... Ward & Lock ... 17
— Friendly Holiday Album ... Warne ... 22
— Friendly Stories ... Warne ... 22
— Friendly's Toy Books ... Warne ... 31
— Jane's Hero ... Ward & Lock ... 23
— Jane's Hero ... Routledge ... 33
— Jane's Verses ... Tubbs ... 4
— Judy, Works by ... Bell ... 19
— Louisa's Choice Books ... Warne ... 25
— Louisa's London Toy Books ... Warne ... 33
Aural Surgery (The Questions of) ... King ... 6
Aurora Leigh ... Smith & El. ... 3
Auspicious Day (The) ... Macmillan ... 42
Austen's Tales and Novels ... Routledge ... 6
— (Miss) Novels ... Routledge ... 36
— Novels, Six Vols. ... Bentley ... 16
Austin (A.) Poems ... W. Blackw'd ... 2
Austin's Jurisprudence ... Murray ... 1
Australia, Church in ... Macmillan ... 29
— Church Life in ... Hodder ... 16
— Colonies, Atlas of ... Philip ... 3
— Colonies ... Rel. Tr. Soc. ... 14
— Dominion of ... Chapman ... 4
— Flora ... Reeve ... 5
— Methodism in ... Hodder ... 24
— and New Zealand ... Chapman ... 4
— Powell ... Bentley ... 11
— Seaweeds ... Reeve ... 9
— South, Map of ... Stanford ... 77
Australian Meats, Cooking of ... Chapman ... 11
— Parsonage ... Stanford ... 61
— Views of England ... Macmillan ... 23
Austria, Armed Strength of ... Harrison ... 7
— History of House ... Bohn's Lib. ... 7
— House of, Ward ... Macmillan ... 40
— Thompson ... Smith & El. ... 25
Austro-Hungarian Empire ... Chapman ... 11
Austro-Italian War of 1866 ... Stanford ... 72
Austro-Prussian War ... Tinsley Bros. ... 8
Authoritative Teaching of Church ... Parker ... 6
Authority and Conscience ... Longmans ... 33
Authorship, Aspects of ... Hodder ... 7
— Gems of Christian ... Nisbet ... 6
Authors, Book of ... Warne ... 33
— (Favourite) Pocket Vols. ... Bell ... 33
— Half Hours with Best ... Warne ... 4
— (Standard) Elzevir Series ... Bell ... 34
— at Work ... W. H. Allen ... 7
Author's Guide ... Wilson ... 7

Autobiography of a Seaman .... *Bentley* 6
Autocrat at the Breakfast Table. *Ibister* 21
Autographs .... *Russell Smith* 4
Autumn at Kurnford .... *Warne* 29
—— Memories .... *Houlston* .. 14
—— Manœuvres, 1871 .... *Trubner* 19
Auvergne ; its Mineral Springs . *Hardwicke*.. 14
Average, Handbook of.......... *Smith & El.* 10
Average Clause, Atkins .... *Layton*...... 7
Awa I. Hind .... *Trubner* 3
Awful Crammers................ *Chatto* 3
Ayrshire Ballads and Songs .... *T. Stevenson* a
Aytoun (W. E.) Poems.......... *W. Blackw'd* 2
Azimuth Tables .... *Ibister* 39

Bab Ballads .... *Routledge* .. 61
Babies (flits about)............ *Ward & Lock* 3
Babies and Ladders .... *Chatto* 3
Babrius, Fables of.............. *Lockwood* .. 43
Back Numbers of Magazines. .. *Wheldon* .. a
—— Numbers of Periodicals .. *Platnauer* .. a
Backwoodsman (The) .... *Ward & Lock* 3
Backwoods Preacher (The)...... *Ibister* 10
Bacon's Advance. Learning .... *Clar. Press*.. 31
—— Essays, Whateley .... *Longmans* .. 11
—— Essays, Wright .... *Macmillan* .. 14
—— (Lord) Life .... *Murray* 7
—— Novum Organum .... *Clar. Press*.. 17
—— Works, by Spedding .... *Longmans* .. 11
Bad English Exposed .... *Hatchard* .. 16
Bailey (P. J.) Poems............ *Bell* 35
Baillie (Rev. John) Works by.. *Nisbet* 3
Baillie's Moohummadan Law... *Smith & El.* 2
Baines (Rev. J.) Works by ...... *Masters* 2
Bairns (The)................... *Hodder* 27
Baker (Chas.) Works by .... *Houlston* .. 29
—— (Sir Samuel) Works by .. *Macmillan*.. 2
Balanstin's Adventure.......... *Smith & El.* 3
Balfour (Clara) Works by...... *Houlston* .. 29
Balfour's (Prof.) Works on Botany *Black* 2
Ballad Book (The) .... *Macmillan*.. 13
—— Romances .... *J. R. Smith* 11
—— Society .... *Trubner* 3
Ballads, Ancient Scottish ...... *Stevenson* .. a
—— Brave Old .... *Ward* 20
—— and Broadsides .... *Sotheran* .. 5
—— Early.................... *Pickering* .. 14
—— of England and Scotland .. *Warne*...... 18
—— and Hymns .... *Cassell*.... a
—— Old .... *J. R. Smith*. 16
Ballantyne, Juvenile Books by .. *Routledge* .. 31
—— (R. M.) Works by ...... *Nelson* 6
—— (R. M.) Works by ...... *Nisbet* 3
Balloon Ascents, Wonderful .. *Cassell* 6
—— Voyages, Glashier........ *Bentley* 15
Ballot Act Explained.......... *Routledge* .. 42
—— Act, 1872 .... *Wilson*...... 5
—— and Corruption at Elections *Macmillan*.. 7
Baltic, Letters from .... *Murray* 20
—— Log of a Cruise .... *Smith & El.* 1
Bamford (S.) Works by .... *A. Heywood*. 8
Bampton Lectures, Eaton ...... *Rivingtons* .. 13
—— Farrar .... *Murray* 11
—— Garbett.................. *Rivingtons* .. 16
—— Hannah .... *Murray* 14
—— Hessey .... *Murray* 14
—— Liddon .... *Rivingtons* .. 14
—— Mansel .... *Murray* 21
—— Morley .... *Rivingtons* .. 11
—— 1838, Woodgate .... *Parker*...... 6
—— 1840, Hawkins .... *Parker*...... 4
—— 1844, Jelf .... *Parker*...... 6
—— 1845, Heurtley .... *Parker*...... 3
—— 1849, Michell .... *Parker*...... 4
—— 1852, Jelf .... *Parker*...... 4
—— 1864, Bernard .... *Macmillan* .. 3
—— 1868, Hamilton .... *Parker*...... 5
—— 1869, Smith............ *Macmillan*.. 33
—— 1871, Curteis .... *Macmillan*.. 8
Bandaging, Essentials of...... *Smith & El.* 10
—— (Surgical) .... *Churchill* .. 20
Band of Hope Publications.... *Tubbs* 8
Banffshire Dialect .... *Asher* 8
Bankers' Cheques .... *Wilson* 11
—— Cheques, Law of .... *Waterlow* .. a

Bankers' Clearing-house System.. *Cassell*...... 4
Banking (London) .... *Cassell*...... 4
—— and Commerce .... *MacPhun* .. 10
—— Notes on, Palgrave ...... *Murray* 24
—— Principles of .... *Wilson* 7
—— Princip. and Practice, Gilbert *Bell* 42
—— Scotland .... *Black* 31
Banks (Saving) Scratchley .... *Layton* 15
—— Theory and Practice of.... *Longmans* .. 44
Bankruptcy, Law, &c.......... *Stevens* 24
—— and Liquidation.......... *Waterlow* .. a
Bannerman (J.) Sermons ...... *Edmonston*.. 1
Bantam Family .... *Mozley*...... 1
Baptism...................... *Parker*...... 40
—— Blackley .... *Hodder* 25
—— Doctrine of, Goode ...... *Hatchard* .. 9
—— Doctrine of, Wilberforce .... *Mozley*.... 13
—— Essay on, Noel .... *Nisbet* 28
—— Explanation of, Rogers .... *Nisbet* 32
—— Old Testament Types of.. *Masters* 30
—— Plain Thoughts on ...... *Bell* 51
—— (Sacramental)............ *Hatchard* .. 8
Baptismal Regeneration ...... *Murray* 23
—— Judgment on .... *Masters* 13
—— Vow, Thoughts on........ *Mozley*.... 12
Baptista...................... *Warne* 25
Baptistery (The) .... *Parker*...... 27
Barbary, Western, Hay .... *Murray* 14
Barbauld (Mrs.) Memoir of .... *Bell* 40
Barbauld's Hymns, Illustrated .. *Murray* 3
Barbour (M. F.) Works by .... *Nisbet* 4
Barclay (Rev. Jas.) Univl. Dicty. *Virtue* 18
Barker (Lady) Works by ...... *Macmillan*.. 2
Barnes's Rev. Alfred, Works .... *Blackie* .. 21
—— Notes .... *Virtue* 18
—— Notes, Cobbin .... *Gall* 10
—— Cobbin .... *Houlston* .. 30
—— Notes, Cobbin.......... *Rel. Tr. Soc.* 3
—— Notes, Cumming .... *Routledge* .. 3
Barnes (Rev. W.) Works ...... *J. R. Smith* 5
Barneveld (John of)............ *Murray* 23
Baronetage, The Shilling...... *Hardwicke*.. 13
Baronetcies, Extinct .... *J. R. Smith* 6
Baronia Anglia .... *J. R. Smith* 5
Baronial Halls................ *Sotheran* .. 5
Baron's Little Daughter ...... *Masters* 1
—— War (The) .... *Bell* 38
Barracouta (Voyage of H.M.S.).. *Smith & El.* 25
Barrett (Rev. A.) Works ...... *Wesleyan* .. 8
Baretti's Italian and Eng. Dict. . *Rivingtons* .. 18
Barlow (Dr. H. C.) Works by.. *Williams* .. 2
Barrow (Isaac) Works of ...... *Cambridge* .. 6
—— (Sir J.) Mem. & Voyages . *Murray* 3
Bartlett (W. H.) Works by .... *Bell* 5
Bashan, Giant Cities of........ *Nelson* 5
Basket of Flowers .... *Milner* 11
—— of Flowers .... *Warne*...... 27
Bastian (H. C.) Works by ...... *Macmillan* .. 3
Bastile, History of............ *Tegg* ...... a
Bate's Illustrated Travels........ *Cassell* 4
Bath Archives, Jackson .... *Bentley* 2
Baths and Wells, Macpherson.. *Macmillan*.. 23
—— of Europe and England .. *Churchill* .. 0
Battle Abbey, Roll of .... *Chatto* 72
—— Fields of 1866 .... *Tinsley Bros.* 8
—— of Dorking .... *W. Blackw'd* 1
Battles, Book of.............. *Houlston*.... 21
—— (Great) of Army and Navy . *Routledge* .. 22
—— Land .... *Warne* 27
—— on Land and Sea .... *Cassell* 4
—— of the World, 15 Decisive .. *Bentley* 5
Baxter (Richard) Works by .... *Rel. Tr. Soc.* 3
Bayldon's Valuing Rents ...... *Longmans* .. 33
Bayley (Mrs.) Works by ...... *Nisbet* 5
Beagle, Voyage of .... *Smith & El.* 5
Beale (Lionel B.) Med. Works by *Churchill* .. 8
Beams and Girders, Strength of.. *Spon* 41
Beasley's Medical Works........ *Churchill*.... 9
Beatitudes (The) of the Kingdom *Nisbet* 12
—— Stories on the............ *Nisbet* 12
—— Tales of, Power............ *Hatchard* .. 22
Beattie's (W.) Scotland .... *Virtue* 12
Beautiful Island .... *S. S. Union* 7
—— Miss Barrington.......... *Smith & El.* 13

Beautiful, Philosophy of the .... *Edmonston* .. 15
— Pictures .... *Chatto* 8
Beauty, On, Blackie .... *Edmonston* .. 3
— Hay .... *W. Black'd* 14
— of Holiness .... *Lockwood* .. 43
— of the Word .... *Nisbet* 5
Bedside Readings .... *Soc. P. C. K.*
Beecher (Henry Ward) Works by *Isbister* 6
— Works .... *Nelson* 8
— Preaching .... *Marr* 15
— Life Thoughts .... *Ward & Lock* 21
— One Thousand Gems .... *Hodder* 2
— Sermons .... *Dickinson* .. 2
Beefsteaks, Sublime Society of .. *Bradbury* .. 12
Beer, a Satirical Sketch .... *Milner* 30
Bee (The) and White Ants ..... *Lockwood* .. 13
Bees, British .... *Reeve* 2
— Pettigrew .... *W. Black'd* 53
— Silkworms, &c. .... *Ward & Lock* 11
Beethoven, Handel, Haydn, &c. *Tinsley Bros.* 3
Beethoven, Life of .... *Bell* 40
Beetles, British .... *Routledge* .. 9
— British .... *Reeve* 2
Beeton's " All About it Books ". *Ward & Lock* 6
— Publications .... *Ward & Lock* 6
Beever (W. H.) Works on Farming *Bradbury* .. 10
Beginning Life .... *Isbister* 43
Beginnings of Evil .... *Masters* 2
— of Life (The) .... *Macmillan* .. 3
Belfries and Ringers .... *Bell* 52
Belief, Bases, Griffith .... *Longmans* .. 33
— Philosophy of Primary .... *Williams* ... 9
— Scientific and Religious .. *Macmillan* .. 39
— What is it? .... *W. Black'd* 37
Believer, The Suffering .... *Wesleyan* .. 42
Believers, Sonship & Brotherhood *Black* 9
Belgian Art, Modern .... *Routledge* .. 3
Belgium & Holland, Few Days in *Stanford* ... 57
Belgium, Spas of .... *Churchill* .. 30
Bell (B.) Life and Character of.. *Edmonston* .. 2
— (C. D.) Tales, &c. .... *Warne* 26
— (M. M.) Novels by .... *Routledge* .. 49
Bell (The) Change Ringing .... *Bell* 52
— its Origin and Uses .... *Bell* 52
— Ringing, Troyte .... *Masters* 28
Bells and Ringing .... *Masters* 16
Bell's Electionary Works ..... *Mullan* ..... a
— (H. G.) Romances, &c. .. *Macmillan* .. 3
Belloc (Parkes) Works by ..... *Isbister* 33
Ben Rhydding, Treat. of Disease *Churchill* .. 25
Benaiah .... *Warne* 28
Benedicite .... *Murray* 7
Benedictine Missal .... *Washbourne* 4
Bengal Civilian .... *Smith & El.* 6
— Famine, Frere .... *King* 14
— Famine .... *Murray* 12
— Famine Aspects, Hunter... *Trubner* 16
— Missions .... *Snow* 7
— (Rural) .... *Smith & El.* 10
Bengali Language .... *Allen* 32
Bengel's Gnomon .... *Williams* ... 2
— Steudel .... *Nutt* 3
— Translation .... *Clark* 29
Bennett Case, Stephens .... *Rivingtons* .. 12
Bennett (Prof.) Medical Works by *Black* 2
Ben Sylvester's Word .... *Mozley* 1
Bentham's Complete Works .... *Sotheran* ... 8
Bentinck (Lord G.) by Disraeli *Longmans* .. 5
Berjeau's Reproductions ...... *Stewart* .... a
Berkeley's (Bishop) Works ..... *Clar. Press..* 17
Berkley's School Histories .... *Laurie* 2
Berkshire, Windsor, Annals .. *J. R. Smith* 5
Bermuda .... *Smith & El.* 5
Bessie Gray ; or, the Dull Child. *Mozley* 5
— at the Sea Side .... *Nisbet* 5
Best of Everything .... *Warne* 42
— of all Good Company ..... *Houlston* ... 23
— (Mrs.) Scripture Tracts .. *Houlston* ... 40
Bethany (Life at) .... *Snow* 10
— Memories of............. *Nisbet* 23
Bethlehem, The Story of ..... *Nisbet* 24
Bethlehem's Three Mothers ... *Hatchard* .. 2
Betsy Lee .... *Macmillan* .. 3
Better Life and How to Find it. *Morgan* 5
Betts' Globes and Atlases...... *Betts* 6

Beust (Count) Policy of......... *Chapman* ... 11
Bewick Collector (The) .... *Reeve* 12
— 2000 Woodcuts .... *Reeve* 12
Bézique, Cavendish's Law of ... *De La Rue..* a
Bhotan and the Dooar War .... *Murray* 26
Biarritz and the Basque Countries *Stanford* .. 65
Bible (The Holy) i............. *Virtue* 18
— List of Editions in English. *Clar. Press..* 12
— Specimen Pages............ *Cambridge* .. 6
— The Child's .... *Cassell* 1
— (The Child's) Narrative ... *Cassell* 1
Bible, The Comprehensive .... *Bagster* 21
— Coverdale's English ...... *Bagster* 61
— The Emphatic .... *Kellaway* .. 11
— The Invalid's .... *Bagster* 24
— Invalid's Large Type ..... *MacPhun* .. 7
— Large Type Closet .... *MacPhun* .. 1
— for MS. Notes .... *Bagster* 25
— Nat. Comprehensive Fam. *MacPhun* .. 4
— Paragraph, Scrivener ..... *Cambridge* .. 3
— Wycliffe .... *Clar. Press..* 8
Bible in various Languages .... *Nutt* ...... o
— German .... *Hagger* 4
— Hebrew, Hooght .... *Nutt* 4
— Hexaglot .... *Dickinson* .. 6
— Polyglot .... *Bagster* 4
— in Eight Languages ...... *Bagster* 1
— (The) of Every Land ..... *Bagster* 62
Bibles and Commentaries...... *Blackie* 13
— and Commentaries .... *Clark* 23
— and Commentaries .... *Dickinson* .. 15
— and Commentaries .... *Masters* .... o
— and Commentaries .... *Rel. Tr. Soc.* 20
— and Commentaries .... *Ward & Lock* 21
— Family, Brown's Self Inter. *Sangster* ... 4
— (Family) .... *Soc. P. C. K.* 4
— Graphic Family .... *Hagger* 3
— Henry's .... *Collins* 1
— Imperial Family .... *Blackie* 5
— Jamieson, Fausset, & Brown *Collins* 1
— Kalisch .... *Longmans* .. 11
— Kitto .... *Sangster* ... 2
— Lange .... *Clark* 9
— Macfarlane .... *Nisbet* 25
— Portable Commentary .... *Collins* 1
— Scott's Notes .... *Nisbet* 2
— " Speaker's " .... *Murray* 4
— Student's Commentary .... *Collins* 1
— Whitney .... *Hodder* 11
— (Wholly Biblical) .... *Bagster* 25
— Wordsworth's Commentary. *Rivingtons*..
— (Youth's) and Commentary. *J. Blackwood* 27
Bible with Illustrations, Doré .. *Cassell* 1
— (Guinea) Illustrated ...... *Cassell* 1
— Illust. Pocket for the Young *Bagster* 53
— Pictorial, Kitto .... *Sangster* ... 2
— Pictorial, Kitto .... *Chambers* .. 31
— Pictorial Illustrations .... *Bagster* 62
— Pictorial Expository Fam. *MacPhun* .. 1
Bible, Roman Catholic (Douai) .. *Washbourne* 4
— Catholic Family .... *Burns* 19
— Reeve and Challoner ..... *Burns* 22
Bible, Account of, Blunt ...... *Rivingtons* .. 2
— Is it The Word of God? .. *Trubner* 27
— (Claims of the) and Science *Macmillan* .. 24
— and Science, Conversation on *Jarrold* 17
— in Harmony with Phy. Sci. *Bell* 61
— and Modern Thought ..... *Rel. Tr. Soc.* 3
— Not of Man .... *Collins* 3
— Short Summary of the Evid. *Parker* 8
— Superhuman Origin ...... *Hodder* 2
— Triumphant .... *Kellaway* .. 8
— Truth & Broad Church Error *Hodder* 17
— Companion to the .... *Rel. Tr. Soc.* 6
— Child's Guide to......... *Macmillan* .. 1
— Concordance to .... *Soc. P. C. K.* 2
— Concordance, Useful ..... *MacPhun* .. 15
— Educator .... *Cassell* 1
— Epitome of .... *Whittaker* .. 15
— Explainer (The) .... *Kellaway* .. 6
— Key to .... *Rivingtons* .. 4
— Knowledge Treasury of .. *Longmans* .. 43
— Manual .... *Nelson* 12
— Nicholls' Help to Reading. *Soc. P. C. K.* 13
— Obsolete Words in....... *Parker* 8

Bible Opened for Children .. ... *Lockwood* .. 38
—— Synonymes of .... *Longmans* .. 34
—— Text Cyclopædia .... *Houlston* ... 36
—— Youth's Key to .... *Snow* 15
Bible Dictionary, Boutell's ...... *Ward & Lock* 32
—— Beeton .... *Ward & Lock* 7
—— Imperial .... *Blackie* 5
—— Pictorial .... *MacPhun* ... 21
—— Smith's .... *Murray* 28
—— Teacher's Pictorial .... *Ward & Lock* 13
Bible, History of the English .... *Macmillan* .. 40
—— History .... *Nelson* 4
—— History.................... *Virtue* 5
—— History Class Books........ *Macmillan* .. 21
—— for the Young.............. *J. Blackwood* 23
—— Plea for a New Version ...... *Macmillan* .. 29
Bible Animals .... *Longmans* .. 24
—— Beacons of the .... *Nisbet* 21
—— Boys of the .... *Warne* 25
—— Doctrine & Development in *Allen* 4
—— Easy Reading.............. *Hogger* 4
—— Female Characters of ...... *Warne* 25
—— First Catechism of.......... *Parker* 8
—— Geography, Wheeler .... *Isbister* 47
—— for Young People, Oort. .... *Williams* ... 10
—— Hours, Duncan .... *Nisbet* 12
—— Illustration Books.......... *Nelson* 20
—— in the Church............. *Macmillan* .. 40
—— in the Counting House .... *Cassell* 1
—— in France................. *Blackie* 6
—— in the Holy Land .... *Murray* 28
—— in Spain .... *Murray* 5
—— Jewels, Newton .... *Partridge* ... 7
—— Lands .... *Nelson* 5
—— Lands, Ruins of .... *MacPhun* ... 5
—— Legends, Old Test. Charac. *Macmillan* .. 2
—— Lessons, Abbott........... *Macmillan* .. 1
—— Life of our Lord........... *Isbister* 5
—— Light from Bible Lands .... *Collins* 3
—— Months, Groser (W. H.).... *S. S. Union* . 42
—— Mountains of, Bell......... *Nisbet* 5
—— Notes by the Wayside...... *Nelson* 12
—— Music .... *Hodder* 10
—— Natural History........... *Cassell* 10
—— Natural History of......... *Soc. P. C. K.* 19
—— Oral Instruction on the .... *MacPhun* ... 5
—— Personal Names n the .... *Isbister* 47
—— Pictures, in Oil Colours .... *Jarrold* 3
—— Sketches .... *Ward & Lock* 20
—— Sketches and their Teachings *Rel. Tr. Soc.* 3
—— Portraits from............. *Hatchard* .. 19
—— Preceptive Illustrations of .. *Stanford* ... 42
—— Proper Names of .... *Wesleyan* .. 37
—— Readings for a Month ..... *Hatchard* .. 7
—— Scenes from the .... *Collins* 3
—— Scenes of the, Clarkson ... *Snow* 5
—— Stories .... *Warne* 29
—— Story, Traits of Character, .. *Hodder* 10
—— Synoptical Lectures on .... *Nisbet* 13
—— Teachings in Nature ...... *Macmillan* .. 21
—— Thoughts in Quiet Hours .. *Yapp* 2
—— Thoughts and Themes..... *Nisbet* 6
—— Truths, Shaksperian Parallels *Hodder* 12
—— Truths, Simple Thoughts on *Hatchard* .. 11
—— Villages of .... *Hodder* 20
—— Wonders, Newton .... *Partridge* ... 7
Bibles for Presentation .... *Bagster* 0
—— for Churches .... *Freud* ...... a
—— in Elegant Bindings .... *Suttaby* .... a
—— Presentation Family .... *MacPhun* .. 1
—— Prayers, and Ch. Services .. *Stevenson* .. a
Bible Class Reader............. *Nicholson* .. 4
—— Class Studies .... *Hodder* 23
—— Class Teachings........... *Macintosh* .. a
Biblia Pauperum .... *J. R. Smith*. 6
Biblical Antiquity of Man ...... *Wesleyan* .. 46
—— Cabinet.................. *Clark* 30
—— Criticism .... *Clark* 11
—— Criticism, Davidson .... *Black* 10
—— Cyclopædia, Eadie (J.) .... *S. S. Union* 42
—— Literature (Library of) .... *S. S. Union*. 43
—— Lexicon, Men & Places .... *Houlston* ... 34
—— Psychology............... *Clark* 13
—— Revision, Alford........... *Isbister* 4
—— Studies, Plumptre.......... *Isbister* 35

Biblical and Theo. Dictionary.... *Wesleyan* .. 37
—— and Theo. Literature ...... *Blackie* 23
—— Theological Works .... *Clark* 13
—— Literature, Kitto .... *Black* 13
—— Museum .... *Stock* ...... a
—— Reason Why .... *Houlston* ... 5
—— Hist. & Archæ. Lennep. .. *Murray* 20
Bibliography .... *Clar. Press* . 13
Bibliographer's Manual .... *Bohn's Lib.* . 11
Bibliography—A Martyr to .... *J. R. Smith* . 1
Bibliolatry, Letters on .... *Trubner* 13
Bibliotheque Asiatique .... *J. R. Smith*. 6
Bibliotheca Classica .... *Bell Ed.* ... 3
—— Classica .... *Whittaker* .. 1
—— Græca, Jacobs and Rose .. *Nutt* 38
Bickersteth (Bishop) Sermons by *Nisbet* 32
—— (Rev. E. H.) Works by .... *Rel. Tr. Soc.* 3
—— (Rev. E. H.) Works by .... *Rivingtons* .. 24
Bidlake's School Books........ *Allman* 5
Bigg's Digest of Statutes....... *Waterlow* .. a
Biglow Papers .... *Chatto* 5
—— Papers .... *Trubner* 5
Billiards, Game of .... *De La Rue*.. a
—— Made Easy .... *Houlston* ... 21
—— Practical .... *Routledge* .. 19
Bingham's Antiquities .... *Clar. Press*. 11
Bingley's Tales .... *Allman* 5
Binney (T.) Memorial of ...... *Hodder* 16
—— Sermons .... *Macmillan* .. 3
—— Works by .... *Nisbet* 5
—— Works by .... *Hodder* 16
Biographical Dictionary ...... *Cassell* 1
—— New, Cooper .... *Bell* 32
—— Series .... *Nelson* 10
—— Sketches, 1852—68 ...... *Macmillan* .. 23
—— Treasury .... *Longmans* .. 41
Biographies .... *Parker* 20
—— Church of England ...... *Soc. P. C. K.* 4
—— of the Day.............. *Isbister* 33
—— Foreign .... *Tinsley Bros.* 6
Biography .... *Chambers* .. 25
Biography .... *Clark* 21
Biography .... *Rivingtons* .. 24
—— British .... *Ward & Lock* 4
—— British .... *Ward* 13
—— Contemporary .... *W. Blackwood* 22
—— Contemporary .... *Routledge* .. 4
—— Dictionary of .... *Ward & Lock* 4
—— General, Cates .... *Longmans* .. 0
—— Index of .... *Ward & Lock* 32
—— Modern .... *King* 1
—— Religious .... *Masters* 0
—— Religious, Catholic ..... *Burns* 33
Biology, Principles of, Spencer . *Williams* ... 13
Bird Fancier .... *Mozley* 1
—— (The) by Michelet ...... *Nelson* 1
—— Preserving and Mounting . *Groombridge.* 20
Birds of America .... *Morgan* .... a
—— Beautiful, their History, &c. *Houlston* ... 14
—— Book of................ *Cassell* 1
—— (British) in their Haunts .. *Soc. P. C. K.* a
—— British Song .... *Ward & Lock* 11
—— Cage and Singing ...... *Bohn's Lib.* .. 13
—— Catalogue of .... *Pickering* ... 17
—— Chamber and Cage ..... *Hardwicke* .. 10
—— Descrip. and Anecdotes of . *Routledge* .. 45
—— Eggs and Nests......... *Routledge* .. 10
—— Fishes, Quadrupeds ..... *Van Voorst* .. a
—— of Europe, Bree........ *Bell* 16
—— Familiar History of ..... *Longmans* .. 24
—— Fishes and Insects...... *J. Blackwood* 13
—— and Flowers .... *Nelson* 2
—— Home and Foreign ..... *Routledge* .. 27
—— of Land and Water ..... *Cassell* 10
—— Morris .... *Bell* 17
—— Natural History of ..... *Warne* 15
Birds' Nests .... *Ward & Lock* 11
—— and their Nests .... *Partridge* ... 11
—— Nests and Eggs .... *Bell* 17
—— Nests and Eggs .... *Soc. P. C. K.* a
—— Out-door .... *Warne* 21
—— Smaller British .... *Bell* 23
—— Song .... *Routledge* .. 13
—— Pratt .... *Soc. P. C. K.* 23
Birks (T. R.) Works by........ *Hatchard* .. 5

Birks (Rev. S.) Works by ...... Rel. Tr. Soc. 4
Birmingham Guide .... Cornish 6
—— Manufacturer, Essays .... Williams 12
Birth of the War God .... Allen 4
Birthday Book for Boys and Girls Lockwood .. 46
—— Cards .... Haddon 6
—— Girl's................. Routledge .. 23
—— Girl's................. Ward 15
—— Little Folks' .... Nimmo 32
—— of Proverbs .... Nimmo 32
—— Present .... Warne 25
—— Scripture Text-Book...... Mack 1
—— Series Gift Book .... Warne 28
—— Stories .... Warne 29
—— Tales for Young People .. Warne 29
—— Tales for Young People .. Virtue 18
—— A Book for .... Nisbet 10
Bit of Bread (A) .... Bell 20
Bivouac, or Martial Lyrist ...... Chapman .. 23
Black (R.) Lady Caroline........ Smith & El. 3
—— (Wm.) Works by .... Macmillan.. 3
Black Ivory, Ballantyne .... Nisbet 3
—— Sea .... W. Blackw'd 22
—— Sea, Cunynghame........ Murray 9
—— Sheep .... Tinsley Bros. 10
Blackmore, Maid of Sker........ W. Blackw'd 4
Blackstone Economised .... Longmans .. 44
—— Abridged by Kerr .... Murray 30
Blackwell's (C. S.) Letters ...... Shaw 3
Blackwood (S. A.) Works by .... Nisbet 5
Blaikie (Dr.) Works by .... Isbister 7
Blake (Wm.) Poetical Works .. Pickering ... 4
—— (Wm.), by Swinburne .... Chatto 35
Blast Furnace, Action of ...... Spon 5
—— Gruner .... King 6
Blazon of Episcopacy.......... J. R. Smith 6
Blending Lights, Fraser .... Nisbet 13
Blessedness of Religion in Earnest Wesleyan C. 46
Blessed Virgin, Works on........ Washbourne 4
Blind People, their Works & Ways Murray 19
Blindness and the Blind ...... Chapman .. 20
Blockade (The) .... Ward&Lock 23
Blomfield's (Alf.) Sermons...... Morley 2
—— (Bishop) Works .... Fellowes 6
—— (Bishop) Memoir ...... Murray 4
Blood, Disorders of the.......... Smith & El. 26
Bloomfield, Selections from .... J. R. Smith 6
—— A Tale .... Nisbet 6
Blowpipe Vade Mecum, Smith .. Williams .. 13
Blue-Bell; or, Tales and Fables.. Mozley.... 4
Blunt (H.) Works by .... Hatchard .. 3
—— (J. H.) Works by .... Rivingtons .. 6
—— (J. J.) Works by .... Murray 4
Boardman (Rev.W. E.) Works by Isbister 7
—— Works by .... Nisbet 6
Boating, Oars and Sculls ...... Bell 24
Boat Races, Oxford and Cam. .. Bell 24
Bob the Shoeblack .... S. S. Union 10
Boccaccio's Decameron.......... Chatto 5
Bodily Strength, Wonders of .... Cassell 8
Bodleian Library, Annals of .... Rivingtons.. 25
—— Catalogues .... Clar. Press.. 19
Body and Mind, Hunter ...... Churchill .. 21
—— Maudsley.............. Macmillan.. 24
Bogatzky's Golden Treasury .... Milner 2
—— Golden Treasury .... Mozley.... 2
—— Treasury .... Warne 39
Bohny's New Picture Book .... Edmonston.. 3
Boke of Nurture (The) .... Trubner .. 5
Bokhara, History and Conquest.. King...... 3
Bombay, Hand-book to.......... Murray 16
Bon Gaultier Ballads.......... W. Blackw'd 5
Bonar (Rev. Hor.) Works by .... Nisbet 6
Bond of Kindness .... S. S. Union. 8
Bonds, their Nature, &c. ...... Stevens 17
Bone-setting, Hood on .... Macmillan.. 16
Bonwicke (Ambrose) Life of.... Bell 39
Book about Boys.............. Nimmo 27
—— of Blunders............ Marr 15
—— of the Church, Southey .. Murray 31
—— by Southey .... Warne 22
—— of Common Prayer, Gaelic.. Edmonston.. 4
—— of Days.............. Chambers .. 26
—— for Every Land .... Snow...... 12
—— of Gems, S. C. Hall ...... Bell 9

Book of Golden Deeds .... Macmillan .. 4
—— of Golden Thoughts........ Macmillan .. 14
—— History of a .... Cassell 10
—— (The) and the Life........ Macmillan.. 38
—— of Marvels .... Wesleyan .. 41
—— of Praise .... Macmillan.. 13
—— of Ratramn .... Parker...... 3
—— of Worthies .... Macmillan.. 74
—— Boxes of .... Routledge .. 6
—— Carlyle on the Choice of .. Chatto 8
—— of Example for Boys ...... Nelson 14
—— the Friendship of .... Macmillan.. 25
—— for the Household ...... Jarrold 1
—— for all Time .... Ward&Lock 19
—— for Young Readers ...... Nelson 14
Books and Forms, Poor Law .... Knight 6
Bookbinding................ Ramage 6
Book-keeping .... Bell 62
—— keeping .... J. Heywood.. 12
—— keeping, Beavis and Jack's.. Houlston .. 6
—— Commercial .... MacPhun .. 18
—— Brewer .... Jarrold 5
—— S. and D. Bryce .... Collins 12
—— by Account, to Bd. of Trade Clar. Press.. 25
—— for Coffee Planters ...... Haddon 6
—— Double Entry .... MacGlashan 4
—— Double Entry.......... Stanford 53
—— Double Entry.......... Stanford 50
—— Double Entry.......... Wilson 3
—— Laws of .... Wilson 5
—— Farm................ W. Blackw'd 53
—— Jones................ Cassell 12
—— New Manual .... Bell Ed. .. 38
Bookmarks and Bookmakers .. Hodder 10
Bookseller, The .... Whitaker .. 6
Booksellers, History of .... Chatto 5
Boole (G.) Mathematical Works by Macmillan.. 4
Booth's Epigrams .... Chatto 5
Borderland of Science .... Smith & El. 17
Born Again, Phelps .... Hodder 7
Borrow (G.) Works by .... Murray 5
Bosanquet (S. R.) Works of...... Hatchard .. 4
Bosphorus (Cimmerian) .... Smith & El. 15
—— and the Danube.......... Virtue 13
Boswell's Johnson .... Routledge .. 4
—— Johnson's Life.......... Nimmo 7
—— Life of Johnson .... Murray 4
Botanic Garden, Maund ...... Bell 17
—— Terms, Cooke .... Hardwicke.. 4
Botanical Diagrams .... Chapman .. 31
—— Dictionary, Paxton ...... Bradbury .. 9
—— Labels .... Hardwicke.. 6
—— Nomenclature .... Reeve 3
Botanist's Companion .... Black 3
—— Pocket Book .... Bell 15
Botany .... Chambers .. 17
—— Balfour's Works on ...... Black 2
—— Bentley's Manual of ...... Churchill .. 9
—— British, Hooker .... Macmillan.. 16
—— Brown .... W. Blackw'd 42
—— Contributions to, Miers .... Williams .. 9
—— Class Book of .... Black 8
—— Descriptive and Analytical.. Longmans .. 25
—— Domestic .... Reeve 3
—— Elementary .... J. Heywood.. 2
—— Elements of .... Longmans .. 24
—— Elements, Oliver........ Macmillan.. 27
—— English, Sowerby .... Bell 15
—— First Book of .... King 7
—— First Lessons in .... Trubner .. 13
—— Garden .... Routledge .. 47
—— of the Himalaya Mountains Allen 4
—— Loudon's First Book of.... Bell 18
—— Outlines of Elementary .. Reeve 3
—— (Palæontological) ...... Black 2
—— Principles of Scientific .. Hardwicke.. 4
—— Rudiments of, Dresser .... Isbister 13
—— Structural .... Hardwicke.. 4
—— Structural, &c. .... Trubner .. 13
—— Systematic and Economic .. Collins 8
—— Treasury of .... Longmans .. 44
—— Works on .... Bradbury .. 9
—— Young Collector .... Reeve 3
Boulogne, Guide to.......... Stanford .. 50
Bound Books for Presents .... Suttaby 6

Bound for the Kingdom......... *Nisbet* 7
Bounty, Mutiny of............. *Tegg*...... 6
Bourdillon (Rev. F.) Works of .. *Rel. Tr. Soc.* 4
Bow in the Cloud (The) .... *Nisbet* 24
Bowen (Bishop) Memorials of .. *Nisbet* 7
Bowes (Rev. G. S.) Works of ... *Nisbet* 7
Bowman's (Hetty) Works ...... *Mack* 5
Bowman's Juvenile Books....... *Routledge* .. 32
Bowra (H.) Works by .... *Hodder* 26
Boy Artist .... *Nelson* 18
—— in the Bush (The).......... *Isbister* ... 21
—— and the Constellations ..... *Warne* 27
—— Grey (The) .... *Isbister* ... 24
—— Makes the Man .... *Nelson* 14
—— Tar (The) .... *Routledge* .. 24
—— Voyagers .... *Routledge* .. 32
—— with an Idea .... *Warne* 24
Boyhood, Great Painters' .... *Nelson* 13
—— of Great Men .... *Routledge* .. 5
Boyle Lectures, Leathes .... *Rivingtons* .. 13
—— 1866, Plumptre .... *Isbister* ... 15
—— 1871 Hessey .... *Soc. P. C. K.* 18
Boyle (Fred.) Works by .... *Chapman* .. 12
Boys of Axelford (The).......... *Isbister* ... 9
—— Facts about .... *Tubbs* 5
Boy's Life Aboard Ship......... *Ward&Lock* 27
—— Adven. in the Baron's War.. *Ward&Lock* 8
—— (The) Birthday Book ...... *Ward&Lock* 15
—— Book of Heroes .... *Warne* 27
—— Book of Science .... *Chapman* .. 23
—— Books .... *Cassell* 11
—— (Every) Book .... *Routledge* .. 18
—— Famous................. *Ward* 27
—— Games and Sports .... *Warne* 3
—— Handybook of Natural Hist. *Ward&Lock* 4
—— of Holy Writ .... *Warne* 25
—— Home Book of Sports ..... *Lockwood* .. 46
—— Locker, Marryat .... *Bell* 22
—— Manual of Seamanship ... *Trubner* ... 6
—— Own Book .... *Lockwood* .. 46
—— Own Library .... *Ward&Lock* 8
—— Own Sea Stories.......... *Ward&Lock* 15
—— Own Story Book .... *Routledge* .. 31
—— Own Treasury............ *Ward&Lock* 15
—— Prize Library .... *Ward* 11
Bradby (Rev. E. H.) Sermons .. *Macmillan* .. 4
Braddon (Miss) Works .... *Ward&Lock* 16
Brahmins, Sacred Hymns of ... *Trubner* ... 21
Brain, Delineations of the ...... *Bradbury* .. 12
—— Diseases of, Elam .... *Churchill* .. 15
—— Works on the .... *Churchill* .. 30
Bramwell (Elizabeth) Memoirs .. *Morgan* ... 5
—— Memoirs .... *Wesleyan* .. 8
Branches Running over the Wall *S. S. Union* .. 8
Brands Plucked from the Burning *Snow* 16
Brakespeare .... *Tinsley Bros.* 10
Brasses (Monumental) .... *Parker* 50
Brassey's Life and Labours..... *Bell* 39
Brave British Soldiers .... *Ward&Lock* 8
—— Deeds (True Stories of) ... *Warne* 27
—— Men's Footsteps .... *King* 2
—— Old Ballads .... *Ward&Lock* 20
—— Tales, &c. .... *Ward&Lock* 12
Brazil and the Plate, Mansfield.. *Macmillan* .. 23
—— Kennedy .... *Stanford* ... 57
—— Explora. of the Highlds. of *Tinsley Bros.* 2
—— Scientific Journey......... *Trubner* ... 1
Brazilian Colonization .... *Stanford* ... 51
Breach Loaders .... *Cassell* 5
Breaking the Rules .... *S. S. Union* 7
Brechin (Bishop of) Works by .. *Masters* ... 3
Brehm's Book of Birds........ *Cassell* 1
Breitmann's Ballads .... *Trubner* ... 18
—— Ballads .... *Chatto* 18
Bremer's Novels in German .... *Nutt* 12
—— (Miss) Works .... *Bohn's Lib.* 7
Brett (R.) Works by .... *Masters* ... 4
Breviaries and Missals .... *Burns* 17
Breviates from Scripture ...... *Parker* 33
Brewer's Dicty. of Phrase, &c .. *Cassell* 2
—— (Dr.) Histories .... *Jarrold* 5
—— English Classics.......... *Clar. Press..* 11
Brewing (Art of) Dobell .... *Spon* 6
—— The Art of .... *Cornish* ... 3
—— Practical .... *Longmans* .. 44

Brewster's (Sir David) Home Life *Edmonston* 3
Briar and the Myrtle .... *Nisbet* 35
Bricklayers' &c. Guide .... *Hagger* ... 15
—— Tables .... *Spon* 6
Bridal Bouquet .... *Lockwood* .. 41
Bride (The) Poems .... *Smith & El.* 7
Brides and Bridals .... *Hurst* 8
Bridges, Construction of ...... *Spon* 6
—— Humber .... *Lockwood* .. 1
—— Haupt .... *Trubner* ... 15
—— Haskoll .... *Lockwood* .. 3
—— of History .... *Hodder* 9
—— (Iron) Campin .... *Lockwood* .. 4
—— Military, Haupt .... *Trubner* ... 15
—— Oblique, Buck .... *Lockwood* .. 4
—— Theory, Practice, &c ..... *Sotheran* .. 6
Bridgewater Treatises .... *Bohn's Lib...* 18
Briefs and Papers .... *King* 33
Brief History of Christian Church *Parker* 12
Brigands, Tales of............ *Burns* 35
Bright Gems for the Young.... *J. Blackwood* 24
—— Light in the Cloud........ *J. Blackwood* 18
—— Rays .... *Nelson* 21
Bright's (Jn.) Speeches........ *Chatto* 7
—— Speeches .... *Macmillan* .. 4
Brightstone Sermons .... *Rivingtons..* 15
Brightwell (Miss) Works by..... *Rel. Tr. Soc.* 5
Brimley's (G.) Essays .... *Macmillan* .. 4
Bringing in Sheaves .... *Morgan* ... 4
Bristol Hand-book .... *Mack* 12
—— Orphan Home .... *Morgan* ... 2
Britain and Her Colonies...... *Stanford* ... 59
—— Conquest and Settlement of *Bemrose* .. 13
—— (Great) Phys. Geog. & Geol. *Stanford* .. 67
British Association Reports .... *Murray* ... 9
—— Columbia, Mission Life in . *Soc. P. C. K.* 14
—— Mayne .... *Murray* ... 22
—— Dramatists, Works of ..... *Nimmo* ... 7
—— Empire, History of .... *Virtue* 21
—— Guiana .... *Isbister* ... 11
—— Islands (Round about) ... *Tinsley Bros.* 2
—— Landscape Painters ...... *Virtue* 10
—— Pharmacopœia, Comp. to . *Churchill* .. 34
—— Poets, Lectures on .... *Skew* 7
—— Portrait Painters .... *Virtue* 3
—— Schools of Art .... *Virtue* 11
—— School of Sculpture ...... *Virtue* 11
—— Senators .... *Tinsley Bros.* 8
British Museum .... *Willoughby* . 9
—— Pickering .... *Pickering* .. 3
—— Handbook .... *J. R. Smith* 22
—— Catalogues of............ *Pickering* .. 3
—— Cowtan .... *Bentley* 5
—— Lives of the Founders..... *Trubner* ... 11
British Wild Flowers.......... *Van Voorst* 9
British Workman .... *Partridge..* 9
British Workwoman .... *Willoughby* . 9
Brittany and its Byways .... *Murray* ... 24
Broad, Broad Ocean .... *Warne* 20
—— Grins, Colman .... *Chatto* 7
Broadchalke Sermon, Essays ... *Williams* .. 16
Broken Bread, Molyneaux ..... *Nisbet* 27
—— Lights, Cobbe .... *Williams* .. 4
Brontë's Works, Lib. Ed....... *Smith & El.* 3
Brook in the Way (The)....... *Morgan* ... 2
Brooke (Rev. Stopford) Works by *King* 34
Brooks (Shirley) Works by .... *Bradbury* .. 4
Brougham (Lord) a Biography.. *Smith & El.* 3
—— Memoirs .... *W. Blackw'd* 5
—— Works .... *Black* 9
Broughton (Miss R.) Novels ... *Bentley* 16
Brown (J. B.) Works by .... *Hodder* 17
—— (J. Baldwin) Works by..... *Smith & El.* 3
—— (John, M.D.) Works by ... *Edmonston* 3
—— Jones, & Robinson, Struggles *Smith & El.* 25
—— Jones, & Robinson .... *Bradbury* .. 10
—— (J. E. A.) Poet, Works by . *Isbister* ... 8
Brown (Peter), Revelations of . *Cassell* 7
Browne (M.) Views and Opinions *Isbister* ... 8
Browne (Sir Thomas) Works of. *Bohn's Lib...* 5
Browning (E. B.) Poems ...... *Smith & El.* 6
Bruce, Days of .... *Groombridge* 3
—— (James) Travels, Adventures *Black* 9
Bruey, a Little Worker for Christ *Nisbet* 17
Brunel (J. K.) Life .... *Longmans* .. 3

Brunton, (Mrs.) Novels by ..... Routledge .. 49
Brussels, Guide to .... Stanford .. 13
Bryan (Ruth) Letters of .... Nisbet .. 8
Bryant's Poems .... King 49
Bubbles from the Brunnens ...... Murray .. 14
Buchan's Domestic Medicine .... Walker ... 3
Buchanan (Dr.) Works by .... Clark ... 19
—— (Robt.) Poetical Works ..... Isbister .. 8
—— Collected Works .... King 22
Buchanites (The) Train .... W. Blackwd 31
Buckle (H. T.) Works of .... Longmans .. 18
Buddha and his Doctrines .... Trubner .. 17
Buddhaghosha's Parables........ Trubner .. 6
Buddhism (Chinese) .... Trubner .. 11
—— Illustrated .... Trubner .. 2
—— in Tibet .... Trubner .. 26
Buddhist Scriptures .... Trubner .. 4
Buddhists, Legends & Theories of Williams .. 7
Budgeyore, Chronicles of........ Allen 13
Buds and Blossom Series .... Greenbridge 23
Buenos Ayres and Argentine .... Stanford .. 49
Buffon's Natural History........ Virtue ... 13
Buhl Work .... Pearce ... 49
Builder's Comprehensive Specator Longmans .. 45
—— Director .... Hagger ... 14
—— Drawing Rules .... Lockwood .. 7
—— Pocket Estimator .... Lockwood .. 8
—— Pocket Technical Guide .... Lockwood .. 8
—— Price Book .... Lockwood .. 8
—— Specifications .... Lockwood .. 8
—— Tables, Laxton .... Spon 9
—— Young .... Spon 8
Building Construction, R. S. Burn Collins .. 6
—— Rudimentary Works ...... Lockwood .. 13
—— Science of, Tarn......... Lockwood .. 7
—— Specifications .... Spon 17
—— Societies, Scratchley ..... Layton ... 14
—— Stones, Treatise on ...... Macmillan .. 16
Bulgaria, Residence in .... Murray ... 26
Bullion and Foreign Exchanges Wilson 9
Bull's Works .... Clar. Press .. 13
—— on Justification .... Parker ... 17
Bunting (Dr.) Memorials .... Hodson ... 42
Bunyan in Large Type .... Book Society .. 8
—— Choice Works .... Milner ... 7
—— Choice Works .... MacPhun .. 5
—— Entire Works .... Virtue ... 18
—— Holy War .... Cassell ... 2
—— Holy War .... Warne 37
—— Leaflets .... Morgan ... 13
—— Pilgrim .... Cassell ... 2
—— Pilgrim .... Milner ... 2
—— Pilgrim .... Warne 37
—— Pilgrim .... Chatto ... 49
—— Pilgrim, by Landels ...... Sangster .. 7
—— Pilgrim, Venables .... Clar. Press .. 32
—— Pilgrim's Progress .... Baxter ... 18
—— Pilgrim's Progress .... Nicholson .. 4
—— Pilgrim's Progress .... Collins ... 4
—— Pilgrim's Progress .... Hagger ... 4
—— Pilgrim's Progress .... Macmillan .. 14
—— Pilgrim's Progress .... Routledge .. 7
—— Pilgrim's Progress .... Virtue ... 15
—— Pilgrim's Progress .... Ward,Lock & Co 16
—— Pilgrimage, Story of ..... Hodder ... 7
—— and Holy War .... Nisbet ... 8
—— Select Works .... Collins ... 2
—— Works .... Allman ... 5
—— Works, Complete .... Blackie ... 13
—— Works, Various .... Rel. Tr. Ss. .. 5
—— Works, Various .... Sangster .. 4
Burden of Human Sin .... Macmillan .. 16
Burgoyne (Sir John) Life, &c. .. Bentley .. 5
Buried Cities of Campania ..... Nelson ... 11
Burke (Edmund) a Hist. Study Macmillan .. 26
—— (Edm.) Lectures on ...... Macmillan ..
—— (E.) Memoirs .... W. Blackwd 5
—— French Revolution, Payne Clar. Press .. 32
Burke's (Edmund) Works ...... Bohn's Lib. .. 11
Burlington Library .... Bentley .. 2
Burnand (F. C.) Works by ..... Bradbury .. 4
Burnet's (Bp.) Works .... Clar. Press .. 15
—— History of his own Time .. Virtue ... 15
—— Reformation .... Clar. Press .. 11
—— Works on Painting........ Sotheran .. 7

Burning Words .... Dickinson .. 13
Burns (Islay) Select Remains of Nisbet 6
—— (James D.) Memoir, &c. .. Nisbet ... 8
—— (Rev. Jabez) Works by ... Houlston .. 31
—— (W. C.) Memoirs, &c. .... Nisbet ... 8
Burns' (Robt.) Complete Works J. Blackwood 3
—— (Robt.) Poetical and Prose. MacPhun .. 11
—— Complete Works .... Collins ... 2
—— Complete Works .... Virtue ... 10
—— Life .... Chambers .. 26
—— Poems and Songs .... Bell 32
—— Poetical Works .... Warne 14
—— Works .... Blackie ... 11
—— Works, with Life .... Nimmo ... 6
Burtons of Burton Hall .... Warne 24
Bury (Lady Charlotte) Novels by Routledge .. 52
Bushnell (Horace) Works by ... Isbister .. 9
Business, by a Merchant .... Edmonston .. 4
—— Man of, in Six Aspects ... Nimmo ... 13
—— Man (Thorough) .... Isbister .. 18
—— Model for Men of........ Hatchard .. 26
Busy Hives Around Us .... Virtue ... 14
Butler's Analogy .... Parker ... 4
—— Analogy, Analysis of ..... Masters .. 8
Butler (Mrs Clifford) Juv. Bks. Nisbet ... 8
—— (M.) Harrow Sermons ..... Macmillan .. 5
—— (Rev. W. A.) Works by ... Macmillan .. 5
Butterflies, British........... Routledge .. 10
—— (British) Morris.......... Bell 17
—— Described .... Groombridge 13
—— European, Kirby .... Williams .. 8
—— and Moths, Kirby .... Jarrold ... 8
—— and Moths .... Reeve ... 1
Buxton (Sir T. F.) Memoirs ... Murray ... 6
Buyers' and Sellers' Guide .... Wilson ... 5
By the Loch and River Side ... Edmonston .. 4
By Order of the King .... Bradbury .. 11
Byeways of Two Cities .... Hodder ... 3
Byron's Complete Poetical Works Virtue ... 13
—— Life, Elze............... Murray ... 21
—— Moore .... Murray ... 6
—— Poetical Works and Life .. Nimmo ... 6
—— Poetical Works .... Warne 18
—— Songs .... Virtue ... 16
—— Works .... Murray ... 6

Cabinet Lawyer .... Longmans .. 45
—— Making, Charles .... Spon 9
—— Pictures in Colours ...... Macmillan .. 5
—— Portraits .... King 5
Cabul, Lawrence's Reminiscences Murray ... 19
Caddell (Miss) Works by ...... Burns 22
Cadore ; or, Titian's Country .. Longmans .. 35
Caerlaverock, Roll of .... Chatto ... 31
Caged Lion (The) .... Macmillan .. 42
Caird's Sermons .... W. Blackwd 35
Cairnes (J. E.) Works by ...... Macmillan .. 5
Caithness, Pre-Historic Remains Williams .. 5
Calais, Annals and Legends of J. R. Smith 6
Calculator and Ready Reckoner Wilson 5
Calculator's Pocket Guide ..... MacPhun .. 10
Calculus, Hemming .... Macmillan .. 15
Calcutta, Port of .... Spon 35
—— (From) to the Snowy Range Tinsley Bros. 8
Calderon's Dramas............ King 21
Calderwood (H.) Works by .... Macmillan .. 5
Caledonia, Illustrated......... Virtue ... 13
Calendar (Perpetual) .... Bell 63
Calendars and Diaries .... De La Rue ..
Californian Trees .... Bradbury .. 11
California and its Resources, Seyd Trubner .. 27
Calverley (C. S.) Poems ...... Bell 35
Calvini Institutio, Tholuck .... Clark 35
Calvin's Works............... Clark ....
Cambist, Modern .... Wilson ... 1
Cambridge in the 17th Century Macmillan .. 26
—— Colleges of .... Rel. Tr. Soc. ..
—— College Exam. Papers .... Hall .....
—— Greek and Latin Texts ... Bell Ed .. 6
—— Greek and Latin Texts ... Whittaker .. 6
—— Senate House Problems ... Macmillan .. 5
—— Student's Guide to........ Bell 61
—— University Local Exam. ... Cambridge .. 2
—— History .... Cambridge .. 4
—— Work, Christian Drift of .. Macmillan .. 42

Camden's Remains (Britain) .... *J. R. Smith*   7
Cameos from English History.... *Macmillan* ..   6
Cameron (Mrs.) Life of .... *Houlston* ...   33
—— Works by.................... *Houlston* ...   18
—— Works by.................... *Houlston* ...   33
Cameroon Mountains .... *Tinsley Bros.*   6
Camp Notes, Boyle .... *Chapman* ...   5
Campania, Buried Cities .... *Nelson*   11
Campbell (Rev. J. M.) Works by *Macmillan* ..   6
—— (Rev. Dr. J.) Works by ... *Snow*   3
—— (Lord) Works of........... *Murray*   7
Campbell's Poems .... *Routledge* ..   28
Campion Court .... *Isbister*   48
Canaan, Walks in .... *Morgan*   2
—— Walks in .... *Tubbs*   2
Canada, Eastern, Adams .... *King*   4
—— First English Conquest .... *Remrose* ...   13
—— Recollections of .... *Chapman* ...   21
—— Sport in, Hardy............ *Chapman* ...   19
—— Tour in, Medley............ *King*   5
—— Travels in................. *Trübner*   17
Canadian Bush, Geikie .... *Isbister*   16
—— Dominion, Guide Book to *Stanford* ...   16
—— Heroine .... *Tinsley Bros.*   15
—— Scenery................... *Virtue*   13
Canary, Management .... *Groombridge* 16
Canal and River Engineering.... *Black*   31
Candlish (Rev. Dr.) Works by .. *Black*   9
Cancer, Arnott on .... *Churchill* ...   7
—— The Origin of............. *Churchill* ...   14
—— Successful Treatment ...... *Churchill* ...   26
Cancerous Growths .... *Churchill* ...   9
Cannes and its Climate......... *Churchill* ...   14
Canoe Travelling, Baltic .... *Smith & El.*   1
Canoness (The) .... *Bell*   35
Canons (The) .... *Parker*   7
Canons in Greek, Latin, and Eng. *Bagster* ...   74
Canonum (Index) Greek and Eng. *Bell*   45
Canterbury, Architectural Hist. .. *Parker*   53
—— Hymnal................... *Houlston* ...   30
Canticum Canticorum .... *Trübner*   7
Cape of Good Hope, Flora of.... *Reeve*   5
—— (To the) for Diamonds .... *Chapman* ...   5
Capital Punishment .... *Smith & El.*   3
—— Punishment, Carson .... *Houlston* ...   21
Captives, The .... *S. S. Union* 6
Carafa (Anna) Court of......... *Tinsley*   4
Carbon Compounds .... *Macmillan* ..   32
Cards and Card Playing .... *De La Rue* ..   a
—— Games of .... *Houlston* ...   18
Cardinals, English .... *Allen*   6
Cardwell's Common Prayer ..... *Clar. Press*.   11
Carey, Marshman and Ward .... *Isbister*   31
Caricatures .... *Pickering* ...   7
Caricature, History of .... *Chatto*   40
Carisbrook Castle, a Tale of ..... *Soc. P. C. K.* 14
Carlyle (A.) Autobiography ..... *W. Blackw'd* 6
—— Tennyson, and Ruskin ..... *Smith & El.*   12
Carlyle's (Thomas) Works ...... *Chapman* ...   13
Carmina Crucis, Greenwell ..... *Bell*   35
Carnarvon (Lord) Works by .... *Murray*   6
Carnatic and Eng. Dictionary ... *Allen*   34
—— Language, Æsop's Fab. .... *Allen*   34
Caroline Matilda, Qn. of Denmark *Allen*   29
Carpathians (The) Hutchinson .. *Chapman* ...   19
Carpenter's Guide .... *Virtue*   20
—— Nicholson .... *Lockwood* ..   9
—— and Joiner's Assistant ..... *Blackie*   10
Carpentry, Principles of .... *Lockwood* ..   9
—— and Joinery .... *Hagger*   15
—— and Joinery .... *Warne*   46
—— Tredgold and Hurst .... *Spon*   10
Carrie's Enemy .... *S. S. Union* 16
Carroll (Lewis) Works by .... *Macmillan* ..   0
Carson (Rev. A.) Works by ..... *Houlston* ...   31
Carswell's Gaelic Prayer Book... *Edmonston*..   4
Carter (Rev. T. T.) Works ...... *Masters*   4
Carthagina, Ruined Cities of .... *Murray*   9
Cartoon Portraits .... *Tinsley*   4
Carver and Gilder's Design Book. *Houlston* ...   21
Carving, Works on .... *Houlston* ...   10
—— made Easy. .... *Groombridge* 18
Casket of Lyric Gems .... *Cameron* ...   0
Caspian, Source of the .... *Murray*   52
Cast up by the Sea............. *Macmillan* ..   2

Caste, Theory of .... *Smith & El.* 10
Castellani Collection (The) ...... *Bell*   4
Castle Builders .... *Mozley*   2
Castlereagh Despatches .... *Murray*   6
Cat (The) History and Diseases.. *Groombridge* 19
Cats and Dogs................. *Ward*   11
—— and Fairlie's Moral Emblems *Longmans*..   29
—— their Points & Characteristics *Dean* ......   a
Cat's Pilgrimage .... *Edmonston* ..   9
Catalogue of Theology......... *Stewart* ....   a
Catechising .... *Parker*   40
Catechism (Church) .... *Mozley*   2
—— Conversations on the...... *Mozley*   3
—— Stories and Catechisings on . *Mozley*   12
—— Thoughts on Church .... *Mozley*   12
—— on Seasons of Church ..... *Parker*   36
—— of the Wesleyan Methodists *Wesleyan*...   35
Catena Aurea .... *Parker*   10
Cate's and Woodward's Encyclop. *Longmans* ...   5
Cathay, the Foreigner in .... *Stanford* ...   61
Cathedra Petri................ *Dickinson* ..   5
Cathedral, Canterbury .... *Murray*   28
—— Exeter, Freeman .... *Bell*   13
—— St. Paul's, Milman .... *Murray*   22
—— Longman's History of ..... *Longmans* ..   30
—— (The) .... *Parker*   27
Cathedrals, English and Welsh .. *Murray*   16
—— Essays on .... *Murray*   11
—— of the Western Church.... *Masters*   28
Catherine II., Memoirs......... *Trübner*   7
Catholic Antidotes .... *Masters*   11
—— Church (Old) History of ... *Clark*   31
—— Prayer Books............. *MacGlashan*   a
—— Quarterly Series........... *Burns*   14
—— Thoughts, Myers .... *Isbister*   32
—— Worship and Devotions .... *Burns*   3
Catholic's Vade Mecum .... *Burns*   10
Catholicism in England......... *Burns*   15
—— and the Vatican........... *King*   28
Catlin (George) Works by ...... *Trübner*   7
Catnach Publications........... *Fortey* .....   a
Cattle Breeder's Assistant ...... *Lockwood* ..   16
—— Dobson .... *Longmans* ..   42
—— Doctor, Clater............ *Warne*   14
—— Doctor, by Clater......... *Houlston* ...   7
—— Doctor and Farrier .... *Walker*   5
—— and Fields, Notes on ...... *Bradbury* ..   9
—— Measurer .... *Blackie*   11
—— M'Combie .... *W. Blackw'd* 50
—— Plagues, Fleming .... *Chapman* ...   8
—— Practical Treatise on, Skillett *Cornish*   3
Caucasus, E., Travels in .... *Murray*   9
—— Mounsey's .... *Smith & El.* 16
Caudle's Curtain Lectures....... *Bradbury* ..   8
Cavaliers, English, Lays of ...... *Parker*   64
Cavalier and his Lady .... *Macmillan* ..   34
Cavalry Field Duty .... *King*   13
—— Service, Notes on .... *Cassell*   5
—— Exercise, Austrian .... *King*   11
—— Manœuvring of .... *Harrison* ...   8
Cave Hunting, Dawkins .... *Macmillan* ..   9
Cavendish, Life and Works of... *Harrison* ...   14
—— on Whist .... *De La Rue*..   a
Caxton Society .... *J. R. Smith* 26
Cecy's Recollections .... *Isbister*   8
Celebrated Claimants .... *Chatto*   8
—— Jumping Frog .... *Routledge* ..   1
Celebrities, Hist. and Literary .. *Chambers* ..   30
—— Modern.................. *Ward & Lock*   7
Celestial Objects for Telescopes.. *Longmans* ..   20
Celt (The), Roman, and Saxon... *Trübner*   32
Celtic Language .... *Smith & El.*   1
—— Studies, Sullivan .... *Williams* ...   14
Census of 1871, Eng. Digest of .. *Stanford* ...   58
Central Idea of Christianity ..... *Morgan*   2
—— Truths .... *Hodder*   22
Centconti and other Poems...... *Wesleyan*...   41
Ceramic Gallery .... *Chapman* ...   30
Cæsar's Invasion of Britain, Lewin *Bell*   11
Ceylon, Coffee Planter of........ *Spon*   11
—— Described .... *Haddon*   8
—— Directory, 1874 .... *Haddon*   8
—— Institutes of the Laws of .. *Trübner*   29
—— Sketches of .... *Hardwicke*..   14
Chaldee Lexicon, Buxterf ...... *Asher*   3

Chaldee Reading Lessons ..... *Bagster* ... 33
Chalmers' Life and Works ..... *Edmonston* .. 3
—— Select Sermons .... *MacPhun* .. 6
Chamber Dramas for Children .. *Isbister* 29
Chambers's Encyclopædia ..... *Chambers* .. 26
—— Miscellany of Tracts ...... *Chambers* ... 33
Chambers (Rev. J. D.) Works by *Masters* 5
—— (Rob.) Memoir of .... *Chambers* ... 28
Champney (H. N.) Works by .... *Bagster* 78
Chancellors, The Three .... *Burns* 23
Chancery Cases .... *Stevens* 16
Chances and Changes .... *Isbister* 23
Chandos Library .... *Warne* 20
Change of Air and Scene ...... *King* 7
Changed Cross, Illuminated .... *Hardwicke* .. 15
Channel Islands .... *Allen* 3
—— Islands, Guide to .... *Black* 5
—— Guide .... *Stanford* 53
Channing's Corresp. with Aiken . *Williams* 4
—— Life .... *Routledge* .. 5
Chants, Ancient and Modern ... *Isbister* 39
Chapel Building, Pract. Hints on *Snow* 4
Chapman (G.) Plays .... *Chatto* 27
Character, Sermons on .... *Hatchard* ... 4
—— Sketches .... *Isbister* 29
—— Sketches .... *Ward & Lock* 17
Characteristics of Belief ...... *Macmillan* .. 39
Charades, Enigmas and Riddles.. *Bell* 24
—— Francis............... *Houlston* 24
Charities of Europe .... *Isbister* 12
—— of London .... *Hardwicke* .. 13
Charity (Protestant) in England.. *Isbister* 14
—— Social Duties Considered .. *Macmillan* .. 33
Charles Dallaway .... *Mozley* 2
Charles I., Wills............ *W. Blackw'd* 33
Charles XII., by Voltaire, Trans. *Black* 32
Charles the Bold (History of)... *Murray* 19
Charlotte (Princess) Memoir of . *Murray* 25
Charms and Countercharms .... *Routledge* .. 36
Charters, Facsimiles .... *Pickering* .. 8
Chateaubriand's Atala, Doré .... *Cassell* 3
Chatterton, A Biographical Study *Macmillan* .. 6
Chaucer, Morris .... *Clar. Press*.. 31
—— Riches from .... *Lockwood* ... 41
—— Poetical Works .... *J. Blackwood* 4
Chaucer and Spenser.......... *Nimmo* 7
Chavasse's Advice to Mothers... *Churchill* ... 13
Cheever (Dr.) Works by ...... *Collins* 3
Cheltenham Coll. Prize Poems .. *Rivingtons* .. 20
Chemical Analysis, Commercial.. *Lockwood* .. 12
—— Crookes .... *Longmans* .. 26
—— Noad .... *Reeve* 15
—— Spencer .... *Macmillan* .. 34
—— History of a Candle ...... *Chatto* 14
—— Philosophy, Catechism of . *Churchill* ... 21
—— Cooke .... *Macmillan* .. 8
—— Physiology .... *Longmans* .. 25
—— Problems, Thorpe .... *Macmillan* .. 36
—— Students, Notes for ...... *Churchill* ... 9
—— Technology .... *Churchill* ... 37
—— Theory, History of ...... *Macmillan* .. 8
Chemist's Pocket Guide .... *MacPhun* .. 17
Chemists, First Lines for ...... *Churchill* ... 34
Chemistry, Hd.-Bk. of, Gmelin.. *Harrison* .. 14
Chemistry, Physiologl., Lehmann *Harrison* .. 14
Chemistry .... *Chambers* .. 17
Chemistry .... *J. Heywood* 41
—— Analytical .... *Lockwood* ... 29
—— The Birth of .... *Macmillan* .. 26
—— Common Life.......... *W. Blackw'd* 17
—— of Creation .... *Soc. P. C. K.* 5
—— Elementary .... *Cassell* 12
—— Elements, Miller .... *Longmans* .. 26
—— Experimental .... *Bell* ED.... 38
—— First Principles of Modern. *Churchill* ... 23
—— Industrial............. *Longmans* .. 30
—— Inorganic............. *Longmans* .. 21
—— Inorganic............. *Philip* 36
—— Introduction .... *Groombridge* 22
—— Introduction to .... *Rivingtons* .. 27
—— (The New) Cooke ...... *King* 8
—— Organic and Inorganic, Stud. *Collins* 8
—— Practical .... *Churchill* ... 10
—— Practical .... *Clar. Press* .. 27
—— Odling .... *Longmans* .. 26

Chemistry, Owens College ..... *Macmillan* .. 1
—— Rudimentary Class Book .. *Stanford* 67
—— for Schools .... *Stanford* 55
—— for Students .... *Clar. Press* .. 27
—— for Students .... *Allen* 4
—— Works on .... *Churchill* ... 0
Chepmell's Histories .... *Whittaker* .. 4
Cheshire Prophecies.......... *A. Heywood* 7
—— Story (A) .... *Hurst* 9
Chess .... *Longmans* .. 44
—— Book of.............. *Houlston* ... 9
—— Game of .... *J. R. Smith* . 7
—— Game of, Caxton .... *Trubner* 7
—— History of .... *Allen* 7
—— Works on .... *Bohn's Lib.* . 18
—— and Chess Problems .... *De La Rue* .. 0
Chest, Works on Diseases of ... *Churchill* ... 0
Chester, Mediæval Architecture *Parker* 53
Chesterfield's Letters .... *Tegg* 0
Cheyne (C. H. H.) Works by... *Macmillan* .. 6
—— (T. K.) Works by ...... *Macmillan* .. 6
Child of the Chosen People, a Tale *Nisbet* 4
—— of the Kingdom (The).... *Nisbet* 4
—— Life, Poems........... *Nisbet* 4
—— Minister (The) .... *Morgan* 4
—— World Library .... *Isbister* 10
Child's Bible Expositor .... *J. Heywood* 35
—— Bookcase .... *Rel. Tr. Soc.* 32
—— Church Service .... *Pickering* .. 9
—— Finger Post........... *Warne* 29
—— Guide to the Bible ...... *Macmillan* .. 1
—— (The) Popular Fairy Tales. *Ward & Lock* 19
Childhood, Diseases of, West.... *Longmans* .. 27
—— of the World .... *Macmillan* .. 7
Children, Addresses to .... *S. S. Union* . 46
—— of Blackberry Hollow ... *Nisbet* 9
—— Celebrated .... *Routledge* .. 34
—— Culture of Observ. Power of *King* 10
—— Diseases of, Braidwood .. *Smith & El.* . 4
—— Day .... *Churchill* ... 14
—— Holmes.............. *Longmans* .. 26
—— of Elf Land........... *Warne* 29
—— Godly Bringing up ..... *Isbister* 9
—— How to Train .... *Jarrold* 14
—— and Jesus............. *Partridge* .. 11
—— Management of......... *Longmans* .. 44
—— Mental Culture and Training *Churchill* .. 13
—— of the Plains .... *Nelson* 17
—— Pleasure Book .... *Virtue* 6
—— of the Pear Tree .... *Warne* 28
—— Sermons to .... *Dickinson* .. 16
—— of the State, Hill ...... *Macmillan* .. 16
—— of the Sun .... *Warne* 29
—— Works on Diseases of ... *Churchill* ... 0
—— Hist. Sketches of, Illustrated *Mozley* ... 10
—— Lectures to, Crawshaw .. *Tubbs* 5
Children's Books............ *Dean* 0
—— Church at Home .... *Nelson* 3
—— Garden .... *Warne* 30
—— Journey (The) .... *Isbister* 14
—— Toy Books .... *Fortey* 0
—— Pets (Our) .... *Partridge* .. 15
—— Pulpit .... *Dickinson* .. 3
—— Sayings .... *Warne* 29
—— Services .... *Sangster* ... 5
—— Voyage .... *M. Ward* ... 7
—— Week .... *Nelson* 16
Chillingworth's Works........ *Clar. Press* . 13
Chimes from Heaven's Belfrey . *Dickinson* .. 7
Chimney Pieces, Designs for ... *Spon* 11
Chimneys, Works on .... *Spon* 0
China, British Arms in Peking .. *Murray* 26
—— Brit. Embassy in, Rennie . *Murray* 26
—— Coasts of, Tronson ..... *Smith & El.* . 25
—— Elgin's and Embassy to .. *Murray* 20
—— and the Gospel .... *Nisbet* 27
—— History of .... *Smith & El.* . 0
—— and Japan .... *W. Blackw'd* 22
—— Naturalists in.......... *Murray* 8
—— North, Campaign, 1860 .. *Smith & El.* . 26
—— Notes on .... *Allen* 17
—— and its People .... *Nisbet* 27
—— Pictorial and Descriptive .. *Bohn's Lib.* . 13
—— its State and Prospects .. *Snow* 10
—— Tea Countries of .... *Murray* 12

China, towards India (Travels in) *Murray* 8
— Views in .... *Allen* 28
— War, 1840–42 .... *Smith & El.* .. 15
— Travels in, De Carné ...... *Chapman* ... 5
China's place in Philology ...... *Trubner* ... 11
Chinese Campaign .... *W. Blackw'd* 33
— Classics .... *Trubner* ... 18
— Conversations.............. *Trubner* ... 16
— Dictionary .... *Trubner* ... 10
— Dict. Lobscheid............ *Trubner* ... 18
— Empire, Williams .... *Trubner* ... 32
— Grammar and Chrestomathy *Clar. Press.* .. 4
— Language .... *Allen* 34
— Novel, Flowery Scroll...... *Allen* 4
— Rebellion, Meadows .... *Smith & El.* .. 15
— Tale in English Verse ...... *Macmillan.* 40
— Vocabulary .... *Trubner* ... 4
Chips and Chapters .... *W. Blackw'd* 46
— from a German Workshop .. *Longmans* ... 12
Chivalry, Days of .... *Cassell* 3
— Tales of .... *Isbister* ... 40
— Tales of .... *Ward* 12
— Tales of .... *Houlston.* ... 17
Chloroform, its Action and Adm. *Churchill* .. 32
— Snow .... *Churchill* .. 33
Choice of a Dwelling.......... *Murray* 32
— Tales .... *J. Blackwood* 16
Choix d'Opuscules Philosoph. .. *Trubner* ... 30
Cholera, Asiatic, Macnamara.. *Churchill* .. 25
— How to Avoid and Treat .. *King* 7
— in its Home, Macpherson .. *Churchill* .. 20
— Macleod .... *Churchill* .. 25
— at Oxford .... *Parker* 62
— Pathology and Treatment .. *Smith & El..* 16
— Symptomatic Treatment of.. *Bell* 18
Choppart (J. P.) Amusing Hist. of *Burns* .. 23
Chorister's Guide .... *Rivingtons* .. 10
Chorley (H. F.) Autobiography.. *Bentley* 5
Christ All in All, Sermons ..... *Dickinson* .. 10
— is All, Law .... *Rel. Tr. Soc.* 11
— the Bread of Life .... *Macmillan.* .. 6
— and the Church .... *Nisbet* 83
— the Consoler .... *Longmans* .. 34
— on the Cross .... *Bagster* 71
— Crucified, Saphir .... *Nisbet* 33
— — Divinity of .... *Clar. Press..* 13
— our Example .... *Hatchard* .. 8
— an Example, Young........ *Stanford.* .. 61
— Footsteps of .... *Clark* 19
— Friends of .... *J. Blackwood* 18
— Genealogies of, Harvey .... *Macmillan..* 15
— Given, Received, and Used. *Nisbet* 9
— of God, Bonar............ *Nisbet* 6
— of the Gospels and Mod.Crit. *Macmillan..* 38
— (The) History of .... *Isbister* ... 48
— Incidents in the Life of ... *Nisbet* 13
— in the Law and Prophets.. *Masters* 5
— the Light of the World..... *Isbister* ... 45
— our Life, Lamb........... *Morgan* 2
— our Light, Graham .... *Morgan* 3
— our Life, Hudson .... *Kellaway* .. 11
— and other Masters .... *Macmillan.* .. 15
— Miracles and Preaching of.. *Masters* 13
— in Modern Life, Sermons .. *King* 30
— in the Old Testament ..... *Bagster* 73
— Presence of............... *Isbister* ... 43
— Personal Reign of .... *Houlston.* .. 33
— and His Salvation......... *Isbister* ... 9
— and the Scriptures........ *Morgan* 2
— at Sychar, Walker......... *Nisbet* 36
— Symbols of .... *Hodder* 22
— Teaching of, King........ *Bell* 60
— Satisfying Instincts of Hum. *Macmillan.* 39
— Wholesome Words of ..... *Macmillan.* .. 39
— in the Word.............. *Nisbet* 37
— and his Work .... *Snow* 6
— The Work of .... *Macmillan..* .. 9
Christ's Atonement .... *Hodder* 25
— Hospital, Annals of .... *Bemrose* 17
— Kingdom .... *W. Blackw'd* 38
— Life .... *Hagger* 4
— Life from Cradle to Cross .. *MacPhun* .. 18
— Life, by Fleetwood .... *MacPhun* .. 6
— Life, Taylor.............. *Mozley* 12
— Life .... *Virtue.* 13

Christ's Life, Andrews .... *Isbister* 5
— By a Layman............... *Murray* 22
— for Children .... *Bell* 27
— Ewald .... *Bell* 60
— Farrar .... *Cassell.* 4
— Fleetwood .... *Sangster* ... 4
— Fleetwood .... *Collins* 2
— Illustrated, Jamieson ..... *Longmans* .. 29
— Lange .... *Clark* 8
— Lectures on, Ellicott ...... *Longmans* .. 35
— Lessons from .... *Nisbet* 17
— Taylor .... *Routledge* ... 5
— Second Advent, Philpot .. *Nisbet* 30
— — Second Coming, Brown .. *Clark* 18
Christabel Hope............... *Warne* 27
Christian Armour agst. Infidelity. *MacPhun* .. 15
— Art and Symbolism .... *Smith & El.* 26
— Brothers, School Books .. *MacGlashan.* 5
— Certainty .... *Hatchard* .. 31
— Character, Sermons ...... *Rivingtons..* 14
— Character............... *Nelson* 13
— Chivalry (Flower of) ...... *Isbister* ... 24
— Church, Brief History .... *Parker* 12
— Church, Hist. of, Robertson *Murray* 26
— Churches, Gould .... *Rivingtons..* 12
— Re-Union of .... *Rivingtons..* 12
— Churches and Sects ...... *Bentley* 10
— Comfort .... *Nimmo* 26
— Companionship .... *Isbister* ... 10
— Cyclopædia.............. *Blackie* 22
— Denomination, ReasonWhy *Houlston.* ... 4
— Devotedness .... *Snow* 3
— Doctrine, Deliv. & Develop. *Clark* 36
— of Prayer for the Departed.. *Isbister* ... 24
— of Sin .... *Clark* 22
— Dogmatics .... *Hodder* 2
— Dogmatics .... *Clark* 12
— Dogmas, Neander .... *Bohn's Lib..* 8
— Eighteen Centuries ...... *W. Blackw'd* 47
— Ethics, Harless .... *Clark* 14
— Ethics, Wuttke .... *Clark* 36
— Evidences and the Bible ... *Macmillan..* 39
— Evidences, Brewer .... *Jarrold* 4
— Evidences, Brewer .... *Parker.* 4
— Evidence Soc. Lectures ... *Hodder* 4
— Faith, Comprehensive .... *Parker.* 4
— Faith, Smith .... *Macmillan.* 33
— Fruitfulness............. *Snow* 16
— Gentleman, Tytler........ *Murray* 5
— Hero (The) .... *Morgan* 5
— Heroism, Tales of........ *Burns* 3
— Householder (The) .... *Mozley* 19
— Instruction, Dalton ...... *Nisbet* 11
— Life, Secret Trials of ..... *Mozley* 5
— Life, Sermons on .... *Mozley.* 10
— Orthodoxy, Donaldson ... *Williams* ... 4
— Thought and Work .... *Block* 1
— Life in the Camp .... *Nisbet* 9
— Endeavours after .... *Longmans* . 36
— Notes of .... *Macmillan.* 30
— Series .... *Ward & Lock* 31
— Living, Plain Words on ... *Isbister* ... 46
— Literature and Doctrine .. *Macmillan..* 5
— Lyrics .... *Warne.* 18
— Manliness .... *Rel. Tr. Soc.* 5
— Merchant (The)........... *Snow* 6
— Ministry Delineated ...... *Longmans* .. 33
— Missionary .... *Nelson* 12
— Morality, Characteristics of. *Parker.* 3
— Nurture .... *Isbister* ... 9
— in Palestine............. *Virtue* 13
— Philosopher (The) .... *Collins* 3
— Triumphing over Death ... *Snow* 7
— Politics................. *Parker.* 4
— Princess (The) .... *Morgan* 5
— Religion, Great Truths of .. *Masters* ... 11
— Religion, Gregory's Eviden. *Bohn's Lib..* 8
— Institutes of .... *Clark* 12
— Sacrifice and Service of Praise *Block* ... 10
— Sanctity .... *Macmillan.* 42
— Scholar .... *Parker.* 27
— Seasons (The)........... *Parker.* 36
— Theology in Apostolic Age *Hodder* 8
— Truth and Duty.......... *Nelson* 12
— Truth, on Attaining ...... *Parker.* 4

Christian Voice of Devotion ...... *MacPhun* 14
  — Vagabond .... *Houlston* 11
  — Vestiges of Creation .... *Parker* 8
  — Work .... *Nelson* 5
  — World Unmasked .... *Isbister* 7
  — Worship, Theory of .... *Masters* 5
  — Year .... *Parker* 26
  — Year .... *Rivingtons* 9
  — (Illustrated) .... *Cassell* 21
  — (Illustrated) .... *Routledge* 7
  — (Illustrated) .... *Ward&Lock* 21
  — Ken .... *Pickering* 24
Christian's Daily Treasury ...... *Snow* 15
  — Day (The) .... *Masters* 20
  — Incidents and Memoirs of .. *Collins* 3
  — Last Hours of .... *Soc. P. C. K.* 6
  — Teachings of .... *Masters* 5
Christianity, First Age of ...... *Allen* 5
  — as Taught by St. Paul ...... *Parker* 9
  — and other Systems .... *Collins* 3
  — Central Idea of .... *Morgan* 2
  — (Early) Milman .... *Murray* 22
  — Early Years of .... *Hodder* 15
  — Essence of .... *Trubner* 12
  — Founders of .... *Trubner* 9
  — Fundamental Truths of ...... *Clark* 10
  — Genius of Unveiled .... *King* 10
  — in Great Britain .... *Hodder* 5
  — in its Homely Aspects ...... *Masters* 9
  — in India .... *Allen* 15
  — (Latin) Milman .... *Murray* 22
  — Moral Truths of.............. *Clark* 30
  — Origin of .... *Trubner* 15
  — Phily. of .... *W. Blackw'd* 40
  — and Positivism .... *Macmillan* .. 23
  — (Primitive) Jones .... *Snow* 8
  — Rise and Progress of........ *Williams* 9
  — Saving Truths of .... *Clark* 10
Christina North .... *Macmillan* .. 2
Christmas Books, Dickens ...... *Chapman* 15
Christmas Eve, Tales for .... *Bentley* 14
Christmas Cake in Four Quarters *Macmillan* .. 2
  — Carol (A) Illuminated ...... *Macmillan* .. 7
  — Carols .... *A. Heywood.* 20
  — Carols and Ballads .... *Chatto* 8
  — Carols with Music.......... *Masters* 32
  — set to Music .... *Routledge* 29
  — Crackers for .... *Macmillan* .. 19
  — with the Poets .... *Ward&Lock* 21
  — Stories .... *Bohn's Lib.* 12
  — Stories .... *Tinsley Bros.* 8
  — Stories .... *Ward* 26
  — Voices of .... *Masters* 24
  — Mummers (The) .... *Mozley* 2
Chronicles and Characters ...... *Chapman* 20
Chronicles of Cosy Nook .... *Ward* 9
Chronicle of Gudrun .... *Edmonston* .. 11
  — of Yeres .... *Sotheran* 8
Chronological Pict. English History *Stanford* .. 52
Chronology .... *Clar. Press.* .. 17
  — English History .... *J. Heywood.* 24
  — of History, Art, &c .... *Lockwood* .. 29
  — History, and Biography .... *Longmans* .. 9
  — of New Testament .... *Parker* 4
Chronos, Mother Earth's Biogphy. *Trubner* 32
Chrysostom, (St.) Life of ...... *Nisbet* 8
Church (The) .... *Parker* 18
  — and the Age, Essays .... *Murray* 6
  — of England .... *Parker* 3
  — Doctrine of .... *Rivingtons* .. 11
  — Antiquities, Bingham ...... *Clar. Press.* 14
  — Association Lectures, 1872. *Hatchard* .. 4
  — Authority, Wilberforce...... *Mozley* 13
  — Bells .... *Smith* 1
  — Catechetical Works .... *Masters* 3
  — Catechism .... *Walker* 6
  — Catechism, Stories of ...... *Houlston* 38
  — Councils, Urwick .... *Tubbs* 4
  — Courts and Ch. Discipline .. *Mozley* 13
  — Lectures on, Nixon .... *Rivingtons* .. 11
  — Works on .... *Bell* 5
  — (Catholic) History, Mossman *Longmans* .. 5
  — of Christ Portrayed .... *Nisbet* 38
  — of the Fathers .... *Newman* 15
  — of the First Days .... *Macmillan* .. 39

Church and Clergy, Pinnock .... *Hall* 3
  — (Dean) Works by .... *Macmillan* .. 7
  — Decoration .... *Bemrose* .. 11
  — Decoration .... *Mozley* 2
  — Barrett .... *Rivingtons* .. 10
  — Masters .... *Masters* 6
  — Designs .... *Smith & El.* 4
  — Dictionary, Hook.......... *Murray* 14
  — Doctrine, Sadler .... *Bell* 50
  — Doctrine, Sadler .... *Rivingtons* .. 11
  — Doctrine, Sadler .... *W. Blackw'd* 41
  — of England Clergy .... *Chapman* .. 25
  — (English) Tales of .... *Houlston* 26
  — (of the) Five Books, Field .. *Harrison* 16
  — (Early) History .... *Longmans* .. 5
  — and the Empires .... *King* 2
  — Apology of .... *Parker* 6
  — and Common Sense .... *Macmillan* .. 17
  — not Established by Law .... *Soc. P. C. K.* 6
  — Freedom in.................. *King* 30
  — Maintenance of .... *Murray* 25
  — Present Position of .... *Macmillan* .. 6
  — Reasons for Returning to .. *Isbister* 10
  — Sermons on.................. *Bell* 48
  — Service Book .... *Parker* 37
  — Government, Potter .... *Bagster* 65
  — Festivals and Fasts .... *Soc. P. C. K.* 17
  — Furniture, Field .... *Rivingtons* .. 10
  — History ...4................ *Hall* 3
  — History .... *Longmans* .. 6
  — History .... *Hodder* 31
  — History .... *Clark* 16
  — History .... *Hagger* 11
  — History .... *Parker* 12
  — History .... *Clar. Press.* .. 9
  — History .... *Macintosh* .. 11
  — History, Neale .... *Mozley* 9
  — Fuller .... *Clar. Press.* 11
  — Grant .... *Hatchard* .. 10
  — Key to .... *Rivingtons* .. 25
  — England .... *Soc. P. C. K.* 12
  — First Three Centuries ...... *Murray* 4
  — 300 Years, Killen .... *Nisbet* 20
  — First Six Centuries .... *Clark* 16
  — Chapters on .... *Nisbet* 21
  — for Children................ *Bell* 27
  — Epitome of, Simpson ...... *Macmillan* .. 33
  — Mahan .... *Rivingtons* .. 73
  — Middle Age .... *Macmillan* .. 15
  — Neander .... *Clark* 17
  — Neander .... *Bohn's Lib.* .. 8
  — under Roman Empire ...... *Rivingtons* .. 24
  — Simple Sketches............ *Stanford* .. 70
  — Stoughton .... *Hodder* 17
  — Time of Reformation ...... *Macmillan* .. 15
  — Works on.................... *Masters* 0
  — in the House, Arnot........ *Nisbet* 3
  — Law, Blunt .... *Rivingtons* .. 10
  — Life, Grounds & Obligations *Isbister* 10
  — Music .... *Masters* 0
  — Music .... *Bemrose* 7
  — Music .... *Harrison* 15
  — Ordinal .... *Rivingtons* .. 12
  — Organs, Sutton .... *Rivingtons* .. 10
  — of Rome, Theology of ...... *Mozley* 6
  — Bishop .... *Rivingtons* .. 10
  — (The) its Origin, its History. *Clark* 15
  — Plate (Ancient) .... *Parker* 54
  — and the People .... *Chapman* .. 24
  — Poetry .... *Mozley* 2
  — Poetry for the Year .... *Mozley* 3
  — Policy, Essays on .... *Macmillan* .. 10
  — Principles, Discussions on .. *Clark* 18
  — Problems .... *Hodder* 24
  — Psalmody .... *Parker* 38
  — Questions, Parker .... *Snow* 12
  — Questions of the Day ...... *Murray* 25
  — Reform .... *Dickinson* .. 2
  — Registers .... *Masters* 24
  — Register of Preacher, &c ... *Letts* 3
  — of Rome .... *Parker* 6
  — Sacraments .... *Rivingtons* .. 5
  — Seasons, Catechism on...... *Parker* 36
  — Seasons : What they Teach . *Mozley* 12
  — Student's Manual .... *Black* 8

Church, Seven Ages of the ...... *Masters* 5
—— and Society, Essays .... *Hodder* 18
—— Spirit of .... *Masters* 26
—— and State, Birks............ *Hatchard* .. 3
—— Services, Bibles, &c......... *Stevenson* .. 0
—— Tales of Ancient British.... *Masters* 9
—— Teacher's Manual........... *Bell* 15
—— Teaching .... *Parker*...... 6
Churches, Colour on Walls, &c .. *Spon*........ 2
—— (Free) Dobney .... *Isbister* 13
—— (Modern Parish) Plan, &c... *King* 33
—— their Structure and Orna. .. *Masters* 21
—— Working Drawings of ...... *Parker*...... 54
Churchill's Series of Manuals.... *Churchill* .. 40
Churchman's Guide to Faith, &c. *Masters* 4
—— Library................... *Masters* 6
—— Instructor .... *Mosley* 3
Churchyard Lyrist............... *Houlston*.... 18
Cicero, De Oratore, Trans....... *Edmonston*.. 4
—— Holden, Purton .... *Cambridge* .. 5
—— Selections from .... *Macmillan* .. 7
—— Long .... *Whittaker* .. 1
Cicero's Life and Times .... *Murray* 7
Circassian Homes .... *Hurst* 9
Circle of the Church's Life ...... *Nisbet* 34
Circling (The) Year .... *Rel. Tr. Soc.* .. 6
Cistercian Order ; its Mission, &c. *Washbourne* .. 6
Cities (Great) of Middle Ages ... *Routledge* .. 34
Citizen Bonaparte .... *Ward&Lock* 23
City of London Directory .... *Wilson* 11
—— Road Chapel.............. *Wesleyan*.... 43
Civilization considered as a Science *Bell* 42
—— Guizot's History .... *Bohn's Lib.*.. 8
—— History of .... *Longmans* .. 2
—— in the 5th Century .... *Allen*...... 8
—— Origin of .... *Longmans* .. 24
Civil Power in Relation to Church *Rivingtons* .. 12
—— Wars in England .... *Clar. Press.* .. 15
—— Service Arithmetic .... *MacGlashan* 4
—— Examination Handy Books *Lockwood* .. 36
—— Examination .... *MacGlashan* 3
—— Guide .... *Cassell* 2
—— Guide .... *J. Blackwood* 25
—— Key to .... *Bell* 63
—— Situations .... *Stanford*.... 54
Clarendon's Rebellion .... *Clar. Press.* .. 15
—— State Papers .... *Clar. Press.* .. 15
Clare Savile .... *Warne*...... 19
Clarke (Rev. J. Erskine) Works.. *Bell* 27
Clarke's Bible and Commentary.. *Tegg*........ 0
Clark's Foreign Theological Lib. *Clark* 2
Class and the Desk............ *Sangster* .. 7
—— and Home Lesson Books.... *Allman* 6
Classic Tales .... *Bohn's Lib.* .. 9
Classics, British .... *Walker* 8
—— Chandos .... *Warne* 15
—— Critical and Annoted Eds... *Bell* 7
—— English .... *Clar. Press.* .. 31
—— English School and College.. *Collins* 11
—— French .... *Hachette*.. 1
—— with German Notes .... *Nutt* 39
—— German.................. *Lockwood* .. 35
—— Grammar School .... *Whittaker* .. 5
—— Greek .... *Clar. Press.* .. 1
—— Greek .... *Clar. Press.* .. 21
—— Greek .... *MacGlashan* 8
—— Greek .... *Lockwood* .. 32
—— and Roman .... *Nutt* 8
—— Italian .... *Nutt* 30
—— Latin .... *Clar. Press.* .. 5
—— Latin .... *Clar. Press.* .. 21
—— Latin .... *Lockwood* .. 31
—— Selections for Schools .... *Clar. Press.* .. 24
—— Our Christian .... *Nisbet* 9
—— Oxford Pocket .... *Parker*...... 55
—— Pocket English .... *Lockwood* .. 45
—— Translations of .... *Parker*...... 58
Classical Biography .... *Nimmo*...... 15
—— Dictionary .... *Milner* 2
—— Dictionary .... *Ward&Lock* 7
—— Smith .... *Murray* 28
—— Examination Papers .... *Rivingtons* .. 20
—— Manual, Baird .... *Whittaker* .. 11
—— Scholarship Considered .... *Bell* 31

Classical Tables .... *Bell* 12
—— Tales and Legends .... *Masters* 9
—— Texts with Short Notes ... *Parker*...... 56
—— Translations .... *Bohn's Lib.* .. 15
Classification, Essay on .... *Trubner* 1
Claude on Composit. of a Sermon *Cornish* 3
Claverhouse, Napier's Memorials *Stevenson* 0
Clematis, Hardy Species, &c. .. *Murray* 23
Clemency Franklin .... *Macmillan* .. 7
Clere (R. G.) Works by .... *Hatchard* .. 5
Clergy, Books for Use of the.... *Masters* 0
—— Charities .... *Rivingtons* .. 11
—— of the First Ten Centuries .. *Macmillan* .. 21
—— Hodgson's Instructions for *Rivingtons* .. 11
—— Sufferings of .... *Parker*...... 13
Clergyman's Instructor .... *Clar. Press.* .. 13
Clergymen of the Church of Eng. *Chapman* .. 25
—— Duration of Life amongst .. *Layton*...... 11
Clerical Anecdotes, &c .... *Chatto* 8
—— Friends and Mod. Thought *Burns* 23
—— Papers .... *Hall* 3
—— Workshops and Tools Used *Nisbet* 32
Clewer Manuals (The) .... *Parker*...... 33
Climatology (Chemical) .... *Longmans* .. 20
—— Donne .... *King* 7
—— Works on .... *Churchill* .. 0
Clinical Medicine, Study of .... *Smith & El.* 22
Clinton's Fasti Hellenici .... *Clar. Press.* .. 17
Clitheroe, History of.......... *Routledge* .. 22
Clock and Watch Makers' Manual *Spon* 13
Cloister Legends............... *Washbourne* .. 6
Clouds, Modification of .... *Churchill* .. 21
Clough (A. H.) Poems and Remains *Macmillan* .. 7
Clubfoot, Brodhurst .... *Churchill* .. 0
Club Night, a Village Record .. *Partridge* .. 9
Clubs and Club Life .... *Chatto* 37
Coal, Autobiography of a Lump of *Cassell*...... 10
—— Fields of Great Britain .. *Stanford* 56
—— of Gloucestershire .... *Stanford*.... 47
—— Mining, Smyth .... *Lockwood* .. 6
—— Question, Jevons .... *Macmillan* .. 17
—— Screening .... *Allen* 2
—— Trade Reckoner .... *Philip* 41
Coast Guard Manual for Boatmen *Harrison* 6
Coast Survey, &c., of Gt. Britain *Virtue* 12
Cobbe (Miss) Works by .... *Williams* .. 4
Cobbin's Commentaries .... *Ward* 14
Cobden (R.) A Biography ...... *Lockwood* .. 43
—— Club Essays .... *Cassell* 22
Cobwebs from an Empty Skull .. *Routledge*.. 43
Cockburn (Lord) Memorials of .. *Black* 10
Cockburn's Memorials .... *Edmonstone* 5
Codex Apocryphus .... *J. R. Smith* 9
—— Canonum Lamburti .... *Dickinson* .. 8
Codrington (Adm. Sir Ed.) Life.. *Longmans* .. 7
Coffee Auctions of Dutch T. Co. *Edmonston* .. 15
—— and Chicory .... *Spon*...... 12
Cohn's Exchange Tables .... *Wilson* 12
Coinage of Great Britain ...... *Sotheran* .. 25
—— Greek Federal .... *Macmillan* .. 40
Coin Collector's Manual .... *Bohn's Lib.* .. 18
Coins .... *Pickering* .. 10
—— (Current) of all Countries .. *Trubner* 9
—— English .... *J. R. Smith* 9
—— Sassanian .... *Trubner* 29
Colburn's Locomotive Engineering *Collins* 2
Colenso (Bishop) Works by .... *Macmillan* .. 7
—— Works by .... *Longmans* .. 0
—— Natal Sermons .... *Trubner* 8
—— Pentateuch Examined, Drew *Bell* 60
Coleoptera, Scotland .... *W. Blackw'd* 22
Coleridge (Rev. H. J.) Works by *Burns* 14
—— (Sara) Memoir and Letters, *King*...... 2
—— (S. T.) Spiritual Phil. .... *Macmillan* .. 14
Colet (Dean) Works by........ *Bell* 46
Colinton, Parish .... *Edmonston*.. 16
Collects, Brief Meditations on .. *Mosley*...... 2
Collects of the Chrch., Floral Design *Macmillan* .. 8
Collects, Commentary on, James *Rivingtons* .. 5
Collects, Sonnets on the ...... *Isbister* 8
—— Stories and Catechisings on *Mosley* 12
Collector's Handy Book of Algæ. *Hardwicke*.. 5
College Life, Whytehead ...... *Masters* 29
Collieries and Colliers .... *Longmans* .. 44
Collins (W.) New Magdalen .... *Bentley* 16

C

Collins's (W.) Works ...... — ...Smith & El. 4
— Poor Miss Finch .... Bentley 16
Colloquia Peripatetica .... Edmonston.. 7
— Critics .... Ibister ... 18
Colonial Adventures and Experienc. Bell 12
Colonial Constitutions .... Longman ... 3
— Empire .... Soc. P. C. K. 7
— Office List .... Harrison ... 2
— Policy and History .... Stanford .. 49
— Questions.............. Isbister ... 3
— Sports and Pastimes........ Tinsley Bros. 2
— Subjects .... Smith & El. 28
— Service, Rules for .... Harrison ... 11
Colonies (British) .... Stanford ... 54
— Geography .... J. Heywood 5
— (The) and Imperial Unity .. Isbister ... 19
— (Tales of) Rowcroft ..... Smith & El. 18
Colonization Circular.......... Stanford .. 53
Colour, Alphabet of .... Chapman .. 27
Colour (Laws of) Chevreul ..... Routledge .. 67
— (Harmony of) .... Bohn's Lib. .. 18
— Hay .... W. Blackw'd 13
Colour, Prin. & Science of, Benson Chapman .. 15
— (Rudiments of) Field .... Isbister ... 11
Colquhoun (Lady) Memoirs of . Nisbet 10
Columbus .... Wilson 7
— (Life of) Helps .... Bell 39
Columbia .... Trubner ... 8
Come to Jesus, Hall .... Nisbet 10
Comfort for Afflicted .... Rivingtons .. 8
Comfort ye, Comfort ye .... Nisbet 23
Comic Annual .... Chatto 10
— History of England ...... Bradbury .. 2
Coming Man (The) .... Isbister ... 44
Commanders (Memoirs of Great) Routledge .. 5
Commandments, Dale .... Hodder 5
— and Nat. Reformation...... Macmillan .. 24
— (Ten), with Prayers....... Hatchard .. 27
— Stories on the............ Nisbet 22
— Tales on .... Masters ... 2
Commentary, Clarke's Bible .... Tegg 6
Commerce, Dictionary of ...... Longmans .. 44
— of the Globe .... Wilson..... 11
— (British) History of ...... Murray 20
— Maritime .... W. Blackw'd 26
— Modern .... Virtue 22
— Raw Materials of .... Virtue 22
— and Science .... Hardwicke.. 10
— Treaties, Laws, &c., of ... Harrison ... 2
— in War .... Smith 25
Commercial Chemical Analysis . Lockwood .. 12
— Correspondent .... Murby 6
— Law, Levi .... Smith & El. 13
— Subjects .... Smith & El. 28
— Terms .... Groombridge 19
— Terms .:.............. Routledge .. 12
— Traveller's Guide .... Walker ... 6
Common Prayer, 1661 .... Pickering .. 10
— 1682 .... Pickering .. 33
— accord. to Text of Sealed Bks. Harrison ... 16
— Annotated .... Rivingtons .. 4
— Arranged as Said .... Bemrose .. 1
— Book of .... Masters ... 3
— Catechetical Lessons ..... Parker 11
— and Church Service ..... Cambridge .. 12
— and Church Service, Spec. pp. Bagster .. 48
— Coloured Borders .... Murray ... 5
— Companion to.......... Parker 11
— Companion to.......... Rivingtons .. 16
— of Edward VI. .... Rivingtons.. 29
— Expository Sermons on ... Macmillan.. 24
— Headpieces and Initials . Bell 47
— History of .... Soc. P. C. K. 21
— History of .... Parker 11
— History, Proctor .... Macmillan.. 29
— History and Principles.... Black 8
— Illuminated............ Rivingtons .. 4
— Interleaved............ Rivingtons .. 4
— Key to .... Rivingtons .. 4
— Latin............... Rivingtons .. 4
— Objections to .... Rivingtons .. 5
— Rational Illustration of . Whittaker .. 15
— with Scripture Proofs .... Bemrose.. .. 1
— Sermons on............ Masters 14
— Specimen Pages.......... Cambridge.. 16

Common Prayer, Students' Book of Bell 47
— Treatise on, Humphry ..... Bell 47
— French, La Liturgie ...... Rivingtons.. 4
— Wheatley on .... Bohn's Lib. 9
— Wheatley on .... Clar. Press.. 14
— Works on.............. Rivingtons.. 4
Common Things Explained .... Lockwood .. 13
Communicant's Manual ...... Mozley 2
Communion Discourses....... MacPhun .. 12
Commutation Tables, Chisholm.. Layton 8
Companies' Act .... Wilson 6
Companies' Act .... Waterlow .. a
— Limited by Guarantee ... Wilson 5
Companions to the Altar ..... Suttaby .... a
— of my Solitude .... Smith & El. 5
Companion Library .... Warne 44
— to Old Testament .... Rivingtons .. 2
— or, Teachings of Life .... Warne..... 27
Compass, Variation, &c., of ... Philip 39
Compensations, Fletcher ..... Spon 17
Compensation Claims (Farm) .. Longmans .. 31
— Law of .... Stevens ... 10
Complete Grazier .... Lockwood .. 16
Composition, Currie .... W. Blackw'd 43
— Theory and Practice...... Sangster ... 7
Comte and Positivism, Mill..... Trubner ... 20
Conceited Pig (The) .... Mozley..... 2
Conchology .... Reeve 10
Concordance to the Christian Year Parker 27
— of Scripture Names and Places Clark ... 22
Concrete, Cement and Mortars .. Spon 12
Confectioner (Royal) .... Chapman .. 18
Confectionary, Modern....... Mozley 6
Confectionary, Nourse ...... W. Blackw'd 22
Conferences of Reformers...... Wesleyan .. 44
Confession in Church of England J. Heywood 37
— Doctrine of .... Masters ... 4
Confessions of the 16th Century.. Bell 48
— of a Clarionet Player ..... Ward & Lock 23
— of Var. Chrchs. of Christendom. Clark ... 22
Confessors, Manual for....... Parker 31
— Two Thousand of, 1662 .... Snow 5
Confirmation .... Parker.'c... 40
— and First Communion .... Masters ... 19
— Lectures, Vaughan ...... Macmillan.. 38
— Lectures on, Villiers ..... Nisbet 36
— Lessons on .... Bell 51
— Manual .... Rivingtons .. 17
— Manual, Maclear .... Macmillan.. 21
— Oxenden .... Hatchard .. 6
— Sewell .... Longmans .. 36
— Tracts .... Mozley..... 2
— Works on............. Masters ... 0
Congratulations and Counsels.. Nisbet 10
Congregational Church Music .. Hodder 34
— History, Waddington ...... Snow 16
— Union Publications .... Hodder 36
Congregationalism in Yorkshire. Snow 11
Conic Sections, Day .... Macmillan.. 9
— Drew .... Macmillan.. 9
— Elementary .... Bell 15
— Jackson .... Macmillan.. 17
— Puckle .... Macmillan.. 29
— Todhunter .... Macmillan.. 37
Conington (John) Mis. Writings Longmans .. 15
— (J.) Translations by........ Bell 35
Conjuring Book, Boy's Own .. Milner..... 2
— Fly, Notes on .... Routledge .. 4
Conqueror and his Companions . Tinsley Bros. 2
Conquest of the Sea .... Chatto 7
Conrad the Squirrel .... Macmillan.. 8
Conscience (The) Maurice ..... Macmillan.. 24
— Examination of .... Rivingtons.. 6
Conscience's Tales .... Burns 24
Conscript (The) .... Ward & Lock 23
Conservation of Energy ...... King...... 8
Consolation for the Bereaved .. Lockwood .. 42
— Grandpierre .... Nisbet 15
— in Sickness, &c.......... Bell 53
— Statutes .... Waterlow .. a
Consolator .... Wesleyan .. 42
Consolatoria (Epistola) Perez .. Nisbet 5
Consoler (The) .... Washbourne 5
Constable (Archibald) .... Edmonston.. 5
— (Rev. H.) Works by........ Kellaway .. 4

Constancia's Household .... S. S. Union   5
Constipated Bowels .... Churchill.... 9
Constitutional Law .... Stevens 4
—— History for Students ...... Stevens 5
—— Progress .... Murray 6
Consult Me, Receipt Book ...... Nicholson 7
Consumption, Curability of ..... Churchill .. 36
—— from First Stages of ...... Churchill .. 15
—— (Pulmonary) .... Black 2
—— in Remediable Stages ...... King 7
—— Treatment of .... Churchill... 6
Contemporary Review .... Strahan 1
Continent, Letters from the .... Isbister 4
—— Hand Books to .... Murray 15
Continental Hand Book .... Cassell 3
Contracts, Law of .... Lockwood ... 28
Contrasts .... Isbister 11
Conundrums .... Lockwood ... 45
Convent Life, Lights & Shadows Morgan 3
Convents and Monasteries ..... Washbourne . 6
Conversation, De Quincey on.... Black 11
Conversation, Guides to Languages Nutt....... 25
Conversion Illustrated from Bible Isbister 38
Conveyancing, Precedents in ... Stevens 15
Convict Ship & England's Exiles Nisbet 8
Convocation (Comedy of) ...... Washbourne . 7
Convocations of the Two Provinces Mozley..... 13
Cook (Captain) Story of .... Cassell 11
—— Voyages .... Black 10
—— (E.) Poems .... Warne 18
—— (Modern) Francatelli..... Bentley 6
Cook's Guide, Francatelli ...... Bentley 6
Cooke (Dr.) of Belfast, Life, &c.. Murray 25
—— (Rev. Corbett) Memorials of Wesleyan ... 43
—— (Gunner, J.L.) Memoir of .. Nisbet 10
Cookery, All About It .... Ward & Lock 6
—— Australian Meats .... Chapman.... 11
—— Books .... Ward & Lock 22
—— Books .... Warne 42
—— Books.................. Bemrose 13
—— Book, Beeton .... Ward & Lock 5
—— Cottage .... Groombridge 18
—— Dainty Dishes .... Edmonston .. 5
—— Delamere .... Lockwood .. 48
—— Domestic .... Milner 3
—— Everybody's Pudding Book Bentley 6
—— Book, Every Family's...... Nicholson .. 9
—— First Lessons in .... Macmillan .. 3
—— German .... Chapman ... 18
—— and Housekeeping Books .. Routledge .. 8
—— Indian Meal Book .... Smith & El. 13
—— for Lent............... Burns 27
—— Little Dinners........... King 31
—— Model .... Warne 16
—— (Modern), Acton......... Longmans .. 44
—— Modern Cook, Francatelli . Bentley 6
—— Modern Domestic .... Murray 8
—— Modern .... Mozley..... 6
—— Nourse .... W. Blackw'd 22
—— Pocket Guide to .... Macl'hun ... 16
—— Rational .... Nimmo 27
—— Turkish .... Allen 28
—— What to do with Cold Mutton Bentley 15
—— Works on .... Houlston.... 10
Cookman's (A) Life .... Hodder 6
Cooley, His Rights and Wrongs.. Isbister 11
Cooper (Mrs. M. S.) Memoirs... Wesleyan ... 43
—— (Thomas) Works by ...... Hodder 9
Co-ordinates, Treatise on ..... Parker 60
Copland's (S.) Agriculture ..... Virtue 19
Copper, Chemistry and Metallurgy Trubner ... 24
Coptic Grammar, Tattam....... Williams ... 14
Copy Books .... Marr 14
—— Books.................. Marby 4
—— Books.................. J. Heywood 13
—— Babbit .... Jarrold 6
—— Farnell .... Jarrold 5
—— German .... Nutt....... 15
—— Harding .... J. Heywood 12
—— Headline .... A. Heywood 17
—— Vere Foster .... M. Ward... 28
—— and Lines .... Chambers .. 10
—— Millard's Gram......... J. Heywood.. 10
—— Orthographical .... Collins 27
—— and Slips .... Philip 44

Copy Books, Waverley .... Marlborough 16
Copy Slips .... J. Heywood 15
—— Wilson's .... Allman 19
Copyhold, Enfranchisement .... Layton 14
Copyright of Designs, Printed Fab. Smith & El. 27
—— Law of .... Stevens 2
Coral Island .... Nelson 7
Corinthians, Epistles to, Thom .. Trubner 26
Corn Merchant's Guide........ MacGlashan 8
Corn in Oxford, Prices of...... Clar. Press.. 14
Corneille's Plays, French....... Clar. Press.. 26
Corner Cupboard .... Houlston.... 5
Corner's Educational Works .... Dean....... 11
Cornhill Library of Fiction .... King 29
Cornish Drama, Stokes .... Trubner 25
—— Drama .... Asher 7
—— Drama .... Clar. Press.. 8
—— Mines (A Tale of the) .... Nisbet 44
—— Names, Bannister........ Williams ... 2
—— Tales and Poems .... Houlston.... 26
Cornish's (G.) Sermons & Remains Mozley 3
Cornishmen, Cat. of Writings of. Longmans .. 7
Cornwall .... J. R. Smith. 7
—— Drolls of Old .... Chatto 30
—— History of .... Chatto 28
—— its Mines .... Spon....... 43
—— (Old) Echoes from....... Masters 11
—— Superstitions and Customs. Bentley 5
—— Survey of............. Sotheran .. 7
Cornwall (Barry) Songs and Lyrics Bell 35
—— Walter White .... Chapman .. 26
Cornwallis's Papers and Corresp. Murray 8
Corpulence, Letter on, Banting.. Harrison... 5
Correggio, Works of .... Bell 3
Correspondence Register........ Letts 2
Corsica, Campbell .... Hatchard .. 4
Cortes (Hernando) Life of ..... Bell 39
Cosmogany of Hebrew Scriptures Hodder 12
Costumes of Highland Claus .... Sotheran.... 19
Costume, Cyclopædia of .... Chatto 9
Cottage by the Creek .... Nisbet 10
Cottage Library .... Milner 7
—— Life in the West of England Macmillan.. 29
—— Management .... Ward & Lock 12
—— Pictures .... Parker 45
—— on the Rock .... Yapp 3
Cottages &c. Designs .... Hagger 4
Cottager's Library .... Nicholson .. 6
Cottagers' Series .... Parker 48
Cottar's Library (The) .... Walker 10
Cotton's (Bishop) Life .... Longmans .. 8
—— Works by .... Macmillan.. 8
Cotton Cultivation, Gibbs ..... Spon....... 13
—— Cultivation, De Coin ..... Chapman... 14
—— Cultivation, Mallet ...... Chapman... 21
—— Culture in Bombay ...... Smith & El. 3
—— India, and Elsewhere ..... Smith & El. 18
—— Manufacture .... A. Heywood. 15
—— of Great Britain .... Bohn's Lib.. 19
Cough (Hooping) Martyn ...... Churchill .. 26
—— (Winter) Dobell......... Churchill .. 15
Councils, Ancient and Modern .. Hodder 21
—— (Christian) .... Clark 16
—— of the Church.......... Parker 12
Council of Florence .... Masters 22
Counsel & Cheer for Battle of Life Isbister 7
—— to a Young Wife .... Cornish ... 1
Counsels on Holiness of Life ... Rivingtons . 6
—— of an Invalid .... Macmillan.. 11
—— to a Newly-Wedded Pair .. Snow 12
—— for Young Students ...... Macmillan.. 39
Counterpoint, Treatise on ..... Clar. Press.. 30
Countess Kate .... Mozley.... 3
Counting House Guide........ Wilson 2
Country Book, Boy's Own ..... Routledge .. 31
—— Books for the .... Routledge .. 9
—— Books for the .... Ward & Lock 11
—— Common Objects of ...... Routledge .. 8
—— of the Dwarfs .... Chatto 8
—— Houses, Designs for ..... Parker 54
—— Life, All About .... Ward & Lock 6
—— Maidens .... M. Ward... 9
—— Stroll, Book for a .... Hardwicke.. 9
—— Towns, their Place in Civili. Bell 42
—— Walks .... Groombridge 13
—— Stories, Old and New ..... Smith & El. 13

County Atlas, Gt. Brit. & Ireland *Virtue* 19
—— Court Guide .... *Lockwood* .. 28
—— Families (The) .... *Hardwicke*.. 12
—— Maps .... *C. Smith*.... 8
—— Geographies .... *Collins* ... 13
—— Geographies .... *Philip* ... 43
—— Histories .... *J. R. Smith* 0
Courage and Cowards ...... *Nisbet* ... 10
Course of Time .... *W. Blackw'd.* 26
Court Beauties of Charles II. *Chatto* ... 2
—— Hand Restored .... *Chatto* ... 40
Courts-Martial, Simmons ... *Murray* ... 28
—— (Clode) .... *Murray* ... 7
—— (Hough and Long) ...... *Allen* 14
Courtnay (Bp.) Works by ... *Hatchard* .. 13
Cousin Annie .... *Warne* ... 29
—— Kate, Works by .... *Warne* ... 26
—— Kate's Library .... *Nelson* ... 22
Covenant of Love .... *Hatchard* .. 13
Cow, The Breeding .... *Cornish* ... 3
Cowper's Complete Works ... *Bohn's Lib.* .. 5
—— (Wm.) Poetical Works .. *J. Blackwood* 6
—— Poems, Griffiths ...... *Clar. Press.* 12
—— Poems & Letters, by Meines *MacPhun* .. 20
—— Poetical Works .... *Warne* ... 18
—— (Lady) Diary .... *Murray* ... 8
Cox (David) A Memoir ...... *Chapman* ... 6
—— (G. W.) Works by ...... *Longmans* .. 0
—— (Rev. Sam.) Works by .. *Isbister* ... 11
Coxe's Christian Ballads ... *Parker* ... 44
Crab, Shrimp, and Lobsters *Routledge* .. 10
Crabbe (Geo.) Poetical Works *J. Blackwood* 7
—— Life and Poetical Works *Murray* ... 8
Cracow (Try) and the Carpathians *Chapman* ... 19
Craik's (Henry) Works ..... *Mack* 9
Cranmer's Works .... *Clar. Press.* 13
—— Strype's Memorials of.. *Harrison* ... 16
Cranston's Tibullus ...... *W. Blackw'd.* 37
Crashaw, Poetical Works.... *J. R. Smith* 8
Craven (Mrs. A.) Sister's Story *Bentley* ... 5
—— Fleurange .... *Smith & El.* 4
Crawley (Capt.) Games for Boys *Tegg* ..... a
Creator (The) and the Creation *Isbister* ... 48
Creation and the Fall ...... *Clark* 11
—— History of .... *King* 6
—— in Plan and Progress ... *Macmillan.* 6
—— Thoughts on .... *Parker* ... 8
—— Vestiges of Nat. History of. *Churchill* . 36
—— The Week of .... *Macmillan.* 40
—— Christian Vestiges of .. *Parker* ... 8
Creasy's Fifteen Decisive Battles *Bentley* ... 5
—— English Constitution ... *Bentley* ... 5
Credibilia .... *Trubner* ... 0
Cree Language, Grammar of .. *Trubner* ... 16
Creed, On the .... *Parker* ... 3
—— Exposition of .... *Clar. Press.* 14
—— Pearson on the .... *Bell* 49
—— Pearson on the .... *Bohn's Lib.* 8
—— Tales on the .... *Masters* ... 19
—— Village Conferences on the. *Masters* ... 2
—— of Christendom .... *Parker* ... 14
—— (The) of the Church & Scrip. *Macmillan.* 35
—— and Church .... *Hall* 4
Creeds and Churches........ *Edmonston.* 19
—— (Collection of)........ *Clar. Press.* 13
—— History of, Lumby ...... *Bell* 48
—— in Scotland .... *W. Blackw'd* 16
Creole Grammar .... *Trubner* ... 29
Cressy and Poictiers ...... *Ward & Lock* 8
Cricket Ground, Selkirk ... *Macmillan.* 32
Cricket, Jerks in from Short Leg *Harrison* ... 4
—— Origin and Laws .... *Bell* 24
Crime, History of in England.. *Smith & El.* 16
Crimea and Astrakan .... *Hurst* 1
—— Kinglake .... *W. Blackw'd* 17
Crimean War, Burgoyne's Life *Bentley* ... 5
—— Nolan .... *Virtue* ... 21
—— Surgery of .... *Churchill* ... 15
Criminal Law of England ... *Macmillan.* 34
—— Law .... *Waterlow* .. a
Cripple of Antioch (The) .. *Nisbet* ... 10
Cris Forbes' Boyhood ...... *Warne* ... 20
Cross-Cross Journeys ...... *Hurst* 2
Criticism, Essays in ...... *Macmillan.* 2
Crochet Work, Designs for .. *Houlston...* 7

Crofton Cousin's Juveniles ...... *Warne* ... 31
Croker (J. W.) Works by ...... *Murray* ... 8
Cromwell's Letters and Speeches *Chapman* .. 12
—— Life, Guizot............ *Bentley* ... 0
—— (Oliver) .... *Wilson* ... 7
Croquemitaine, Doré .... *Cassell* ... 3
Croquet and other Games, Prior. *Williams* .. 11
Cross of Christ (The) Landels.. *Nisbet* ... 20
—— and Passion, Lessons of the. *Macmillan.* 32
—— Practical Science of .... *Masters* ... 22
—— and the Serpent .... *Parker* ... 13
—— Seven Words from, Ireland. *Nisbet* ... 19
—— Seven Sayings of, Watson.. *Masters* ... 23
—— Seven Words of Christ on the *Macmillan.* 8
—— Some Aspects of the ..... *Masters* ... 12
—— The Story of the .... *Mozley* ... 13
—— The Words from the...... *Masters* ... 12
Crossing the River .... *Nisbet* ... 25
Crown (The) and its Advisers.... *W. Blackw'd* 5
Croydon Church............. *Sotheran* ... 1
Cruden's Concordance .... *Bagster* ... 63
—— Trade Edition .... *Rivingtons* ... 4
—— Hannay .... *Bell* 43
—— King .... *Warne* ... 39
—— Eadie .... *S. S. Union* 42
—— Smith .... *J. Blackwood* 5
—— Carey .... *Routledge* .. 64
Cruikshank (G.) Works Illus. by *Bell* 8
Cruise of the Daring .... *Ward & Lock* 28
Crumbs Swept Up .... *Hodder* ... 10
—— Swept Up .... *Nicholson* ... 3
Crusaders, Chronicles of the .... *Bohn's Lib.* 12
Crusades, Stories of .... *Masters* ... 10
—— and Crusaders .... *Ward & Lock* 27
—— History .... *Longmans* .. 5
Crushed Hopes Crowned in Death *Nisbet* ... 8
Crustacea .... *Van Voorst* a
Crystallography .... *Clar. Press.* 27
Cuba, Gallenga .... *Chapman* .. 4
—— Goodman .... *King* 4
Cubitt (Rev. G.) Works ..... *Wesleyan* .. 10
Cues from All Quarters ..... *Hodder* ... 10
Culpepper Com. Herbal ...... *Virtue* ... 19
—— Brit. Herbal .... *Nicholson* .. 4
—— Herbal .... *Milner* ... 2
Culture and Anarchy .... *Smith & El.* 1
Cumberland Worthies .... *Routledge* .. 5
Cumming's (J.) Seventh Vial ... *Hurst* 9
—— Works .... *Bentley* ... 5
Cuneiform Inscriptions, Smith ... *Williams* .. 13
Cunningham Lectures .... *Clark* 12
Cupples (Mrs. Geo.) Works .. *Nelson* ... 22
Cur Deus Homo............. *Parker* ... 7
—— Anselm .... *Williams* .. 1
Curate's Wife (The) .... *Mozley* ... 3
Curfew Chimes, Macduff ..... *Nisbet* ... 23
Curiosities of Natural History ... *Bentley* ... 4
—— of the Pulpit .... *Virtue* ... 15
—— of Savage Life .... *Ward & Lock* 8
—— of Science .... *Lockwood* .. 44
—— of Street Literature .... *Sotheran* .. 9
—— of Toil, Wynter .... *Chapman* .. 26
Currency .... *Parker* ... 62
—— Paper and Metallic ..... *Black* ... 14
—— Question .... *Wilson* ... 5
Curse of Immortality ...... *Macmillan.* 19
Curtius (Prof.) Greek Language. *Murray* ... 9
Curve Tracing, Frost .... *Macmillan.* 17
—— Tables of .... *Lockwood* .. 5
Curzon (Hon. R.) Books of Travel *Murray* ... 4
Cushions and Corners .... *Warne* ... 28
Customs' Duties Tariff ..... *Wilson* ... 9
Cust's Annals of the Wars .. *Murray* ... 9
Cuyler (Dr.) Works by...... *Hodder* ... 22
Cyclopædia of Anecdote ..... *Stock* ... a
—— of English Literature .... *Chambers* .. 29
—— of Moral and Rel. Anecdotes *Wesleyan* .. 41
—— of Moral and Rel. Truths .. *Jarrold* ... 3
—— of Practical Receipts .... *Churchill* .. 13
—— of Useful &c. Plants .... *Sangster* ... 5
Cycle of Life (The) .... *Soc. P. C. K.* 8
Cyril Ashley .... *Nelson* ... 9

Dahomé, 3 Months' Residence at *Tinsley* 6
Dahomey As It Is .... *Chapman* ... 3

Daily Devotion (Household) .... Cassell 2
—— Lessons for Church .... Freud ..... a
—— Lessons for Daily Life .... Hatchard 7
—— Light on the Daily Path .... Bagster 58
—— Meditations, Bowen .... Edmonston 3
—— Meditations .... Masters 25
—— Readings for a Year .... Bell 53
—— Wants, Dicty. of .... Houlston 3
Dairyman's Daughter (The) .... Partridge 7
—— Guide .... Groombridge 16
Daisy and her Friends .... Warne 29
Daisy, by Author of W. W. World Nisbet 11
—— Library .... Bell 26
Dale (R. W.) Works .... Hodder 5
Dallas (A. R. C.) Life and Works Nisbet 11
Dalton (Rev. T.) Arith. and Algebra Macmillan .. 8
Dalyell's Musical Memoirs .... Stevenson .. a
Damages, Law of .... Stevens 4
Damascus and Jordan, Rivers of Burns 33
—— Porter .... Murray 25
Dames of High Estate .... Warne 19
Dana (J. D.) Works by .... Trubner 9
Danbury Newsman .... Chatto 11
Dance Album (The) .... Routledge 44
Daniel, or, Apocalypse of OldTest. Williams .. 4
—— Dissertations on .... Clark 11
—— (The Prophet) Gaussen ... Mozley 3
—— the Prophet .... Parker 9
Daniel's Prophetic Visions .... Bagster 64
Daniell and Ayton's Voyage Gt. B. Sotheran .. 9
Danish Ballads, Ancient .... Williams 11
—— Language, Guide to .... Trubner 5
—— Legends .... Bohn's Lib... 13
—— Pract. Introd. to .... Williams 6
—— Speaker and Dialogues .... Williams 3
—— War, A Story of .... Hatchard 31
Dante, by Ford .... Smith & El. .. 4
—— Doré's Illustrations .... Cassell 3
—— Flaxman's Illustrations .. Bell 2
—— Inferno, Selections (Italian) Clar. Press.. 29
—— Intro. to Study of .... Smith & El. 22
—— Shadow of .... Rivingtons .. 27
—— Trans. by Carey .... Bell 29
—— by Carlyle .... Chapman 12
—— Study of, Barlow .... Williams 2
Dante's Comedy, Rosetti .... Macmillan.. 8
Dare to do Right .... Nisbet 11
Daring Deeds .... Warne 27
—— Library .... Warne 27
Dark Sayings of Old, M'Caul .. Nisbet 23
Darwin (C.) Geological Observa. Smith & El. .
—— Works by .... Murray 9
Darwinian Theory Examined.... Nisbet 11
Darwinism and Design .... Hodder 6
—— in Morals .... Williams 4
Date Book .... Ward 7
Dates, Book of .... J. Blackwood 25
—— Dictionary of, Hadyn .... Ward 32
—— and Events in Eng. History Lockwood .. 29
—— (Index of) Chron. of World Bohn's Lib... 17
—— Manual of .... Warne 6
—— Rules and Tables for Verifying Bell 62
Dathavanso (The) .... Trubner 27
Dauphin & Companions in Temple Burns 14
Davenport (E.) Grandmamma .. Hatchard 7
David (Critical History of) .... Clar. Press.. 13
—— (King) Life of .... Wesleyan 49
—— King of Israel .... Masters 27
—— Wright .... Macmillan .. 42
Davidson (Dr. S.) Works by .... Williams 5
Davies (Rev. J. Ll.) Works by .. Macmillan.. 8
Davies' Scripture Manuals .... Philip 38
Davis (Rev. Richard) Memoir .. Nisbet 11
Davy (Sir H.) Works by .... Murray 9
Dawn of Day Books .... Warne 32
Dawn of Light, Leslie .... Snow 9
Dawn of Love (The) .... Nisbet 31
Dawning Lights, Cobbe .... Williams 4
Dawson (J. W.) Works by .... Hodder 12
Daybreak in Spain .... Cassell 3
Day with Christ .... Cassell 2
—— after Death .... Bentley 6
—— Hours of the Church of Eng. Masters 7
—— of the Lord (The) .... Nisbet 29
—— Office of the Church .... Masters 8

Day of Rest .... Strahan 2
—— Sanctified (The) .... Burns 24
Days and Seasons .... Mozley 3
—— Book of .... Chambers 26
—— of a Father's Sorrow .... Smith & El. 3
—— and Nights in the East .... Nisbet 6
—— of Old .... Macmillan .. 9
—— of the Son of Man .... W. Blackw'd 30
—— of Yore .... Isbister 44
D'Azeglio (Massimo) Recollections Chapman .. 14
De Balzac, Selections, Van Laun Rivingtons .. 18
De Beauvoisin's French Works .. Marlborough 14
De Chantal's Life, by Bowles .. Burns 14
De Fide et Symbolo .... Parker 7
De Fiva's French School Books.. Lockwood .. 34
De Gasparin (Countess) Works .. Isbister 12
De Guérin (M. & E.) Monograph Chapman .. 14
De Guerin's Journal and Letters Isbister 17
De La Voye's French Read. Bks. Allman 2
De Leikle, Works by .... Isbister 16
De Morgan's Budget of Paradoxes Longmans .. 14
De Pressensé (E.) Works by .... Hodder 11
De Quincy's Works .... Black 10
De Ros (Lord) Works by .... Murray 13
De Sévigné (Mde.) Correspond. Tinsley 9
—— Selections, French .... Clar. Press. 29
De Teissier (Rev. G. F.) Works by Macmillan .. 2
De Tocqueville, Correspondence King 8
Deaconship, Presbyterian Church Macl'hun .. 13
Dead Shot (The) .... Longmans .. 46
Deafness, Allen .... Churchill .. 2
Deaf and Dumb, Education of .. Bell 46
Dean's (The) English .... Hatchard 11
Dear Old England Described .... Nisbet 11
Death of Self the Life of Service Nisbet 33
Debatable Land .... Trubner 23
Debility and Defective Nutrition Churchill .. 35
Debrett's Peerage, &c. .... Dean ..... a
Debt and Grace .... Kellaway 11
Decalogue as Christian's Law .. Macmillan .. 35
Decimal Currency .... Smith & El. 10
—— Coinage, Bryce .... Black 9
—— System .... Stanford .. 52
—— System, Table of .... Layton 10
Decoration, Flower and Fruit.... Harrison 4
Decorative Design .... Cassell 2
Decorator (Universal) .... Houlston 10
Decorator's &c. Guide .... Hagger 15
Deep Down, Ballantyne .... Nisbet 4
—— Roots for Pleasant Fruits .. Nisbet 11
—— Sea Soundings in Philosophy Edmonston .. 7
Deer and Deer Parks .... Murray 37
—— Forest, Lays of the .... W. Blackw'd 39
Defence of Holy Orders in Ch. Eng. Parker 7
Defoe's Life .... J. R. Smith 8
—— Works .... Bohn's Lib .. 11
—— Works, with Life .... Nimmo 7
Deformity, Works on .... Churchill .. o
Deity, Views of the .... Williams 12
Delepierre (Octave) Works by .... Trubner 9
Delhi, Brown .... W. Blackw'd 6
—— Pathan Kings of .... Trubner 29
Delille's French School Books .. Whittaker .. 7
Delitzsch (Prof.) Works by .... Clark ..
Del Mar's Spanish Language .... Nutt 30
Deluge (The) Lucas .... Hodder 19
Delusions (Popular) .... Routledge .. 21
Democracy in Europe .... Longmans .. 2
Demonology, Sir W. Scott .... Tegg ..... a
Demosthenes, by Heslop .... Rivingtons .. 23
—— Holmes .... Rivingtons .. 23
—— Whiston .... Whittaker .. 1
Denison's (E.) Letters, &c. .... Bentley 6
Denman (Lord Chief Justice) Life Longmans .. 7
Demaus (Rev. R.) Works by .... Black 11
Denmark, History of .... Nisbet 12
—— Hymns of .... Isbister 42
—— in the Early Iron Age .... Williams ..... r
Denominational Statistics .... Stanford .. 63
Dentistry, Principles, &c. .... Tenber 15
—— Operative .... Trubner 28
—— Works on .... Churchill .. o
Denton's Comment. Gospels & Ep. Bell 47
Der Vetter, Comedy in 3 Acts .. Trubner 5
Derby (Countess of) Life of .... Smith & El. 13

Derby Day .... *Chatto* 12
Derbyshire Ballads and Songs .. *Bemrose* .. 16
—— Croston .... *J. Heywood*.. 44
—— Domesday Book .... *Bemrose* .. 16
—— Guide Book, Adams .... *Mozley* 4
—— History of, Glover .... *Mozley* 4
Derry and Enniskillen .... *Mullan* 6
—— A Tale of the Revolution .. *Nisbet* 9
Dervishes (The) .... *Trubner* .. 6
Desert of the Exodus .... *Bell* 11
—— Pastor (The)............ *King* 17
—— World .... *Nelson* 1
Deserted Ship (The) .... *King* 17
Desk Diary .... *De La Rue*.. 0
Detached Links .... *Dickinson* .. 9
Determinants, Elem. Treatise on *Macmillan* .. 8
Development of Anti-Christ.... *Nisbet* 6
Devil (The) his Origin, &c.... *Williams* .. 11
Devon, King's (R. J.) .... *J. R. Smith* 8
—— S., Climate of .... *Churchill* .. 32
—— Superstitions and Customs .. *Bentley* .. 5
Devoniensis (Lyra) .... *Macmillan*.. 41
Devotion, Private .... *Parker* 32
—— Treasury of .... *Rivingtons*.. 6
Devotions for Morning & Evening *Mozley* .. 3
Devotional Books .... *Masters* 0
—— Daily Reading .... *Shaw* 6
—— Comment. on Gos. Narrative *Rivingtons*.. 3
—— Help, Young Persons...... *Rivingtons*.. 10
—— Reading, Orme .... *Isbister* .. 32
—— Works .... *Bell* 53
—— (Oxford Editions) .... *Parker* 35
—— Works .... *Parker* 30
—— Series .... *Rivingtons*.. 6
Devout Thoughts, &c........ *Nisbet* 12
Dewdrop and the Mist ...... *Soc. P. C. K.* 8
Diabetes, Pavy .... *Churchill*.. 28
Dialects, Local............ *J. R. Smith* 18
Dialogues on Pulpit Preparation.. *Wesleyan* .. 43
Diamagnetism, Researches on .. *Longmans* .. 22
Diamond Necklace.......... *Tinsley Bros.* 5
—— Rose (The) .... *Isbister* .. 44
—— The Story of a.......... *Rel. Tr. Soc.* 19
—— Wedding (The) .... *Houlston*.. 15
Diamonds, To the Cape for .... *Chapman* .. 5
—— and Precious Stones .... *Blackie* .. 17
—— and Precious Stones .... *Chatto* 14
Diane: A Drama in Verse .... *Trubner* .. 3
Diary of Mrs. Kitty Trevylyan.. *Nelson* 7
—— of Physician .... *W. Blackw'd* 32
Diaries and Pocket Books .... *De La Rue*.. 0
Diatessaron .... *Parker*.... 10
—— White .... *Clar. Press*.. 9
Dick Roblins .... *S. S. Union* 8
—— (Dr. Thos.) Works by .... *Collins* 4
Dickens (Chas.) as a Reader .. *Chapman* .. 19
—— Works .... *Chapman* .. 15
—— Story of................ *Chatto* 11
—— Speeches .... *Chatto* 12
Dictation Exercises, Beasley .. *Whittaker* .. 12
Dictionaries, On Deficiences in .. *Macmillan* .. 37
—— Walker and Johnson .... *Routledge* .. 13
—— Various .... *Warne* 40
—— Writer's and Student's.... *Whittaker* .. 11
Dictionary Appendix........ *Shaw* 7
—— Barclay .... *Virtue* 13
—— Cabinet .... *Collins* 5
—— Comprehensive .... *Blackie* 2
—— Craig's Universal ...... *Routledge* .. 12
—— of the English Language.... *Trubner* .. 31
—— Eng. Etymol., Wedgwood .. *Trubner* .. 31
—— Etymological .... *Cassell*.... 15
—— Etymological .... *Chambers* .. 7
—— Etymological, Oswald .... *Black* 15
—— Globe .... *Collins* 5
—— and Grammar .... *Lockwood* .. 29
—— (Illustrated) Webster .... *Bell* 64
—— Imperial .... *Blackie* 1
—— Knowles', large type .... *Routledge* .. 12
—— Latham's Johnson ...... *Longmans* .. 12
—— Library .... *Collins* 5
—— (New) Richardson ...... *Bell* 63
—— Pocket Pronouncing .... *Collins* 5
—— Stormmouth .... *W. Blackw'd* 47
—— of Terms in Arch. &c... *Lockwood* .. 6

Dictionary, Webster & Worcester *Routledge* .. 12
—— J. T. White .... *Longmans* .. 13
—— Vest Pocket .... *Trubner* .. 17
—— of Derivations.......... *Collins* 7
—— of Engineering .... *Spon* 15
—— in Four Languages ...... *Nutt* 21
—— Household, 1,000 Illust. .. *Collins* 1
—— of Illust. Chr. Teaching .. *Dickinson* .. 4
—— Mechanic's .... *Blackie* .. 10
—— Naval & Military Terms.. *Murray* 5
—— of the Old Eng. Language .. *Trubner* .. 34
—— of Poetical Chr. Teaching .. *Dickinson* .. 4
—— Scientific Terms .... *Isbister* .. 32
—— Scripture Names and Places *Clark* 22
—— Student's English ...... *Blackie* 2
—— Terms of Art .... *Isbister* .. 14
—— of Theology .... *Rivingtons*.. 11
—— Trade and Commerce .... *Ward & Lock* 7
—— of Vulgar Tongue ...... *Chatto* 17
—— Johnson................ *Mozley* 5
—— of Proper Names, Old Test. *Williams* .. 5
—— of Terms in Medicine .... *Whittaker* .. 16
—— Walker .... *Mozley* 13
Diet and Regimen .... *Churchill*.. 30
Dietaries (Practical) for Families *King* 7
Digestion (Chambers) ...... *Churchill*.. 8
—— (Imperfect) .... *Churchill*.. 23
—— Pavy .... *Churchill*.. 28
Dilapidations, Fletcher ...... *Spon* 15
Dinner Question (The) ...... *Routledge* .. 8
Dinners (Little), Hooper ...... *King* 31
Diogenes among the D. D. S. .. *Marr* 15
Diplomacy, Lectures on ...... *Macmillan*.. 5
Diplomatist, Experiences of a.. *Macmillan* .. 8
Diphtheria, Walker on ...... *Churchill*.. 37
Disciple among the Poor .... *Wesleyan*.. 41
Disciples (The) A New Poem .. *King* 20
—— of Jesus, Bruce .... *Clark* 12
Discipline and Drill .... *King* 13
Discount Tables, Evans ...... *Mozley* 3
Discovery and Adventure...... *Burns* 24
Disease Germs, Beale........ *Churchill* .. 8
—— Germs and Vestiges of .. *Churchill*.. 15
Disraeli's Curiosities of Literature *Routledge* .. 43
—— Speeches .... *Chatto* 12
Disraeli, Works by .... *Longmans* .. 0
Dissections, Holden on ...... *Churchill*.. 22
—— Illustrations of.......... *Smith & El.* 6
Dissent in its Relation to the Ch. *Macmillan* .. 8
Dissertation, Validity of Ordinations *Parker*.... 5
District Visitors, Alphabetical List *Soc. P. C. K.* 8
—— Visitors, Bible Reading for .. *Nisbet* 21
—— Visitor's Hand Book .... *J. Heywood* 37
—— Visitor's Note Book ...... *Letts*...... 3
—— Visiting, Hilton .... *Mozley*.... 1
Divers and Diving .... *Chatto* 7
Diversions of Echo Club .... *Chatto* 3
Divine Footsteps .... *W. Blackw'd* 37
—— Government, Method of .. *Macmillan*.. 23
—— (The) Human in the Scriptures *Nisbet* .. 21
—— Kingdom on Earth........ *King* 23
—— Master (The)............ *Masters* .. 8
—— Service, Principles of .... *Parker* 11
Divinity, Hey's Lectures .... *Cambridge*.. 7
—— Hill .... *W. Blackw'd* 38
Dixon (Hepworth) Works by .. *Hurst* 1
Dobell (H.) Medical Works by .. *Churchill* .. 15
—— (Sydney) Works .... *Smith & El.* 5
Doctors, Book About ...... *Hurst* 15
Doctrinal Definitions........ *Burns* 35
Doctrine of the Real Presence .. *Parker*.... 3
Doctrines & Conf. of Communities *Clark* .. 36
Documentary Works .... *Clar. Press*.. 15
Doda's Birthday............ *M. Ward* .. 8
Dodsley's Collection of Old Plays *Reeves & T.* 4
Dog Crusoe .... *Nelson*.... 6
—— and Gun, "Craven" .... *Bell* 24
—— by Idstone .... *Cassell* 4
—— Works on the .... *Longmans* .. 42
Dog-Breaking, Method of .... *Murray* .. 10
Dogs .... *W. Blackw'd* 24
—— Anecdotes of .... *Bell* 23
—— Jesse .... *Bohn's Lib.* 5
—— and Cats .... *Ward & Lock* 11
—— (Clever), Horses, &c. ...... *Partridge* .. 15

Dogs, their Sagacity .... *J. Blackwood* 11
— and their Ways .... *Routledge* .. 34
— Whims, Points, and Instincts *Dean* .. a
Doing Good .... *Nelson* .. 10
Dollars and Cents .... *Nisbet* .. 14
— Tables .... *Wilson* .. 12
Dollinger, Works by .... *Rivingtons* .. 12
Dolomite Mountains .... *Longmans* .. 37
Domus Dei, Story of the .... *Parker* .. 53
Domestic Addresses .... *Partridge* .. 6
— Commentary .... *Macintosh* .. a
— Economy .... *Bemrose* .. 13
— Law .... *Longmans* .. 45
— Manners in Middle Ages .. *Trubner* .. 32
— Medicine, Buchan .... *Milner* .. 2
— Compendium of .... *Churchill* .. 32
— Handbook .... *Bohn's Lib.* 18
— Medicine .... *Routledge* .. 20
— Medicine, Walsh .... *Warne* .. 8
— Medicine, Fullerton .... *Chapman* .. 18
— Pets (Our) .... *Routledge* .. 33
— Service Guide.. .... *Lockwood* .. 48
— Stories, by A. John Halifax *Smith & El.* 5
Dominican Artist .... *Rivingtons* .. 26
Doomsday Book of England .. *Pickering* .. 13
— Book, Oxfordshire .... *Parker* .. 51
Don Quixote .... *Routledge* .. 72
— Illustrated .... *Ward&Lock* 22
— Illustrated by Doré .... *Cassell* .. 3
— Spanish .... *Cassell* .. 2
Donegal, Scenery of .... *MacGlashan* a
Doran (Dr.) Works by .... *Bentley* .. 6
Doré's Illustrated Works .... *Cassell* .. 2
Dorothea Trudel .... *Morgan* .. 3
Dorset Dialect, Grammar of .. *Asher* .. 8
— Warne's (Charles) .... *J. R. Smith* 8
Doudney's (Dr.) Works .... *Mack* .. 7
Douglas Family .... *Warne* .. 29
— (Gavin) Poetical Works .. *Sotheran* .. 10
— (Sir H.) Works by .... *Murray* .. 10
Dove on the Cross (The) .... *Nisbet* .. 12
Dovecot and Rabbit Warren .. *Bemrose* .. 19
Dover—Church and Fortress .. *Parker* .. 53
Draining .... *W. Blackw'd* 53
— for Profit and Health .... *Spon* .. 14
Drama, Annals of .... *Allen* .. 6
— English Actors in, in Germany *Asher* .. 3
— Essays on .... *J. R. Smith* 9
— of Kings (The) .... *Isbister* .. 5
— (The) .... *Tinsley Bros.* 5
Dramas for Boys and Girls .. *Washbourne* 7
— for Children .... *W. Blackw'd* 33
— Judicial .... *Tinsley Bros.* 7
Dramatic Literature .... *Bohn's Lib.* 9
— of England .... *J. R. Smith* 1
Dramatists (Old) .... *Routledge* .. 62
— of the Present Day .... *Chapman* .. 14
— Works of British .... *Nimmo* .. 7
Draper (D. J.) Life of .... *Hodder* .. 24
Dravidian, Comparat. Grammar of *Trubner* .. 7
Drawing-Books .... *Collins* .. 23
Drawing-Books and Cards .. *J. Heywood* .. 20
Drawing-Book .... *Ward&Lock* 26
Drawing and Geometry .... *Kempster* .. a
— Broad-line .... *J. Blackwood* 26
— Beginner's .... *Macmillan* .. a
— George's .... *Allman* .. 16
— Society of Art's .... *Bell* .. 7
— of Design .... *Chapman* .. 17
Drawing Copy Books .... *Chapman* .. 17
Drawing Copies, Delamotte .. *Bell* .. 7
Drawing, Elementary .... *Cassell* .. 12
— Free Hand .... *Morby* .. 8
— Instruction in .... *Chambers* .. 9
— Vere Foster's Course .. *M. Ward* .. 19
Drawings of Churches .... *Parker* .. 54
Drawing-room Charades .... *Routledge* .. 7
— Plays .... *Ward* .. 13
— Plays .... *Isbister* .. 15
— Plays .... *Isbister* .. 29
Drayton Hall .... *Nisbet* .. 19
Dream-book and Fortune-teller .. *Routledge* .. 7
— Book .... *Milner* .. 3
Dreamland .... *Warne* .. 99
Dreams Lit. and Curiosities...... *Lockwood* .. 43

Dreamthorp: A Book of Essays.. *Isbister* .. 40
Drew (Rev. G. S.) Works by.... *King* .. 29
— (W. H.) Works by .... *Macmillan* .. 9
Drifted and Sifted .... *Nimmo* .. 12
Drill, Company and Battalion.. *Bemrose* .. 19
— School .... *J. Heywood* .. 19
Droll Stories .... *Chatto* .. 12
Dropsy, Basham on .... *Churchill* .. 8
Drunkenness, Anatomy of .... *MacPhun* .. 7
Drummond of Hawthornden .. *Macmillan* .. 24
Drummond's (T.) Memoir .... *Edmonston* .. 6
Druses of Lebanon .... *Murray* .. 6
Dryden, Select Poems .... *Clar. Press.* . 32
Du Chaillu, Works by .... *Murray* .. 10
Dublin Mission, Story of the .. *Nisbet* .. 34
Duchess Agnes .... *Isbister* .. 12
Duff (Grant-) Political Works.... *Edmonston* .. 7
Du Guesclin, Life and Times .. *Trubner* .. 17
Dulce Domum .... *Isbister* .. 34
Dumb Companions (Our) .... *Partridge* .. 14
Dumfriesshire, History of .... *Black* .. 14
Duncan (John), Memoir, by Brown *Edmonston* .. 8
— by Stuart .... *Edmonston* .. 8
Dundonald (Lord) Life of .... *J. Blackwood* 20
Dunham's Tables .... *Wilson* .. 10
Durer (Albert) Life and Works .. *Longmans* .. 28
— Life, Letters, and Works .. *Macmillan* 10
— Passion of our Lord .... *Bell* .. 7
D'Urfey's Pills to Purge Melancholy *Sotheran* .. 10
— Wit and Mirth .... *Chatto* .. 13
Durham, Antiquities of .... *J. R. Smith* 8
— Illustrations &c. of the Co. of *Parker* .. 53
Dutch Admirals (Great) .... *King* .. 18
— Language, Easy Method .. *Trubner* .. 2
— Republic, Motley .... *Routledge* .. 20
Duties, Legacy and Succession .. *Waterlow* .. a
Dyeing and Calico Printing .... *Longmans* .. 32
Dye-Wares and Colours .... *Lockwood* .. 12
Dykes (Rev. J. O.) Works by .. *Nisbet* .. 12
Dynamical Formation of Earth .. *Isbister* .. 38
Dynamics of Rigid Bodies .... *Macmillan* .. 31
— of a Particle .... *Macmillan* .. 35

Eagle and Dove .... *Washbourne.* 8
Eagles (John) Works by .... *W. Blackw'd* 8
Ear, Diseases and Injuries of.. *Churchill* .. 14
Earl & the Doctor, S. S. Bubbles *Bentley* .. 13
Earlswood, a Tale .... *Hatchard* .. 2
Early Death not Premature .... *Nisbet* .. 25
Early English, Specimens of .. *Clar. Press.* . 28
— History of Mankind .... *Murray* .. 32
— Rising, a Duty .... *Nisbet* .. 12
Earnest Missionary .... *Wesleyan* .. 50
— Words for Earnest Men .. *Isbister* .. 45
Earth, Attraction and Figure of.. *Macmillan* .. 37
— Dynamical Theory of .... *Isbister* .. 38
— Figure of the .... *Macmillan* .. 99
— and its Inhabitants .... *Routledge* .. 14
— and Man, Dawson .... *Hodder* .. 12
— (The) and Man .... *Longmans* .. 24
— (The) its Physical Condition *J. Blackwood* 11
— Physical History of the .. *Bagster* .. 71
— and Sea .... *Nelson* .. 1
Earth's History .... *Allen* .. 3
— Many Voices .... *Soc. P. C. K.* 9
— (Mother) Biography .... *Trubner* .. 32
— Motion of Rotation .... *Macmillan* .. 7
— (The) Reclus .... *Chapman* .. 6
Earthly Shad. of Heavenly King. *Nisbet* .. 37
Earthquakes, Mallett .... *Asher* .. 5
— and Volcanoes .... *Nelson* .. 9
— (The Coming) .... *Kellaway* .. 9
— (Neapolitan) of 1857 .... *Chapman* .. 25
Earthward Pilgrimage .... *Chatto* .. 13
Earthwork Measurement .... *Lockwood* .. 6
— Tables, Various .... *Spon* .. 16
Eastbourne, Handbook for .... *Stanford.* . 52
Easter Subjects, Sermons on .. *Masters* .. 2
Eastertide Sermons, Alford .. *Isbister* .. 4
Eastern Archipelago, Travels in . *Murray* .. 4
— Church, Neale .... *Masters* .. 18
— Church, Offices of .... *Williams* .. 9
— Experiences, Bowring .... *King* .. 14
— Legends and Stories. .. .. *King* .. 21
— Manners and Customs...... *Nelson* .. 80

Eastern Monachism .... *Williams* .. 7
—— Love Story .... *Trubner* .. 27
—— Questions, Essays on .... *Macmillan*. 27
—— Seas (In the) .... *Nelson* 6
East Lynne .... *Bentley* ... 16
Eastward, Macleod .... *Ibbister* ... 29
Ecce Homo .... *Macmillan* .. 12
—— Homo, Examination of .... *Nisbet* 33
—— Gladstone on .... *Ibbister* ... 17
—— Gladstone on .... *Macmillan*.. 10
—— Messias, Higginson ...... *Williams* .. 7
Eccentrics and Eccentricities ... *Chatto* 37
Ecclesia..................... *Hodder* 24
—— Dei .... *Ibbister* ... 14
—— the Bride .... *Houlston*... 15
Ecclesiastes, Commentary on... *Rivingtons*.. 3
—— Lectures on .... *Ibbister* ... 11
—— Lectures on .... *Nisbet* 17
Ecclesiastical Dilapidation Act . *Rivingtons*.. 10
—— (Greek) Historians ...... *Bagster* ... 60
—— History .... *Bohn's Lib*.. 11
—— History .... *Clar. Press*.. 9
—— Maurice .... *Macmillan*.. 14
—— P. Smith .... *Murray* ... 30
—— Compendium .... *Clark* 16
—— Judgments, Brook .... *King* 28
—— Joyce .... *Rivingtons* .. 12
—— Jurisdiction .... *Masters* ... 13
—— Polity .... *Clark* 18
—— Polity of New Testament .. *Ibbister* ... 23
—— Princ. &c. of the Wes. Meth. *Wesleyan* .. 43
—— Privy Council Judgments .. *Murray* ... 26
—— Terms, Shipley .... *Rivingtons*.. 31
—— Truth .... *Hodder* 18
—— Year .... *Washbourne*. 7
Ecclesiology, Works on ...... *Masters* ... 0
Echo Français .... *Trubner* ... 10
Echoes of a Famous Year .... *King* 3
—— of the Night .... *Ward & Lock* 23
—— of the Past .... *Hatchards* .. 7
—— of Holy Thoughts .... *Williams* .. 5
Eclipse of Faith .... *Longmans* .. 16
Eco Italiano .... *Trubner* ... 10
—— de Madrid .... *Trubner* ... 11
Economic Policy, M'Culloch .. *Black* 14
—— Position of Brit. Labourer .. *Macmillan*.. 11
Economy of Capital .... *W. Blackw'd.* 25
Ecumenical Councils, Urwich... *Tubbs* 4
Eda May .... *S. S. Union.* 8
Edda Sæmundar Hinus Frodd .. *Trubner* ... 11
Edda : Tales of a Grandmother. *Nisbet* 12
Edersheim (Dr.) Works by .... *Rel. Tr. Soc.* 7
Edgar (J. G.) Juvenile Books by *Routledge* .. 33
Edgeworth Library .... *Chambers* .. 29
Edgeworth's Books .... *Routledge* .. 32
—— Juvenile Stories.......... *Milner* 11
—— Tales................... *Allman* 7
—— (Miss) Works........... *Houlston*... 22
Edinburgh Byeways.......... *Hodder* 3
—— Castle .... *W. Blackw'd.* 10
—— (Duke) Cruise of the Galatea *Allen* 6
—— Geological and Historical .. *Nimmo*..... 4
—— Plans of .... *Johnston*... 6
—— Traditions of .... *Chambers* .. 27
—— University .... *Edmonston*.. 6
—— Flora of .... *Black* 2
Edith and her Ayah, &c...... *Nelson*..... 19
Edmunds (J.) Works .... *Hatchard* .. 8
Education Act Explained...... *Routledge* .. 42
—— The Conflict of, Studies ... *Macmillan*.. 37
—— Defects in .... *Macmillan*.. 29
—— Early, Mrs. Hoare ...... *Hatchard* .. 11
—— Hooper .... *Hatchard* .. 12
—— in Early England .... *Trubner* ... 13
—— of Girls............... *Trubner* ... 16
—— Harmony of, Jolly ...... *Nisbet* 19
—— Health and .... *Ibbister* ... 23
—— of the Heart .... *Hodder* 26
—— (Home) Taylor .... *Bell* 41
—— Intellectual, Moral, and Phys. *Williams* .. 14
—— (Middle Class) .... *Macmillan*.. 2
—— (National) Schools ...... *Ibbister*..... 38
—— Practical Essays on ..... *Ibbister* ... 30
—— and School .... *Macmillan*.. 36
—— Scripture Principles of.... *Nisbet* 13

Education, Symmetrical ...... *Smith & El.* 25
—— Struggles for National...... *Chapman* .. 22
—— (Technical) .... *Bradbury* .. 12
—— True Words on .... *Nisbet* 20
—— (The Void in Modern).... *Macmillan*.. 16
—— of Women, Sherriff ...... *Smith & El.* 19
Educational Books............ *Bell* 1
—— Books .... *Cassell* 14
—— Books .... *Masters* ... 0
—— Illust. .... *M. Ward* .. 26
—— Course .... *Chambers* .. 4
—— Minor .... *Chambers* .. 23
—— Manuals .... *Routledge* .. 14
—— Works .... *Bemrose* ... 12
—— Works .... *Hodder* 30
—— Works .... *Laurie* 1
—— Works .... *Murby* 1
—— Works .... *Rel. Tr. Soc.* 21
—— Works .... *Houlston*... 43
Edward VI. Common Prayer. *Rivingtons* .. 4
—— (King) Latin Grammar .. *Murray* ... 19
Edwardes (Mrs. A.) Novels .. *Bentley*..... 16
Edwards (Edward) Works by .. *Trubner* ... 11
Edwin of Deira, Smith....... *Macmillan* .. 33
Effie's Friends and Effie's Year.. *Nisbet* 12
Egan's Book of Sports ...... *Tegg*...... 6
Eggleston (Edward) Works by .. *Routledge* .. 2
Eggs and Nests .... *Van Voorst* 2
Egypt, Ancient .... *Rel. Tr. Soc.* 7
—— Ancient .... *Fellowes* .. 11
—— Artists in .... *King*...... 5
—— Bartlett's Nile Boat ...... *Bell* 12
—— Country, People and Produce *Snow* 2
—— from Earliest Times to A.D. 640 *Bell* 11
—— Eden's The Nile........ *King*...... 5
—— as a Health Resort........ *Churchill* .. 27
—— Journal of a Visit to .... *Smith & El.* 9
—— Lindsay's Letters on .... *Bohn's Lib* .. 13
—— and the Nile........... *Murray* ... 16
—— Nubia, and Ethiopia .... *Smith & El.* 6
—— of the Pharaohs......... *Smith & El.* 27
—— Photo. Views, Past & Present *Collins*..... 3
—— Smith's Nile........... *Murray* ... 79
—— (Ten Plagues of)........ *Murray* ... 22
—— Travels in, Maughan .... *King*...... 4
—— as Winter Resort for Invalids *Churchill* .. 28
Egypt's Record of Time ..... *Rivingtons* .. 26
Egyptian Dictionary .... *Smith & El.* 27
—— Revolution .... *Trubner* ... 24
—— Sketch Book .... *Ibbister* ... 25
—— Grammar, Tattam....... *Williams* .. 14
Egyptians (Ancient) .... *Murray* ... 32
—— (Modern) Manners and Cus. *Murray* ... 19
Eight Months on Duty .... *Ibbister* ... 14
Eighty Years Ago, Cave ...... *Hatchard* .. 4
Eildon Manor .... *Warne* 27
Eiloart (Mrs. Jno.) Books by .. *Routledge* .. 33
Eirenicon .... *Parker*..... 6
Elder (Jno.) Memoirs........ *W. Blackw'd.* 9
Eldergowan .... *M. Ward* .. 9
Election, Ballot and Corruption at *Macmillan*.. 7
—— Law .... *Stevens* ... 14
—— Manual .... *Virtue* 5
—— of Representatives, Hare .. *Longmans* .. 14
Electric Telegraph .... *Lockwood* .. 13
—— Telegraph .... *Longmans* .. 21
—— Cables .... *Spon* 42
—— Cully .... *Longmans* .. 31
—— Sabine .... *Ibbister* ... 38
—— Service Handbook ...... *Lockwood* .. 37
—— Wilson .... *Macmillan*.. 41
—— Works on .... *Spon* 16
Electrical Standard.......... *Spon* 16
Electricity................. *Chambers* .. 17
—— Essen .... *Clar. Press*.. 27
—— (Frictional) .... *Ibbister* ... 20
—— and Magnetism .... *Clar. Press*.. 25
—— and Magnetism .... *Longmans* .. 21
—— Thomson .... *Macmillan*.. 35
—— Manual of............. *Lockwood* .. 12
—— Tyndall................ *Longmans* .. 23
Elegant Extracts............ *Nimmo* 10
Elegantly Bound Books ...... *Ramage* ... 0
Elementary Education Act ... *Waterlow* .. 2
Elgin's (Lord) Letters & Journals *Murray* 11

Elia, Essays of............... Chatto 21
Elijah, Life and Times of........ Nisbet 23
—— the Prophet, Aveling .... Snow 1
—— Sermons, Shirley .... Macmillan .. 32
Elijer Goff.................... J. Heywood 44
Eliot (Sir John) by Forster ..... Chpman ... 7
Eliot (George) Romola .... Smith & El. 17
—— Works by............. W. Blackw'd 8
Elisha, Prophet, History of ..... Hodder 25
—— Scenes from Life of ..... W. Blackw'd 40
Elia and Marian .... Warne 26
Ellenborough's Admin. in India . Bentley 6
Ellen Montgomery's Book-shelf. Routledge ... 35
Ellen Strong's Victory .... S. S. Union. 9
Ellerslie House .... Partridge .. 8
Elliott (Bishop) Works by ...... Longmans ... 0
Elliott (Char) Select. from Poems Rel. Tr. Soc. 7
—— (H. Venn) Life of .... Macmillan .. 10
Elliot's Memoir by Ctss. Minto . Edmonston . 8
Ellis's (W.) Memoir .... Murray 11
Ellis (W.) Works .... Smith & El. 6
Elocution, Bell's Works on ...... Mullan 0
Elocution made Easy.......... Groombridge 20
—— System of, Ross .... Laurie 1
Elsie Dinsmore .... King...... 16
Ely Cathedral .... Van Voorst a
Elzevir Series of Stan. Authors . Bell 33
Ember Hours .... Masters 11
Emblems from Eden .... Nisbet 17
—— by Gottbold .... Clark 19
Embroiderer's Book of Design . Lockwood .. 15
Embroidery, Ecclesiastical ...... Masters 9
Emerson's Complete Works ..... Bohn's Lib . 7
—— Orations .... J. Blackwood 21
Emigrant (The) Gentleman .... Tinsley Bros. 2
—— Sir Francis Head .... Murray 14
Emigrants, Letters of Intro. for . Soc. P. C. K. 3
Emigration Maps .... Johnston .. 6
—— Works on .... Lockwood .. 24
Emmanuel ; or, Father Revealed Nisbet 11
—— A Poem .... Yapp 3
Emma Wellford .... S. S. Union 9
Empire (The) .... Parker.... 64
—— and Cities of Asia .... Virtue 8
—— of the Church .... Parker.... 13
Enchanted Toasting Fork ..... Tinsley Bros. 8
Escombe Stories .... Warne 25
Encyclopædia Britannica........ Black 12
—— of Chron. His. Bio. ...... Longmans .. 4
—— of Universal Knowledge... Chambers .. 26
Endymion, by Keats......... Ward & Lock 31
Engineer and Machinist's Drawing Blackie..... 10
Engineers (Brit.) Lives of ...... Murray 27
—— (Royal) Head.......... Murray 14
Engineer's Companion, Marine . Spon 19
—— and Con. Estimate Price Bk. Lockwood .. 5
—— Field Book .... Lockwood .. 6
—— Hand Book.......... Longmant .. 31
—— (Marine) Useful Tables .. Lockwood .. 4
—— Pocket Book .... Lockwood .. 6
—— Pocket Book .... Spon 19
—— Tables for the Use of ..... Stanford .. 50
—— Useful Information ...... Longmans .. 37
—— Pocket Guide .... MacPhun .. 15
Engineering (Civil) Encyclopædia Longmans .. 31
—— Civil & Mechanical, Works on Spon 17
—— Canal and River .... Black 31
—— Rud. Works on .... Lockwood .. 19
—— Dictionary of .... Spon 14
—— Drawing .... Lockwood .. 6
—— Field Work .... Lockwood .. 5
—— Locomotive, Colburn ..... Collins 2
—— Marine, Rud. Works...... Lockwood .. 22
—— Notes for Practice........ Spon 11
—— Works .... Lockwood .. 1
England, Agriculture, Prices, &c. Clar. Press.. 16
—— Antiquities of, Brand ...... Bohn's Lib .. 12
—— Baths and Wells of ...... Macmillan.. 23
—— Birchall's History .... A. Heywood 16
—— Border History of .... Sotheran .. 23
—— Cameos from History of .. Macmillan .. 6
—— Charity in .... Isbister 14
—— Compendium of History .. Chapman .. 7
—— Comprehensive History ... Blackie 8
—— Constitutional History...... Clar. Press 25

England, 1760–1870 .... Longmans .. 2
—— in Early and Middle Ages .. Bell 38
—— Female Sovereigns of .... Routledge .. 4
—— and France, Chronicles of . Routledge .. 20
—— The Great Schools of .... Isbister .. 41
—— Handy History for Young .. Routledge .. 32
—— History .... Hogger 2
—— History.............. J. Heywood 33
—— History............... Nelson 4
—— Outlines of History ...... Lockwood .. 29
—— (Popular History) .... Sangster .. 3
—— in Reign of Queen Anne.... Murray .. 31
—— Synoptical History ...... Lockwood .. 37
—— Historical Works .... Clar. Press.. 2
—— (Aunt Charlotte's Stories) .. M. Ward .. 2
—— Half Hours.............. Warne.... 4
—— (Old).............. Macmillan.. 12
—— Pearce and Hague ...... Murby 2
—— Pictures from .... Routledge .. 78
—— Romantic Tales from ..... Isbister .. 7
—— Stories from .... Murray .. 8
—— Histories of............ Routledge .. 21
—— History of, 1830 to 1874 .. Chapman .. 3
—— History, Goldsmith, by Coxe Mozley .. 15
—— History for the Young...... Mozley .. 15
—— from Acc. James II.......... Longmans .. 2
—— Dr. Smith .... Murray .. 29
—— to Edward III........... Longmans .. 2
—— E. Thompson .... Macmillan.. 36
—— Howell (J.) .... W. Blackw'd 15
—— Illustrated .... Cassell.... 2
—— from Invasion to Victoria .. Masters 21
—— Keightley .... Whittaker... 9
—— in Reign of George III..... Isbister .. 34
—— Wolsey to Spanish Armada . Longmans .. 1
—— of, for the Young .... Burns .. 25
—— Hume and Smollett ...... Virtue.... 20
—— Illustrated History .... J. Heywood 33
—— Invasions of............ Stanford.... 54
—— (Judges of) .... Murray .. 12
—— Lake Country............ Smith & El. 14
—— Lake Scenery............ Allman .. 10
—— Littlewood (W. E.) ...... Cassell.... 13
—— (Merry).............. Tinsley Bros. 14
—— (Merrie) Olden Time ...... Warne.... 23
—— Pastimes of............ Cassell.... 6
—— National History .... Collins .. 2
—— Notes on, Taine.......... Isbister .. 42
—— (Old).............. Sangster .. 3
—— Student's Text Book ...... Bell 24
—— Synopsis of............ Bell 24
—— and its People, Miller ..... Nimmo .. 4
—— (Queens of) Strickland .... Longmans .. 9
—— Religious Thought in ...... Isbister .. 21
—— and Rome, Waterworth .... Burns .. 36
—— Royal Princesses of ...... Routledge .. 3
—— Rural Life of .... Longmans .. 38
—— Stately Homes of .... Virtue .. 3
—— Visit to Fields of Battle .... J. R. Smith 6
—— Voyage Round .... Sotheran .. 9
—— and Wales, Picturesque Views Bell 4
—— West of (Cottage Life in) . Macmillan.. 29
—— West, Romances of ...... Chatto.... 20
—— under Norman Occupation.. Williams .. 10
—— from Thames to Humber.... Chapman .. 26
—— and Wales, Guide to........ Black 5
England's Antiphon .... Macmillan.. 34
—— Foreign Policy .... Stanford .. 61
—— Workshops .... Groombridge 17
English Accidence, Morris ...... Macmillan.. 26
—— Affairs, 1625-1660........ Clar. Press.. 16
—— Anecdote .... Routledge .. 3
—— Art, Masterpieces of ...... Bell 9
—— Art of the 19th Century ... Routledge .. 3
—— Authors, Typ. Selections .. Clar. Press.. 29
—— Church History.......... Parker .. 12
—— Charters, Thorpe .... Trubner .. 29
—— Classics, Cheap Reprints .. Chambers .. 6
—— Code (An) .... Isbister .. 5
—— Constitution, Bagehot .... King.... 31
—— Creasy .... Bentley.. 5
—— De Lolme .... Bohn's Lib .. 7
—— Growth of .... Macmillan.. 12
—— Primer of .... Longmans .. 10
—— Rowlands .... Murray 26

English Cyclopædia .... *Bradbury* .. 6
—— Divines, Lives of .... *Masters* ... 27
—— (Early) Meals and Manners *Trubner* .. 10
—— (Early) Metrical Romances *Bohn's Lib.*.. 12
—— Flora, Hooker .... *Macmillan* .. 16
—— Govt. and Constitution .... *Longmans* .. 2
—— Heroes in the 13th Century *Nimmo* ... 12
—— Idylls, Ellice .... *Macmillan* .. 10
—— in India .... *Trubner* ... 4
—— Lake District .... *Stanford* ... 56
—— Lakes, Hand-Book to ...... *Murray* ... 17
—— Lakes, Guide to .... *Black* 5
—— Landscape, B. Foster ...... *Routledge* .. 27
—— Language, Changes in ...... *Macmillan* .. 4
—— Language, Outlines of ..... *Chapman* .. 14
—— Lewis .... *Stanford* ... 57
—— and Literature .... *Clar. Press.*. 28
—— Lost Beauties of .... *Chatto* ... 23
—— Rogue .... *Chatto* ... 14
—— Leaders, Langton .... *King* 2
—— Literature .... *Shaw* 7
—— (Modern) Hall .... *Williams* .. 7
—— (Old) Chronicles .... *Bohn's Lib.*. 12
—— Orders and Papal Supremacy *Parker* .. 5
—— Ordinal, Churton .... *Rivingtons* .. 12
—— Past and Present .... *Macmillan* .. 37
—— People, History of .... *Macmillan* .. 14
—— Photographs .... *Tinsley Bros.* 8
—— Premiers, Earle .... *Chapman* .. 17
—— Prize Class Bk, Demaus... *Black* ... 11
—— Psychology, Ribot .... *King* 6
—— Rebellion .... *Clar. Press.*. 15
—— Revolution, 1640 .... *Bohn's Lib.*. 8
—— Revolution, 1688 .... *King* 2
—— Sonnets .... *King* 20
—— (Standard) Sources of .... *Macmillan* .. 19
—— Studies in .... *Trubner* ... 26
—— Specimens .... *Clar. Press.*. 12
—— Writers, Morley .... *Chapman* .. 28
—— (Aunt Charlotte's Stories of) *M. Ward* .. 3
Englishman's (The) Concordance *Bagster* ... 34
—— House .... *Chatto* .. 14
Englishmen, Lives of .... *Masters* ... 15
Englishwoman's Cookery Book . *Ward & Lock* 5
Enigmas of Life .... *Trubner* ... 14
Epoch, Book of .... *Trubner* ... 5
Enquire Within Series .... *Houlston* .. 3
Enterprise and Adventure ..... *Groombridge* 25
Entertaining and Instructive Bks.*Cassell*... 10
Entomology .... *Reeve* ... 10
—— American .... *Sotheran* ... 25
—— Works on .... *Longmans* .. 23
Envelope Series of Small Books . *Morgan* ... 15
Eothen, Eastern Travel .... *Harrison* .. 4
Ephemera, Lyttleton .... *Murray* ... 21
Epic of Women .... *Chatto* ... 26
Epidemic Disease, Howe ...... *Churchill* ... 21
—— Remote Cause .... *Churchill* ... 28
Epidemics of the Middle Ages . *Trubner* ... 15
—— Pestilences, History of ... *Churchill* ... 8
Epigrams, Book of .... *Chatto* ... 5
—— Common Place Book of .... *Tegg* ... 2
Epigrammatists, Selections from *Bell* 37
Epilepsy, Althaus .... *Churchill* ... 7
Epiphany Sermons, Vaughan... *Macmillan* .. 38
Episodes in an Obscure Life ... *Ibister* ... 14
Epistles and Gospels .... *Parker* ... 11
—— Paraph. and Comment. ... *Clar. Press.*. 14
—— of New Testament .... *Shaw* 8
Epitaphs .... *J. R. Smith.* 9
—— for Country Churchyards .. *Parker* ... 64
—— Palliser .... *Murray* ... 24
—— Quaint, Curious, &c....... *Tegg* ... 2
—— Queer .... *Marr* ... 15
—— Remarkable .... *Bohn's Lib.*. 12
Epoch Men .... *Nimmo* ... 14
Equity, Principles of .... *Stevens* ... 5
Erasmus ; his Life and Char.... *Smith & El.* 5
Erastianism, History of ...... *Mozley* ... 13
Erckmann-Chatrian Library ... *Ward&Lock* 23
—— Works of, in French ...... *Nutt* ... 23
—— Works .... *Smith & El.* 7
Erewhon ; or, Over the Range .. *Trubner* ... 6
Eric .... *Black* 8
Erith ; its Natural, Civil &c. Hist. *Virtue* 5

Erling the Bald .... *Nisbet* 4
Erskine's (Thomas) Works .... *Edmonston*.. 8
Essays by a Barrister .... *Smith & El.* 7
—— Theological and Literary . *Ibister* ... 22
Essex .... *J. R. Smith,* 9
Estate Valuation, Biden ...... *Layton* ... 7
Esther West .... *Cassell* ... 11
Etchings .... *Tegg* ... 6
Eternal Life, Gift of .... *Macmillan* .. 6
—— (Graham) .... *Shaw* 1
—— (The) Sermons .... *King* 23
—— Purpose of God, Kelly .... *Nisbet* ... 21
—— Newton .... *Nisbet* ... 23
Ethel's Strange Lodger ...... *S. S. Union.* 8
Ethical Inquiry .... *Longmans* .. 17
—— Philosophy, Macintosh ... *Black* ... 14
Ethics (Physical) Barratt .... *Williams* .. 2
—— Old Fashioned .... *Macmillan* .. 26
—— Philosophy of .... *Edmonston*.. 14
—— Smith .... *W. Blackw'd.* 18
Ethnic Inspiration, 7 Homilies on *Williams* .. 7
Ethnographical Essays, Latham.. *Williams* .. 8
Ethnological Soc. Trans....... *Murray* ... 11
Ethnology, Manual of .... *Murray* ... 5
Etiquette .... *Lockwood* ... 45
—— Works on .... *Houlston* ... 10
—— Habits of Good Society ... *Virtue* ... 14
—— Miniature Library of ..... *Routledge* .. 44
—— Modern .... *Warne* ... 35
—— of the Present Day ...... *Cassell* ... 5
—— Series .... *Milner* ... 14
—— Series .... *Walker* ... 14
Eton Books .... *Williams* .. 2
Etruria, History of, Gray .... *Hatchard* .. 10
Etruscan Inscriptions, Lindsay . *Murray* ... 22
—— Researches, Taylor ...... *Macmillan* .. 35
—— Catechism of Holy .... *Mozley* ... 2
Eucharist Doctrine .... *Clar. Press.*. 14
—— Doctrine .... *Masters* ... 4
—— Nature of Christ's Presence. *Hatchard* .. 9
Eucharistica .... *Suttaby* ... 2
Eucharistical Adoration ...... *Parker* ... 3
Eucharistic Manuals .... *Masters* ... 9
Euchologion .... *W. Blackw'd.* 38
Euclid .... *Chambers* .. 16
Euclid .... *Parker* 60
—— Elements of .... *Cassell* ... 23
—— Green .... *J. Heywood.* 23
Euripides, Andromache, Edwards *Bentley* ... 3
—— Paley .... *Whittaker* .. 1
—— Plays of, Lit. Translated .. *Hall* ... 1
—— Plays of, by Badham ..... *Williams* .. 6
Europe from 1814-1867 .... *Edmonston*.. 16
—— Art in Northern Capitals.. *Macmillan* .. 2
—— Baths and Wells of ...... *Macmillan* .. 23
—— Charities of .... *Ibister* ... 12
—— Early Geog. of .... *Reeve* ... 14
—— during French Revolution . *Murray* ... 31
—— History of, Koch .... *Whittaker* .. 10
—— Intellectual Development .. *Bell* 42
—— Literature of South of ... *Bohn's Lib.*. 9
—— Modern, Bullock .... *J. Heywood.* 34
—— (Modern) History, Dyer ... *Murray* ... 10
—— Nationalities of .... *Allen* ... 15
—— Richmond's Tour in ...... *Routledge* .. 35
—— Royal Gems from Galleries of *Virtue* 11
—— Sketches in North........ *King* 4
—— (Six Years in) .... *Chapman* .. 21
—— South of, Word Sketches .. *Bentley* ... 15
—— The Spas of .... *Trubner* ... 2
—— (S.) Watering Places of ... *King* 7
—— Winter in the South of ... *Churchill* ... 9
European Celebrities......... *Ward&Lock* .. 7
—— History, Freeman .... *Macmillan* .. 12
—— Sewell and Yonge .... *Macmillan* .. 10
—— in India, Med. Guide to ... *King* 2
—— Morals, Lecky .... *Longmans* .. 5
Europe's Crisis .... *Houlston* ... 30
Eusebius's Eccles. History .... *Clar. Press.*. 9
Evans (Rev. James H.) Sermons *Nisbet* 22
—— (R. W.) Church of God ... *Smith & El.* 7
Evelyn's Diary .... *Warne* ... 23
—— and Correspondence ...... *Bohn's Lib.* 10
Evelyn Grey .... *Nisbet* 13
Evening Hours with my Children *Nisbet* 13

Evening Hymn .... Nelson 21
—— of Life .... Masters 11
—— Meetings .... Masters 9
—— Rest .... Mozley 3
—— Words .... Parker 30
Evenings at Home .... Nimmo 19
—— at Home .... Warne 26
—— at the Tea-table .... Isbister 14
Events to be Rememb. : Eng. Hist. Lockwood 43
Everlasting Destruction .... Shaw 2
—— Righteousness .... Nisbet 6
Ever Victorious Army .... W. Blackw'd 33
—— Working, Never Resting.. Hodder 20
Everyday Companion .... Parker 30
—— Book .... Tegg ...... a
—— Difficulties, Dictionary of .. Ward 22
—— Lessons.................. Partridge .. 6
—— Objects .... Nimmo 12
Every Man's Own Lawyer .... Lockwood .. 48
—— Morning .... Tegg ...... a
—— Saturday .... Warne 28
Evil Thoughts, Chilcot on ...... Rivingtons.. 8
Evolution of Living Things ...... Macmillan .. 15
Ewing (Mrs.) Books for the Young Bell 21
Examination of Conscience ...... Rivingtons .. 6
Example and Encourage. for Boys Nelson 14
Excelsior Library .... Warne 39
Exchange and Bullion Tables.... Wilson 6
Exchange, Science of .... Cassell 7
—— Tables Adams............ Wilson 7
—— Cohn .... Wilson 12
—— Garrett.................. Wilson 10
—— Tea and Silks .... Smith & El. 4
Executors' Account Book ...... Bell 63
—— Account Book .... Houlston .. 10
Exeter Hall Lectures .... Nisbet 13
—— Cathedral, Freeman ...... Bell 13
Exiles (The) .... S. S. Union 7
—— of Lucerna, Macduff...... Nisbet 24
—— of St. Germains .... Hurst 9
Exodus, Cottage Readings on.... Nisbet 19
Expanse of Heaven .... King 6
Exploratio Philosophica ...... Bell 41
Explorers (Early) .... Cassell 11
Explorer's, Miner's &c. Guide .. Trubner .. 24
Expositor's Note-Book .... Hodder 11
Extempore Speaking .... Lockwood .. 29
Extemporaneous Speaking ...... Washbourne 8
Extradition Law .... Stevens 6
Eye, Diseases of, Dixon ...... Churchill .. 15
—— Macnamara .... Churchill .. 25
—— Natural and Morbid Changes Trubner .. 3
—— Near Sight & ImpairedVision Churchill .. 13
—— Principal Diseases of, Power Churchill .. 29
—— Works on Diseases of the . Churchill .. 0
—— Wounds and Injuries of .... Churchill .. 13
Eyes and Ears, Beecher ...... Isbister 6

Faber's Hymns, Selections from Isbister 14
Fabiola : a Tale of the Catacombs Burns 25
Fable and Fiction Dictionary.... Cassell 2
—— Picture Book .... M. Ward .. 13
Fables, Books of.............. Routledge .. 43
—— and Fancies, Francis ...... Isbister 15
—— for Old and Young ...... Isbister 33
—— in Song .... W. Blackw'd 19
—— in Verse, Croly .... Bell 35
Facets of Truth .... Hodder 25
Fact, Fiction, History, &c..... Ward&Lock 11
Facta non Verba .... Isbister 14
Factory Books................ Nicholson .. 15
—— Books and Forms .... Tubbs 6
—— Girl .... S. S. Union. 9
—— Legislation .... Chapman .. 26
Facts and Dates.............. W. Blackw'd. 44
—— and Fancies.............. S. S. Union. 7
—— and Hints, Everyday Life.. Cassell 3
—— (A Million of)............ Ward&Lock 24
Fah-Hian & Sung-Yun, Travels Trubner 3
Fairchild Family (The).......... Hatchard .. 25
Fairfax (Lord) Life of .... Macmillan .. 10
Fair and False .... J. Blackwood 29
—— Haven (The) .... Trubner .. 6
—— Women.................. Cassell 3
Fairies, Dealings with the ...... Isbister 28

Fairy Book (The) .... Macmillan .. 10
—— Family (The) .... Macmillan .. 21
—— Series of Gift Books........ Warne 29
—— Stories, Hugessen .... Macmillan .. 19
—— Tales .... Bell 22
—— Tales .... Warne 27
—— Andersen .... Warne 29
—— Gammer Grethel .... John's Lib.. 11
—— Greek, Kingsley .... Macmillan .. 18
—— by H. Lee .... Warne 19
—— Our Favourite .... Ward&Lock 20
—— Popular .... Ward&Lock 1
—— (Seven)................ Parker 44
—— told Again .... Cassell 3
—— Various .... Routledge .. 29
—— Tales, Lemon .... Bradbury .. 4
—— Tree .... Nelson 16
Fairyland (in) Doyle .... Longmans .. 28
Faithful unto Death .... Nisbet 13
—— Promiser (The) .... Nisbet 24
Faith, Aids to................ Murray 1
—— (Christian) Cranbrook .... Trubner .. 9
Faith, Deeds of .... Mozley 9
—— Smith .... Macmillan .. 33
—— and Doubts............ Hodder 13
—— Foundations of Our ...... Isbister 15
—— and Free Thought ...... Hodder 4
—— Gartney's Girlhood ...... Ward&Lock 28
—— in God and Mod. Atheism . Clark 10
—— Harrowby .... S. S. Union. 6
—— and Life .... Rivingtons .. 6
—— Mysteries of .... Masters 25
—— Phases of, Newman ...... Trubner .. 21
—— and Practice .... Rivingtons .. 15
—— and Practice, Divine Rule of Hatchard.. 9
—— Practical Power.......... Hodder 16
—— and Providence, Tales of .. Masters 9
—— and Reason .... Burns 25
—— (Reasons of) Drew ...... Longmans .. 33
—— (Saving) The Ground of ... Nisbet 10
—— Sermons on, West........ Masters 16
—— Scientific Bases.......... Macmillan .. 26
—— Shipwrecks of.......... Macmillan .. 33
—— and Victory .... Nisbet 28
—— Warrant of .... Bagster .. 61
—— The Way of .... Bagster .. 63
—— Westminster Confession of . Williams .. 7
—— Work, Boardman .... Isbister 7
Falcon Family (The) .... Warne 25
Falconburst .... Warne 28
Falconry, Salvin and Brodrick .. Van Voorst. a
Falkland (Lady) Life of ...... Burns 14
Fall of Jerusalem, &c.......... Nelson 20
—— Man (The) .... Macmillan .. 10
Familiar Things, History, &c.... Isbister 47
Families of England .... W. Blackw'd. 27
—— (Great) Rise of .... Longmans .. 9
—— (Vicissitudes of)........ Longmans .. 9
Family Altar .... MacPhun .. 9
—— Altar, Campbell .... MacPhun .. 9
—— Circle (The) .... Kelloway .. 9
—— Devotion .... Cassell 2
—— Devotion .... Hodder 22
—— Catholic .... Burns 9
—— Clerke .... Rivingtons .. 9
—— Duncombe .... Rivingtons .. 9
—— Fletcher .... Virtue 19
—— Devotions, Morison ...... Collins 2
—— Doctor (The) .... Routledge .. 20
—— (The) and " The Church " . Morgan .. 4
—— (The), its Duties .... Hodder 24
—— Prayer, Alford .... Isbister 4
—— Prayer Book .... Cassell 3
—— Prayer, Hook .... Rivingtons .. 9
—— Prayer, Hour of .... Rivingtons .. 8
—— Prayer, Rickards ...... Mozley 10
—— Medd .... Rivingtons .. 9
—— Prayers .... Bell 53
—— Prayers .... J. Blackwood 18
—— Prayers .... Masters 0
—— Prayers .... Parker 32
—— Prayers .... Wesleyan .. 18
—— Prayers, Arden .... Mozley 1
—— Bunsen .... Longmans .. 34
—— Prayers, Canon Barnes .... Houlston.... 30

Family Prayers (Ch. of Scotland) W. Blackw'd. 35
— for a Fortnight, Kennaway.. Nisbet 20
— for Four Weeks ...... Hatchard 18
— for Four Weeks ...... Hatchard 19
— Goulburn........... Rivingtons 9
— Hart .... Walker 4
— Law .... Nisbet 21
— Lord Portman ...... Hatchard 22
— Macduff .... Nisbet 24
— for a Month .... Ragster 78
— Reeve .... Nisbet 31
— (Unsectarian)....... King 29
— Various .... Hatchard .. 23
— Vaughan .... Isbister 45
— Villiers .... Nisbet 36
— for a Week, from Com. Prayer Nisbet .. 22
— Readings, Molyneaux .. Nisbet 27
— Register .... Letts 1
— Register .... Ward&Lock 9
— Sermons, Bonar ...... Nisbet 6
— Walking Sticks ...... Partridge ... 6
— Worship .... Blackie .. 24
— Worship .... Hagger 6
— Book (The) .... Ragster .. 76
— Dialogues on ...... Macmillan .. 24
— Lady Grovenor ...... Hatchard .. 11
— Medical Guide ...... Chapman .. 18
— Reading, Short Sermons for Mosley .. 10
— Save All .... Houlston 5
Famous Boys .... Ward&Lock 27
— London Merchants .... Virtue 14
Fanny Fern's New Stories .... Ward&Lock 27
Fanti and Ashanti ...... W. Blackw'd. 5
Faraday, by J. H. Gladstone.... Macmillan .. 10
Farm Ballads .... Routledge .. 2
— — Bookkeeping ...... Chambers .. 15
— Crops, Wilson ...... Blackie .. 11
— Expenses Book ...... Letts 2
— (The) Seller's, ... W. Blackw'd. 52
— Book of. See Agriculture .. W. Blackw'd. 52
Farmer's Account Book, Webb.. Jarrold .. 20
— Account Books, Wyley .... Houlston .. 27
— Assistant, Youatt .... Lockwood .. 16
— Calendar .... Warne .. 11
— Friend (The) ...... Walker 4
— Guide, Webb's ...... Blackie .. 11
— Ready Reckoner ...... Virtue .. 31
Farming (Amateur) ...... Lockwood .. 16
— British, Wilson ...... Black .. 32
— Manuals .... Routledge .. 10
— Modern, Burn ...... Lockwood .. 16
— Pleasant Talk about .... Isbister 6
— Profitable, Mechi .... Routledge .. 1
— Successful .... Bradbury .. 9
Farnham (Lord) Works by .. Yapp 3
Far Off: Asia, Aust., &c., Descri. Hatchard .. 7
Farrar (Rev. F. W.) Works by .. Macmillan .. 10
— Books for Boys ...... Black .. 12
— Life of Christ ...... Cassell 0
Farrier, by Laurence ...... Virtue .. 20
Farriery, Brown ...... Virtue .. 13
Fascicules .... Parker .. 64
Fasti Ecclesiæ Hibernæ .... Parker .. 13
— Monastici Aevi Saxonici .. Trubner .. 5
— Sacri, Lewin ...... Bell .. 47
Fate, Royal Book of ...... Cornish 4
Fatherhood of God ...... W. Blackw'd. 37
— of God .... Hatchard .. 10
Fathers of the Church .... Clar. Press.. 9
— of the Church ...... Soc. P. C. K. 6
— (Early) on Study of .... Bell .. 45
— Extracts from the ...... Washbourne. .. 8
— Library of .... Parker .. 16
— (Our) Wisdom of .... Rel. Tr. Soc. 19
Fawcett (Prof.) Works by .. Macmillan .. 11
Fecundity, Fertility, &c., Duncan Black .. 12
Feed My Lambs ...... Nisbet .. 13
Fellowship .... Macmillan .. 11
— among Men ...... Macmillan .. 42
Female Characters of Holy Writ Warne .. 25
— Disciple .... Houlston .. 39
— Sovereigns ...... Routledge .. 4
Fenelon, Religious Extracts .... Hatchard .. 8
Fern Collector's Album......... Hardwicke.. 2
— Every Known............ Hardwicke.. 1

Fern Garden.................Groombridge 7
— Leaves.................Ward&Lock 27
Ferns and Allied Plants ...... Routledge .. 9
— British .... Reeve .. 7
— and Fern Allies, Sowerby .. Bell .. 15
— British, Culture of...... Houlston .. 12
— British and Foreign ...... Hardwicke. .. 1
— Geographical Handbook .. Murray .. 22
— of Great Britain, Pratt.... Warne .. 7
— Hooker .... Sotheran. .. 15
— Lowe .... Bell .. 16
— Plain Account of British .. Hardwicke. .. 2
— Synopsis of the Genera of .. Williams .. 10
Fertilizers, Pure ...... Trubner .. 20
Festivals of the Church of England Hatchard .. 19
— and Feasts, Nelson ...... Soc. P. C. K. 3
Festus: A Poem ...... Bell .. 36
Fevers (Continued) Murchison .. Longmans .. 23
— Tweedie .... Churchill .. 34
Fever, Lectures on, Stokes .... Longmans .. 27
— (Relapsing) Lyons...... King .. 7
Fichte (J. G.) Works ...... Trubner .. 12
Fiction, Masterpieces of .... J. Blackwood .. 3
Fictitious Names, Handbook for J. R. Smith 7
— Persons and Places ...... Bohn's Lib. .. 11
Field Exercises ...... Allen .. 37
— & Garden, MonthlyGleanings Soc. P. C. K. 18
— Manœuvres ...... W. Blackw'd .. 20
— (E. W.) A Memorial Sketch Macmillan .. 11
— Pocket, for Auxiliary Forces Macmillan .. 41
Fields and Woodlands (The) .. Ward&Lock 24
Fielding (Henry) Works, Complete Bell .. 34
— Works .... Sotheran. .. 12
— Writings of ...... Nimmo .. 7
Fiend's Delight ...... Chatto .. 15
Fife and the Lothians, Geology of Black .. 14
Fifine at the Fair ...... Smith & El. 3
FiftyThous. MilesRoundtheWorld Bentley .. 14
Fighting the Flames ...... Nisbet .. 4
Figuier's Human Race ...... Chapman .. 13
Figurative Language in Scripture Parker .. 8
Figures Made Easy ...... Clar. Press. 25
Fiji and the Fijians ...... Hodder .. 26
— Islands .... Parker .. 64
— Flora of.......... Reeve .. 4
Fijian Dictionary ...... Wesleyan .. 44
Filling up the Chinks ...... Warne .. 27
Finance, Patterson (R. H.) .. W. Blackw'd 25
Financial and Monetary History Wilson .. 4
Fine Art Annual ...... Virtue .. 7
— Arts, Rudimentary Works .. Lockwood .. 25
Fingers and Toes. Diseases of .. Edmonston. .. 5
Finn's (Mrs.) Works on Palestine Nisbet .. 13
Fire Brigade: A Tale of London Nisbet .. 4
— Insurance Law, Bunyon .... Layton .. 8
— and Life Assurance, Law of Layton .. 7
— Surveys.......... Wilson .. 4
Fire-Engines and Brigades .... Lockwood .. 4
Fires, Notes on Causes of...... Layton .. 13
Fireside Chats, &c. ...... Warne .. 25
— Series .... S. S. Union 8
Firework Making ...... Spon .. 46
Fireworks, Art of Making .... Ward&Lock 9
— How to Make ...... Routledge .. 19
First Heroes of the Cross...... S. S. Union 5
— Principles of Ecclesias. Truth Hodder .. 18
Fish Cook (Continental) ...... Washbourne 6
Fishes of British Islands, Couch Bell .. 16
— (Food) British ...... Murray .. 20
Fishing Girl (The) ...... Cassell .. 11
— (Sea) Wilcocks ...... Longmans .. 42
Fisk (Fidelia) Records of...... Morgan .. 2
Fistula, Allingham on ...... Churchill. .. 6
Fitful Gleams from Fancy Land Houlston .. 22
FiveDays' Entertainment ...... Macmillan .. 3
— Day's Frolic ...... Chatto .. 20
— Gateways of Knowledge .. Macmillan .. 41
— Great Monarchies ...... Murray .. 20
— Old Friends ...... Smith & El. 31
Fixtures, Laws of ...... Stevens .. 6
Flagellation, &c. ...... Chatto .. 15
Flat Iron for a Farthing ...... Bell .. 21
Flax and Hemp ...... Routledge .. 4
Flaxman's Illustrations...... Bell .. 7
Fleming (G.) Veterinary Works by Chapman .. 18

Flemish Literature............ Murray 10
—— Painters (Early)........ Murray 7
Fleetwood's Life of Christ ...... Virtue.... 19
Fleury's France, Beljamo ...... Williams.... 6
—— Histories .... Allman 9
—— Histories .... Edmonston .. 9
Flint Chips, Stevens .... Bell 12
Floating Light of Goodwin Sands Nisbet 4
Flora Antarctica .... Sotheran.... 15
— — British .... Reeve 3
—— of British Islands ...... Macmillan.. 16
—— Symbolica .... Warne 4
—— of Middlesex .... Hardwicke.. 2
—— Tourist's, Brit. and Cont. .. Reeve 4
Floral World and Garden Guide.. Groombridge 11
—— Literarum .... Wilson 10
Flowering Plants, &c. .... Warne 6
Flowers, Alpine .... W. Blackw'd 54
—— Birds, & Insects of the Month Ward & Lock 28
—— Burbidge .... W. Blackw'd 28
—— Choice Garden .... Houlston 5
—— Common Wayside .... Routledge .. 28
—— English Wild .... Warne 13
—— and Festivals .... Rivingtons.. 10
— — Field .... Groombridge 12
—— of Foreign Lands .... Houlston 12
—— & Fruit gath.by Loving Hands Houlston.... 18
—— and Gardens .... Isbister 46
—— Grasses, and Shrubs .... J. Blackwood 9
—— Handy .... Warne 13
—— and Heraldry .... Houlston.... 14
—— from the Holy Land ...... Houlston.... 14
—— Language of .... Warne 3
— — Language, Tyas .... Routledge .. 28
—— Pleasant Talk About .... Isbister 6
—— Sentiment of .... Houlston.... 14
—— Wild .... Reeve 3
—— Wild .... Routledge .. 9
—— (Wild) of England, Tyas.. Howlston.... 14
—— Pratt .... Soc. P.C.K. 29
—— worth Notice .... Hardwicke.. 3
—— and Fruit Decoration .... Harrison.... 4
Flower Seekers (Little) ...... M. Ward 6
Flying from a Shadow ...... Smith & El. 15
Fly-Fisher's Entomology ...... Longmans.. 43
Fly-Leaves, Poems.......... Bell 35
Foa (Med. Eug.) Works of, French Nutt...... 24
Foes of Faith, Vaughan .... Macmillan.. 39
Foliorum Silvula............ Bell 11
Following Fully .... Morgan 3
Fontaine's Fables, Doré ...... Cassell...... 4
Food Adulterations .... Isbister 5
—— Lankester's Lectures on .. Hardwicke.. 15
—— for My Flock, Sermons .. Hatchard .. 11
Foods, Dr. F. Smith........ King...... 7
Fool of Quality (The) .... Macmillan.. 4
Fools' Paradise, a Series .... Chatto 16
Foot and Ankle, Surgery of.... Churchill .. 19
—— of the Cross, Winslow.... Nisbet 38
Footfalls on Another World.... Trubner 23
Foot-notes from Page of Nature Macmillan.. 21
Footsteps of Error, Close ...... Hatchard .. 4
—— of the Flock .... Morgan 3
—— of Our Lord and His Apostles Bell........ 12
For Liberty's Sake.......... Isbister 30
—— the Work of the Ministry .. Isbister 7
Forbes (Bishop) Works by .... Masters 3
—— (Edward) Life of .... Macmillan.. 12
—— (J. D.) Life and Letters of .. Macmillan.. 12
Force, Mental & Moral Correlates Longmans.. 16
—— and Matter .... Trubner 6
—— and Nature .... Macmillan.. 41
Forces of Nature, Guillemin .. Macmillan.. 15
Ford (Rev. J.) Works by........ Masters 10
Foreign Armies & Home Reserves Chapman.. 12
—— Books and Periodicals .. Barthes .... a
—— Countries (Peeps at) .... Isbister 34
—— Exchanges .... Wilson 7
—— Office List & Consular Hd.Bk Harrison.. 2
—— Phrases Familiarised ...... Cornish 4

Foreign Prot. Pulpit .... Dickinson .. 5
—— Theological Pulpit ...... Clark 2
Forest Cantons (The).......... Smith & El. 27
—— and Field .... Chatto 17
—— (the), Jungle and the Prairie Nelson 6
—— Life in Acadie............ Chapman .. 19
—— Ranger, Campbell .... Routledge .. 31
Forester, Brown .... W. Blackw'd 43
Forget thine Own People........ King...... 27
Forgiveness, Life, and Glory .. Nisbet 6
Forgotten Themes, Brown .... Kellaway .. 5
Formby (Rev. Henry) Works by Burns 12
Forms of Praise and Prayer .. Parker 30
—— of Prayer, &c., Oxford.... Mozley.... 9
—— of Prayer, &c., Winchester. Mozley.... 3
Forster (John) Works by ...... Chapman .. 13
Forsyth (W.) Essays .... Longmans.. 9
—— Works of .... Murray 12
Fortescue Family .... Houlston.... 17
Fortification .... W. Blackw'd 34
—— Field .... Allen 19
—— Field .... Isbister 24
—— Instruction in .... Harrison .. 19
—— O'Brien .... Cassell...... 5
Fortune Teller .... Milner 3
—— Raphael .... Cornish 4
Forty Days in the Desert...... Bell 12
Forum and the Vatican........ Nisbet 16
Fosbery's Hymns for the Sick .. Rivingtons.. 7
Fossils, Cambrian and Sil. .... Cambridge .. 5
Foster (Birket) Summer Scenes.. Bell 9
—— Works Illustrated ...... Routledge .. 27
—— (Frank) Works by ...... Snow 6
—— (John) Life and Works .. Bohn's Lib.. 7
Foster's Plain Sermons........ Wesleyan.... 44
Foundling of Fevecot ...... S. S. Union 9
Fountain of Living Waters...... J. Blackwood 24
—— of Truth (The) .... Macmillan.. 11
Fouque's Works, in German .... Nutt...... 14
—— Works, in German .... Williams.... 6
Fox (W. J.) Works .... Trubner 12
Fox's Works .... Wilson 5
—— (Rev. G. T.) Sermons .... Nisbet 13
—— (Wilson) Works .... Macmillan.. 11
Foxe's Book of Martyrs ...... Cassell...... 4
—— Book of Martyrs........ Routledge .. 65
—— Book of Martyrs........ Warne 37
Fox Hunting, Scrutator ...... Routledge .. 71
—— Vyner (R. C.)........ Chatto 37
Fractional Calculator........ Mozley.... 9
Frädersdorff's Eng.-Grk. Lexicon Rivingtons.. 22
Français (Questionnaire) ...... Trubner 17
France, Church of .... Murray 19
—— Domestic Life in ...... W. Blackw'd 9
—— and Eng., Parallel History.. Macmillan.. 43
— — Geology and Ext. Volcanoes Murray 27
—— Glimpses of Life in .... Bell 24
—— Great Christians of ...... Macmillan.. 34
—— History................ W. Blackw'd 47
—— History................ Routledge .. 21
—— History of, Brewer ...... Jarrold 27
—— History to 1453 .... Clar. Press.. 26
—— of, Taylor .... Whittaker .. 11
—— and Italy, 1848-52, Senior .. King...... 3
—— (La Belle) .... Isbister 33
—— Les Ecrivains Militaires .... Trubner 17
—— Les Ecossais en .... Trubner 20
—— Military Institutions of .. Chapman .. 14
— — Under Nap. III., Court, &c. Tinsley Bros. 3
—— Old Court Life in ...... Chapman .. 18
—— (Old) Ballads and Lyrics.... Longmans.. 42
—— Poets and Prose Writers of.. Black 15
—— Priestly Life in .... Rivingtons.. 25
—— Religion and Literature in .. Williams.... 2
—— under Richelieu.......... Edmonston.. 3
—— Society in, Davies........ Hurst 4
—— (Society in) before Revolution Murray 31
—— (Southern) Archæology of .. Williams.... 11
—— Tales of .... Burns 3
—— Tales of the South of .... Mozley.... 13
—— Women of .... Bradbury .. 4
—— History of under the Bourbons Tinsley Bros. 6
Franco-German War .... Asher 3
—— War, Chapelle .... Chapman .. 14
—— German War............ Cassell...... 8

Franco-German War .... *Hagger* 10
—— German War .... *Tinsley Bros.* 5
— Battle of Sedan .... *Stanford*.... 54
— Besieged Residents in Paris *Macmillan*.. 19
— " Daily News " Corres. .... *Macmillan*.. 8
— Eight Months on Duty .... *Isbister* 14
— Fall of Metz .... *Bradbury* .. 11
— German Operations ...... *King*........ 11
— Gov. of the Nat. Defence .. *King* 3
— — Letters on .... *Trübner* 18
— On Trail of the War, Shand *Smith & El.* 19
— Paris during Siege ...... *Macmillan*.. 17
—— Rough Notes, Ashton ...... *King*........ 4
— Rustow .... *W. Blackw'd* 27
— Scenes, Sketches & Incidents *Nisbet* 10
—— A Tale of .... *Hodder* 26
— " Times " Correspondent .. *Bentley* 5
— Versailles .... *Trübner* 15
—— War, German Official Accnt. *Harrison*... 22
—— War, Roberts............. *Chapman* .. 24
—— War, Siege of Paris...... *Chapman* .. 24
Franklin (Benj.) a Biography *Nimmo* 14
—— Young Benjamin .... *J. Blackwood* 5
— — Expedition .... *W. Blackw'd* 23
— (Sir J.) Search for .... *Murray* 21
Frank Oldfield .... *Nelson* 13
— Record of a Happy Life.... *Morgan* 2
Fraser Portraits .... *Chatto* 3
Fred and his Relations ...... *S. S. Union* . 9
Frederick the Second, Carlyle .. *Chapman* .. 13
Free Churches .... *Isbister* 13
Freedom of the Will .... *Wesleyan* ... 51
Free-Hand Drawing .... *Laurie* 4
—— Ornament, Hulme ...... *Chapman* .. 19
— — Copham .... *Jarrold* 6
—— Ornament .... *M. Ward* .. 13
Freeman's Historical Works .... *Macmillan* .. 12
—— Norman Conquest ...... *Clar. Press*.. 15
Freemasonry, Works on ...... *Reeves & T.* 2
Freethinking, Essays on ...... *Longmans* .. 9
Free Thought in Christian Rel... *Murray* 11
Freighter's Guide .... *Philip* 39
French Academy, History of .... *Trübner* 11
— Book, Little Boys'...... *Stanford* ... 54
— Class Books .... *Bell* 33
—— Classics................ *Hachette* ... 1
—— Commune, History of .... *Chapman* .. 26
— Comparative Gram., Eugene *Williams* .. 6
— Conversation for Schools, Roy *Williams* .. 12
— — Didot's Ed. .... *Nutt*........ 23
—— Commercial Letter Writer .. *Trübner* 4
—— Conversation, Easy Lessons *Stanford* ... 54
—— Fruston................ *Trübner* 10
—— and German Books ...... *Dulau* 2
—— Grammar .... *Nutt*........ 26
— Country Family.......... *Isbister* 13
—— Grammar, Brasseur ...... *Williams* ... 3
—— Goods, Tables of Eng. Prices *Houlston* .. 25
—— Grammar (French Academy) *Black* 14
—— Grammar, Noel & Chapsal.. *Williams* .. 10
—— House .... *Smith & El.* 18
— Ed. Course, Chardenal .. *Collins* 12
—— Dialogues.............. *Hachette* ... 5
—— Letters for Trans. into Eng. *Williams* .. 10
—— Literature, Masson ...... *Black* 15
—— Naval Tactics.......... *Harrison*.... 6
— Plays, Buchheim .... *Williams* ... 4
—— Primer, Beaumont ...... *Williams* ... 2
—— Revolution, Carlyle ...... *Chapman* .. 13
French Dictionaries .... *Hachette*... 6
—— Dictionaries .... *Routledge* .. 14
—— Dicty., Bona Fide Pocket .. *Trübner* 4
—— Dictionary, Contanseau .... *Longmans* .. 12
—— Elwe.................. *Lockwood* .. 30
—— Masson .... *Macmillan* .. 24
—— Nugent................ *Rivingtons*.. 28
—— Spiers .... *Whittaker* .. 9
—— Weller .... *Trübner* 31
—— Gase .... *Bell* 34
—— International Dictionary .. *Nutt*........ 28
—— Technical Dictionary ...... *Spon*....... 21
—— Eton (A) .... *Macmillan*.. 2
—— Etymological Dictionary .. *Clar. Press*.. 29
—— Pick .... *Murray* 25
— — Drama, Gombert .... *Bell* 30

French Educational Books ...... *Nutt*........ 22
—— Course .... *Hachette* .. 3
—— Le Page .... *Isbister* 25
—— Works .... *Parker*..... 59
—— Works .... *Whittaker* .. 6
—— Elementary Books ...... *Lockwood* .. 38
—— Course .... *J. Heywood* 30
—— Empire, Last Days of...... *Bentley* 13
—— and English Conversations.. *Trübner* 2
—— and English Conversations.. *Whittaker* .. 7
French Examination Papers, Brette *Trübner* 6
—— Ruhle .... *Nutt*........ 22
French Grammar, Brachet ...... *Hachette*... 3
—— Brette .... *Hachette* ... 3
—— Roche .... *Trübner* 26
—— at Sight .... *Macmillan*.. 9
—— Van Laun .... *Trübner* 20
—— Historical Grammar...... *Clar. Press*.. 29
French History .... *Chambers* .. 13
—— Home Life .... *W. Blackw'd.* 9
—— Idioms, Hue .... *Hachette* ... 3
—— Language, Greene ...... *Trübner* 13
—— and Literature .... *Clar. Press*.. 29
—— Philosophy of.......... *Hachette* ... 5
—— Lessons in .... *Cassell* 13
—— Literature, Poitevin...... *Asher* 5
—— Memoirs .... *Bohn's Lib.*.. 10
—— (Modern) Conversation .. *Lockwood* .. 34
—— Palaces............... *Bradbury* .. 4
—— Periodicals .... *Hachette* .. 7
—— Phrase and Word Book ... *Nutt*....... 26
—— Plays, Brette .... *Trübner* .. 28
—— Poetry .... *Hachette* .. 3
—— Early .... *Macmillan* .. 3
—— Polishing .... *Spon* 21
—— Prayer Books .... *Burns*...... 8
—— Prose and Poetry, Studies in *Isbister* 47
—— Readers .... *Hachette* ... 4
—— Reader, Karcher ...... *Trübner* 20
—— Republic, Men of ...... *Isbister* 31
French Revolution .... *Bentley* 10
—— in 1848 .... *Bohn's Lib.*. 8
—— 1848 to 1852, Senior ...... *King* 3
—— Baker .... *Bentley* 6
—— Burke .... *Rivingtons* .. 26
—— Early Period .... *Murray* 8
—— Michelet .... *Bohn's Lib.*.. 8
—— Morris .... *Longmans* .. 6
—— Recollections of.......... *Washbourne.* 7
—— Story of .... *Bell* 25
—— Tales of .... *Burns* 35
—— Thiers .... *Bentley* 14
—— A Woman's Lot in ...... *Isbister* 44
French School Books .... *Jarrold* 19
—— De Fivas............. *Lockwood* .. 44
—— Classics, Tauchnitz ...... *Nutt*........ 27
—— School Life .... *Nimmo* 13
—— Self Teaching Grammar .. *Nutt*........ 28
—— Society, Baker .... *Bentley* 6
—— Stories, with Notes ...... *Asher* 2
—— Teacher, Pontet ...... *MacGlashan.* 6
—— without a Teacher...... *Lockwood* .. 30
—— Testament and Com. Prayer *Ragster* ... 17
—— Tourist's Pronounc. Hd. Bk. *Routledge* .. 44
—— Verbs .... *Wilson* 8
—— Bellew's .... *Trübner* 4
—— Verbs at a Glance........ *Stanford* ... 50
—— Versions .... *Stanford* ... 52
Frere (Sir B.) Works by .... *Murray* 12
Frere's (John Hookham) Works.. *Pickering* .. 15
Fresh Religious Thoughts ...... *Houlston* .. 36
Fret Cutting .... *Bemrose* ... 10
Freytag's Our Forefathers .. *Asher* 14
—— Works in German ...... *Nutt*....... 14
Friarswood Post Office ...... *Mozley*..... 3
Friction, Theory of, Jellet .. *Macmillan* .. 17
Friend Fritz.............. *Ward & Lock* 23
Friend in Need Papers...... *Hatchard* .. 3
Friends in Council.......... *Smith & El.* 10
—— in Fur and Feather ...... *Bell* 23
Friendly Hands & Kindly Words *Isbister* .. 15
—— Societies' Accounts ...... *Layton* 13
—— Societies, Ansell ...... *Layton* 7
—— Societies' Law .... *Lockwood* .. 28
Friendship of Books .... *Macmillan* .. 25

Friendship's Garland............ Smith & El. 1
Frithiof, Tale of, Spalding ..... Murray 30
Froissart's Chronicles .... Routledge .. 21
From Morning to Evening ...... Rivingtons .. 7
From Seventeen to Thirty ...... Nisbet 3
From Tent to Palace........... S. S. Union. 5
Frost and Fire .... Edmonston .. 8
—— King................. J. Blackwood 22
—— (Rev. P.) Works by .... Macmillan .. 12
Frost's Greek & Lat. School Bks. Bell 10
Froude, Refutation of .... Cameron 1
Froude's Historical Works ..... Longmans ... 1
Fruit Culture .... W. Blackw'd. 54
—— Manual .... Houlston 12
—— Trees, Culture of .... Lockwood ... 16
Fry (Caroline) Works by....... Nisbet 13
Fry (E.) Memoir by Cresswell .. Nisbet 14
Fuel, How to Save........... Chapman ... 8
Fugitive Poems .... Parker..... 64
Fuller (W. H.) Medical Works by Churchill .. 16
Fullerton (Lady G.) Novels .... Bentley 16
—— Works by............... Burns 26
Fullom (S. W.) Last Days Jerus. Hatchard .. 8
Fun, Books of .... Nicholson .. 14
—— for the Million .... Chatto 16
Fundamentals, Mental, Moral ... Longmans .. 33
Funds, Compendium of .... Wilson 2
—— (Sinking) Apology for ... Williams .. 12
Fungi (British) Cook .... Macmillan .. 8
—— Edible and Poisonous .... Hardwicke.. 3
—— (Microscopic) .... Hardwicke.. 3
—— Plain Account of Brit..... Hardwicke.. 4
Fungology .... Reeve 9
Fur, Wool, and Hair, Prop. of .. Spon....... 23
Furniture, Decorative Designs for Houlston ... 21
—— Taste in Household ...... Longmans .. 30
Future Life (The) .... Kellaway .. 11
—— Doctrine of .... Trubner ... 2
—— Punishment, Constable ... Kellaway .. 4
—— State.................. Parker..... 4
—— Courtesy .... Hatchard .. 13
—— Philosophy of .... Collins 3

Gabrielle Hastings, a Tale ...... Hatchard .. 8
Gaelic Dictionary .... W. Blackw'd. 15
—— and English Dictionary ... MacPhun .. 13
—— Poetry .... Edmonston .. 14
—— Prayer Book .... Edmonston .. 4
Gahu, Com. Abridged .... Cambridge .. 5
—— Commentaries of .... Stevens ... 6
Galatea, Cruise of H.M.S. ..... Allen 5
Galbraith & Haughton's Manuals Cassell 13
Galileo, Private Life of........ Macmillan .. 12
Gallery of Illust. Lit. Characters Chatto 1
—— of Modern Sculpture .... Virtue 11
—— of Nature.............. Chambers .. 30
—— of Pictures............. Sotheran .. 13
Gallican Church, Jervis .... Murray 19
Galt (J.) Novels by .... W. Blackw'd. 10
Galton (Francis) Works by ..... Macmillan .. 12
Gamble (Rev. H. J.) Works by .. Snow 6
Game Book .... W. Blackw'd. 51
—— Register .... Letts...... 2
Games for all Seasons .... J. Blackwood 5
—— for Children .... Routledge .. 18
—— for Family Parties....... Warne 46
—— Handbook of .... Bohn's Lib.. 18
—— (New) and Amusements .. Chatto 25
—— and Pastimes, Handbooks of Routledge .. 19
—— of Skill................ Routledge .. 37
—— and Tricks .... Chatto 3
—— and Tricks .... Chatto 18
Gaol Cradle (The) Who Rocks it? Isbister ... 15
Garbett (Rev. Ed.) Works by .... Rel. Tr. Soc. 8
Garden, Alpine Flowers for Eng. Murray 27
—— The Children's .... Warne 30
—— and the City .... Smith & El. 14
—— (Cottage) Adamson ...... Black...... 1
—— (Flower) .... W. Blackw'd. 54
—— Beauty of Form in....... Murray 27
—— Flower and Kitchen...... Routledge .. 11
—— Loudon .... Bradbury .. 9
—— Fruit, Flower, and Kitchen. Black 15
—— and Greenhouse Botany... Routledge .. 47
—— Hardy Exotic Plants ..... Murray 27

Garden (The) Hole (S. R.) ..... W. Blackw'd. 50
—— How to Lay Out .... Bradbury .. 9
—— Management .... Ward&Lock 5
—— Manuals, Cuthill .... Groombridge. 8
—— M'Intosh (C.).......... W. Blackw'd. 51
—— of Sorrows (The) .... Morgan 3
—— of the Soul (The) .... Burns 9
—— of the Soul (The) .... Washbourne. 15
Gardener (Cottage) Dictionary . Bell 15
—— Thomson's .... W. Blackw'd. 49
—— and Farmer's Reason Why. Houlston ... 6
Gardener's (Amateur) Calendar . Warne 12
—— Assistant .... Blackie ... 16
—— Receipt Book .... Groombridge. 6
Gardening, All About It ...... Ward&Lock 6
—— for Amateurs .... Groombridge. 4
—— Book, Beeton .... Ward&Lock 5
—— Encyclopedia .... Longmans .. 33
—— Hardy Flowers .... Warne 13
—— for Ladies, Loudon ...... Murray 21
—— Market .... Groombridge. 2
—— Plain Path to Good ...... Lockwood .. 16
—— Practical .... Groombridge. 8
—— Profitable .... Groombridge. 7
—— (Scientific) Rennie ...... Cornish ... 4
—— Vegetables and Flowers .. Warne 13
—— (Window).............. W. Blackw'd. 48
—— (Window).............. Routledge .. 11
—— Works on............... Bradbury .. 9
—— Works on, Glenny .... Houlston ... 11
Gardiner (Com. Allen) Memoir . Nisbet 16
Gardner&Sharpe'sHomeLessons. Philip 40
Garibaldi's Campaign .... W. Blackw'd. 8
Garland of Poetry and Prose ... Nimmo 11
—— of the Year .... M. Ward .. 4
Garnet Island .... Warne 98
Garnston .... Wilson 10
Garrett (Ed.) Works of Fiction by Isbister ... 16
Garrick (David) Life.......... Tinsley Bros. 5
Gas and Gasworks, Hughes .... Lockwood .. 4
—— Manufacture of, Clegg .... Trubner ... 8
—— Works on............... Spon...... 22
Gasc's French School Books ... Bell 33
Gascoyne, the Sandalwood Trader Nisbet 6
Gaskell's (Mrs.) Works........ Smith & El. 8
Gate Lodges, Designs for...... Spon...... 12
Gates Ajar (The) .... Routledge .. 34
—— Antidotes to .... Hodder 26
—— Critically Examined ..... Hatchard .. 8
Gathered Leaves .... Isbister ... 40
—— Together .... Warne 10
Gatherings from a Ministry, Milne Nisbet 27
Gatty's Parables from Nature . Bell 9
—— (Mrs.) Popular Works.... Bell 19
Gaultier (L.) Works by, French . Nutt 24
Gay's Fables .... Warne 20
Gazetteer, Beeton .... Ward&Lock 4
—— (Bijou) .... Warne 46
—— British .... Ward&Lock 7
—— of the Central Prov. of India Trubner ... 13
—— Cotton .... Clar. Press. 19
—— Imperial .... Blackie ... 4
—— of India .... Allen 8
—— of the Punjaub, &c. ..... Allen 8
—— of the United Kingdom ... Longmans .. 20
—— of the World .... Johnston .. 47
—— of the World, Diamond ... MacPhun .. 16
Geikie (Arch.) Works by ...... Macmillan .. 12
—— (Dr.) Works by .... Isbister ... 16
Geldart's (Mrs.) Stories....... Jarrold ... 7
—— Stories .... Routledge .. 37
Gelfie, Mission to .... Tinsley Bros. 6
Gem of the Peak............. Moxley ... 4
Gems of Literature........... Nimmo 10
—— of National Poetry ...... Warne 21
—— and Rings .... Bell 14
—— of Sacred Melody .... Walker ... 15
Genealogy and Surnames ...... J. R. Smith 2
Genealogical Stemma, Hola .... Macmillan . 18
—— Tables, Modern History ... Clar. Press. 25
Genera Plantarum .... Williams .. 3
Generative Organs, Works on the Churchill... 1
Gennesaret, Memoirs of .... Nisbet 23
Genesis, its Authenticity & Auth. Nisbet 14
—— and its Authorship ...... Williams .. 81

Genesis, Book of, Alford .... *Isbister* 3
— (Book of) in Hebrew........ *Williams* .. 16
— of the Church .... *W. Blackw'd* 36
— of the Earth and Man ...... *Williams* 6
— Paul's Analysis .... *W. Blackw'd* 40
— of Species, Mivart .... *Macmillan* .. 25
— Book of, Candlish .... *Black* 10
Genial Showman .... *Chatto* 17
Genius of the Gospel .... *Dickinson* .. 13
Gentiles, The Times of the .... *Nisbet* 5
Gentle Shepherd (The) .... *Black* 16
Gentleman Emigrant .... *Tinsley Bros.* 2
Gentleman's House, Kerr ...... *Murray* 19
Geographical Pronunciation .... *Stanford* 64
— Society Journal .... *Murray* 13
— Text Books .... *Chambers* .. 13
Geographies for Children ...... *Hatchard* .. 9
Geography.................... *Clar. Press.* 17
Geography.................... *Whittaker* .. 11
— for Beginners .... *Cornwall* .. a
— Comparative .... *W. Blackw'd* 47
— Curiosities of Physical...... *J. Blackwood* 12
— Dictionary of .... *Johnston* 47
— Dictionary .... *Ward & Lock* 4
— (Ecclesiastical) .... *Masters* 14
— Educational Handbooks .... *Johnston* 9
— Elementary .... *Murby* 7
— Elementary .... *Philip* 35
— Ansted .... *Cassell* 13
— Elementary Course .... *J. Heywood* 31
— English Cyclopædia .... *Bradbury* .. 6
— European .... *MacGlashan* 6
— Gallery of, Milner .... *MacL'hun* .. 11
— Historical................ *Longmans* .. 6
— Horn's Scholar's.......... *J. Heywood* 11
— Mackay.................. *W. Blackw'd* 43
— Maunder .... *Longmans* .. 41
— Mathematical .... *Murray* 30
— Military .... *Whittaker* .. 12
— of Old and New Testaments *Isbister* 47
— Physical .... *Allen* 3
— Physical .... *W. Blackw'd* 46
— Physical .... *Chambers* .. 12
— Physical .... *J. Heywood* 32
— (Pictorial) Handbook ...... *Bohn's Lib.* 14
— Pictorial Illustrations of .. *C. Smith* 6
— (Progressive) for Children .. *Murray* 8
Geological Diagrams .... *Chapman* .. 31
— Maps .... *Johnston* 5
— British Isles............. *W. Blackw'd* 10
— Sketches .... *Trubner* 1
— Stories .... *Hardwicke* .. 8
— Survey of the British Isles .. *Stanford* 44
Geology .... *Chambers* .. 17
— Applied to Arts and Manufac. *Hardwicke* .. 8
— Chem. & Phys. Bischof .... *Harrison* .. 14
— for Beginners .... *Longmans* .. 24
— (Class Book of) .... *Lockwood* .. 15
— Dana .... *Trubner* 9
— Elementary .... *Trubner* 31
— and Genesis .... *Lockwood* .. 42
— and History.............. *Trubner* 8
— Last Glacial Epoch of .... *Chapman* .. 7
— Lyell .... *Murray* 21
— Manual of, Jukes .... *Black* 13
— Mantell's Works on ...... *Bohn's Lib.* 19
— for the Million............ *Routledge* .. 68
— Minerals, Mines, &c. ...... *Houlston* .. 22
— Natural and Revealed .... *Nimmo* 4
— Newer Pliocene, Smith .... *Williams* .. 13
— (Our World) .... *Jarrold* 12
— Page .... *W. Blackw'd* 45
— Popular Sketch-book of .... *Nimmo* 4
— Religion of .... *J. Blackwood* 19
— and Scripture .... *Bohn's Lib.* 19
— for Students, J. Young .... *Collins* 8
— and Theology, Gloag ...... *Clark* 22
— (Town) .... *Isbister* 24
Geometrical Drawing, Bradley .. *Chapman* .. 12
— Drawings, De Rheims ...... *Williams* .. 5
— Note Book, Kitchener ...... *Macmillan* .. 19
— Optics, Airy .... *Macmillan* .. 1
Geometry.................... *J. Heywood* 29
— Elementary Works on .... *Laurie* 3
— and Euclid .... *Bell* 17

Geometry, Inventional .... *Mosley* 1
— Note Book on.............. *Macmillan* .. 1
— Plane and Solid .... *Longmans* .. 25
— (Practical) Burchett ...... *Chapman* .. 12
— Tarn .... *Lockwood* .. 11
— Pure, Lectures .... *Clar. Press.* 25
— Rudimentary .... *Lockwood* .. 26
George III. Corres., Ld. North.. *Murray* 19
— Desmond .... *Houlston* .. 33
— Opposition under .... *Isbister* 37
George and Lizzie .... *Warne* 29
George's Enemies .... *Nimmo* 15
Georges (The) History of .... *Chatto* 40
Gerard, the Lion Killer........ *Burns* 26
Gerard's Monument, Poems.... *Trubner* 24
Gerhardt's (Paul) Spiritual Songs *Isbister* 16
German Art, Modern.......... *Routledge* .. 3
— Ballads from the.......... *W. Blackw'd* 15
— Caligraphist .... *Trubner* 27
— Carlyle's Trans. from ...... *Chapman* .. 13
— Class Books.............. *Bell* 35
— Class-Book, Schlutter ...... *Williams* .. 12
— Commercial Letter Writer .. *Trubner* 1
— Conversation, Busch........ *Trubner* 6
— Conversation .... *Trubner* 1
— Conversation .... *Whittaker* .. 7
— Cookery for Eng. Kitchens.. *Chapman* .. 19
— Crabb .... *Nutt* 13
— Dict., Black's Theime's .... *Williams* .. 3
— Ed. Course, Apel .... *Williams* .. 2
— Ed. Course, Ravensberg.... *Williams* .. 1
— Grammar................ *Nutt* 19
— New Guide .... *Macmillan* .. 1
— Wolfram .... *Trubner* 10
— Conversational Grammar.... *Asher* 3
— Conversation, Travelling.... *Nutt* 12
— Declension, Theory of ...... *Asher* 4
— Dialogues................ *Hachette* .. 5
German Dictionaries .... *Routledge* .. 13
— Dictionary .... *Cassell* 14
— Blackley .... *Longmans* .. 14
— Cauvin.................. *W. Blackw'd* 42
— Elwell .... *Nutt* 13
— Dictionary, Flugel .... *Whittaker* .. 7
— Hilpert.................. *Nutt* 16
— Koehler .... *Asher* 4
— James' Schneider's .... *Nutt* 16
— Lucas .... *Nutt* 17
— Pocket Dictionary, Feller .. *Nutt* 13
— Thiemes, Black............ *Nutt* 19
— Triglot .... *Lockwood* .. 30
German and Dutch Schools.... *Murray* 9
— Echo .... *Trubner* 10
— Ed. Course, Maier .... *Collins* 12
— Educational Works .... *Whittaker* .. 6
— Elementary Books.......... *Lockwood* .. 38
— Empire (New) Bryce ...... *Macmillan* .. 4
— for the English .... *Nutt* 20
— Equivalts. for Eng. Thoughts *Nutt* 12
— in Fifty Lessons, Bran...... *Harrison* 14
— Grammar, Ahn .... *Trubner* 1
— Grammar, Becker .... *Williams* .. 2
— Demmler .... *Nutt* 13
— Eulenstein .... *Nutt* 13
— and Key, Andlaw........ *Stanford* 49
— Tiark.................... *Nutt* 21
— Whitney .... *Macmillan* .. 41
— Grammar and Exer., Weisse *Williams* .. 15
— Gram. Philosophically Devel. *Williams* .. 7
— Higher Schools and Univ.... *Macmillan* .. 9
— Guide for Begin., Schmidt .. *Williams* .. 12
— Language, Friedrich ...... *Trubner* 12
— Frambling .... *Trubner* 12
— and Literature .... *Clar. Press.* 30
— Literature, Outlines of...... *Williams* .. 7
— Lessons .... *Cassell* 14
— Life and Manners........ *Allen* 8
— Life, Gordon .... *Murray* 12
— Literature .... *Nutt* 12
— Literature, Solling .... *Trubner* 9
— Method, Duicken's Ollendorff *Williams* .. 10
— Mountains, On the .... *Chapman* .. 23
— Poetry, with Translation.... *Williams* .. 7
— Poetry .... *W. Blackw'd.* 12
— Thesaurus of .... *Nutt* 15

German Plays Buchheim .... *Williams* .. 3
—— Popular Stories .... *Chatto* .. 17
—— Prose Writers .... *Murray* .. 1
—— Protestantism .... *Clark* .. 17
—— Prose Specimens .... *Trubner* .. 2
—— Series .... *Chambers* .. 18
—— Songs .... *Ward&Lock* 24
—— Stories, with Notes .... *Asher* .. 2
—— Studies .... *Asher* .. 5
—— Studies, Plate............. *Nutt* .. 19
—— Tales for Beginners .... *Nutt* .. 21
—— for English Students ...... *Nutt* .. 12
—— Test. and Common Prayer. *Bagster* .. 16
German-English Conversation .. *Williams* .. 16
—— English Dictionary, Flugel *Nutt* .. 13
Germany, Art Treasures .... *Hagger* .. 16
—— Christian Singers of .... *Macmillan* .. 35
—— and France .... *Hagger* .. 10
—— School and Army in .... *Trubner* .. 13
—— History to Close Mid. Ages. *Clar. Press* .. 26
—— History of, Menzel ...... *Bohn's Lib.* .. 8
—— from Reformation .... *Clar. Press* .. 27
—— Minnesinger of .... *Trubner* .. 17
—— Poetry of, Baskerville ... *Nutt* .. 11
—— Religious Life in .... *Isbister* .. 6
—— Thought in .... *Tinsley Bros.* 8
—— Spas of .... *Churchill* .. 39
Gesta Romanorum .... *Chatto* .. 17
—— Romanorum .... *Sotheran* .. 11
Gethsemane, Molyneaux ...... *Nisbet* .. 2
Ghost Seer .... *J. Blackwood* 23
Giant Conquered .... *S. S. Union.* 9
—— Killer .... *Nelson* .. 9
Giants and How to Fight Them.. *Partridge* .. 10
Gib, Stories from .... *Tinsley Bros.* 7
Gibbon's Life and Correspondence *Warne* .. 23
—— Roman Empire .... *Murray* .. 12
—— by Smith .... *Virtue* .. 19
Gibraltar, Siege of .... *Murray* .. 10
Gideon, Life of .... *Edmonston* .. 4
Gideon's Rock .... *King* .. 33
Gift Books, Elegant .... *Nimmo* .. 10
—— Illustrated .... *Nimmo* .. 13
—— Illustrated .... *Routledge* .. 27
—— Religious .... *Nimmo* .. 25
Gift for the Young............ *Rel. Tr. Soc.* 32
Gifts for Men .... *Edmonston* .. 10
Gilbert (Wm.) Works by ...... *Isbister* .. 16
Gil Blas............. *Routledge* .. 72
—— Adventures of .... *Bohn's Lib.* .. 13
Giles's Keys to the Classics ...... *Cornish* .. 1
Gillespie (W. H.) Works by .... *Houlston* .. 35
Gillray (James) Works ...... *Chatto* .. 2
Ginx's Baby............. *King* .. 32
Gipsies (Eng.) in Norway ...... *King* .. 4
—— of Spain .... *Murray* .. 5
Gipsy Language (English) .... *Murray* .. 3
Girlhood and Womanhood .... *Isbister* .. 44
Girl's Birthday Book .... *Routledge* .. 33
—— (Every) Book......... *Routledge* .. 19
—— Life, Thoughts from a .... *Macmillan* .. 11
Girls' Books............. *Cassell* .. 11
Girls, Education of .... *Trubner* .. 16
—— Papers for Thoughtful .. *Isbister* .. 44
Gish the Outlaw .... *Edmonston* .. 6
Glacial Epoch of Geology .... *Chapman* .. 7
Glaciers, Forms of Water in .. *King* .. 8
—— Theory of, Forbes .... *Black* .. 12
Gladness in Jesus .... *Morgan* .. 3
Gladstone (W. E.) On Ecce Homo *Isbister* .. 17
—— Juventus Mundi......... *Macmillan* .. 13
—— Speeches .... *Chatto* .. 17
Glass Painting .... *Parker* .. 50
Glastonbury Abbey, Willis .. *Bell* .. 13
Glaucus, Kingsley......... *Macmillan* .. 19
Glazier's Booke......... *Pickering* .. 35
Gleams from the Lamp of Life .. *Morgan* .. 3
Gleanings from Nature......... *Hatchard* .. 32
Greig (G. R.) Works by ...... *Murray* .. 13
Glendower (Owen), a Biography. *Williams* .. 16
Gleo Luna .... *Nisbet* .. 24
Glenmahra, Roberts ...... *Chapman* .. 26
Glenny (Geo.) Works on Gardening *Houlston* .. 11
Glimpses of our Heavenly Home Snow. .. 7
Globe Editions .... *Macmillan* .. 13

Globes and Quadrants .... *C. Smith* 11
—— in Various Mountings ...... *Johnston* .. 38
—— and Maps .... *Betts* .... a
Glory of Christ, Minton ...... *Kellaway* .. 5
—— of God in Man .... *Macmillan* .. 12
Glossary, Nare's .... *R. Smith* .. 15
—— (Select) of Eng. Words .. *Macmillan* .. 37
Gloucestershire, Coal Fields of . *Stanford* .. 49
Glover (R.) Works by .... *Hatchard* .. 9
Gnostics and their Remains.... *Bell* .. 13
Goblin Market .... *Macmillan* .. 31
God, Book of .... *Trubner* .. 5
—— in Disease, Duncan ...... *Nisbet* .. 12
—— Fatherhood of......... *Black* .. 9
—— and Man .... *Chapman* .. 27
—— Misunderstood .... *Kellaway* .. 7
—— Soul, and a Future State .. *Hodder* .. a
Godhead, Being and Attributes of *Hardwick* .. 8
Golley (J. R.) Writings, Selectns. *Stanford* .. 55
God's Glory in the Heavens .. *Isbister* .. 25
—— Jewels, Balfour .... *Nisbet* .. 3
—— Message in Low London .. *Nisbet* .. 14
—— Trial by Fire .... *Houlston* .. 37
—— Way of Peace and Holiness *Nisbet* .. a
Gods of the North .... *Sotheran* .. 26
Godwin (J. H.) Works by ...... *Hodder* .. a
Goethe and Mendelssohn......... *Macmillan* .. 13
—— Poems .... *W. Blackw'd* 10
—— Works by, in German .. *Nutt* .. 14
—— Egmont, German ...... *Clar. Press* .. 31
—— Faust, Eng. .... *W. Blackw'd* 20
—— Gallery .... *Bruckmann* .. a
—— Taylor .... *Isbister* .. 43
—— Trans. by Paul ...... *King* .. 22
—— Works by, in German .. *Williams* .. 7
Goethe's Heroines .... *Cassell* .. a
—— Life, by Lewis ...... *Smith & El.* 13
—— Works, Trans. ...... *Bohn's Lib.* .. 8
Gold Digger's Story .... *Burns* .. 26
—— Else .... *Isbister* .. 30
—— Fields, Advts. in Search of.. *Cassell* .. 5
—— and the Gospel ...... *Nisbet* .. 15
—— Serious Fall in the Value of *Stanford* .. 57
—— Thread (The) .... *Isbister* .. 27
—— Tried in the Fire ...... *Nisbet* .. 34
—— Values, Watherston .... *Smith & El.* 26
Golden Days .... *Cassell* .. 11
—— Deeds .... *Macmillan* .. 14
—— Dream, Tale of the Diggings *Nisbet* .. 4
—— Crown Series .... *Cassell* .. 4
—— Fleece .... *Nelson* .. 9
—— Fountain .... *Nelson* .. 13
—— Gift .... *Nimmo* .. 11
—— Histories .... *Smith & El.* a
—— Ladder Series .... *Nisbet* .. 39
—— Link Series .... *Warne* .. 27
—— Links .... *Warne* .. 27
—— Lives .... *Isbister* .. 33
—— Mill .... *S. S. Union* 6
—— Picture Book .... *M. Ward* .. 13
—— Sheaf (The) Poems ...... *Houlston* .. 15
—— Sunset (A) .... *Nisbet* .. 23
—— Thoughts .... *Warne* .. a
—— Treasury Series .... *Macmillan* .. 13
—— of Thought .... *Chatto* .. 17
—— for the Young......... *Nisbet* .. 25
—— Words .... *Ward&Lock* 26
—— Year (A) and its Lessons ... *Partridge* .. a
Goldsmith's England, by Walker *Walker* 4
—— Histories .... *Allman* .. 5
—— Pinnock .... *Whittaker* .. 10
Goldsmiths and Jewellers ...... *Chatto* .. 30
Gold-smith (O.) Complete Works *J. Blackwood* .3
Goldsmith's Complete Works ... *Routledge* .. 43
—— Life, Forster .... *Chapman* .. 2
—— Histories, by Coxe ...... *Moxley* .. 16
—— Miscellaneous Works...... *Nimmo* .. 6
—— Works .... *Ward&Lock* 25
—— Works, Cunningham ...... *Murray* .. 31
Gone Before............. *Lockwood* .. 42
Gongora, Churton .... *Murray* .. 7
Good Aim Series............. *Ward&Lock* 9
—— Devices, Book of ...... *Cassell* .. 4
—— Friday .... *Parker* .. 36
—— Little Hearts .... *Lawrence* .. 9

D

Good News of God, Kingsley .. *Macmillan* .. 18
—— Night and Good Morning .. *Ward & Lock* 26
—— Steward (The) .... *S. S. Union* 45
—— Things .... *Strahan* 4
—— Tidings of Great Joy ...... *Nisbet* 15
—— Voices (The) .... *Macmillan* .. 1
—— Words, Essays from .... *Isbister* ... 38
Good-bye Sweetheart .... *Bentley* 16
Goode (Dean) Works by .... *Hatchard* .. 9
Goodeve, School Text Books by .. *Longmans* .. 21
Goodsir, Anatomical Memoirs .. *Black* 12
—— (J. T.) Works by .... *Williams* ... 7
Goodwin (Bishop) Mathl. Works *Bell* 21
—— (Bishop) Sermons by ...... *Bell* 52
—— Works by .... *Bell* 51
—— (John) Life of .... *Wesleyan* .. 44
Goodwin Sands, Floating Light.. *Nisbet* 4
—— Life Boat Work........... *Macmillan* .. 13
Goodwyn (Gen.) Rel. Works by.. *Kelloway* .. 6
Gooroo Simple, Adventures of ... *Trubner* 13
Gordian Knot .... *Bradbury* .. 4
Gordon (Duchess of) Life, &c. .. *Nisbet* 15
—— (M. M.) Works by .... *Edmonston* .. 10
Gorle's (J.) Analysis of Hooker *Hall* 1
Gospel (The) and its Fruits...... *Nisbet* 38
—— (Fourth) Character of ..... *Williams* ... 15
—— (Fourth) Authorship of .... *Macmillan* .. 31
—— History, Critical Investigatn. *Clark* 10
—— of the Kingdom of Heaven *Macmillan* .. 34
—— and Modern Life .... *Macmillan* .. 9
—— Narratives, if Mythical .... *Edmonston* .. 12
—— of the Pentateuch, Kingsley *Macmillan* .. 18
—— of the Resurrection .... *Macmillan* .. 40
—— Seeds, Malan .... *Nisbet* 25
—— of St Matthew, Quesnel.... *Rivingtons* .. 3
—— and Mark Explained .... *Nisbet* 3
—— Story, Conversation on the.. *Nisbet* 13
—— Studies................. *Collins* 3
Gospels, Anglo-Saxon .... *Cambridge* .. 6
—— Apocryphal, Cowper....... *Williams* ... 5
—— Characteristic Differences of *Nisbet* 19
—— Choice Notes on .... *Macmillan* .. 7
—— Consolidated (The) .... *Bagster* 74
—— Discussions on .... *Macmillan* .. 30
—— and Epistles, Commenty. on *Bell* 47
—— (Four) .... *Parker* 10
—— (The Four) in Greek, Adams *Nutt* 3
—— (Four) and One Christ .... *S. S. Union* 42
—— Greek Text, Notes .... *Hall* 4
—— Harmony of.............. *Hatchard* .. 13
—— Leading Idea of........... *Macmillan* .. 2
—— Norris's Key to........... *Rivingtons* .. 2
—— Pantheistic Prin. Applied to *Bell* 60
—— Readings on the .... *Hatchard* .. 15
—— Studies in the .... *Macmillan* .. 38
—— Words from.............. *Macmillan* .. 39
Gosse (Emily) Recollections of .. *Morgan* 4
—— (P. H.) Works by......... *Nisbet* 15
Gothic Ornament .... *Parker* 54
—— Mouldings, Paley .... *Van Voorst* .. 6
Gotthold's Emblems .... *Clark* 19
Goulburn (Dean) Works by..... *Rivingtons* .. 0
Gould (Baring) Works by ...... *Macmillan* .. 2
—— Works by .... *Masters* 2
—— Works by .... *Rivingtons* .. 0
Gout, Barclay on .... *Churchill* .. 7
—— (Rheumatic) .... *Churchill* .. 6
—— and Rheumatism, Hood .... *Churchill* .. 21
Government (English) .... *Longmans* .. 3
—— Ewald .... *W. Blackw'd.* 9
—— (Parliamentary)........... *Longmans* .. 2
—— of the National Defence.... *King* 3
—— Premiers (English) .... *Chapman* .. 17
—— (Representative) .... *Longmans* .. 10
—— Situations, Handbook to.... *Stanford* .. 55
—— Sphere and Duties of ...... *Trubner* 16
—— (State) Abolition of .... *Trubner* ... 12
—— Thoughts upon .... *Bell* 42
Grace All-sufficient .... *Nisbet* 15
—— Martin, Neame .... *Morgan* 3
—— of the Ministry .... *Bell* 49
Gradus ad Parnassum .... *Whittaker* .. 5
Graffiti D'Italia .... *W. Blackw'd* 30
Grahams (The).............. *Warne* 26
Graham's (Sir James) Life ...... *Routledge* .. 5

Grammar of Assent, Newman .. *Burns* 15
—— Comparative .... *Macmillan* .. 15
—— Comparative, Bopp ...... *Williams* ... 3
—— made Easy .... *Nicholson* .. 10
—— Murray's .... *Mozley* 16
—— Composition, &c. .... *Chambers* .. 7
—— English .... *Whittaker* .. 11
—— for Classical Schools ...... *Clar. Press*.. 28
—— English Elementary ...... *J. Heywood* 23
—— Horn's English .... *J. Heywood* 24
—— Introductory .... *Murby* 3
—— Methodical, Analytical, &c. *Murray* 21
—— Principles of .... *Clar. Press*.. 28
Grammar-School Classics....... *Bell* 4
—— School Classics .... *Whittaker* .. 3
Grammatical Analysis .... *Collins* 12
Grammatography .... *Trubner* 13
Granny's Chapters on Scripture. *Rush* 6
Grant (Eld. Miles) Works by ... *Kelloway* .. 5
—— (Horace) Instrucfor the Young *Bell* 40
—— (James) Juvenile Books by.. *Routledge* .. 33
—— (Sir W.) Memoirs .... *W. Blackw'd* 10
Grant's (Bishop) Life .... *Smith & El.* 17
Grantley Manor .... *Burns* 26
Granville (Dr. A. B.) Autobio. by *King* 4
Grape Vine .... *W. Blackw'd* 54
Grapes of Eschcol (The) .... *Nisbet* 24
Grasses (British) Lowe .... *Bell* 17
—— (British) .... *Reeve*...2 & 4
Gratitude, Stevenson .... *Bagster* 71
Gratry (Père) Last Days of..... *Rivingtons* .. 26
Grave Crosses, &c. .... *Hagger* 13
Gravestones, Remarks on....... *Masters* 3
Gray (Asa) Botanical Works .... *Trubner* 13
—— Beattie, Blair, &c., Works.. *J. Blackwood* 3
—— (J. E.) Works .... *Pickering* .. 17
—— (Mrs. H.) Works by...... *Hatchard* .. 10
Grazier's (Complete) Assistant .. *Lockwood* .. 16
Great Britain, Administration of.. *Smith & El.* 2
—— Coast Scenery of .... *Virtue*..... 12
—— Little Book about .... *Bradbury* .. 11
Great (The) Country........... *Tinsley Bros.* 7
—— Duel (The) .... *Trubner* 14
—— Facts, by F. C. Bakewell .. *Houlston* .. 7
—— Lives for Young Readers.... *Nelson* 13
—— Missionaries .... *Nelson* 10
—— Painters, Homely Scenes from *Cassell* 4
—— Pilot and His Lessons ..... *Partridge* .. 8
—— Sahara, Tristram .... *Murray* 32
—— Unwashed .... *Tinsley Bros.* 9
Greater Britain .... *Macmillan* .. 9
Grecian and Roman History .... *Rivingtons* .. 26
—— Stories, Hack .... *Isbister* 19
Greco-Russian Church, Romanoff *Rivingtons* .. 25
Greece (Ancient) Description .... *Clar. Press*.. 17
—— Ancient History.......... *Chambers* .. 13
—— Finlay .... *W. Blackw'd* 9
—— Geography of, Tozer....... *Murray* 31
—— Handbook to .... *Murray* 16
—— History, Arnold .... *Rel. Tr. Soc.* 3
—— History of, Goldsmith, by Coxe *Mozley*.. 13
—— Cox .... *Longmans* .. 4
—— History of, Curtius .... *Bentley* 6
—— Freeman .... *Clar. Press*.. 26
—— Knightley .... *Whittaker* .. 10
—— in Greek .... *Macmillan* .. 42
—— National Education in..... *Isbister* 47
—— Pictorial, &c. .... *Murray* 32
—— Tales of Ancient .... *Longmans* .. 39
Greek Accentuation .... *Clar. Prest.* 19
—— Accidence, Jessopp .... *Williams* ... 8
—— Antiquities, Rich .... *Longmans* .. 12
—— Anthology .... *Macmillan* .. 12
—— (Choice) Poetry .... *Bell* 12
—— Church, Neale .... *Masters* 18
—— Stanley .... *Murray* 28
—— Classics, Literal Trans. .... *Hall* 4
—— Class-Books............ *Bell* 10
—— Coins, Fox .... *Bell* 12
—— Concordance to New Test... *Bagster* 37
—— Educational Works (Smith).. *Murray* 29
—— Educational Works .... *Parker* 59
—— Educational Works .... *Whittaker* .. 5
—— English Vocabulary .... *Clar. Press* 2. 28
—— (Modern) and Eng. Dict... *Williams* .. 4

Greek Exercises in Attic	Black	10
—— Exercises, Robson	Stanford	68
—— Grammar, Buttman	Whittaker	5
—— Curtius	Murray	9
—— Elementary, Greenwood	Macmillan	14
—— Schmitz	Black	16
—— Matthiæ	Murray	22
—— Thiersch	W. Blackw'd	47
—— Wordsworth	Clar. Press	2
—— History, from Plutarch	Longmans	4
—— Introduction to Study	Murray	17
—— Language	Rivingtons	21
—— and Latin Classics, Teubners	Nutt	17
—— and Latin Etymology	Macmillan	28
—— and Latin Quotations	Shaw	7
—— Lexicon	Lockwood	37
—— Lexicon, English-Greek	Rivingtons	22
—— Lexicon, Liddell and Scott..	Longmans	14
—— Lexicon to New Testament	Kellaway	1
—— Lexicon to New Test.	Bagster	37
—— Lexicon, Yonge	Longmans	13
—— (Modern) Language	Clar. Press	31
—— (Modern) Lexicon	Trubner	8
—— Ollendorff, Method	Trubner	17
—— Plays, Scenes from	Rivingtons	23
—— Poets, Studies of	Smith & El.	22
—— Poetry, Golden Treas.	Clar. Press	19
—— Primer	Clar. Press	2
—— Prose, Golden Treas.	Clar. Press	19
—— and Roman Antiquities	Murray	28
—— and Roman Geography	Murray	28
—— Sceptics, Maccoll	Macmillan	21
—— Septuagint	Soc. P. C. K.	11
—— Synonymes, Pillon	Rivingtons	21
—— Syntax, Madvig	Rivingtons	21
—— Test. and Common Prayer	Bagster	13
—— Test. for Schools, Alford	Rivingtons	2
—— Verb made Easy, for Schools	Nutt	10
—— Verbs, Irregular	Murray	6
—— Verbs, Storr	Rivingtons	21
—— Verbs, Veitch	Clar. Press	19
—— Words in Homer and Hesiod	Murray	6
—— Heroes, Niebuhr	Williams	19
Green (Geo.) Mathematical Papers	Macmillan	14
—— (J. H.) Spiritual Phil.	Macmillan	14
—— Lanes, Half Hours in	Hardwicke	9
Greenwell (Dora) Carmina Crucis	Bell	36
—— Works by	Isbister	17
Greg (W. Rathbone) Works by	Trubner	13
Gregory the Seventh, Life of	Bentley	6
Grenadier Guards, History of	Murray	14
Gresham (Sir Thos.) Life	Wilson	4
Gresley (Rev. W.) Works by	Masters	11
Greswell's Harmonia	Clar. Press	13
Grey (Earl) Works by	Murray	13
Greyhound (The) Stonehenge	Longmans	42
Griffith (T.) Religious Works by..	Hatchard	10
Grimaldi's Life	Routledge	5
Grimboth (Baron) Experiences	Tinsley Bros.	8
Grimm's German Stories	Chatto	17
—— Tales and Stories	Warne	20
Gronow's Recollections	Smith & El.	9
Grosvenor, Simple Thoughts	Hatchard	2
Grote (J.) Works by	Bell	41
Grote's Examination of Mill	Trubner	14
—— Works	Murray	13
Grotius (Trans. by Clark)	Hall	3
—— Whewell	Cambridge	7
Ground and Object of Hope	Macmillan	25
Groves (A. N.) Memoir	Nisbet	4
Growth of Trade	Virtue	22
Guesses at Truth	Macmillan	14
Guide to Heaven	Rivingtons	6
—— (Penny) Books	A. Heywood	
—— (Tourist's) Books	A. Heywood	
—— to the Unprotected	Macmillan	15
Guiding Hand (The)	Kellaway	9
Guilman of Inglismill	Edmonston	12
Guilds, on the History of	Trubner	6
Gurlemin's (A.) Works	Bentley	8
Guillotine, History, Essay on	Murray	7
Guizot, Works by, Trans.	Bohn's Lib.	5
—— Works by, in French	Nutt	55
Gulliver's Travels	Cassell	4
Gulliver's Travels	Black	13
Gunnery, Principles of	Allen	18
—— and Projectiles	Spon	22
—— Theory and Practice	Murray	10
—— Manual of, H.M.S.Fleet..	Harrison	5
Gunpowder	Allen	19
—— Manufacturing	Sotheran	4
—— Handbook of Manufacture	Harrison	11
Guns and Steel	Longmans	32
Gun-Shot Wounds	Churchill	25
Gustavus Adolphus in Germany	Macmillan	37
Guthrie (Dr.) Memoir and Works	Isbister	18
—— (Rev. T.) Life of	Marr	15
—— (Rev. T.) Anecdotes, &c	Houlston	22
Guy's Hospital Int. Lect. 1873-74	King	32
—— (John) School Books	Allman	9
Guy Livingstone	Tinsley Bros.	10
—— Works by Author of	Routledge	68
Guzratee Language	Allen	34
Gwynn and Otway	J. R. Smith	10
Gymnastic Exercises	Harrison	9
Gymnastics	J. Heywood	19
—— and Athletics	Trubner	25
—— Military	Allen	19
Gypsies (English) Dialect of	Asher	8
Gypsy, Series (The)	Isbister	19
Haberdashery, Perkins	Tegg	0
Habits of Good Society	Virtue	14
Habit and Intelligence	Macmillan	26
Hacket (Bishop) Life of	Masters	11
Haddon Hall, Evenings at	Bohn's Lib.	13
—— History, &c.	Bemrose	10
Hades ; the Intermediate State	Kellaway	4
Hagenbach (Prof.) Works by	Clark	14
Half Hours Best Authors	Warne	31
—— with Early Explorers	Cassell	11
—— Pictorial, Knight	Houlston	23
Hall (Newman) Works by	Nisbet	16
—— Works by	Snow	7
—— (Rev. Rob.) Mis. Works..	Bohn's Lib.	8
—— (Robert) Works	Routledge	65
—— (S. C.) Book of the Thames	Isbister	19
—— Ireland : Its Scenery	Virtue	20
—— (Mrs. S. C.) Tales	Nelson	16
—— (T. D.) Educat. Works by	Murray	13
Hall's (Bp.) Works	Clar. Press	13
—— Contemplations	Soc. P. C. K.	11
Hallam's Histories	Murray	14
Hallelujah (The) Waite	Haddon	2
Halliwell (J. O.) Works	J. R. Smith	10
Hamel's French Grammar	Whittaker	7
Hamerton (P. G.) Works by	Macmillan	15
Hamilton (Rev. James) Works of	Nisbet	16
—— (Sir W.) Works	W. Blackw'd	11
—— of Baugour, Poems	Stevenson	0
Hamley (E. B.) Works	W. Blackw'd	12
Hammond (Capt.) Memoir	Nisbet	17
Hampden, Memorials of	Bohn's Lib.	19
Hanbury Mills	Warne	19
Handbooks for Travellers	Murray	15
Hand of God in History	J. Blackwood	19
—— in History	Collins	3
Handley Cross	Bradbury	2
Handmaid of the Lord	Morgan	5
Handrailing	Hagger	14
—— New Elements of	Trubner	25
Handy Volume Library	Bradbury	5
Hankinson (T. E.) Poems	Hatchard	11
Hanky Panky	Chatto	18
Hanna 's (Rev. Wm.) Works	Edmonston	11
Hannibal's Alps, Law	Macmillan	20
Hannibal, A Historical Drama..	Macmillan	27
Hanoverian and Italian War	Stanford	71
Hansard's Parliamentary Debates	Sotheran	14
Happiness of the Blessed	Rivingtons	12
Happy Evenings	Houlston	29
—— Home (The)	Nisbet	17
—— Spring Time	Macmillan	15
—— Thought Hall	Bradbury	2
Harbord (Rev. J. R.) Works by..	W. Blackw'd	13
Harbours, Design and Construc.	Black	31
—— Design and Construction	Lockwood	3
Harding's Sketches	Chapman	4
Hardwick (Archdeacon) Works by	Macmillan	13
Hare (Aug. J. C.) Works by	Isbister	19

Harem, Thirty Years in the...... *Chapman* ... 19
Harmonies of Nature, Hartwig . *Longmans* .. 23
Harmony .... *Craven* ...... a
—— Treatise on .... *Clar. Press*. 30
—— Treatise on, Day .... *Harrison* ... 16
Harris (J.) Sermons by .... *Nisbet* 17
—— (S. S.) Novels .... *Warne* 44
Harrogate Mineral Springs .... *Churchill* .. 23
Harrow Schoolboy, Memorials of *Nisbet* 27
—— School Days at .... *Routledge* .. 37
—— Sundays, Vaughan ...... *Macmillan*.. 38
Harry Lawley .... *S. S. Union*. 6
—— Lorrequer .... *Chapman* .. 20
Harry's Catechism........... *Nelson* 12
—— Ladder to Learning .... *Ward&Lock* 30
Hart (The) and the Water Brook. *Nisbet* 24
Harte (Bret) Works .... *Chatto* 6
—— Works .... *Routledge* .. 3
Hartwig (Dr. G.) Works by .... *Longmans* .. 0
Harvest of the Sea............ *Murray* 4
Haste to the Rescue .... *Nisbet* 37
Hastings (H. L.) Works by .... *Kellaway* .. 9
—— (Warren) Speeches ...... *Sotheran*... 13
Hatchard (Bp.) Works by ...... *Hatchard* .. 11
Hatherley's Cont. of Scripture .. *Murray* ... 14
Hat Making, Practical......... *Spon*...... 23
Haughton's School Books ...... *Philip* 40
Haunted Crest (The). .... *Isbister* 38
Haupt (H.) Works by .... *Trubner* ... 15
Haussen's Period of the Reforma. *Isbister* ... 20
Havelock (Sir H.) Biog. Sketch . *Nisbet* 17
—— Life .... *Longmans* .. 9
Havergal (F. R.) Works by .... *Nisbet* 17
Hawaiian Dictionary.......... *Trubner* ... 2
Haweis (Rev. H. R.) Works by.. *Isbister* 20
—— Works .... *King* 29
Hawker's Poor Man's Portion .. *Routledge* .. 64
Hawthorne (Nathaniel) .... *King* 2
—— Works of .... *Smith & El.* 9
—— Passages fm. Eng. Note Bks. *Isbister* 20
—— Tales .... *Bohn's Lib.*. 9
Hay Asthma and Hay Fever.... *Churchill* .. 29
—— (Bishop) Works. .... *W. Blackw'd*. 38
—— (D. R.) Works .... *W. Blackw'd*. 13
—— Measurer............... *Blackie*.... 11
Haydn's Dictionary of Dates.... *Ward&Lock* 32
Haydn Series of Manuals ...... *Ward&Lock* 32
Hayman (Dr. H.) Exercises .... *Nutt*...... 9
Hayslop Grange............. *S. S. Union*. 8
Hayward (A.) Essays .... *Longmans* .. 8
Hazlitt (W.) Works by .... *Bohn's Lib.*. 8
—— (W. C.) Various Works .. *Reeves & T.* a
Head (Sir E.) Ballads .... *Smith & El.* 9
—— (Sir Francis) Works by .... *Murray* 14
Heads & Hands in World of Labor *Isbister* ... 7
Headache (Nervous) Latham.... *Bell* 18
—— (Sick) .... *Churchill* .. 24
Headaches, their Cause and Cure *Churchill* .. 39
Healing Waters of Israel........ *Nisbet* 23
Health, Books on .... *Routledge* .. 10
—— and Disease .... *King*...... 7
—— and Education .... *Isbister* 23
—— First Lessons on .... *Macmillan*.. 3
—— for Households and Schools. *Isbister* ... 40
—— Industry and Handicraft .. *Bradbury* .. 11
—— Maintenance of.......... *Churchill* .. 25
—— Management of .... *Lockwood* .. 28
—— Plain Words on.......... *Churchill* ..
—— School Manual of .... *Hardwicke*.. 15
—— Thoughts on .... *Smith & El.* 10
Heart Culture............... *Hodder* 22
—— Diseases of, Fuller ...... *Churchill* .. 16
—— Markham............... *Churchill* .. 26
—— Sawyer................. *Hardwicke*.. 16
—— Disease among Soldiers .. *Churchill* .. 16
—— Walsh .... *Smith & El.* 26
—— Bright's Diseases of ..... *Churchill* .. 10
—— and Mind (The). .... *Nisbet* 29
—— Whispers .... *Yapp* 2
Heat, Applications of .... *Longmans* .. 21
—— a Mode of Motion........ *Longmans* .. 72
—— Practical Treatise on .... *Spon*...... 22
—— Science of, Orme .... *Groombridge.* 22
—— Theory of, Maxwell...... *Longmans* .. 21
—— Treatise on .... *Clar. Press.*. 27

Heaven, Aspects of .... *Shaw* 1
—— of the Bible .... *Collins* 3
—— our Home Series .... *Nimmo* 24
Heavens (The) .... *Bentley* 7
Heavenly Jerusalem.......... *Nelson* 21
—— Life .... *Nisbet* 3
—— Peace .... *Nisbet* 5
—— Thoughts.............. *Nisbet* 22
Heber (Bishop) Works of...... *Murray* 14
Hebraist's Vade Mecum (The) . *Bagster* ... 34
Hebrew Accentation, Davidson.. *Williams* ... 5
—— and Chaldee Concordance. *Bagster* ... 34
—— and Chaldee Lexicon, Fuerst *Williams* ... 6
—— Dictionary............. *Lockwood* .. 30
—— Educational Works ...... *Parker*..... 50
—— Grammar,.............. *W. Blackw'd* 36
—— Gesenius .... *Asher* 4
—— Introductory, Davidson .. *Clark* 35
—— Leathes .... *Murray* 30
—— Grammars and Lexicons... *Bagster* ... 98
—— Grammar, Stewart ...... *W. Blackw'd* 47
—— Language .... *Mask* 9
—— Language .... *Rivingtons* .. 18
—— Lexicon, Gesenius ...... *Asher* 7
—— Monarchy, Newman ..... *Trubner* ... 21
—— Prophets, Williams ...... *Williams* ... 15
—— Roots .... *Clar. Press.*. 4
—— Scripture, Essays on ..... *Nisbet* 42
—— Student's Manual .... *Bagster* ... 27
—— Without a Master....... *Cornish* ... 2
Hebrides, Miller's Cruise ..... *Nimmo* 4
Hedaya, by Hamilton .... *Allen* 0
Hegel, The Secret of......... *Longmans* .. 26
—— Logic .... *Clar. Press.*. 17
Heimann's German Elem. Works *Nutt* 15
Heine's Gedichte .... *Nutt* 16
—— Poems .... *Bohn's Lib.*. 8
Heir of Redclyffe. See Yonge .. *Moxley* 14
Helena's Household .... *Nelson* 8
Hellenica, Hist. of Greece in Greek *Macmillan*.. 8
Help Heavenward .... *Nisbet* 38
Helping Hand.............. *J. Blackwood* 42
Helps (Sir A.) Works by ...... *Bell* 42
—— Biographical Works ..... *Bell* 39
—— Works by .... *Smith & El.* 10
—— Some Talk about Animals . *Isbister* ... 14
Hemans (Mrs.) Poems .... *W. Blackw'd* 14
—— Poetical Works .... *Warne* 18
Henderson (James, M.D.) Mem. *Nisbet* 17
Hengstenberg (Prof.) Works by.. *Clark* 0
Henry Burton.............. *Warne* 29
—— Dunbar .... *Ward&Lock* 16
—— Earl of Morland .... *Macmillan*.. 4
—— (Matthew) Commentary.. *Virtue* ... 13
—— Commentary .... *Cassell* 5
—— (Prince) of Portugal..... *Asher* 5
Henrys (The) .... *Warne* 25
—— Histories, Paris Ed....... *Nutt* 24
Hepburn (Sir Jno.) Memoirs ... *W. Blackw'd* 10
Heraldic Dict. of Landed Gentry *Harrison* .. 1
Heraldry .... *J. R. Smith.* 8
—— Anecdotes of .... *Bell* 14
—— Boutell .... *Warne* 15
—— English, Boutell .... *Cassell* 3
—— Handbook .... *Chatto* 10
—— Introduction to .... *Bohn's Lib.*. 8
—— (Manual of)........... *Isbister* 30
—— Planché (J. R.) .... *Chatto* 70
Herbal (Family) Robinson .... *Nicholson* .. 8
—— and Family Physician .... *Nicholson* .. 4
Herbert's (G.) Poems and Provb. *Rivingtons*.. 7
—— (George) Works of ..... *Bell* 32
Herd's Scottish Songs .... *Sotheran.* 13
Hereditary Genius........... *Macmillan*.. 12
Heresy and Christian Doctrine.. *Hodder* 5
Her Majesty's Tower .... *Hurst* 16
Hermeneutics of New Testament. *Clark* 11
Hermits (The) Kingsley ...... *Macmillan*.. 34
Herodotus, Blakesley .... *Whittaker* .. 1
—— Edited by Woods ...... *Rivingtons*.. 12
—— English, Rawlinson ..... *Murray* 26
Heroic Age in England ...... *Isbister* 3
Hero of Elstow .... *Hodder* 7
—— Soldiers, Sailors, &c...... *Ward&Lock* 12
Heroes of Asgard, Keary ..... *Macmillan*.. 18

Heroes, Ancient and Modern .... *Chapman* .. 26
— (Boy's Book of) .... *Warne* 27
— (British) in Foreign Wars .. *Routledge* .. 5
— Greek Fairy Tales .... *Macmillan* .. 18
— of Hebrew History .... *Isbister* 47
— and Hero Worship, Carlyle .. *Chapman* .. 13
— of the Laboratory .... *Routledge* .. 5
Heroines of Domestic Life ...... *Routledge* .. 5
— of History .... *Routledge* .. 5
— of the Household .... *Isbister* 20
— in Obscurity .... *Isbister* 44
Heroism and Adventure .... *Warne* 24
Herring, its Nat. Hist. &c...... *Edmonston.* 16
Hertfordshire History .... *Chatto* 11
— Pedigrees and Arms of .... *J. R. Smith.* 6
Hervey's Meditations .... *Cornish* 3
Hesiod, Paley .... *Whittaker* .. 1
Hesperus, by Richter .... *Trubner* 25
Hester's Fortune .... *Warne* 27
Hester Kirton .... *Smith & El.* 14
He that Overcometh .... *Nisbet* 6
Hewitson (Rev. W. H.) Memoir *Nisbet* 3
Heygate (Rev. W. E.) Works by *Masters* .. 11
— Works .... *Rivingtons* ..0
Hiatus, the Void in Mod. Educa. *Macmillan.* 16
Hibberd's Works on Gardening.. *Groombridge.* 4
Hidden Life (The).............. *Masters* 12
Hierurgia Anglicana .... *Masters* 12
High Church .... *Kemrose* .. 5
High and Low .... *S. S. Union.* 7
Higher Christian Life .... *Nisbet* 6
— Law .... *Tinsley Bros.* 9
— Ministry of Nature .... *Hodder* 12
Highways and Hedges .... *Tubbs* 6
Hill (Rev. Rowley) Works by .. *Nisbet* 18
Himalaya Mountains, Botany of *Allen* 4
— Range, Calvert .... *Span* 36
— Districts .... *Allen* 9
Hindi and Braj Bhakha Grammar *Trubner* .. 3
Hind's (Bishop) Works .... *Fellowes* .. a
Hindoo (Memoir of a) Frere .. *Isbister* 32
— Tales .... *Isbister* 23
Hindoostanee-Eng. Dict., Tayler *Smith & El.* 22
— Interpreter .... *Smith & El.* 21
— Jest Book .... *Smith & El.* 21
Hindu Castes, Law and Customs. *Allen* 15
— Grammar for Students...... *Trubner* .. 12
— Law .... *Allen* 8
— Law .... *Allen* 9
— and Moham. Law .... *Williams* .. 9
— Pantheon, Moor............ *Williams* .. 10
— System of Medicine ...... *Trubner* .. 32
Hindus, Essays on the Architect. *Trubner* .. 24
— Religion of, Wilson ...... *Trubner* .. 32
— Religion & Philosophy of .. *Williams* .. 4
— Sacred City of .... *Trubner* .. 27
Hindustan (Emperor) Memoirs .. *Allen* 16
— Races and Tribes .... *Allen* 23
Hindustani Exercise Book ...... *Trubner* .. 10
— Grammar, Dawson .... *Trubner* .. 10
— Language .... *Allen* 30
— Made Easy .... *King* 15
Hinton (J.) Works of.......... *Smith & El.* 10
— (Rev. J.) Works by ...... *Houlston* .. 35
Hips and Haws, Acrostics ...... *Hatchard* .. 11
Historic Ninepins .... *Lockwood* .. 44
Historic (Pre-) Times, Lubbock . *Williams* .. 9
Historical Books.............. *Masters* 0
— Characters, Bulwer ...... *Bentley* 4
— Course for Schools ...... *Macmillan* .. 16
— Essays, Freeman .... *Macmillan* .. 12
— Finger Post .... *Lockwood* .. 49
— Gleanings, Rogers .... *Macmillan* .. 31
— Library, Juv. Englishman's *Masters* .. 13
— Manuals .... *Murray* 30
— Manuals, Davies .... *Philip* 38
— and Miscellaneous Questions *Chambers* .. 13
— Reason Why .... *Houlston* .. 6
— Results .... *Allen* 23
— Romances .... *Ward & Lock* 12
— Tales .... *Parker...* .. 42
— Tales .... *Routledge* .. 35
— Tales of British Children ... *Jarrold* 18
— Theology .... *Clarke* 15
— Works .... *Parker* 63

Historical Works .... *Eel. Tr. Soc.* 9
— Works, English .... *Clar. Press.* 9
Historicus, Letters by .... *Macmillan* .. 16
History Ancient, Manual of .. *Clar. Press.* 26
— Ancient & Modern, Bridges *Burns* 22
— and Art, Essays on ...... *W. Blackw'd.* 25
— for Boys .... *Routledge* .. 22
— Compendium of .... *Jarrold* 7
— Elementary .... *Chambers* .. 13
— Elementary .... *Jarrold* 27
— England, Elementary...... *J. Heywood* 33
— Epochs of.............. *Longmans* .. 7
— The Hand of God in...... *J. Blackwood* 17
— Hand of God in.......... *Collins* 3
— for Junior Classes ...... *Collins* 13
— Landmarks of............ *Mozley* 14
— Maunder .... *Longmans* .. 43
— Mediæval .... *Chambers* .. 13
— Modern .... *Allen* 6
— Modern, Yonge .... *Longmans* .. 5
— Outlines, A. and M. Tytler *Black* 32
— (Philosophy of) Schlegel .. *Bohn's Lib.* 9
History of Progress in Gt. Britain *Houlston...* 9
— Romance of.............. *Warne* 21
— Short Stories in.......... *Soc. P. C. K.* 5
— System of Modern, Reynolds *Black* 16
— Tales and Legends from.... *Burns* 35
— Theories of .... *Allen* 3
— and Travel .... *Nelson* 4
— Unity of .... *Macmillan* .. 12
— Universal .... *Bagster* 50
— Universal, Outlines of.... *Mozley* 16
— Universal, Weber .... *Whittaker* .. 11
Hoarseness and Loss of Voice .. *Churchill...* 25
Hodder (E.) On Holy Ground .. *Nimmo* 31
Hodge (Rev. C.) Works by.... *Nisbet* 18
Holgson (Rev. C.) Memorial Vol. *Nisbet* 18
Hoffmann's Juvenile Books .... *Nutt* 16
Hogarth's Works .... *Bell* 4
— Works .... *Chatto* 20
Hogg's (James) Works .... *Blackie* 14
Holbeach (H.) Student in Life,&c. *Isbister* 20
Holbein's Dance of Death .... *Bohn's Lib.* 13
— Life, Wornum............ *Chapman* .. 19
Holiday Adventures .... *Virtue* 14
— Album .... *Warne* 22
— Book, Young Student's .... *J. Blackwood* 19
— House .... *Ward & Lock* 28
— Letters .... *Isbister* 14
— Stories .... *Routledge* .. 30
Holidays on Highlands........ *Macmillan..* 21
— with Hobgoblins .... *Chatto* 18
Holiness through Faith........ *Morgan* 4
Holland, Church of .... *Parker...* .. 12
Holland House .... *Macmillan* .. 29
Holland (Sir H.) Recollections .. *Longmans* .. 7
Hollingshead's Mis. Works .... *Tinsley Bros.* 2
Holly Berries, Acrostics ...... *Hatchard* .. 11
Holmes (O. W.) Works........ *Chatto* 19
Holt (E. S.) Works by ...... *Shaw* 3
Holt (M. A.) Juvenile Books .... *Marlborough* 0
Holy Communion .... *Rivingtons* .. 5
— Communion .... *Wesleyan* .. 18
— Communion, Comment. on.. *Rivingtons* .. 5
— Communion, Goulburn .... *Rivingtons* .. 5
— Communion, Ridley ...... *Mozley* 21
— Communion, Plain Guide to *Rivingtons* .. 5
— Communion, Sewell ...... *Longmans* .. 32
— Eucharist, Cath. Doctrine of *Mozley* 13
— Footsteps .... *King* 20
— Ghost, Divinity of........ *Clar. Press.* 13
— Ghost, Person and Work of.. *Masters* 12
— Grail, Origin .... *Edmonston* 2
— Land, Home in the ...... *Nisbet* 12
— Sacrament, Malan........ *Nutt* 5
— Scriptures .... *Parker...* .. 8
— Spirit, Office and Work of .. *Clark* 19
— Spirit, Script. Testimony to *Clark* 20
— Virginity .... *Parker...* .. 7
Home and Abroad............ *Marr* 15
Home Affections, Mackay .... *Routledge* .. 28
— amid the Snow .... *Nelson* 15
— Book of Pleasure .... *Warne* 21
— Books of Christian Truth, &c. *Nelson* 12
— Books of Example, &c. .... *Nelson* 13

Home Circle Gift Books .... *Warne* 28
—— Circle, Tales for the .... *Nelson* 16
—— and Colonial Library ...... *Murray* 18
—— Exercises, Willie's .... *J. Heywood* 25
—— and Foreign Service ...... *Nisbet* 19
—— Influence .... *Groombridge* .. 3
—— Lesson Books.......... *J. Heywood* 26
—— Life, Essays on .... *Isbister* 34
—— Life, Relative Duties of .... *Black* 10
—— Missions, Sermons for ...... *Dickinson* .. 6
—— Pets .... *Ward & Lock* 5
—— Reading, Papers for...... *Nisbet* 15
—— Recreations, &c. .... *Warne* 27
—— Rule, Jenkins............ *Isbister* 5
—— Sunshine .... *Warne* 26
—— Sunshine Library .... *Warne* 25
—— Temper................ *Hodder* 26
—— Trials .... *Masters* ... 28
Homely Scenes, Great Painters.. *Cassell* 4
Homer, by Hayman .... *Nutt* 9
—— and the Iliad .... *Edmonston*.. 2
—— Paley .... *Whittaker* .. 2
—— Worsley .... *W. Blackw'd* 15
—— Lexicon .... *Rivingtons* .. 22
—— Iliad, First Six Books ...... *Stanford*.... 19
—— Iliad, Derby .... *Murray* 10
—— Iliad, Eng. Rhyme and Verse *Isbister* 31
—— Iliad, Trans., Cordery ...... *Rivingtons*.. 27
—— Translation by Norgate .... *Williams*.. 7
Homes of Other Days .... *Trübner* 32
—— without Hands .... *Longmans* .. 23
Homeward Bound, Sermons .... *Nisbet* 10
Homiletics, Kidder .... *Dickinson* .. 7
—— Vinet................ *Clark* 20
Homiletical & Pastoral Theology *Isbister* 7
Homilies .... *Clar. Press..* 13
Homilies .... *Soc. P. C. K.* 13
Homœopathy, Handy Book on .. *Houlston*.... 7
Honduras, Descriptive, &c.... *Trübner* 27
Hone's Every Day Book .... *Tegg* ..... a
—— Scrap Books .... *Chatto* 19
Hong-Kong Flora .... *Reeve* 5
Honora's Sunday Book.......... *Mozley*...... 4
Hood (Thomas) Works.......... *Ward & Lock* 31
—— (P.) Lamps of the Temple .. *Snow* 8
—— Works by .... *Hodder* 20
Hook's (Dean) Devotional Lib.. *Bell* 55
—— Archbishops .... *Bentley* 8
Hook (T.) Works .... *Chatto* 37
Hooker's Century of Ferns...... *Sotheran* .. 15
—— Flora Antarctica .... *Sotheran* .. 15
—— Polity .... *Clar. Press.* 31
—— Works .... *Clar. Press..* 14
Hooper's (Bp. G.) Works........ *Clar. Press.* 14
Hoosier Schoolmaster .... *Routledge* .. 2
Hope (A. R.) Works by .... *Nimmo* 27
—— Campbell .... *Warne*..... 26
—— (Mrs.) Works by .... *Burns* 27
Hope on .... *Nelson* 18
Hopeful Enterprize Library .... *Warne*...... 24
Horace and May .... *Warne*...... 26
Horace, by Dean Milman........ *Murray* 27
—— Lyrics, Trans. from ...... *Smith & El.* 3
—— Macleane .... *Whittaker* .. 2
—— Trans.Eng Verse,Connington *Bell* 35
—— Odes................ *Wilson* 10
—— Works, Trans., Globe Ed. .. *Macmillan*.. 23
Horæ Hebraicæ, Crawford...... *Williams* .. 4
Horeb, Idol in .... *Tinsley Bros.* 8
Horse Doctor .... *Allen* 10
—— Book, Handy .... *W. Blackw'd* 13
—— Management .... *Allen* 10
—— Riding, Graceful .... *Hardwicke*.. 11
—— in the Stable and Field .... *Routledge* .. 1
—— Taming, Rarey .... *Routledge* .. 11
—— Warranty .... *Hardwicke*.. 11
—— Works on the .... *Longmans* .. 42
Horses of Sahara .... *Allen* 12
—— (Clever) and Dogs.......... *Partridge* .. 16
—— and Horse-Shoeing, Fleming *Chapman* .. 7
—— and Hounds .... *Routledge* .. 71
—— (Race) Descent of .... *King*..... 31
—— and Stables .... *Longmans* .. 42
—— Stewart............ *W. Blackw'd* 30
—— Shoeing .... *Longmans* .. 42

Horse Shoeing.............. *Smith & El.* 7
—— Shoeing, The, Charlier...... *MacGlashan* 4
—— Shoeing, Douglas .... *Murray* 10
Horseowner & Stableman's Comp.*Warne*...... 13
Hortense (Queen) .... *Hurst & B.* 9
Horticulturist, Loudon ...... *Warne*...... 12
Hosea, Lessons from Book of.... *Nisbet* 34
Hospital Hygiene .... *Churchill* .. 23
—— Training for Ladies ...... *Harrison* ... 4
—— Nurses, Manual for ...... *Churchill* .. 15
—— Pharmacopæias .... *Churchill* .. 34
—— Practice .... *Churchill* .. 6
—— Prayer Book .... *Churchill* .. 37
—— Sisters, Handbook for .... *Isbister* 24
—— Statistics .... *Churchill* .. 11
Hospitals, Construction of ...... *Macmillan* .. 12
—— Prescriptions, Mil. ...... *Harrison*.... 9
—— Sermons for .... *W. Blackw'd* 18
Hot & Green House Construction *Spon* 23
Hour (The) of Death.......... *Masters* 29
—— of Prayer.............. *Rivingtons* .. 8
Hours with My Class .... *S. S. Union* 46
—— of Christian Devotion .... *W. Blackw'd* 41
House of Commons, History, &c. *Macmillan* .. 26
—— of Commons, The Shilling.. *Hardwicke* .. 13
—— Decoration .... *A. Heywood* 15
—— Israel, by Auth. W. W.World *Nisbet* 19
—— Owner's Estimator ...... *Lockwood* .. 7
—— of Prayer (The)........ *Macmillan*.. 9
Household Amusements ...... *Ward & Lock* 13
—— Book English Poetry ...... *Macmillan*.. 38
—— Guide .... *Cassell* 4
—— Education .... *Smith & El.* 15
—— Guide to Fam. & Civil Rights *Letts* 1
—— Management .... *Smith & El.* 12
—— Management .... *Ward & Lock* 4
—— Medicine .... *Smith & El.* 8
—— Prayer .... *Rivingtons* .. 9
—— Stories .... *Ward & Lock* 27
—— Surgery, South .... *Murray* 31
—— Tales and Fairy Stories .... *Routledge* .. 29
—— Theology .... *Rivingtons* .. 16
—— Tracts for the People ...... *Jarrold* 8
—— Truths .... *Jarrold* 8
—— Words Christmas Stories .. *Ward & Lock* 26
Householder (Modern) ...... *Warne*...... 16
Housekeeper's Account Books .. *Letts* 1
—— Account Book, Bell ...... *Mozley*...... 1
—— Pocket Guide .... *MacPhun* .. 15
Housewife (Practical) .... *Houlston*.... 5
Housewife's Reason Why ...... *Houlston*.... 5
How to be Happy .... *Warne*...... 5
—— we are Governed .... *Warne*...... 46
—— a Penny Became £1000 .... *Houlston*.... 5
Howard (T.) Sermons by ...... *Nisbet* 19
Howe (John) Works of.......... *Rel. Tr. Soc.* 9
Howitt (W. & M.) Juv. Books by *Routledge* .. 33
Howson (Dean) Works by ...... *Isbister* 21
—— Works by.............. *Rel. Tr. Soc.* 10
Hoyle (Modern, The) .... *Warne*...... 35
Hubert Ellis.............. *Ward & Lock* 8
Hudibras, Butler .... *Bohn's Lib..* 11
Hudson (River) .... *Isbister*..... 20
Hugessen (Knatchbull) Works by *Macmillan* .. 19
Hugo's By Order of the King .. *Bradbury* .. 11
—— Les Miserables .... *Chatto* 38
—— Miserables .... *Hurst & B.* 15
Huguenot Family .... *Warne*...... 27
—— Family in the Eng. Village *Isbister*..... 44
Huguenots, Browning .... *Whittaker* .. 9
—— in 17th Century, Bray ...... *Murray* 5
—— in France.............. *Isbister*..... 40
Hull (E. L.) Sermons by ...... *Nisbet* 19
Hulsean Lectures, 1859, Ellicott *Longmans* .. 32
—— Lectures, 1865, Moorhouse.. *Macmillan*.. 25
—— Lectures, 1867-68 .... *Bell* 25
—— Lectures, 1874, Farrar...... *Macmillan*.. 10
—— Lectures, Moore .... *Rivingtons*.. 15
—— Lectures, Trench .... *Macmillan*.. 37
Human and Animal Frame ...... *Chapman*.. 10
—— Body, Wonders of.......... *Blackie*..... 17
—— Brain, Ecker .... *Smith & El.* 5
—— Culture, Garvey .... *Bell* 42
—— Destiny, Hudson .... *Kellaway* .. 11
—— Frame, Proportions of the .. *Chapman*.... 25

Human Hives, Peeps into the .. *Chapman*.... 7
— Intellect (The) .... *Isbister* 35
— Mind, Carlile .... *Isbister* 10
— Mind, Mill .... *Longmans* 10
— Nature, Hume .... *Longmans* 17
— Nature, Sermons on .... *Bell* 57
— Physiology .... *Smith & El.* 4
— Physiology, Nichols.. *Trubner* 22
— Power in Divine Life .. *Hodder* 13
— Race (The), Figuier .... *Chapman*.. 18
— Race, Future of.......... *Smith & El.* 0
— Sadness .... *Isbister* 12
— Skeleton, Humphrey.. *Macmillan*.. 17
— Skeleton, Norton .... *Hardwicke*.. 16
Humber's Engineering Works .. *Lockwood* .. 1
Humboldt, Life of .... *Longmans* .. 8
— Cosmos.......... *Bohn's Lib.*.. 18
— Letters .... *Trubner* .. 16
— Life and Travels .. *J. Blackwood* 9
Hume & Smollett's England .. *Virtue* 20
Humility, Virtue of .... *Masters* 25
Humming Birds .... *Groombridge* 13
Humour, Modern .... *Warne*.... 35
— Wit, and Satire .... *J. Blackwood* 28
Humorous Books .... *Ward & Lock* 9
Humphreys' Masterpieces .... *Sotheran* .. 15
— Works by .... *Macmillan* .. 16
Hungarian Life, Tale of .... *Isbister*.... 13
— Grammar, Csink .... *Williams*.... 5
Hungary, its History .... *Bohn's Lib.*.. 8
— Patterson's Magyars.. *Smith & El.* 16
Hunt (Rev. J.) Contemp. Essays *Isbister* 22
— (L.) Old Court Suburb.... *Hurst & B.* 14
— (Leigh) Works of .... *Smith & El.* 11
Hunt the Slipper, Acrostics.. *Hatchard* .. 12
Hunter's Life in S. Africa .. *Murray* 9
Hunter, The Solitary .... *Routledge* .. 72
Hunting-Box, Notes from .. *Bradbury* .. 3
Hunting Field, Sketches .... *Routledge* .. 72
— Grounds of Old World .. *Routledge* .. 31
— Sketches .... *Chapman*.. 25
— Sketches, Illust. .... *Bradbury* .. 3
— Songs .... *Pickering* .. 40
Huntington's (W.) Works .... *Allman* .. 9
Hurricanes, Conversations about.. *Williams*.. 11
Husenbeth (Rev. Dr.) Works by *Washbourne* 9
Hutton's (R. H.) Essays .... *Isbister*...... 22
— (W.) Life of .... *Warne*...... 23
Huxley (Prof.) Works by.... *Macmillan* .. 17
Hyacinthe's Life and Orations .. *Morgan* 3
Hydraulic Tables, Neville .... *Lockwood* .. 3
Hydraulics, Works on .... *Spon*...... 4
Hydropathy .... *J. Blackwood* 27
Hydrophobia, Fleming.......... *Chapman*.. 8
Hydrostatics .... *Chambers* .. 17
— — Elementary.......... *Groombridge* 22
— Pbear .... *Macmillan*.. 28
Hygiene of Air and Water .. *Hardwicke*.. 16
— and Dietetics .... *Burns* 0
— Pickford .... *Churchill* .. 29
— Works on .... *Churchill* .. 0
Hymnal, Churchman's .... *Bemrose* 5
— for English Church .... *Mozley* .. 5
— (People's).......... *Masters* 21
— Scottish .... *W. Blackw'd* 36
— Treasures of the Church.. *Nisbet* 46
— with Tunes, Grey .... *Mozley* .. 5
Hymni Ecclesiæ.......... *Macmillan* .. 17
Hymnology (English) .... *Mozley* .. 3
Hymns .... *Parker*...... 38
— (Ancient) Mant .... *Rivingtons* .. 12
— Ancient and Modern .... *Stevenson* .. 0
— of Christ, Smith .... *Macmillan*.. 33
— Church .... *Soc. P. C. K.* 31
— for Church and Home .... *King*...... 28
— of the Church Militant .. *Nisbet* 19
— for the Day of Sorrow .. *Nisbet* 6
— of Denmark, Trans. .... *Isbister* 42
— of Faith and Hope .... *Nisbet* 7
— on Holy Communion ...... *Houlston* .. 10
— for Household of Faith .. *Macintosh* .. 0
— for Infant Classes .... *Wesleyan* .. 36
— for Infant Minds .... *Hodder* .. 29
— Latin, Trans. .... *Masters* 5
— for Little Children .... *Masters* 1

Hymns of Love and Praise ...... *Bell* 36
— and Lyrics, Church Seasons *Masters* 18
— Mediæval.......... *Masters* 19
— and Meditations.......... *Isbister* 46
— Narrative.......... *Masters* 1
— and Pictures .... *Soc. P. C. K.* 13
— and Poems for Sick .... *Rivingtons* .. 7
— of Praise and Prayer .... *Longmans* .. 36
— of Praise, Reid .... *Nisbet* 32
— for Public Worship, Westbrk. *Nisbet* .. 37
— Worship, Alexander .... *Black* 1
— of Salvation, with Tunes.. *Morgan* 4
— Selection from Best Authors *Isbister* .. 38
— and Songs of Pilgrim Life .. *Nisbet* .. 14
— for the Sorrowing .... *Haddon* .. 6
— for Special Services .... *Yapp* 6
— for Sundays and Holidays .. *Isbister* .. 4
— for the Week and Seasons .. *Parker* .. 36
Hymn Book for Sailors ...... *Snow* 14
— Wesleyan Methodist .... *Haddon* .. 2
— Books .... *Bell* 56
— Books .... *Masters* 0
— Books .... *Routledge* .. 23
— Books .... *S. S. Union* 36
— Books .... *Rel. Tr. Soc.* 31
— Books .... *Wesleyan* .. 35
— Books, Catholic .... *Burns* 27
— Books, Eng. Presbyterian .. *Nisbet* .. 45
— Books and Hymns .... *Morgan* .. 19
— Books, Wesleyan .... *Wesleyan* .. 37
— and Tune Books, Welsh .. *Haddon* .. 4
— Tunes, Modern .... *Morgan* .. 4
— Writers, Selections from Best *Macmillan* .. 13
— Selections from Best .... *Macmillan* .. 32
Hymn Books, Rippon and Watts *Houlston* .. 41

"I Ams" (The) of Christ........ *Yapp* 2
I Can Because I Ought .... *Warne* 26
Ice, Forms of Water in........ *King* 8
— A Lecture .... *Trubner* .. 31
Iceland, Dufferin .... *Murray* 10
— Painter's Journal in .... *Macmillan* .. 39
Icelandic-English Dictionary .. *Clar. Press.*. 4
— Burnt Njal, Trans........ *Edmonston*.. 6
— Gisli the Outlaw, Trans... *Edmonston*.. 6
— Grammar, Bayldon .... *Williams*.... 2
— Religious Poems .... *Williams* .. 8
— Translation, Head........ *Williams*.... 15
Iconography (Christian) .... *Bohn's Lib.*.. 13
Idioms and Usage, Alford .... *Isbister* .. 4
Idolatries, Old and New .... *Hodder* 18
Idylls and Epigrams .... *Macmillan*.. 12
— of the King .... *Ward & Lock* 31
Ignatius (Father) Leonard Morris *Bentley* .. 10
Ikhwânu-S. Safâ .... *Trubner* .. 16
'Ilam En Nas, Arabian Tales... *King* 31
Iliad of the East.......... *Macmillan*.. 30
Illuminated Book Com. Prayer .. *Rivingtons*.. 4
— Legends .... *M. Ward* .. 16
— Tablets .... *Tract Society* 33
— Texts .... *Tract Society* 34
Illuminating .... *M. Ward* .. 12
Illumination, Alphabets for.... *Spon* 26
— Art of .... *Lockwood* .. 15
— Art of, Shaw .... *Bell* 4
Illustrated Diagrams .... *Philip* 18
— Sheets and Diagrams ...... *Soc. P. C. K.* 36
— Story Books .... *Nelson* 17
Illustrative Gatherings .... *Nisbet* 7
— Scripture Readings .... *Nisbet* 10
— Teaching .... *S. S. Union* 44
— Texts and Texts Illustrated *Nisbet* 4
Imagination and Fancy .... *Smith & El.* 11
Imauddeen: and other Poems .. *Nisbet* 19
Imbecile, A Day at Earlswood .. *Isbister* .. 33
— Education of the .... *Isbister* .. 18
Imitation of Christ.......... *Parker* 30
Immaculate Conception, R. Doc. *Clark* .. 15
Imperial Bible Dictionary .... *Blackie* 3
— and Colonial Constitutions.. *Longmans* .. 3
— Dictionary .... *Blackie*.... 1
Improvement of Time .... *Hodder* .. 21
In the Eastern Seas .... *Nelson* 10
In Exitu Israel .... *Macmillan* .. 2
In the Golden Shell, a Tale.... *Macmillan* .. 25

In Memoriam Album.......... *Mack* 4
In the Plain and on the Mountain *Hardwicke*.. 6
In Strange Company .... *King* 10
In the Wilds of Africa .... *Nelson* 6
Incarnation, Doctrine of .... *Mozley*.... 13
— Sermons on .... *Masters* 3
Incense for the Altar .... *Masters* 23
Inchmahome Priory .... *W. Blackw'd* 30
Incident and Adventure Library.. *Warne* 23
Incidents in Life of Our Saviour *Nisbet* 13
Income and Property, Guide .. *Macmillan* .. 13
Income Tax .... *Wilson* 9
Increase of Faith .... *W. Blackw'd* 33
Independent Church (Story of an) *Isbister* 36
Independency in England .... *Snow* 6
Index Geographicus .... *Johnston* 48
India, Administration of Justice *Williams*.... 10
— Ancient and Modern, Taylor *Houlston*.... 26
— Analytical History of ...... *Allen* 25
— British History .... *Clar. Press.* 26
— Ancient Geography of ...... *Trubner* 9
— Ancient and Mediæval...... *Allen* 3
— Analytical History .... *Allen* 3
— (British) .... *Nelson* 4
— (British), History of ...... *Routledge* 21
— (British) Flora of .... *Reeve* 5
— British Rule in .... *Smith & El.* 15
— (British) to 1783 .... *Murray* 31
— Childhood in .... *Hodder* .. 28
— Clinical Surgery in .... *Churchill* .. 15
— and Christian Missions .... *Snow* 12
— Christianity in .... *Allen* 15
— Civil Service, Educa. Course *King* 15
— Service, Examination Papers *Stanford*.... 54
— Comprehensive History .. *Blackie* 8
— Currency (Drain of to East) *Allen* 6
— Dalhousie's Administration.. *Smith & El.* 10
— Directory .... *Allen* 11
— Diseases of, Moore .... *Churchill* .. 26
— Diseases of .... *Smith & El.* 8
— East, Calculator .... *Allen* 6
— Ellenborough's Administratn. *Bentley* 6
— Empire in, Bell .... *Trubner* 4
— The English in .... *Trubner* 4
— English Homes in .... *Allen* 7
— Englishwoman in .... *Smith & El.* 6
— and Europe Compared ...... *Allen* 4
— (European Officer in) Reg for *Harrison*.... 11
— on the Eve of British Conquest *Allen* 22
— Folk Lore of, Elliot .... *Trubner* 12
— S., Fairy Legends of .... *Murray* 12
— Farming in .... *Smith & El.* 9
— Forty-three Years' Service .. *Murray* 19
— Gazetteer of the Cen. Prov... *Trubner* 13
— Gazetteer of .... *Allen* 8
— Geography of .... *Allen* 3
— Gold Currency for .... *Layton* 15
— The Retention of .... *Tinsley Bros.* 8
— Highlands of Central .... *Chapman* 6
— Hindu Medicine .... *Smith & El.* 18
— Historical Sketch .... *Rel. Tr. Soc.* 10
— History of, Elphinstone .. *Murray* 11
— History of, Elliot .... *Trubner* 11
— History of, Keightley .... *Whittaker* 10
— History, Marshman .... *Longmans* 3
— History of, Wheeler .... *Trubner* 31
— Irrigation.......... *Smith & El.* 17
— Land Tax of .... *Smith & El.* 2
— Law Relating to.......... *Allen* 15
— Medical Guide to European *King* 14
— Mercantile Ex. Tables .... *Smith & El.* 19
— Military Transactions in .. *Allen* 23
— Muhammadanism in .... *Macmillan* .. 4
— (Modern) Campbell .... *Murray* .. 7
— Naturalist in .... *Edmonston* .. 1
— Notes on the N. W. Provs... *Allen* 22
— Our Last Years in, Speid .. *Smith & El.* 21
— Pen and Pencil Sketches of.. *Murray* 23
— Pharmacopœia of .... *Allen* 2
— Pictorial and Descriptive ... *Bohn's Lib.* 13
— Picturesque Scenery .... *Allman* 12
— Productive Resources ...... *Smith & El.* 18
— Roads in .... *Smith & El.* 5
— Sport in .... *Edmonston.* .. 4
— Southern Folk Songs of .... *Trubner* 13

India, Success in.......... *Wilson* 8
— — Tree and Serpent Worship.. *Allen* 2
— — Textile Manufactures, &c .. *Allen* 26
— — Thug, &c. of .... *Allen* 27
— — (South) Today, Customs, &c. *Longmans* .. 17
— — Venomous Snakes of ...... *Churchill* 15
— — (Western) English in .... *Allen* 3
— — (Western) Geol. Papers on *Allen* 8
— — (Western) Travels in .. *Allen* 27
— — Wild Races.......... *Allen* 15
— — Wild Sports of .... *Smith & El.* 11
— — Yesterday and To-Day in .. *Allen* 4
Indian Administration .... *Allen* 12
— Administration, 1859-68 ... *Macmillan* .. 29
— Affairs, 1859-66 .... *Smith & El.* 27
— Affairs, Concerning John's.. *Chapman* ... 17
— Army and Civil Service List *Allen* 12
— Army, Vital Statistics of... *Smith & El.* 7
— Ballads .... *Smith & El.* 29
— Beauty, Oliver .... *Macmillan* .. 27
— Civil Service Guide .... *Cassell* .. 2
— Code of Civil Procedure... *Allen* 12
— Criminal Law and Procedure *Allen* 12
Indian (East) Ready Reckoner .. *Smith & El.* 5
— Evangelization, Wilson .... *Stewart* ... 9
— Evidence Act .... *Macmillan* .. 34
— Exchange Tables, Fraser .. *King* 15
— Experiences .... *King* 14
— (S.) Grammar.......... *Trubner* ... 6
— Government Memorials .... *Allen* 15
— History, by own Historians *Trubner* ... 11
— History, Outlines of... *Bell* 25
— Infanticide .... *Allen* 14
— Islands, Crawford .... *Bradbury* ... 2
— Jails .... *Smith & El.* 7
— Missions, Freer .... *Murray* ... 12
— and Military Law .... *Allen* 12
— Musalmans .... *Trubner* ... 16
— Mutiny .... *Allen* 25
— Mutiny, Jacob .... *King* ... 15
— Mutiny, MacPherson .... *Murray* 24
— Mutiny .... *Smith & El.* 5
— Mutiny, Grant .... *W. Blackw'd* 11
— Mutiny, Havelock's March *Smith & El.* 16
— Mutiny, Siege of Lucknow.. *Murray* 21
— Mutiny, Sketch of, Cooke .. *Nisbet* ... 20
— Mutiny, A Tale of, by Una *Hatchard* ... 7
— Non-Aryan Language Dict. *Trubner* 16
— Ocean, Slave Catching .... *Longmans* .. 30
— Ocean, Storms in .... *Smith & El.* 25
— Officer, Autobiography of an *Morgan* ... 2
— Officers, Lives of .... *Isbister* ... 23
— and Eastern Plants, Index to *Trubner* ... 31
— Penal Code .... *Allen* 12
— Philology.......... *Trubner* ... 3
— Pilgrim's Progress .... *Houlston* ... 31
— Plantations, Quinology of .. *Reeve* ... 6
— Polity, Chesney .... *Longmans* .. 3
— Subjects, Essays on .... *Allen* 15
— Tales, Meadows Taylor .... *King* 24
Indians, Boy Life Among .... *Routledge* ... 79
Indies (West) Flora of .... *Reeve* 5
Indications of the Creator ...... *Collins* ... 3
Indicator, Inland Postal .... *Wilson* ... 11
Indigenism, Chambers.......... *Churchill* .. 12
Indo-China, Travels in.......... *Chapman* ... 5
Indo-European Languages, Attwell *Williams* .. 2
Indo-European Comparative Gram. *Trubner* ... 26
Indus to the Tigris (Frens) .. *Trubner* ... 4
Industrial Chemistry .... *Longmans* .. 33
— Library .... *Houlston* .. 6
— Schools, Manuals for ...... *Masters* ... 13
Industry (Native) Protection of .. *Stanford* ... 70
Infancy, Works on Diseases of .. *Churchill* ... 11
Infant Baptism .... *Clar. Press.* 14
— Bridal (The) .... *Macmillan.* .. 9
— Feeding .... *Churchill* ... 12
Infants and Children, Diseases... *Smith & El.* 24
Infant's Pilgrim's Progress .... *Houlston* ... 38
Infantile Diseases, Norton .... *Churchill* ... 27
Infantry, Frontal Attack of .... *King* 12
— Tactics (Prussian) .... *Harrison* ... 12
— Tactics.......... *W. Blackw'd* 20
— Tactics, Studies in.......... *King* 12
Infinitesimal Calculus .... *Clar. Press.* 18

Information for the People ...... Chambers .. 31
Ingelow (Jean) Works by........ Ibister 22
Ingoldsby Legends.............. Bentley 8
—— Legends, Life of Author ...... Bentley 3
Ingraham's (Rev. J. H.) Works.. Routledge .. 65
In Heaven...................... Houlston..<.. 35
Initials, The.................... Bentley 16
Injunctions, Law, &c. of .... Stevens 8
Inland Postal Indicator.......... Wilson 11
Inman (Thos.) Work by .... Trubner 27
Inoes (Cosmo) Works by .... Edmonston.. 12
Innocents at Home.............. Routledge .. 1
Inquiry into the Means of Grace Parker...... 6
Inquisitio Philosophica .... Chapman .. 12
Inquisition, Spanish .... Nimmo 14
Insane in Private Dwellings ...... Edmonston.. 16
Insanity in Europe and America.. Murray 7
—— Legal Tests of .... Churchill.... 30
—— Sanky .... Churchill.... 31
—— Sheppard .... Churchill.... 33
Insect Architecture, Rennie ...... Bell 23
—— World, Figuier (L.) .... Cassell 4
Insects .... Pickering .. 39
—— Abroad .... Longmans .. 23
—— British .... Routledge .. 46
—— A Guide to the Study of .. Trubner 23
—— at Home .... Longmans .. 23
—— Kirby and Spence .... Longmans .. 22
—— Origin and Metamorphoses of Macmillan .. 20
—— Origin and Metamorphoses of Macmillan .. 26
—— British .... Reeve 10
Inspiration, Bannerman .... Clark 10
Inspiration and Interpretation .. Parker...... 8
—— Lee's Discourses on .... Rivingtons .. 14
—— of Scripture .... W. Blackw'd 38
Institute of Actuaries' Life Tables Layton 2
Instructive Picture Books........ Edmonston.. 12
—— Shilling Books .... Nelson 17
Insurance .... Stevens 23
—— (Compound)Tables,Turnbulls Layton 15
—— Cyclopædia (The).......... Layton 4
—— Guide and Hand Book...... Layton 16
—— Marine .... Smith & El. 10
—— Register (The) .... Layton 5
Intellect, Progress of the .... Williams.... 9
Intellectual Development, Draper Bell 42
—— Life (The) .... Macmillan.. 15
—— Observer .... Sotheran .. 15
Intelligence (Taine) .... Reeve 13
International Law, Letters on .. Macmillan.. 16
—— Law, Kent .... Bell 41
—— Reading Books .... Asher 2
—— Relations before War 1870.. Tinsley Bros. 5
—— Scientific Series .... King...... 8
—— Story of the .... Ibister 48
Interest (Compound) Thoman .... Lockwood .. 11
—— Tables .... Chambers .. 30
—— Tables .... Wilson 3
—— Tables .... Wilson 9
—— Tables, by Booth .... Wilson 5
—— Tables, Laurie .... Routledge .. 68
—— Tables, Green .... Smith & El. 9
—— Tables, King .... Bell 62
—— Table for all Rates........ Layton 10
—— Tables, any Rate .... Mozley.... 2
—— Time Tables .... Letts...... 2
Interview (The) .... Houlston .. 5
Invalids, How to Amuse out .... King 32
Invasions of England .... Stanford .. 54
Invention and Discovery .... Groombridge 25
—— Triumphs of .... Nelson 11
Inventions, History of .... Bohn's Lib... 7
—— Wonderful .... Routledge .. 31
Inventors, Great .... Ward 27
—— and Inventions .... Spon 26
Investing Money................ Ward&Lock 7
—— Guide to .... Ward&Lock 13
—— Hints on .... Lockwood .. 28
Investment, Safe Guide to ...... Wilson 7
Inwood's Tables for Estates...... Lockwood .. 11
Iona, Argyll.................... Ibister 5
Ionian Islands .... Allen 5
—— in 1863 .... Allen 14
Ireland in 1872 .... King...... 5
—— Ancient, Fine Arts of...... Smith & El. 16

Ireland, Ballads of.............. MacGlashan 1
—— and the American Centenary Wesleyan .. 43
—— (English) in 18th Century .. Longmans .. 1
—— Fraser's Handbook .... MacGlashan 2
—— Guide to .... Black 6
—— Handbook to .... Murray 17
—— Handbook of Railway Dis... Harrison .. 13
—— History of .... Cameron .. 1
—— History of .... Masters .. 13
—— History for Students ...... Longmans .. 3
—— Lawrence Bloomfield in .. Macmillan.. 3
—— Letters from Martineau .... Trubner .. 15
—— Leaders of Public Opinion .. Longmans .. 8
—— A Little Tour in.......... Bradbury .. 3
—— Lyrics of .... Houlston .. 16
—— Old Folk Lore of .... Cameron .. 1
—— Picturesque Scenery in.... Virtue.... 4
—— Religious History of........ King...... 3
—— its Scenery, &c .... Virtue 12
—— Its Scenery .... Virtue 20
—— Works on .... Cameron .. 1
—— Works Relating to .... MacGlashan 1
Irish Anecdote .... Routledge .. 3
—— Brigades, History of........ Cameron .. 4
—— Character, Sketches of...... Chatto .. 18
—— Chieftains (The) .... MacGlashan 1
—— Church History .... Mullan .. 6
—— before the Conquest ...... Bell 38
—— Glossaries (Old).......... Williams .. 14
—— Glosses, Prose and Verse.. Trubner .. 27
—— Grammar .... MacGlashan 3
—— Grammar of Modern...... Williams .. 10
—— History and Irish Character Parker.... 63
—— Hist., Social Life, O'Curry Williams.. 30
—— Life, Realities of .... Longmans .. 3
—— Melodies, Moore .... Longmans .. 40
—— Music, Joyce .... MacGlashan 3
—— Names and Places.......... MacGlashan 3
—— National School Books...... Collins .. 15
—— Peasantry, Hall............ Chambers .. 30
—— Rebellion, Maxwell .... Bell 32
—— State Church .... Ibister .. 8
Irma, Tale of Hungarian Life .. Ibister 13
Iron Armour Plates & Steel Shot Harrison .. 6
—— Beams, Armour .... Lockwood .. 4
—— (Cast and Wrought) for Build. Longmans .. 22
—— its History and Manufacture Black .. 12
—— Horse (The), a Railway Tale Nisbet .. 4
—— Metallurgy of .... Ibister .. 5
—— and Steel Assaying .... Chapman .. 14
—— Strength of .... Murray .. 31
—— Strength of .... Spon 41
—— Table of Weight.......... Hagger .. 15
—— Weight .... Spon 48
—— Works on .... Spon 27
Irons (Rev. W. J.) Works by .... Masters .. 13
Ironwork (Mediæval).......... Parker .. 50
—— Shield's.................. Lockwood .. 3
Irrigation, Italian .... W. Blackw'd 52
Irritability, Hints for Management Churchill .. 27
Irving (C.) Catechisms .... Stanford .. 56
—— (Edward) Life of.......... Hurst .. 15
—— (Edward) Writings of...... Ibister .. 23
—— (Washington) Complete Wks. Bohn's Lib. 10
Irving's Sketch Book, Illust. .... Bell 10
Irvingism, its Pretensions, &c... Kelloway .. 12
Is it Possible to Make the Best.. Nisbet 4
Isabel's Secret .... Nelson 16
Isaiah, Birks' Commentary .... Rivingtons .. 2
—— Chronologically Arranged .. Macmillan .. 6
—— Codd's Lectures on ...... Rivingtons .. 13
—— Notes on Unfulfilled Proph.. Nisbet .. 29
—— Prophecies of .... Parker .. 9
Isaiah's Testimony for Jesus .... Bell 43
Isham Reprints .... Sotheran .. 10
Isle of Man, Ecclesiological Notes Masters .. 19
—— of Man, Guide to .... Stanford .. 53
—— of Wight .... Virtue .. 20
—— of Wight, Chapters on...... Masters .. 23
—— of Wight, Geology of ...... Bohn's Lib. 9
—— of Wight, Geology, &c..... Stanford .. 71
Israel, Antiquities of .... Longmans .. 35
—— The Religion of.......... Williams .. 8
—— History of, Ewald .... Longmans .. 35
Israel's Exodus Alleg. Considered Hakkard .. 4

Israelites, History and Lit. ...... Longmans .. 35
It's His Way .... Nelson 19
It is Written Again, Breay ..... Nisbet 7
It is Your Life .... Isbister 23
Italian Art, Masterpieces of... Bell 9
—— Anecdotes, &c., Rossetti.. Williams... 12
—— Conversational Course.. Trubner 19
—— Conversation .... Trubner 7
—— Conversation Grammar.. Nutt 32
—— Conversation, Millhouse.. Trubner ... 20
—— Conversation, Skelton .. Trubner 10
—— Dictionary .... Rivingtons . 18
—— Dictionaries .... Routledge .. 14
—— Dictionary, Graglia ..... Rivingtons.. 18
—— Dictionary, Millhouse ... Trubner 20
—— Dictionary, Triglot ..... Lockwood .. 30
—— Educational Literature..... Nutt 30
—— Educational Works ..... Whittaker .. 6
—— English Dictionary, Roberts Nutt 31
—— (First) Book.......... Rivingtons .. 18
—— Grammar (Eton) Volpe..... Williams.. 15
—— Grammar, Mariotti ..... Williams.. 9
—— Language, Biaggi ..... Williams.. 3
—— Language, Easy Method.. Trubner .. 2
—— Painters, Early ..... Murray 19
—— Pictures .... Rel. Tr. Soc. 10
—— Poets, Glassford ..... Black 12
—— Poets, Modern .... Williams.. 10
—— School of Painting ..... Murray 9
—— Sculpture, Robinson ..... Chapman .. 24
—— Stories, with Notes ..... Asher 2
—— Testament and Com. Prayer Bagster 18
—— War, 1848-9, Lushington.. Macmillan .. 21
—— War, 1866......... Stanford... 71
Italiani (Prosatori), Biaggi ..... Williams.. 3
Italics (Notes on Italy in 1864).. Williams.. 4
Italy (Art Guide to Painting in).. Murray .. 5
—— Art in, Taine ..... Williams.. 14
—— in England .... Houlston .. 12
—— Mediaeval Christianity in... Williams.. 7
—— (Cent.) Mineral Resources of Stanford... 57
—— Climate of......... Churchill .. 12
—— Dawn to Dark in ..... Rel. Tr. Soc. 6
—— Diary of an Idle Woman in.. Chapman .. 18
—— Englishwoman in ..... Hurst & Bl. 14
—— History of the Liberators .. Virtue 21
—— History of, Hunt .... Macmillan .. 17
—— Illustrated and Described .. Blackie.... 15
—— Old and New .... Tinsley Bros. 2
—— (Painting in) .... Murray 7
—— Poems on .... King 9
—— The Red Shirt Episodes .... Smith & El. 17
—— Reformation......... W. Blackw'd 19
—— Terra-Cotta Architecture.. Murray .. 13
—— (Visits to) Broughton....... Murray .. 5
Ithuriel's Spear .... Nisbet 33
Ivan de Biron .... Isbister 22
Ivy (The), its History, Uses, &c.. Groombridge 10

Jack the Conqueror .... Partridge .. 12
—— Hazard, &c .... Warne.... 28
Jackson (Sir G.) Diaries & Letters Bentley ... 9
—— (Stonewall) Memoir of ..... Nisbet 19
—— (Rev. T.) Works .... Wesleyan .. 14
—— (Dr. T.) Works ..... Clar. Press.. 14
Jacob, Sermons .... Macmillan .. 26
Jacob's Well, The Story of ..... Nisbet 23
Jacox (F.) Works by .... Hodder .. 10
Jade Chaplet (The) .... Trubner .. 27
Jamaica, Baptist Mission in..... Snow 16
—— Letters from......... Edmonston.. 14
James (Canon) Works by ..... Rivingtons.. 0
—— (Rev. J. A.) Works by..... Rel. Tr. Soc. 10
Jameson's (Mrs.) Art Works.... Longmans .. 0
Jane Eyre, Library Edition..... Smith & El. 3
Janet's Home .... Macmillan .. 17
—— Love and Sacrifice......... Hodder .. 27
Jansenists .... Parker.... 12
—— (The) Tregelles .... Bagster 62
January to December (From)..... Longmans .. 21
Japan, the Amoor and Pacific .. Allen 14
—— Dickson......... W. Blackw'd 7
—— Elgin's Mission ..... W. Blackw'd 72
—— History of, Adams......... King 3
—— (New)......... Murray 23

Japan Our Life in .... Chapman .. 19
—— Pines and Firs of .... Bradbury .. 11
—— Tales of Old .... Macmillan .. 25
—— Voyage, Tronson .... Smith & El. 25
Japanese Dictionary, Hepburn .. Trubner .. 15
—— Grammar .... Trubner .. 3
—— Picture Book .... M. Ward .. 13
Jar of Honey from Mount Hybla Smith & El. 11
Jarwin and Cuffy......... Warne.... 18
Jason Legend .... Parker.... 64
Jasper (Sir) Trial of .... Virtue.... 20
Jaundice, MacLeod......... Churchill .. 25
Jaws, Injuries of the .... Churchill .. 20
Jeannie Barker......... S. S. Union. 9
Jeffrey (Lord) Life of......... Black 10
Jelf, Humbert .... Bentley .. 9
Jelf (Rev. G. E.) Works by ..... Mozley..... 5
Jenkins (Edward) Works by ..... King 32
Jenny's Geranium .... Partridge .. 6
Jeremiah (Prophet)......... Marlborough 11
—— and Ezekiel, Shesheth's .. Williams... 10
Jerrold (Douglas) Works by ..... Bradbury .. 8
Jersey and Guernsey, Guide to .. Stanford .. 53
Jersey, Guernsey, Alderney, &c.. Allen 14
Jerusalem, The Child's History of Isbister 11
—— and its Environs......... Nelson 12
—— Explained......... Sotheran.... 22
—— History, Besant .... Bentley .. 4
—— Holy Sepulchre at .... Murray .. 12
—— or the Holy City......... Nelson 20
—— Last Days of .... Routledge .. 27
—— of the Evangelists .... Williams... 12
—— of History (The)......... Williams... 8
—— of Nazara, Keim......... Williams... 8
—— New Life of, Strauss......... Williams... 14
—— Ordnance Survey of ..... Stanford .. 63
—— Our Work in Palestine ..... Bentley .. 12
—— Recovery of .... Bentley .. 12
—— Scamper to .... Bentley .. 13
—— Scenes from, Holland ..... Soc. P. C. K. 24
—— Siege of, Lewis .... Bell 47
—— A Third Year in .... Nisbet 13
—— Walks about .... Isbister 5
Jessica's Prayer, Wks. by Author Rel. Tr. Soc. 6
Jest Book (The) .... Macmillan .. 14
Jest and Earnest, Dasent......... Chapman .. 14
Jesu (Institutum Societatis) ..... Nutt 5
Jesuits, History of the .... Bohn's Lib.. 14
—— (The), their Origin, &c... Houlston .. 37
Jesus Christ in Glory......... Parker.... 31
—— Christ, Lacordaire......... Chapman .. 20
—— Christ, His Times, Life, &c. Hodder .. 15
— — Christ, Doctrine of, Reville Williams.... 11
—— the Good Shepherd .... Masters .. 4
—— Sinlessness of .... Clark .. 11
—— Home Life of .... Rivingtons . 14
—— Lambs, Hammond .... Morgan .. 5
—— Life of .... Nelson 8
—— Life of, by Renan .... Trubner .. 35
—— Mighty to Save .... Nisbet .. 15
—— Saviour .... Isbister .. 23
—— Scenes from Life......... Edmonston.. 11
—— (Society of) Wks. by Fathers Burns 15
—— Sufferings of......... Parker.... 30
—— the Way .... S. S. Union. 7
Jevons (Prof.) Works by .... Macmillan .. 17
Jeweller and Goldsmith......... Chatto .. 30
Jewellery, Hall Marks on......... Chatto .. 5
Jewels .... Blackie .. 17
Jewels .... Chatto .. 14
—— and Gems .... Bell 13
—— Stories in Precious Stones . King 18
Jewel's Apology, with Memoir .. Bell 47
—— Works, Jelf .... Clar. Press.. 14
Jewish Church, Stanley......... Murray .. 28
—— History, Heroes of .... Isbister .. 47
—— History and Politics .... Isbister .. 41
—— Nation, History of .... Clark .. 0
—— Temple and Christian Church Hodder .. 4
Jews (British) .... Houlston .. 24
—— History of, Milman .... Murray .. 22
—— Manners and Customs ..... Soc. P. C. K. 9
Jews' Orphan Colony in China .. Nisbet .. 13
Job, Book of, Froude......... Trubner .. 13
—— Book of, Trans. by Rodwell Williams .. 12

Job, Commentary on, Davidson.. Williams.... 5
—— Book of, Trans. by Coleman Nisbet 10
—— Sermons on Book of, Wagner Nisbet 36
—— Story of, Thiselton .... Nisbet 34
Jobson (Rev. Dr.) Works .... Wesleyan .. 45
Jocular Tenures, Blount .... Reeve 8
Joe Miller, Modern .... Warne.... 35
Joe Witless : A Book for Boys Morgan ... 3
John of the Golden Mouth ..... Nisbet 9
—— Halifax, Novels by Author. Hurst & B.. 13
Johnson (Samuel) Life .... J. Blackwood 3
—— Life and Conversations ... Chapman ... 7
—— Life, Boswell .... Routledge .. 4
—— Lives of the Poets .... Murray 19
—— Lives of the Poets .... Warne.... 23
—— Prayers & Meditations .... Masters ... 13
—— Rasselas, Daniel........... Clar. Press.. 32
Johnston (J. F. W.) Agrl. Works W. Blackw'd 50
Joined to an Idol .... Mozley 5
Joints, Bryant's Diseases of..... Churchill .. 11
Joinery, &c. .... Hagger ... 15
Jokes and Jests .... Lockwood .. 45
Jonah, Book of, in 4 languages.. Williams.... 16
—— Lectures on .... Hatchard .. 34
—— (The Prophet) .... Isbister ... 31
—— The Story of .... Black 16
Jones (Agnes Eliz.) Memorials of Isbister ... 23
—— (T. Rymer) Works by ...... Warne.... 15
—— (T. Wharton) Med. Works by Churchill .. 23
Jonson (Ben) Works .... Chatto 27
Jordan and its Valley .... Nelson 20
Jorrocks's Jaunts and Jollities.. Routledge .. 72
Joseph and His Brethren ..... Masters ... 24
—— History of, Smith .... Snow 14
—— Lessons from Life of....... Nisbet 5
—— Overton's Lectures on ..... Nisbet 29
Josephus, Traill .... Houlston .. 39
Josephus .... Routledge .. 72
—— Translation by Whiston ... Nimmo 6
—— Works of .... Milner 3
—— Works .... Virtue 10
Josh Billings .... Chatto 21
Joshua, Miracle in 10th Chapter. Hatchard .. 34
Journey to Herat and Khiva .. Smith & El. 7
—— of Discovery Round House Houlston .. 5
Journeyman Engineer, Works by Isbister 33
Joyce (P. W.) Works by ...... MacGlashan 3
Jubilee Singers .... Hodder 19
Judea(Mod.)Comp. with Prophecy Collins 30
Judges, Book of .... Hodder 6
—— of England, Foss .... Murray 12
—— of Israel .... Warne.... 28
Judicial and Revenue Terms .. Allen 34
Judson's (Dr.) Missionary Life .. Nisbet 19
Jukes (J. Beete) Letters & Writings Chapman .. 19
Julian Home .... Black 8
—— or Scenes in Judea ...... Warne.... 70
Junius's Handwriting .... Murray 20
—— Letters .... Bohn's Lib.. 8
Juno Stories (The)........... Isbister ... 23
Jupiter's Daughters .... Smith & El. 12
Jurisdiction of Ang. Episcopate.. Parker.... 7
Jurisprudence, Amos .... Isbister ... 5
—— Elements .... Clar. Press.. 26
—— Science of .... Longmans .. 14
Justification .... Parker.... 6
—— Doctrine of............... Clark 12
—— by Faith .... Macmillan.. 37
Justin Martyr and other Poems. Macmillan.. 37
Justinian's Institutes, Sanders .. Longman .. 11
—— Institutes, Translation... Clar. Press.. 26
Jutland Life, Story of .... Bell 25
Juvenal and Persius, Macleane . Whittaker .. 2
Juvenalis Satirae, Lewis ...... Trubner ... 17
Juvenile Books .... Bell 19
—— Books .... Bell 26
—— Books .... Bemrose .. 9
—— Books .... Black 8
—— Books .... J. Blackwood 22
—— Books .... Cassell 8
—— Books .... Chambers .. 32
—— Books .... Gall .... 4 to 6
—— Books .... Isbister ... 10
—— Books .... Isbister ... 24
—— Books .... Mozley 3

Juvenile Books .... Houlston 17
—— Books .... Nicholson .. 2
—— Books .... King 16
—— Books .... Macmillan.. 22
—— Books .... Masters ... 44
—— Books .... Masters ... 0
—— Books .... Nisbet 40
—— Books .... Partridge .. 2
—— Books .... Rel. Tr. Soc. 25
—— Books .... Routledge .. 29
—— Books .... S. S. Union 1
—— Books .... M. Ward .. 2
—— Books .... Ward & Lock 9
—— Books .... Warne.... 29
—— Books, Aunt Fanny ..... Edmonston.. 16
—— Books, Coloured .... Routledge .. 30
—— Books, large Type...... Rel. Tr. Soc. 23
—— Englishman's Library .... Masters ... 14
—— Gift Book .... Warne.... 35
—— Gift Books .... Groombridge 23
—— Gift Books .... Hatchard .. 0
—— Gift Books .... Lockwood .. 46
—— Gift Books .... Marlborough 3
—— Gift Books .... Marlborough 4
—— Gift Books .... Nelson 10
—— Gift Books .... Nimmo 14
—— Gift Books .... Parker.... 43
—— Gift Books .... Shaw 5
—— Gift Books .... Soc. P. C. K. 39
—— Indestructible Books .... Ward 18
—— Library .... Edmonston.. 8
—— Libraries .... Soc. P. C. K. 32
—— Library, Arthur's .... Milner 12
—— Prize Books .... Virtue 13
—— Reward Books .... Nimmo 16
—— Reward Packets .... Walker 14
—— Series .... Walker 11
—— Tales, Edgeworth ...... Milner 11
—— Tales, Sherwood .... Milner 10
—— Works .... Hodder 27
Juventus Mundi .... Macmillan.. 13

Kaffir Dictionary .... Wesleyan .. 43
—— Grammar .... Wesleyan .. 42
—— Races .... Wesleyan .. 45
Kaffraria, Visit to British..... Soc. P. C. K. 14
Kaiteur Falls, British Guiana.. Stanford.... 71
Kalendars of Gwynedd .... Chatto 21
Kalendar of Scottish Saints.... Edmonston.. 9
Kant's Critique of Pure Reason. Bohn's Lib.. 16
Kant and Hamilton, Bolton ... Chapman ... 12
Kant, Philosophy of .... Trubner ... 8
Kashmir (Illust.of Anc. Buildings) Allen 2
Katherine's Trial............. Smith & El. 13
Kathie Brand .... Smith & El. 13
Katie, or the Simple Heart .... Bell 24
Kattern's Sermons .... Snow 9
Katy Lester .... M. Ward .. 2
Kavanagh (Miss) Novels by.... Hurst & B.. 14
—— (Julia) Works of .... Smith & El. 12
Kaye (J. W.) Works of....... Smith & El. 12
Kean (Edmund) Life .... Tinsley Bros. 5
Kearey (A. and E.) Works by.. Macmillan.. 18
Keble's Christian Year .... Rivingtons.. 9
—— Christian Year.......... Routledge .. 7
—— Works .... Parker.... 0
Keeling's Sermons .... Wesleyan .. 40
Keepsake Text-book .... Mack 3
—— for the Young.......... Ward 22
Keightley's Histories......... Whittaker .. 9
Kelly (J.) Sermons, various Subs. Snow 9
Kelso Tracts (The)........... Nisbet 7
Kembles (The) Lives of ...... Tinsley Bros. 7
Kempis, ed. Keble .... Parker.... 30
Kempis, ed. Wesley .... Wesleyan .. 30
—— The Following of Christ .. Burns 21
—— Following of Christ ..... Washbourne 3
—— Imitation of Christ...... Rivingtons.. 7
—— Imitation of Christ...... Bell 33
—— Imitation............... MacGlashan 1
—— Ornamented Ed. .... Macmillan.. 18
Ken's (Bishop) Life .... Murray 10
Kenmare Publications .... Burns 18
Kenneth and Hugh .... Warne.... 26
Kenny's School Books .... Allman 10

Kenrick's (John) Works .... *Fellowes* .... a
Kensington Museum Edu. Works *Chapman* .. 27
Kent, Lambarde's .... *J. R. Smith* 13
Kentish Dialect .... *Asher* 8
—— Bibliography .... *J. R. Smith*. o
Kenyon (Lord) Life .... *Longmans* .. 7
Ker (John) Sermons by .... *Edmonston* .. 13
Keramic Gallery .... *Chapman* .. 20
Kerr's (Rob.) Works on Architect. *Murray* 19
Kertch, Antiquities of .... *Smith & El.* 15
Kew Herbarium .... *Williams* .... a
Key to Church History, &c. .... *Rivingtons* .. o
—— Every Lock, The Apocalypse *Hatchard* .. 32
—— Heaven, Epistles & Gospels *Burns* 11
—— Notes Every Day in the Year *So. P. C. K.* 14
Keyworth (James) Life of ...... *Morgan* 5
Khirad Afroz .... *Trubner* 10
Khiva, On the Road to.......... *King* 4
—— and Turkestan .... *Chapman* 4
Kidney Diseases .... *Churchill* .. 8
Kind Words Annual .... *S. S. Union.* 5
—— Words Awaken Kind Echoes *Nelson* 13
King Arthur, Furnival .... *Macmillan* .. 12
—— Arthur, Legends of .... *Isbister* 24
—— of the Earth, Kingsley .... *Macmillan*.. 18
—— of Topsy Turvy .... *Tinsley Bros.* 8
King's College Chapel, History, *Macmillan*.. 6
—— Highway (The) .... *Nisbet* 28
—— Own Borderers, Records of.. *Chapman* .. 23
—— Study Bk. of Mediæval Arch. *Sotheran&Co* 17
Kings of England .... *Mozley* 14
Kings of Israel and Judah ...... *Hatchard* .. 13
—— and Prophets of Judah..... *Masters* 13
—— and Queens of Eng., Chart of C. *Smith*.... 10
—— and Queens, Tales of ...... *Burns* 3
—— and Queens, Tales of ...... *Routledge* .. 21
Kingdom of God, Constable .... *Kellaway* .. 9
Kingsley (Rev. C.) Works by ... *Macmillan* .. 18
—— (Canon) Works by .... *Isbister* 23
—— (Henry) Works by .... *Macmillan* .. 19
Kingston (W. H. G.) Works .... *Nelson* 6
—— Juvenile Books by......... *Routledge* .. 4
—— Tales for Boys .... *Isbister* 24
Kinloch (Lord) Works by...... *Edmonston* .. 13
Kinsale Tracts (The) .... *Nisbet* 10
Kirstin's Adventures .... *Bell* 25
Kiss (A) for a Blow .... *Partridge* .. 10
Kitto's Cyclop. of Bib. Lit. .... *Black* 13
Knight of Intercession .... *Rivingtons* .. 27
Knight (Charles) Works by..... *Routledge* .. 4
—— Animated Nature .... *Sangster* 6
—— Half Hours .... *Warne* 4
—— Pictorial London .... *Sotheran* .. 16
—— Popular History of England *Sotheran* .. 17
—— Popular History of England *Sangster* .. 3
Knight's Ransom .... *Warne* 19
Knights of St. John .... *Burns* 27
Knightage, The Shilling ...... *Hardwicke* .. 13
Knots, The Book of .... *Hardwicke* .. 7
Knowing & Known, New Theory of *Black* 10
—— Ones at Home............ *Chatto* 21
Knowledge, Five Gateways of .. *Macmillan* .. 41
—— (General) .... *Soc. P. C. K.* 10
—— (General) Mitchell ...... *Whittaker* .. 14
—— and Love Compared ...... *Cornish* 3
—— Oral Training Lessons in.. *Hardwicke* .. 12
—— is Power .... *Bohn's Lib.* 19
—— (Pursuit of) Craik .... *Bohn's Lib.*.. 19
—— Scraps of .... *Cassell* 10
—— Threads of .... *Cassell* 10
—— Treasury of.............. *Longmans* .. 43
—— Useful, Blair .... *Whittaker* .. 14
Knowles (J. S.) Dramatic Works *Routledge* .. 61
Knox (John) Works, by Laing .. *Stevenson* .. a
—— Life .... *W. Blackw'd* 19
—— and His Times .... *Nisbet* 20
—— (Days of) .... *Nelson* 8
—— (Robert) Life and Writings.. *Macmillan* .. 19
Kollock's Sermons .... *Dickinson* .. 8
Koran, Arabic-Eng. Dict. of the *King*...... 7
—— (The) Arabic Text........ *Trubner* .. 17
Korner (Theodore) Biography of *Cassell* 6
Krause (Rev. W. H.) 19 Discourses *Nisbet* .. 20
Krilof and His Fables .... *Isbister* 24
Kruuuuacher, an Autobiography *Clark* 21

Kugler's Hand-Books .... *Murray* 13

Labour Applied to Production .. *Virtue* 22
—— Heads and Hands in World *Isbister* 7
—— Stands on Golden Feet .... *Cassell* 11
—— (On) Thornton .... *Macmillan* .. 36
—— and Wait .... *Houlston* .. 17
Labourers' Cottages, Examples of *Stanford* 50
—— Cottages, Plans for ...... *Hatchard* .. 12
Lacordaire's Life, Grenwell.... *Edmonston* .. 11
Lacroix (Alp. F.) Memorials of .. *Nisbet* 20
—— (Paul) Arts of Middle Ages *Sotheran* .. 19
—— (Paul) Middle Ages ...... *Chapman* .. 20
Ladakh, by Cunningham ...... *Allen* 5
Ladies, Lectures, Pract. Subjects *Macmillan* .. 20
—— in Parliament .... *Bell* 37
Lady Audley's Secret .... *Ward & Lock* 16
—— Betty .... *Warne* 19
—— Caroline .... *Smith & El.* 3
—— of La Garaye .... *Macmillan* .. 27
—— of Last Century .... *Bentley* 6
—— of Latham .... *Smith & El.* 12
—— of the Manor .... *Houlston* .. 38
—— of Provence .... *Nelson* 9
Ladye Shakerley .... *Hurst & B.* 9
Lady's Guide to Household .... *Smith & El.* 12
—— Own Book .... *MacPhun* .. 10
—— (Young) Elegant Recreations *Bohn's Lib.*. 15
Lahore to Yarkland .... *Reeve* 13
Lake Country, Linton .... *Smith & El.* 14
—— District, English Guide to .. *Stanford* .. 56
—— Scenery .... *Allman* 10
—— Victoria .... *W. Blackw'd* 31
Lakes (English) Guide to...... *Black* 5
Lalla Rookh, Illustrated ...... *Longmans* .. 40
Lamartine, Life .... *Bentley* 9
—— Works by .... *Bohn's Lib.*. 8
Lamb (Charles) by Talfourd .. *Bell* 34
—— Tales from Shakespeare .. *J. Blackwood* 10
—— (M. & C.) Poems .... *Chatto* 22
Lambeth Library, MSS. in .... *Pickering* .. 3
Lamplighter (The) .... *Routledge* .. 35
Lamps of the Temple .... *Snow* 8
Lancashire Dialect .... *A. Heywood.* 8
—— Folk, Song and Speech of .. *Tubbs* 6
—— History, Baines .... *Routledge* .. 22
—— Life, Sketches of .... *A. Heywood* 6
—— Puritanism & Nonconformity *Tubbs* 3
—— Songs and Poems .... *Bell* 37
—— Sunday School Songs ..... *Tubbs* 7
—— Worthies .... *A. Heywood* 7
—— Sixty Years Ago .... *Smith & El.* 19
Lancaster (Wm.) Poems by ... *Macmillan* .. 19
—— Portfolio .... *Routledge* .. 22
Land Culture .... *W. Blackw'd* 33
—— and the Book .... *Nelson* 5
—— of Ham, Millington ...... *Murray* 22
—— and Houses.............. *Wilson* 11
—— of Israel, Tristram........ *So. P. C. K.* 15
—— Laws, Lectures on........ *King* 10
—— Measurer's Reckoner ..... *Whittaker* .. 15
—— of Moab .... *Murray* 32
—— of the Nile .... *Nelson* 11
—— Question, Eng. and Scotland *Macmillan*.. 23
—— and Sea .... *Nisbet* 15
—— Valuer's Assistant .... *Lockwood* .. 10
Land of Charity (The) .... *Snow*...... 10
Landed Gentry, Burke .... *Harrison* .. 1
Landels (Rev. Wm.) Works by .. *Nisbet* 20
—— Women of Scripture ..... *Shaw* 3
Landor (Walter Savage), a Biog. *Chapman* .. 20
Lands of the Bible, Wilson .... *Stewart* .. a
Landseer Gallery and Memoir .. *Bell* 5
—— (Sir E.) Pictures.......... *Virtue* 3
Lange's Commentaries .... *Clark* 9
Language, Farrar .... *Longmans* .. 12
—— of Flowers .... *Houlston* .. 14
—— of Flowers .... *Nicholson* .. 9
—— of Flowers .... *Warne* 3
—— of Flowers, Tyas .... *Routledge* .. 28
—— and Sentiment of Flowers .. *Warne* 20
—— (Foreign) Mastery of .... *Longmans* .. 14
—— Formation, &c., Prim. Laws *Allen* 1
—— and Literature .... *Chambers* .. 7
—— (Origin of) .... *Murray* 11

Language (Origin of), Wedgwood *Trubner* 31
—— Science of .... *Longmans* .. 12
—— and Study of Language .... *Trubner* .. 32
Languages, Modern .... *Rivingtons.* 18
—— (Modern) on the Study of .. *Trubner* .. 3
Lankester (Dr.) Works by .... *Hardwicke.* 15
La Parodie chez les Grecs ...... *Trubner* .. 10
Lapland, Notes of a Journey to.. *Chapman* .. 25
—— for Summer Tourists ...... *Chapman* .. 19
La Plata, Brazil during the War.. *Stanford* .. 57
Lardner (Dr.) Works by ...... *Lockwood* .. 13
Larousse (P.) French Ed. Works *Nutt* 25
Laryngoscope, Gibbon .... *Churchill* .. 17
Las Casas, Life of, Helps........ *Bell* 39
Last Adam (The) .... *Kellaway* .. 7
—— Blessing (The) .... *Morgan* 3
—— Chronicle of Barset ...... *Smith & El.* 25
—— Days of Jerusalem .... *Hatchard* .. 8
Latham (Dr. R. G.) Essays by .. *Williams* .. 8
Lathe (The) and its Uses ...... *Trubner* .. 18
Latimer, Life of .... *Rel. Tr. Soc.* 6
Latin Class Books .... *Bell* 10
—— Classics, Lat. Trans. ...... *Hall* 4
—— Course, Vulgate .... *J. Heywood* 5
—— Dictionaries .... *Longmans* .. 13
—— Dictionary .... *Cassell* 14
—— Dictionary .... *Lockwood* .. 31
—— Dictionaries, Smith ...... *Murray* 28
—— Dictionary, Vine .... *Routledge* .. 14
—— Dictionary, Yonge .... *Bentley* 15
—— Educational Works ...... *Parker* 59
—— Educational Works ...... *Whittaker* .. 2
—— Educational Wks., Dr. Smith *Murray* 29
—— Elementary Course .... *J. Heywood* 30
—— Elementary Course .... *Mozley* 8
—— Grammar, Ahn's Course .. *Trubner* .. 2
—— Grammar, Ihne .... *Trubner* .. 16
—— Grammar, Elem., Allen .. *Clar. Press.* 19
—— Grammar, Help to .... *Macmillan* .. 42
—— Grammar, H. Key .... *Bell* 9
—— and Greek Accidence ...... *Hall* 3
—— and Greek Classics, Teubner *Nutt* 17
—— Hymns .... *Macmillan* .. 17
—— Hymns, Trans. .... *Masters* 5
—— Ladder to, Thompson .. *Williams* .. 15
—— Language .... *Rivingtons* .. 19
—— Language, Roby .... *Macmillan* .. 31
—— Lexion, Scheller .... *Clar. Press.* 2
—— Lexicon, Eng.-Lat. .... *Rivingtons* .. 17
—— (Choice) Poetry .... *Bell* 22
—— Sacred Poetry, Trench .... *Macmillan* .. 38
—— School Books .... *MacGlashan* 9
—— Series .... *Chambers* .. 18
—— Steps, Wright .... *Macmillan* .. 43
—— Synonymes .... *Rivingtons* .. 20
—— Syntax, Ihne .... *Williams* .. 43
—— Test. and Common Prayer .. *Bagster* 15
Laud (Archbishop) Life of .... *Masters* 5
Lauda Syon .... *Masters* 5
Laura and Lucy .... *Warne* 27
Laurel Leaves .... *Houlston* .. 16
Lavengro and Sequel........ *Murray* 4
Law .... *Clar. Press.* 26
—— (Ancient) Maine .... *Murray* 21
—— Book .... *Ward & Lock* 5
—— Books, List of.......... *Stevens* 0
—— (Domestic) .... *Longmans* .. 45
—— Elements of .... *Clar. Press.* 26
—— English & Scotch, Paterson *Black* 15
—— Institutes of, Lorimer .... *Clark* 10
—— of the Love of God ...... *Nutt* 5
—— Manuals .... *A. Heywood* .. 1
—— Science of, Amos ...... *King* 8
—— of Storms .... *Smith & El.* 5
—— Twelve True Tales of .... *Wilson* 5
Law (Jean) Works by .... *Nisbet* 21
Lawrence Bloomfield in Ireland.. *Macmillan* .. 2
Lawrence's (Sir Henry) Life .. *Smith & El.* 12
Laws Affecting Medical Men.... *Churchill* .. 13
—— of Church and Clergy ...... *Hall* 4
—— (The) of the Kingdom, Dykes *Nisbet* .. 13
—— The Spirit of .... *Stevens* 2
—— of War, Commerce & Ship. *Smith & El.* 25
Lawyer, Cabinet.......... *Longmans* .. 45
Lays, Lytton.......... *Murray* 20

Lays of Ancient Rome........ *Longmans* .. 40
—— of Deer Forest .... *W. Blackw'd* 57
—— of the English Cavaliers .. *Parker* 65
—— of the Holy Land ...... *Nisbet* 21
—— of the Kirk & Covenant .. *Nisbet* 33
—— of the Pious Minstrels .. *Houlston* .. 16
Leach (John) Works Illustrated by *Bradbury* .. 2
Lead Ore in Swaledale, Yorkshire *Stanford* .. 57
—— in Water (Poison of)...... *Churchill* .. 13
Leaflets .... *Masters* 41
Leaflets .... *Morgan* 2
Leaflets .... *Washbourne* 11
—— and Handbills .... *S. S. Union.* 10
—— and Postscripts .... *Rel. Tr. Soc.* 32
Learning and Science, Essays .. *Smith & El.* 27
—— and Working .... *Macmillan* .. 25
Lear's Books of Nonsense ...... *Warne* 36
Leathe's Popular Essays ...... *Hodder* 7
—— (S.) Truth and Life ...... *Hatchard* .. 11
Leaves of Grass .... *Chatto* 21
—— from Our Life in Highlands.. *Smith & El.* 11
Le Bahn's German School Books *Lockwood* .. 35
Lecky (W. E. H.) Works by .... *Longmans* .. 27
L'Eco Italiano .... *Trubner* .. 7
Lectionary, Companion to the.. *Macmillan* .. 42
Lectures on Great Men .... *Nisbet* 25
—— to Young Men .... *Collins* 3
—— to Young Men .... *Hodder* 6
—— to Young Men .... *Nisbet* 12
Lexicon, Vest Pocket, English .. *Trubner* .. 17
Lexicons and Grammars ...... *Clar. Press.* 3
Lee (Dr.) Exercise and Training .. *Smith & El.* 12
—— (H.) Fairy Tales .... *Warne* 22
—— (H.) Fairy Tales .... *Warne* 22
—— (Holme) Works of ...... *Smith & El.* 11
Leeds Castle, Kent.......... *Sotheran* .. 56
Legal Anecdotes .... *Routledge* .. 4
—— Forms for Common Use .. *Wilson* 5
—— Handy Books .... *Wilson* 5
—— Hand Books .... *Ward & Lock* 7
Legacy and Succession Duties .. *Waterlow* .. 12
Legend of the Mount........ *Wilson* 7
—— of Number Nip .... *Macmillan* .. 20
—— of Saint Ursula .... *Sotheran* .. 11
Legends of Saints and Martyrs .. *Longmans* .. 20
—— of Testament Characters... *Macmillan* .. 2
Legendary Ballads of Eng. & Scot. *Warne* 18
Legislation, Theory of .... *Trubner* .. 5
Leicester, Church of Saint Martin *Bell* 11
Leigh (Rev. S.) Life .... *Wesleyan* .. 46
Leila, or the Island.......... *Hatchard* .. 8
Leisure Hour (The) .... *Rel. Tr. Soc.* 40
Leisure Hour Library ...... *Rel. Tr. Soc.* 12
Leland (C. G.) Works by ...... *Trubner* .. 18
Lemon (Mark) Works by ...... *Bradbury* .. 4
Le Morte D'Arthur .... *Macmillan* .. 12
Lempriere's Classical Dictionary .. *Milner* 3
Lennox's Recollections, 1806-1873 *Hurst & B..* 5
Lent & Easter Sermons, Vaughan *Macmillan* .. 33
—— Guide for Passing Holily .. *Parker* 30
—— Lectures, Carter.......... *Masters* 4
—— Lectures, Edmunds ...... *Hatchard* .. 8
—— Lectures, Reeve .... *Nisbet* 31
—— Legends .... *Masters* 13
—— Passion Week) Sermons.. *Nisbet* 29
—— Readings for, Sewell...... *Longmans* .. 5
—— Sermons .... *Bell* 3
—— Sermons, Cambridge .... *Macmillan* .. 2
—— Sermons, Jackson ...... *Rivingtons* .. 15
—— Sermons, Roswell ...... *Macmillan* .. 1
—— Warnings of Holy Week.. *Rivingtons* .. 11
Lenten Thoughts.......... *Washbourne* 3
Leonards (The) .... *Warne* 22
Leonora Christina of Denmark .. *King* 2
Le Page's (French Ed.) Course .. *Isbister* 25
Leper of Aosta (The).......... *Williams* .. 9
Les Faux Bonshommes, a Comedy *Trubner* .. 5
Leslie's Pictures .... *Virtue* 62
Lessing's Works, in German .. *Nutt* 17
Lessons from the Great Biography *Nisbet* 17
—— from Great Lives .... *Nelson* 22
—— of Life and Godliness .... *Macmillan* .. 31
Letters from Abroad .... *Isbister* 4
—— for Little Folks .... *Mozley* 8
—— to the Young .... *Rel. Tr. Soc.* 12

Letter Writer .... *Ward & Lock* 9
—— Writer, Commercial .... *Murby* 6
—— Writer, Cooke .... *Milner* 2
—— Writer, Cooke .... *Nicholson* 1
—— Writer, English Com. ..... *Williams* 16
—— Writer, English-German ... *Nutt* 19
—— Writer, French and English *Trubner* 2
—— Writer, French-English Com. *Williams* 16
—— Writer, German and English *Trubner* 1
—— Writer, Mercantile .... *Trubner* 2
—— Writer, Schoolboy's ...... *Stanford* 68
—— Writers .... *Marr* 13
—— Writers .... *Warne* 43
—— Writers .... *Mozley* 6
—— Writers .... *Routledge* 43
—— Writers, Eng. & Fr. Com... *Nutt* 14
—— Writers, Foreign and Eng.. *Asher* 2
—— Writers, Ger.-Eng. Com.... *Williams* 16
—— Writers, Half-hours with Best *Routledge* 4
—— Writing, Beard .... *A. Heywood* 17
—— Writing, Hints on .... *Houlston* 7
Lettice Lisle .... *Smith & El.* 13
Letts's Diaries .... *Letts* 3
Levana, by Richter .... *Trubner* 25
Levant, Monasteries of ..... *Murray* 9
Levelling, Simm's Treatise on *Lockwood* 3
Lever's (Charles) Works .... *Chapman* 29
Levi (L.) History of B. Commerce *Murray* 20
—— (L.) Works of .... *Smith & El.* 13
Leviticus, Law of Offerings in *Nisbet* 20
Lewes (G. H.) Works of ..... *Smith & El.* 13
Lewis (W. H.) Sermons ...... *Dickinson* 8
Liberty, Mill .... *Longmans* 10
—— Equality, Fraternity .... *Smith & El.* 21
Library of Anglo-Cath. Theology *Parker* 16
—— Catalogue .... *Letts* 2
—— of Excellent Literature.. *J. Blackwood* 18
—— of the Fathers .... *Parker* 14
—— of Old Authors .... *J. R. Smith* 13
—— Registers .... *Soc. P.C.K.* 15
—— for Young People .... *Chambers* 32
Libraries, Memoirs of ...... *Trubner* 11
Libri Enoch, Versio Æthiopica *Parker* 9
Libyan Desert .... *Murray* 30
Licensed Victualler's Handy Book *Routledge* 43
Lichens, British .... *Routledge* 48
Lichfield Cathedral .... *Bemrose* 17
Liddell and Scott's Greek Lexicon *Longmans* 14
—— Lexicon .... *Clar. Press.* 2
Liddon (Canon) Works by .... *Rivingtons* 0
Life Assurance, Annals, &c.. *Layton* 9
—— Law, Bunyon .... *Layton* 8
—— Medical Adviser in ..... *Churchill* 33
—— Mortality Experience ... *Layton* 2
—— Tables .... *Layton* 2
—— Table, Farr .... *Harrison* 13
—— and Accident Insur. Reports *Stevens* 22
Life a Book for Young Men .. *Isbister* 16
—— in Danebury .... *Routledge* 2
—— and Death, Medical Lectures *Smith & El.* 19
—— Divine Wisdom in Form, &c. *Nisbet* 15
—— Doubled by Econ. of Time. *Houlston* 5
—— Drama (A), Smith .... *Macmillan* 33
—— of Justification .... *Rivingtons* 13
—— in the Light of God's Word *Murray* 31
—— (The) and Light of Men .. *Isbister* 48
—— on the Line, Ballantyne.. *Nisbet* 4
—— Lost or Saved .... *Hatchard* 7
—— of Man Symbolised ...... *Longmans* 28
—— of our Life, Coleridge .. *Burns* 14
—— Père Lacordaire .... *King* 28
—— (Prolonging) after Mid. Age *King* 33
—— in a Risen Saviour ..... *Black* 10
—— Science, Thoughts on ... *Macmillan* 36
—— Thoughts, Beecher ...... *Collins* 3
—— Thoughts .... *Isbister* 6
—— Work, by L. N. R. ...... *Nisbet* 21
—— in the World .... *Rivingtons* 14
Life's Assize .... *Tinsley Bros.* 10
Life's a Dream, Calderon ... *Macmillan* 38
—— Search (A) .... *Masters* 27
—— Voyage .... *Warne* 27
—— True Beatitude .... *Wesleyan* 43
—— Work and God's Discipline. *Macmillan* 39
—— Work, in Preparation, &c. *Macmillan* 17

Lifeboat (The), A Tale of, &c.... *Nisbet* 4
—— Work on Goodwin Sands.... *Macmillan* 13
Lifted Up, Douglas .... *Morgan* 5
Light from Calvary......... *Nisbet* 19
—— from the Cross......... *Clark* 20
—— for the Dark Alleys .... *Nisbet* 21
—— in the Dwelling .... *Hatchard* 13
—— at Eventide .... *Hatchard* 13
—— at Evening Time....... *Nelson* 5
—— in the Grave .... *Nimmo* 16
—— Lectures on .... *Longmans* 22
—— and Life in Christ .... *Nisbet* 37
—— in Life's Shadows .... *Haddon* 6
—— Polarized .... *Spon* 27
—— to the Path .... *Nisbet* 16
—— and Truth, Bonar ..... *Nisbet* 6
—— Wave Theory .... *Longmans* 22
—— (The) of the World, Wilkins.. *Macmillan* 41
Lights through a Lattice ... *Isbister* 8
Lighted Way .... *J. Blackwood* 24
Lightfoot (Rev. Dr.) Works by . *Macmillan* 20
Lighthouse Illumination .... *Black* 31
—— (The), or Man and the Sea.. *Nisbet* 4
Lighthouses, Stevenson on .. *Black* 31
—— and Lightships .... *Nelson* 11
Lilias Lee .... *W. Blackw'd* 8
Lilies of the Valley, &c. .. *Nisbet* 21
Lilla's Relations .... *Mozley* 6
Lilliput Levee .... *Isbister* 26
Lily among Thorns .... *S. S. Union* 10
—— (The), An Icelandic Poem . *Williams* 8
—— Gordon .... *Warne* 27
—— Series .... *Ward & Lock* 29
Limes and Cements .... *Trubner* 3
Limits of Exact Science, &c.. *Macmillan* 19
—— of Religious Thought ... *Murray* 21
Lincoln's Inn, Account of .. *Pickering* 36
Lindsay's Lives of the Lindsays *Murray* 2
Linen Yarn Trade's Reckoner. *Wilson* 8
Linguist, Boileau's German . *Nutt* 11
—— (Modern) Bartel .... *Nutt* 11
—— (Practical) Nasmith ... *Nutt* 18
Linguistic Essays, Garnett . *Williams* 6
Link Motion .... *Spon* 28
—— and the Rivet .... *Nisbet* 21
Linnet's Trial .... *Isbister* 40
Linton (Rev. H. P.) Works by . *Bagster* 78
Lion and the Elephant .... *Hurst & B.* 5
—— of War .... *J. Blackwood* 8
Liquidation by Arrangement . *Waterlow* 2
Lisle (Anna) Works by ..... *Groombridge* 2
Lismore, Dean of, Gaelic Poetry *Edmonston* 2
Lispings from Low Latitudes . *Murray* 20
Listener (The), Fry .... *Nisbet* 13
Litanies .... *Masters* 15
Literary Bouquet .... *Nimmo* 11
—— Characters, Gallery of .. *Chatto* 6
—— and Scientific Class Book . *Whittaker* 10
—— Scraps .... *Chatto* 22
—— and Social Judgments ... *Trubner* 14
Literature of American Abor. Lan. *Trubner* 18
—— Chaucer to Wordsworth .. *Murby* 3
—— Curiosities of .... *Routledge* 43
—— Cyclopædia of English... *Chambers* 89
—— Dictionary of English .. *Trubner* 2
—— and Dogma .... *Smith & El.* 1
—— English .... *W. Blackw'd* 44
—— English .... *Tinsley Bros.* 2
—— (English) Compendium ... *Laurie* 1
—— English, Dr. Smith .... *Murray* 29
—— English, Morley ...... *Cassell* 3
—— (English) Pictures from. *Cassell* 6
—— English, Yonge .... *Longmans* 12
—— Gems of .... *Nimmo* 10
—— Modern .... *Warne* 10
—— Morley's English ..... *Chapman* 22
—— Poetical .... *W. Blackw'd* 21
—— Roman Classical....... *Bentley* 2
—— Schlegel .... *W. Blackw'd* 27
—— Specimens of English .. *Murray* 2
Littéraire des Fous .... *Trubner* 9
Little Alice's Library ..... *Nelson* 22
—— Breeches .... *Chatto* 22
—— Buttercup and Jenny Wren *Morgan* 3
—— Castle Maiden .... *Warne* 38

Little Camp on Eagle Hill ...... Nisbet 20
—— Crowns, & How to Win Them Nisbet 10
—— Elsie's Summer at Malvern.. Nisbet 9
—— Flower Seekers .... M. Ward 6
—— Folk's Library .... Warne 22
—— Foxes, Stowe .... Bell 26
—— Gems Series .... Cassell .. 5
—— Ladders to Learning...... Routledge .. 15
—— Lays for Little Folk ...... Routledge .. 26
—— Library .... Rel. Tr. Soc. 32
Little Lou's Sayings and Doings.. Nisbet 22
—— Lucy's Wonderful Globe.... Macmillan.. 20
—— Maggie .... Nisbet 8
—— Mr. Bouncer .... J. Blackwood 23
—— Ones in the Fold .... Morgan 5
—— People, and other Tales .... Chapman .. 23
—— Sanctuary (The) .... Isbister 37
—— Songs for Me to Sing ...... Cassell 9
—— Lucy's Six Birthdays ...... Nelson 20
— — Susy's Six Birthdays ...... Nisbet 22
—— Threads .... Nisbet 22
—— While, and other Poems .... Tubbs 4
—— Women .... Routledge 20
—— Women .... Ward & Lock 28
Liturgia Domestica .... Parker 32
—— Domestica .... Nisbet 22
Liturgies .... Masters 15
Liturgy Compared with Bible.. Soc. P. C. K. 3
—— How Shall we Conform to the Murray 26
Liturgy, Knox (John) .... W. Blackw'd 39
—— Trollope .... Hall 4
—— and Worship, Discourses on Macmillan .. 38
Lives of the Saints............ Sotheran .. 19
—— made Sublime .... Nelson 10
Liver, Diseases of .... Churchill .. 18
—— Diseases of .... Longmans .. 27
—— On Some Affections of .... Churchill .. 22
Liverpool, Account of .... J. R. Smith 6
Living Epistle (A) .... J F. Shaw.. 3
— — Voices .... Isbister 20
Livingstone, Life and Labours .. Hodder 28
—— Africa .... Murray 20
—— Life and Adventures........ J. Blackwood 11
L'lanely Reefs .... Smith & El. 14
Local Government Forms...... Knight 2
—— Government and Taxation.. Bush 2
—— Legends............ Masters 15
Locke on the Understanding.... Bell 34
Locke's Philosophical Works .... Bohn's Lib.. 8
—— Theology .... Wesleyan .. 46
Lockhart's Scott and Abbotsford.. Virtue 29
Lockyer (J. Norman) Works by.. Macmillan.. 20
Lodge's Portraits............ Bohn's Lib.. 13
Log of the Fortuna............ Cassell 4
—— of the Water Lily .... Chatto 23
Logarithmic Tables, Vega...... Williams .. 15
Logarithms (Anti-)............ Bell 22
—— and Anti-Logarithms.... Layton 9
—— Babbage .... Spon 42
—— Elementary .... Laurie 2
—— Hannyngton............ Layton 6
—— New Manual, Bruhns ...... Williams .. 3
—— Sang .... Layton 13
—— Schron .... Williams .. 13
—— Shortrede .... Layton 15
Logic .... Parker...... 60
Logic .... Rivingtons.. 23
—— Mill .... Longmans .. 10
—— New System of .... Hatchard .. 4
—— Ueberweg's System .... Longmans .. 16
—— Whately .... Longmans .. 11
—— Compendium of .... MacGlashan 5
—— Elementary Lessons, Jevons Macmillan.. 17
—— Elements, Fowler .... Clar. Press.. 24
—— Manual of, Turrell .... Rivingtons .. 24
—— Outline of............ Rivingtons .. 23
—— (For: Royal) .... W. Blackw'd 24
Lombard Street .... King...... 31
London Arbitrageur, Haupt.... Trübner 15
—— Byeways .... Hodder 3
—— and Calcutta Compared .. Nisbet 27
—— Characters .... Chatto 24
—— Charities, Fry............ Hardwicke.. 13
—— Churches, Guide to .... Mozley...... 6
—— Churches, Map of .... Masters 26

London Clubs and Club Life .... Chatto 38
—— Court of, 1819 to 1825, Rush.. Bentley .. 4
—— (Dens of), Vanderkiste.... Nisbet 35
—— Directory (Little), 1677 .... Chatto 22
—— and Environs, Maps ...... C. Smith.. 8
—— Fire Engine Establishment.. Wilson 8
—— Flora .... Smith & El. 8
—— Geology of .... Stanford .. 71
—— Guide to .... Routledge .. 44
—— Heterodox .... Tinsley Bros. 3
—— Library .... J. Blackwood 39
—— Life .... Chatto 22
—— Life, Finish to .... Chatto 15
—— Lyrics .... Isbister 20
—— Mediæval, Riley .... Trübner 26
—— Medical Record, 1873 ...... Smith & El. 14
—— Merchants .... Virtue 14
—— Missions Soc., Fruits of Toil Snow 6
—— Multum in Parvo Guide .. Stanford .. 53
—— Night Side of .... Tinsley Bros. 9
—— and North-Western Railway Murray 14
—— Old and New .... Cassell 5
—— (Old), by various Authors.. Murray 24
—— Orthodox .... Tinsley Bros. 3
—— Parish, Tales of a .... Masters 2
—— Picture Story Book of .... Jarrold 12
—— Parks, Larwood .... Chatto 34
—— Play-Hours in .... Mozley...... 9
—— Poems .... Isbister 8
—— People .... Smith & El. 3
—— Rambler, Works by ...... Hodder 3
—— Ratepayers .... Isbister 11
—— Religious Life in.......... Tinsley Bros. 8
—— Shilling Handy Book of .. Hartwicke.. 14
—— Streets, Romance of ...... Hodder 3
—— The Town .... Smith & El. 11
—— Tower of .... Murray 10
—— Unorthodox .... Tinsley Bros. 3
—— (West) Life .... Chatto 20
—— Works on .... J. R. Smith 14
Londoner's Walk to Land's End.. Chapman.. 26
Long, Long Ago, &c........... Mozley 6
—— Evenings and Work to do, &c. Nisbet 5
Longevity, Secret of Long Life . King 33
—— Gardner .... King 33
—— Hufeland .... Churchill .. 21
—— of Man .... Murray 31
—— in Man and Lower Animals.. Macmillan.. 19
—— A Short Tractate, Rask .. Trübner 25
Longfellow's Evangeline ...... Bell 29
—— Poems, Illustrated.......... Bell 9
—— Poetical Works .... J. Blackwood 6
—— Poetical Works .... Warne 18
—— Prose Works .... Chatto 23
—— Works .... Bohn's Lib.. 13
—— Works .... Routledge .. 44
Longman's History of England .. Longmans .. 2
Lonsdale's (Bishop) Life ...... Isbister 13
—— Life .... Murray 21
Looking Unto Jesus .... Nisbet 31
Lord's Prayer .... Parker...... 11
—— Prayer (The) .... Macmillan.. 25
—— Prayer (Anderson on the).. Mozley...... 1
—— Prayer, Denton .... Rivingtons .. 5
—— Prayer, Exposition of .... Smith & El. 14
—— Prayer, Familiarly Explained Nisbet 38
—— Prayer, Griffith .... Hatchard .. 10
—— Prayer, Lectures on .... Nisbet 33
—— Prayer, Stories Illustrative of Morgan 5
—— Prayer, Stories Illustrative of Nisbet 28
—— Prayer, Thoughts on........ Collins 3
—— Supper .... Parker 24
—— Supper .... Parker...... 40
—— Supper .... Wesleyan .. 18
—— Supper from a Layman's, &c. Williams .. 3
—— Supper, Wilson .... Mozley...... 13
Lord (The) our Shepherd ...... Bagster 71
— — (Our) Sayings Ascribed to .. Parker...... 10
Loss and Value .... C. S. Union 2
Loss and Gain .... Burns 25
Lost Beauties of Eng. Language Chatto 23
—— Brooch (The) .... Mozley...... 6
—— Gip .... King 16
—— Heir (The) .... Warne 29
—— Tales of Miletus............ Murray 22

Lottie Lonsdale .... Isbister 48
London's Encyclopædias .... Longmans .. o
—— Encyclopædias .... Warne 10
Lough Corrib, its Shores, &c. ... MacGlashan 4
Louie Atterbury .... Warne 23
Louisa, or, the Bride .... Mozley 6
—— Queen of Prussia.......... Isbister 21
Louise, Madame, Life of .... Rivingtons. . 26
Love Fulfilling the Law.......... Nisbet 22
—— and Life in Norway .... Cassell 11
Lover (Samuel) Life, &c. .... King 1
—— Lyrics of Ireland .... Houlston 16
Lover's Language of Flowers .... Nicholson .. 9
Loving Work for Christ.......... Wesleyan ... 44
Lowell (James R.) Works by .... Macmillan .. 20
Lowencester, a Tale .... Nisbet 22
Lower (M. A.) Works .... J. R. Smith. 14
Lubke on Art .... Smith & El. 14
Luchmee and Dilloo .... King 32
Lawian, Selections from .... Rivingtons. 23
Luck of Roaring Camp.......... Routledge ... 2
Lucknow, Defence of .... Smith & El. 5
—— Lady's Diary of Siege...... Murray 21
Lucy, or, the Housemaid .... Mozley 6
Lucy West .... Warne 27
Lumbago, Lawson on .... Hardwicke .. 16
Luna, A Mere Love Story ...... Smith & El. 13
Lunacy (Handbook) Law........ Churchill ... 31
—— Manual of, Winslow........ Smith & El. 27
Lunar and Horary Tables ...... Allen 26
—— Theory .... Macmillan .. 13
Lungs, Anatomy of the.......... Churchill ... 0
—— Diseases of .... Churchill ... 16
—— Diseases of, Walsh .... Smith & El. 26
—— and Heart, Diseases of .... Hardwicke .. 16
Lushai Expedition, 1871-72 ...... Hurst & B. 9
Luther's Life, Michelet.......... Bohn's Lib. 8
Luttrell's Diary, State Affairs.... Clar. Press. 16
Lyell (Sir Charles) Works by .... Murray 21
Lynch (Rev. T. T.) Works by .... Isbister 27
Lyon (Mary), a Noble Woman ... Morgan 2
Lyra Americana .... Rel. Tr. Soc. 12
—— Anglicana .... Houlston 16
—— Apostolica .... Mozley 6
—— Apostolica .... Rivingtons . 7
—— Christiana .... Houlston ... 36
—— Consolationis .... Nisbet 6
—— Devoniensis .... Macmillan .. 41
—— Germanica, Illustrated...... Longmans .. 29
—— Innocentium .... Parker 20
—— Sanctorum .... Masters 15
Lyre of David .... Whittaker .. 15
Lyric Gems of Scotland .... Cameron... o
Lyrical Poems .... Edmonston.. 3
—— Poems, Palgrave .... Macmillan .. 28
Lyrics of Ancient Palestine...... Rel. Tr. Soc. 12
—— from a Country Lane ...... J. Heywood. 44
—— of Ireland .... Houlston ... 16
—— Legal and Miscellaneous ... W. Blackw'd 24
—— of a Lifetime .... Chapman ... 25
—— of Love, Adams .... King 20
Lytes' Poems .... Rivingtons.. 7
Lyth (Mrs. Mary) Memoirs of .. Wesleyan ... 46
Lyttelton (Lord) Works by ...... Macmillan .. 21
Lytton (Lord) Works .... W. Blackw'd 19
—— Works by .... Murray 21
—— Dramatic Works .... Routledge .. 62
—— (Hon. Rob.) Works by...... Chapman ... 29

Macaulay's (Lord) Biographies .. Black 14
—— Public Life .... Tinsley Bros. 9
—— Reviews and Essays .... Ward & Lock 11
—— Works by .... Longmans .. o
Macdonald (G.) Novels by .... Hurst & B. 16
—— Works by .... Isbister 27
Macduff (Rev. J. R.) Works by .. Nisbet 23
Macfarlane (Rev. J.) Works by .. Nisbet 25
Machine Design .... Longmans .. 21
—— Details, Coloured Diagrams of Chapman .. 31
Machines, Wood-Working ...... Spon 48
Macintosh (Miss) Juvenile Tales.. Routledge .. 36
Mackay's (Dr. C.) Hist. of U. S. Virtue...... 20
Mackay (R. W.) Works by ...... Williams .. 9
Mackenzie's Travels in Turkey .. Isbister 29
Mackonsie Bishop) Life of ...... —— 40

Mackintosh (C. C.) Memorials.... Edmonston.. 15
Maclaren (Alex.) Sermons........ Macmillan .. 22
Maclaren's (C.) Select Writings .. Edmonston.. 15
Maclear (Rev. G. F.) Works by .. Macmillan .. 22
Macleod (Norman) Works by .... Isbister 29
Maclise's Gallery .... Chatto 2
—— Pictures.................. Virtue 10
Macmillan (Rev. Hugh) Works by Macmillan .. 21
Macerocana Andra .... Trubner 9
Macpherson's Services in India .. Murray 21
Macqood's Novels .... Smith & El. 14
Macrae (D.) Works of .... Marr 16
Maetzner's English Grammar.... Murray 21
Madagascar, Ellis .... Murray 11
—— Martyr Church of .... Snow....... 5
—— Country Life in .... Snow....... 9
—— its Missions and Martyrs .. Snow 13
—— and its People .... Rel. Tr. Soc. 12
Madam How, and Lady Why.... Isbister 23
Madame Fontenoy .... Mozley 5
—— Therese.................. Ward & Lock 21
Madeira, Climate of .... Churchill .. 15
Madeline, with other Poems .... Chapman ... 19
Madeline's Trials.............. Warne 27
Madness, Medical, Legal, &c. ... Churchill .. 33
Madonna, Legends of the....... Longmans .. 29
Madonna's Child .... W. Blackw'd 19
Madras, Handbook to .... Murray 16
—— Irrigation .... Smith & El. 19
—— Letters from.............. Murray 29
—— Letters from.............. Trubner 4
—— Mission to .... Wesleyan ... 45
Magdala, March to............. Tinsley Bros. 7
Magic, History of .... Bohn's Lib. 18
—— Lantern .... Houlston ... 24
Magician's Own Book .... Chatto 23
Magisterial and Police Guide .... Stevens 2
Magna Charta .... Chatto 23
—— Charta, Reprint .... Clar. Press. 14
Magnet Stories................ Groombridge. 27
Magnetism and Electricity ..... Clar. Press. 25
—— and Electricity .... J. Heywood. 40
—— and Electricity, Guthrie .. Collins 8
—— for Students............. Macmillan .. 22
Magyars (The), Patterson's .... Smith & El. 16
Maha-Vira Charita .... Trubner 19
Mahomet's Life, Muir's .... Smith & El. 16
Mahometanism, Palgrave ..... Macmillan .. 27
Mahratta, Language .... Allen 34
Maid of Sker .... W. Blackw'd 19
Maine's (E. S.) Novels .... Smith & El. 14
Maine (Sir H. S.) Works by ... Murray 21
Majolica Wares, Fortnum..... Chapman ... 18
Major's (Dr.) School Books..... Fellowes ... o
Make Up for Lost Time, Sermons Mozley 5
Malan (Rev. Dr.) Works by..... Nisbet 25
—— (Rev. S. C.) Works by..... Masters 16
—— Works by .... Nutt 5
Malay Archipelago (The) ...... Macmillan .. 32
—— Language .... Allen 34
—— Language .... Smith & El. 14
Malayalam Reader .... Allen 34
Maling's Hand-books for Ladies.. Smith & El. 14
Malta, Naturalist in .... Edmonston.. 1
Mammalia, Jones .... Warne 15
Man and Animals, Emotions in . Murray 0
—— and the Apes .... Hardwicke . 8
—— Biblical Antiquity of ..... Wesleyan .. 46
—— in Early Times .... Macmillan .. 7
—— of the Future............ Chapman .. 12
—— Glory of God in .... Macmillan .. 12
—— and the Gospel .... Isbister..... 13
—— with the Iron Mask ...... Smith & El. 14
—— among the Monkeys ..... Ward & Lock 8
—— Natural History, Races of . Bohn's Lib. 14
—— in the Past, Present & Future Asher 3
—— (Pre-Adamite) .... Nisbet 12
—— his Religion and his World . Nisbet 7
—— Science of............... Longmans .. 16
—— of Sorrows .... Parker 36
—— Study of .... Hodder 8
—— about Town .... J. Blackw'd 19
—— Tripartite Nature of...... Clar....... 14
—— and Wife .... Smith & El. 4
Man's Age in the World .... Reece 13

Man's Belief (A)	Williams	9
— Nature, Treatise on	Hodder	7
— Renewal	Isbister	36
Manchester Life, Tales from	Tubbs	4
— Psalter	A. Heywood	13
Mangnall's Questions	Hardwicke	12
Manhood (True), its Nature, &c.	Nisbet	21
Manipulus Vocabulorum	Trubner	19
Mankind, Early History of	Murray	23
— Ground and Object of Hope	Macmillan	25
— Physical History of	Houlston	14
Manly Exercises, Walker	Bell	23
Mann (Dr.) Works by	Jarrold	11
Manners of Good Society	Cassell	5
Manning (Archbishop) Works by	Burns	15
— Works by	Pickering	25
— Works by	Washbourne	11
Manor Farm	Rivingtons	17
— House Exhibition	Warne	20
Manse Garden	J. Blackwood	25
Mansel's (Dean) Letters, &c.	Murray	21
— Philosophy of the Conditioned	Isbister	30
Mansions of England	Sotheran	21
Manuals for the Chris. Household	Nelson	21
Manual of Scientific Inquiry	Murray	2
Manufactures, Dictionary of	Isbister	13
— Influence of Science, &c.	Hardwicke	10
— Philosophy of	Bohn's Lib.	19
Manufacturers' Receipts	Spon	46
Manufacturing Terms	Routledge	12
Maoria, Johnstone	Chapman	4
Map and Plan Drawing	Cassell	5
Maps, Educational	C. Smith	5
— Geological	Johnston	2
— Handy District	Houlston	8
— Library and Office	Johnston	5
— (Relief)	C. Smith	9
— Travelling	Black	7
— Useful Knowledge Society	Stanford	34
— (Wall)	Collins	21
— (Wall)	Nelson	0
— (Wall)	Stanford	13
— (Wall) and History Sheets	Murby	5
— (Wall) School Series	Johnston	6
Marathi Grammar, Bellair's	Trubner	4
March (Com. C.) Memorials of	Nisbet	25
Marco Polo's Travels	Bohn's Lib.	22
— Travels	Murray	22
Margaret Cecil	Warne	26
Margaret Ford	S. S. Union	8
Marie, Glimpses of Life in France	Bell	24
Marienbad Spa	Trubner	17
Marine Engine, Burgh	Spon	28
— Insurance Pop. Explained	Layton	12
— Surveying, Stevenson	Black	31
Mariner's Compass	Longmans	19
— Compass	Philip	39
Marion Grey	S. S. Union	9
— Morley	S. S. Union	9
— and her Pupils	Warne	27
Marion's Three Crowns	S. S. Union	8
Marjory, Milly Deane	Macmillan	9
Markham's Histories	Allman	12
— Histories	Murray	22
Markhams of Ollerton	M. Ward	9
Marks (R.) Works by	Nisbet	25
Marlborough (Duke of) Memoirs	Bohn's Lib.	7
Marlowe's Works	Chatto	27
Marriage Customs	Hurst	8
— and Divorce Laws	Stevens	2
— Gift Book, Burns	Houlston	32
— and Home	Morgan	3
Married, Devotional Manual for	Masters	11
— Life, Holiness in	Rivingtons	13
— Life, Morison	Snow	12
— (Newly) A Book for	Morgan	3
— Pair, Whisper to	Houlston	29
— Women's Property Act, 1870	Stevens	6
Marryat's (Capt.) Books for Boys	Bell	22
— Works	Routledge	30
— (Florence) Novels	Warne	44
Marsden (J. B.) Works by	Hatchard	14
Marsh (Rev. Dr.) Life of	Nisbet	25
— (J. B.) Works by	Isbister	31
— (Miss) Works by	Nisbet	25
Marshall (Mrs.) Tales by	Jarrold	11
— Tales by	Nisbet	26
Marshfield Maidens	Murby	2
Martha's Home	Nelson	18
Martial's Epigrams	Whittaker	3
Martin's (S.) Sermons	Hodder	11
Martin (T.) Translations	W. Blackw'd	20
— (W.) School Books by	Jarrold	11
Martineau (H.) Works of	Smith & El.	15
— (Miss) Playfellow	Routledge	37
Martyr Times	Nelson	8
Martyrdom of Man	Trubner	25
Martyrs, Age of	Parker	12
— and Apologists	Holder	15
— Book of, Fox	Cassell	4
— Memorials of English	Rel. Tr. Soc.	12
— Noble Army of	Masters	10
— in Palestine, Eusebius	Williams	5
— of Science	Chatto	6
— of Spain	Nelson	7
Marvels of the Heavens	Bentley	10
— from Nature	Hatchard	32
— of Nature	Ward & Lock	27
Mary, the Handmaid of the Lord	Nisbet	26
— the Mother of Jesus	Hodder	21
— Elliot	Warne	28
— Leigh	Warne	28
— Queen of Scots, Mignet	Bentley	10
— Stuart, Queen of Scots	Longmans	3
Mason (C. P.) Educational Works	Bell	36
Mason's, Bricklayer's, &c., Guide	Hagger	15
Massey's (Gerald) Tale of Eternity	Isbister	31
Massinger's Plays	Chatto	27
Masson (David) Works by	Macmillan	24
Master John Bull	Nimmo	27
— Spirits	King	10
Mastery of Foreign Languages	Longmans	14
Materia Medica	Churchill	0
— Medica, Pereira	Longmans	28
Materials for Trans. Eng. into Fr.	Trubner	18
Mathematics	Parker	60
Mathematics	Rivingtons	23
— for Beginners, Todhunter	Macmillan	36
— Elementary	Allen	6
— Elementary	Murby	6
— First Book of	Black	16
— for Practical Men	Lockwood	10
— Pure, Sergeant	Collins	7
— Rudimentary Works	Lockwood	26
Mathematical Books	J. Heywood	28
— Course	Chambers	16
— and Drawing Instruments	Lockwood	11
— Examinations	Murray	24
— Instruments	Chapman	31
— Problems and Exercises	Macmillan	26
— Problems, Cambridge Course	Macmillan	42
— Works	Bell	0
— Works, Boole	Macmillan	4
Mathematician's Pt. Pocket Guide	MacPhun	17
Mathews' Catechisms	Houlston	45
Mathison (Duncan) Life of	Morgan	2
Matter and Ether	Macmillan	3
— and Force, Jones	Churchill	22
— and Motion	Chambers	17
— The Mystery of	Macmillan	28
Matthews (Joanna H.) Works by	Nisbet	5
Maud, or Anglican Sister of Mercy	Harrison	3
— Latimer	Warne	29
Maude Talbot	Smith & El.	13
Maule, Sir William	Bentley	10
Maum Guinea	Routledge	2
Maunder's Treasuries	Longmans	43
Maurice (F. D.) Conflict, &c.	Smith & El.	15
— (F. D.) Works by	Macmillan	24
Mavor's (J.) Young Man's Comp.	Virtue	20
Max Havelaar	Edmonston	15
Maxims	W. Blackw'd	21
— by a Man of the World	Tinsley Bros.	9
Maxwell Drewitt	Tinsley Bros.	10
May (E. J.) Juvenile Books	Marlborough	3
— (E. J.) Juvenile Books by	Routledge	33
— and her Friends	Warne	19
— Queen, Tennyson	Warne	2
Mayor (J. B.) Works by	Macmillan	25
Mazzini's Life and Writings	Smith & El.	15

F.

McCausland's Works .... *Bentley* 10
McCulloch (J. R.) Works by .... *Black* 14
—— Dictionary .... *Longmans* 17
McCosh (James) Works by..... *Macmillan* .. 23
McCrie (Thos.) Works .... *W. Blackwd* 10
McPherson's Kertch .... *Smith & El.* 15
Meals and Manners .... *Trübner* 10
Measurer (Complete) Horton .. *Lockwood* .. 2
—— (Hoppus's) .... *Warne* 46
—— Peddie's Practical .... *Blackie* .. 10
—— Universal .... *Nicholson* .. 10
Measuring Artificer's Work .... *Lockwood* .. 8
Measurement (Superficial) .... *Lockwood* .. 10
Mecca, Pilgrimage to .... *Allen* 22
Mechanic (The Young)......... *Trübner* .. 10
Mechanics .... *Chambers* .. 17
—— Applied, Reynolds .... *Collins* .. 7
—— of Construction .... *Bell* 10
—— Elementary .... *Bell* 19
—— Elementary .... *Cambridge* .. 21
—— Elementary .... *J. Heywood* .. 20
—— Elementary, Parkinson .... *Macmillan* .. 28
—— Elements of, Newth ...... *Murray* 24
—— Experimental............. *Macmillan* .. 7
—— and Mechanism .... *Ward & Lock* 26
—— Molecular .... *Macmillan* .. 3
—— Practical, Byrne .... *Spon* 24
Mechanic's Dictionary .... *Blackie* .. 10
—— Pocket Book, Nystrom .... *Trübner* .. 22
—— Pocket Guide .... *MacPhun* .. 15
—— Workshop (Amateur) .... *Trübner* .. 19
—— Workshop Companion .... *Lockwood* .. 10
Mechanical Arts.............. *W. Blackwd* 48
—— Diagrams............... *Chapman* .. 11
—— Drawing .... *Longmans* .. 21
—— Engineering............ *Lockwood* .. 4
—— Engineering, Rud. Works . *Lockwood* .. 21
—— Movements .... *Spon* 29
—— Philosophy .... *Parker* 60
—— Philosophy .... *Reid's Lib.* .. 18
—— Philosophy, Buckmaster .. *Chapman* .. 12
—— Tables .... *Whittaker* .. 15
Mechanism, Goodeve .... *Longmans* .. 21
—— Principles of .... *Longmans* .. 31
Mecklenburgh, Duchess of .... *Morgan* 5
Medals, Ancient and Modern .. *Bell* 13
Mediæval Manners, &c. ...... *Parker* 50
Mediatorial Sovereignty ...... *Clark* 15
Medical Diagnosis, Da Costa .. *Smith & El.* 6
—— Dictionary .... *Ward & Lock* 7
—— Electricity .... *Churchill* .. 36
—— Electricity, Althaus ..... *Longmans* .. 27
—— Errors .... *Churchill* .. 7
—— Guide, Pocket .... *MacPhun* .. 15
—— Hand-Book .... *Churchill* .. 19
—— Information .... *Nelson* 3
—— Jurisprudence, Traill .... *Black* 32
—— Lexicon .... *Churchill* .. 15
—— Men, Laws affecting..... *Churchill* .. 18
—— and Surgical Knowledge... *Houlston* .. 3
—— Terminology, Dictionary of. *Trübner* .. 15
—— Visiting Lists .... *Letts* 3
—— Vocabulary............. *Churchill* .. 26
—— Works .... *Churchill* .. 0
—— Works .... *Smith & El.* 1
—— Works, Simpson .... *Black* 31
Medicine among Asiatic Nations *Churchill* .. 38
—— Clinical Lect., Prin. & Pract. *Black* .. 2
—— Contributions to Practical . *Black* 2
—— Dictionary of, Copland .... *Longmans* .. 27
—— Dictionary of, Lankester .. *Ward & Lock* 32
—— Disease, and Death ...... *Churchill* .. 15
—— First Principles of....... *Bell* 18
—— Household .... *Houlston* .. 9
—— (Household), Fullerton ... *Chapman* .. 13
—— Introduction to Study of... *Black* 2
—— New Theory of .... *Churchill* .. 22
—— and Psychology......... *Bell* 18
—— in Spain, 15 and 16 Centuries *Churchill* .. 17
—— System of, Reynolds..... *Macmillan* .. 30
—— (Unity of) .... *Churchill* .. 14
Meditations, Alford .... *Isbister* .. 4
—— Book of................ *Bemrose* .. 3
—— for Christian Comfort .... *Isbister* .. 23
—— on Death and Eternity..... *Trübner* .. 19

Meditations on Life and Rel. Duties *Trübner* 19
—— (Noomlay) .... *Nisbet* 30
Mediterranean, Coasting Voyage *Hatchard* .. 14
—— Sea Kings of .... *Soc. P. C. K.* 24
—— (Shores of) .... *Churchill* .. 9
Meeting the Sun............. *Longmans* .. 37
Megha-Duta (The) .... *Trübner* .. 19
Melbourne House .... *Nisbet* 26
—— House .... *Routledge* .. 35
Melodies of Zion .... *Morgan* 4
Melvill (Canon) Sermons by .. *Rivingtons* .. 14
Melville, Novels by .... *Longmans* .. 39
Memoir of a Brother, Hughes... *Macmillan* .. 16
Memoirs of a Life .... *Stanford* .. 60
Memorabilia Ecclesiæ ...... *Hatchard* .. 10
Memorials of a Quiet Life .... *Isbister* .. 20
Memoranda Parochialia ...... *Masters* .. 20
Memory, Aids to............ *Isbister* .. 32
—— by Fitch (J. G.) .... *S. S. Union.* 44
—— of Language .... *J. Heywood* .. 4
Memory's Pictures .... *Nisbet* 26
Men, Boyhood of Great ...... *Routledge* .. 5
—— of Capital .... *J. Blackwood* 10
—— Celebrated .... *Ward & Lock* 27
—— of the Day (Cartoon Portraits) *Tinsley Bros.* 4
—— Extraordinary .... *Routledge* .. 4
—— of Faith .... *Hodder* .. 6
—— Footprints of Famous .... *Routledge* .. 5
—— of History .... *Nimmo* .. 15
—— Illustrious .... *J. Blackwood* 15
—— Lectures on Great....... *Nisbet* 28
—— Ministering .... *J. Blackwood* 17
—— Tales of Celebrated ..... *Burns* 35
—— of the Third Republic .... *Isbister* .. 31
—— of the Time .... *Routledge* .. 4
—— Women, and Books ...... *Smith & El.* 11
—— and Women, Modern ..... *Ward & Lock* 4
—— Worth Imitating .... *S. S. Union.* 6
—— who have Risen .... *Virtue* 14
—— who have Made Themselves *J. Blackwood* 5
Mendelssohn's Letters .... *Longmans* .. 8
Mensuration .... *Chambers* .. 16
—— Elementary .... *Bell* 15
—— Elementary, Young ..... *Mozley* 15
—— for Schools, Tebay ...... *Macmillan* .. 35
—— Treatise on .... *Virtue* 21
Mental Disease (Responsibility in) *King* 8
—— Diseases, Sankey ...... *Churchill* .. 31
—— and Moral Phil., Coleman . *Harrison* .. 13
—— and Moral Science ...... *Snow* .. 12
—— and Moral Science, Bain . *Longmans* .. 17
—— Philosophy, Morell ...... *Longmans* .. 14
—— Physiology, Principles of . *King* 6
Mentone, Flora of .... *Reeves* 4
—— in its Medical Aspect .... *Churchill* .. 33
—— Wintering at .... *Chambers* .. 28
—— Wintering at .... *Churchill* .. 11
Menu, Institutes of .... *Allen* 8
Mercantile Correspondence ... *Trübner* .. 2
—— Morals .... *J. Blackwood* 10
—— Law .... *Stevens* .. 14
—— Tables .... *Wilson* 11
—— Telegraphic Code ...... *Wilson* .. 6
Merchant Enterprise .... *Nelson* .. 11
—— Shippers of London .... *Dean* .. a
—— and Trader's Profit Book . *Houlston* .. 7
Merchant's Assistant .... *Smith & El.*
—— Clerk .... *Wilson* .. 2
—— Clerk .... *Ward & Lock* 28
—— Handbook .... *Stanford* .. 51
Mercury in Treatment of Disease *Churchill* .. 13
Mercy Seat (The) .... *Collins* .. 3
Meredith (George) Works by .. *Chapman* .. 23
Meredith (Owen), Works by .. *Chapman* .. 20
Merivale (C.) Works by ...... *Macmillan* .. 25
—— (Dean), Histories .... *Longmans* .. 4
Merrifield (C. W.) Sc. Text-Bks. *Longmans* .. 21
Merry Circle (The) .... *Chatto* .. 15
—— Companion (The) ...... *Nicholson* .. 14
—— England .... *Tinsley Bros.* 16
—— Tales for Little Folk..... *Lockwood* .. 46
Mesmerism and Clairvoyance.. *Burns* 21
Messiah (The), by a Layman .. *Murray* .. 23
—— Footsteps of............ *Snow* .. 9
—— as Foretold .... *Bell* 60

Metal (Sheet) Worker's Instructor *Spon* 37
Metals, Bloxam .... *Longmans* .. 22
— Book of .... *Routledge* .. 67
— Useful .... *Houlston* 10
Metallurgy, Greenwood .... *Collins* 8
— Percy .... *Murray* 25
— Practical .... *Longmans* .. 32
— Rudimental Works ...... *Lockwood* .. 24
— Treatise on .... *Trubner* 23
Metaphysics of Ethics .... *Clark* 20
— Mansel .... *Black* 15
— Speculations on .... *Trubner* 7
Meteorographica, Galton ...... *Macmillan* .. 12
Meteorological Office Publication *Stanford* .. 59
Meteorology .... *W. Blackw'd* 31
Meteorology .... *Chambers* .. 17
— Buchan .... *W. Blackw'd* 5
— Herschell .... *Black* 13
— and Law of Storms .... *Smith&El.* 5
— Steinmetz .... *Reeve* 15
Meteors and Falling Stars .... *Reeve* 15
Methodism As it Is.......... *Walker* 5
— in America .... *Wesleyan* .. 43
— History .... *Hagger* 11
— in Isle of Wight .... *Wesleyan* .. 43
— Women of .... *Tegg* 0
Methodist Family Library .... *Wesleyan* .. 16
Methuen (T. A.) Autobiography *Hatchard* .. 14
Metric System .... *J. Heywood.* 9
— System .... *Murby* 6
— System .... *Philip* 18
— System, Brint .... *Hardwicke.* 11
— System, Dowling ...... *Lockwood* .. 11
— System, Piper.......... *Collins* 11
— System, Smith .... *Macmillan* .. 11
— System, Tables of ...... *Chambers* .. 14
— Weights and Measures .. *Spon* 27
Metrical System of Weights, &c. *Wilton* 6
Metropolis Local Manage. Act. *Lockwood* .. 28
Metz, Fall of, Robinson ...... *Bradbury* .. 11
Mexico in 1864-5 .... *Macmillan* .. 4
— Conquest of, Helps ...... *Bell* 39
— Country and People .... *Rel. Tr. Soc.* 12
— Landscapes and Sketches *Trubner* 26
— Stories of the Conquests .. *J. Blackwood* 5
— Travels in.............. *Allen* 17
— Travels in.............. *Murray* 26
Meyer's Commentary of New Test. *Clark* 33
Michael Kemp.............. *Bell* 25
Michelet (Jules) Works by .... *Nelson* 1
Microscope (The) .... *Lockwood* .. 5
— applied to Medicine .... *Churchill* .. 8
— Carpenter.............. *Churchill* .. 12
— Gosse's Evenings at .... *Soc. P. C. K.* 7
— Half-Hours with .... *Hardwicke.* 6
— Hogg on .... *Routledge* .. 67
— Houghton .... *Cassell* 11
— How to Work with .... *Harrison* 4
— Pereira .... *Spon* 27
— Works on the .... *Churchill* .. 0
— Object Mounting ...... *Hardwicke.* 6
Microscopic Science .... *Murray* 31
Middle Ages, Arts of the .... *Chapman* .. 20
— Ages, Great Cities of .... *Routledge* .. 34
— Manners and Customs of *Chapman* .. 5
— Popular Romances of .. *Longmans* .. 39
— Scenes and Characters in *Virtue* 9
Middle Kingdom (The) ...... *Trubner* 32
Middlemarch.............. *W. Blackw'd* 8
Middlesex, Church Walks in .. *Masters* 26
— Flora .... *Hardwicke* ..
Midnight Cry (The) .... *Nisbet* 5
— Sky (The) .... *Rel. Tr. Soc.* 7
Midshipman (The), Hall ...... *Bell* 32
Midwifery, Elements of Practical *Churchill* .. 37
— Leishman .... *Macmillan* .. 20
Midwives (English) .... *Churchill* .. 7
Milestones of Life.......... *Warne* 79
Military Adventure, Stories of *King* 18
— Architecture .... *Parker* 49
— Arithmetic .... *Stanford* 51
— Autumn Manoeuvres.... *Trubner* 19
— Biography .... *Longmans* .. 7
— Bridges, Haupt .... *Trubner* 15
— Drawing, Treatise on .... *Trubner* 24

Military Duties and Qualities.... *Murray* .. 10
— Ends and Moral Means .... *Smith & El.* 9
— Estates, Gleig .... *Chapman* .. 19
— Field Manoeuvres ...... *Blackwood* .. 21
— Forces of the Crown...... *Murray* 7
— (French) Reports, 1866-1870 *Harrison* .. 12
— Geography .... *Whittaker* .. 12
— Geography, Recon. and Sket. *King* 12
— Grenadier Guards ...... *Murray* 12
— Gymnastics .... *Allen* 19
— Heroes of England ...... *J. Blackwood* 9
— Hygiene, Gorum .... *Churchill* .. 12
— Hygiene, Parkes .... *Churchill* .. 28
— Institutions of France .... *Chapman* .. 14
— Instruction Books ...... *Harrison* .. 7
— Law, Clode .... *Murray* 7
— Law, Precedents in ...... *Allen* 10
— Life, Tales of .... *Soc. P. C. K.* 18
— Manuals .... *Cassell* 7
— Memoir of 83rd Regiment. *Smith & El.* 15
— Men I have Met........ *Tinsley Bros.* 9
— and Political Essays .... *Allen* 7
— Reconnaissance .... *Chapman* .. 23
— Religious Biog., Hammond *Nisbet* 17
— Religious Biography, Cooke *Nisbet* 20
— Religious Biog., Harington *Nisbet* 17
— Religious Biog., Havelock. *Nisbet* 17
— Religious Biography, Holden *Nisbet* .. 19
— Religious Biography, Latter *Nisbet* .. 21
— Religious Biog., Macbeth.. *Nisbet* 23
— Rel. Biog., Stonewall Jackson *Nisbet* .. 19
— Rel. Biography, Vandeleur. *Nisbet* .. 26
— Rel. Biography, H. Vicars .. *Nisbet* .. 26
— Royal Engineer.......... *Murray* 14
— Sciences .... *Lockwood* .. 12
— Songs and Epigrams .... *Chapman* .. 23
— Students, Text Book for .. *Harrison* .. 13
— Surveying .... *Allen* 18
— Surveying .... *Trubner* 24
— Tactics, Modern .... *Harrison* .. 12
— Technical Terms .... *Murray* 5
— Technological Dictionary .. *Williams* .. 5
— Terms, Dictionary of.... *Spon* 29
— Trials................ *Allen* 5
— Victories and Defeats .... *King* 12
— Works .... *Allen* 17
— Works .... *Blackwood* .. 12
— Works .... *King* 11
— Works, Douglas .... *Murray* 10
Militia Orders .... *Harrison* .. 12
— Reforms .... *King* 17
Milk, Analysis of .... *Trubner* 31
Millais' Illustrations .... *Isbister* 31
Mill (J. S.) Autobiography .... *Longmans* .. 7
— Review of the Works of .... *Trubner* .. 14
— Works by .... *Longman* .. 9
Mill's British India........ *Setheran* .. 20
— Philoso. Examined, McCosh *Macmillan* .. 23
— (Rev. W. H.) Sermons.... *Masters* .. 16
Mill Work .... *Spon* 30
Mills and Millwork .... *Longmans* .. 32
Miller's Chemistry .... *Longmans* .. 26
Miller (Hugh) Life and Letters.. *Isbister* .. 6
— Works .... *Nimmo* 3
— (Thos.) Juvenile Books by .. *Routledge* .. 33
Million of Facts (A) .... *Ward&Lock* 24
Millwright's Guide .... *Spon* 30
Milman (Bishop) Works by .... *Masters* .. 17
Milman (Dean) Life .... *Murray* 17
— Works by .... *Murray* 22
Milne (Rev. John) Life of .... *Nisbet* 27
Milner (Rev. Thos.) Works by *Rel. Tr. Soc.* 13
Milton's Complete Poetical Wrks. *J. Blackwood* 3
— Life and Works, Masson.. *Macmillan* .. 25
— Comus and Samson ...... *Macmillan* .. 21
— Paradise Lost, Doré ...... *Cassell* 2
— Poems, Browne .... *Clar. Press.* 31
— Poetical Works .... *Warne* 13
— Works, by Montgomery .. *Bohn's Lib.* 14
— Works, Pocket Edition .. *Bell* 32
Milton (Viscountess) Readings.. *Hatchard* .. 14
Mind and Body, Bain ...... *King* 8
— (Influence of) on the Body .. *Churchill* .. 30
— Physiology and Pathology of *Macmillan* .. 21
Mind Whom you Marry ...... *Partridge* .. 5

Mineral Agent's Handbook...... *Williams* 9
—— Deposits .... *Stanford*.... 70
—— Statistics of the United King. *Stanford*.... 61
—— Surveyor's Complete Guide *Lockwood* .. 5
—— Waters, Wilson .... *Churchill*... 39
Mineralogy .... *Clar. Press*... 27
—— Dana .... *Trubner* 9
— — Elements of, Nicol. ...... *Black* 15
Miner's and Metallurgist's Guide *Trubner* ... 24
Mine Engineering .... *Spon* 30
Mines, Conversation on .... *A. Heywood* 15
—— Laws of .... *Lockwood* .. 5
—— Minerals, and Metals ...... *Routledge* .. 29
Mining and Metallurgy .... *Spon*...... 51
—— Practical .... *Wilson* 9
—— Rudimentary Works on .... *Lockwood*.. 21
Mining (Silver) Calvert .... *Spon* 36
—— Surveyor's Field Book .... *Lockwood* .. 6
—— Tools .... *Lockwood* .. 10
Minister's Family .... *MacVicar* .. 16
Ministering Men .... *J. Blackw'd* 17
Ministry, Grace of the .... *Bell* 41
—— of Nature .... *Macmillan* .. 21
Minnesinger of Germany ...... *Trubner* 17
Minor Prophets .... *Parker* 9
Minto (Earl) Life and Letters.... *Longmans* .. 7
Minton, (Rev. S.) Works by .... *Kellaway* .. 5
Minutes of Methodist Conference *Wesleyan* .. 17
Miracles .... *W. Blackw'd* 38
—— of Christ, Irons .... *Masters* 13
—— Conversations on .... *Mozley*.... 4
—— Defence of, Butler's ...... *Trubner* 6
—— of Our Lord .... *Isbister* 27
—— of Our Lord, Trench ...... *Macmillan* .. 37
—— of Our Lord, Walker ...... *Nisbet* 36
—— Sermons on, Hook .... *Bell* 59
Miramion (Madame) Life ...... *Bentley* 2
Miriam's Marriage .... *Smith & El.* 14
Mirror of Character .... *Nimmo* 14
—— for Monks, Blosius........ *Stewart* 8
— — for Young Christians ...... *Masters* 3
Miscellany of Enter. & Inst. Tales *Nisbet* 4
Mishmee Hills (The) .... *King*...... 4
Miss Brown .... *J. Blackw'd* 28
—— Forrester .... *Tinsley Bros.* 10
—— Herbert's Keys .... *S. S. Union*. 7
Misread Passages of Scripture .. *Hodder* 18
Missale ad usum Ecclesia Sarum. *Stewart* 8
Missals and Breviaries .... *Burns* 12
Missing Link (The) .... *Nisbet* 27
Mission (Baptist) in Jamaica .. *Snow* 16
—— to Bengal (The First Bap.).. *Macmillan*.. 35
—— (Bengal) Pioneers of .... *Snow* 7
—— (The) Hymn Book .... *Jarrold* 9
—— Labour, North Europe.... *Snow* 12
—— Labours, &c., Moffatt .... *Snow* 11
—— Life in Bengal, Weitbrecht *Nisbet* 15
—— Life at Bombay, Nesbit .. *Nisbet* 28
—— Life in South Seas........ *Snow* 3
—— (Medical) China, Henderson. *Nisbet* .. 18
—— (Medical) to Jews in Turkey. *Snow* 10
—— to N. W. America ...... *Soc. P. C. K.* 17
—— to Polynesia .... *Snow* 13
—— (Presbyter.) China, Matheson *Nisbet* .. 26
—— Sandwich Islands .... *Hodder* 34
—— Sermons .... *Masters* 29
—— (Six Years) to Dens of London *Nisbet* .. 35
—— Story of the Life .... *Nisbet* 25
—— to Tinnevelly, Tucker .. *Nisbet* 35
—— to Travancore .... *Snow* 10
—— (Zenana) in India ...... *Snow* 9
Missions in Africa .... *Rel. Tr. Soc.* 16
—— An Appeal for, Vaughan.. *King* 29
—— in Bengal, Mullins ...... *Nisbet* 28
—— in Calcutta, Mullins .... *Nisbet* 27
—— in China, Muirhead ...... *Nisbet* 27
—— (Christian) in India .... *Snow* 14
—— (Christian) in Middle Ages *Macmillan*.. 21
—— Considered, Three Aspects .. *Clark* .. 36
—— History of Christian .... *Nisbet* 17
—— in Japan and Paraguay .. *Burns* 22
—— to Madagascar .... *Snow* 13
—— and Maritime Discovery .. *Snow* 3
— — (Parochial) .... *Isbister* 43
—— (Prospect of Christian).... *Isbister* 41

Missions before the Reformation. *Soc. P. C. K.* 6
—— Romance of Modern........ *Rel. Tr. Soc.* 4
—— to S. Africa, Thomas...... *Snow* 15
—— Siberia, Letters on .... *Snow* 15
—— to the Women of China .. *Nisbet* .. 27
—— in Wrong Places.......... *Nisbet* .. 14
Missionaries, Dictionary for.... *Trubner* .. 4
—— Outline Dictionary for .. *Trubner* .. 20
—— Lives of .... *Snow* 2
—— Lives of.................. *Soc. P. C. K.* 13
—— in S. Sea Islands........ *Hatchard* .. 17
Missionary Centres of Mid. Ages. *Soc. P. C. K.* 26
—— Earnest (The)............ *Wesleyan* .. 50
—— Enterprise in the East .... *King* 28
—— Enterprise S. Sea Islands .. *Snow* .. 16
—— History of Sierra Leone .. *Hatchard* .. 25
—— (Home) Life and Work .. *Snow* 12
—— of Kilmany .... *Nisbet* .. 3
—— Letters to a Young ...... *Masters* .. 10
—— Life in British Columbia .. *Soc. P. C. K.* 14
—— Life in Burmah, Judson .. *Nisbet* .. 19
—— Life in Calcutta, Lacroix.. *Nisbet* .. 20
—— Life, Home and Foreign .. *Nisbet* .. 19
—— Life in India, Groves .. *Nisbet* .. 15
—— Life, Islands of the Pacific .. *Snow* .. 16
—— Lives, Catholic .... *Burns* .. 28
—— (London) Society .... *Snow* 6
—— in Many Lands .... *J. Blackwood* 15
—— in N. American Colonies .. *Murray* .. 1
—— Life in New Zealand, Davis. *Nisbet* .. 11
—— Pioneers .... *Wesleyan* .. 47
—— Stories for the Young .... *Snow* .. 7
—— Travels in Asia Minor .... *Murray* .. 20
—— Voyage Round the World .. *Snow* .. 16
—— Work of the Church .... *Snow* .. 15
—— Work of Modern Times .. *Soc. P. C. K.* 28
—— Work in S. America, Gardiner. *Nisbet* .. 14
Missionary's Wife, Henderson .. *Snow* .. 6
Mississippi, Valleys of the .... *Murray* .. 24
Misunderstood, Works by A .. *Bentley* .. 11
Mitford (Mary R.) Life........ *Bentley* .. 9
Mitford, Our Village .... *Bohn's Lib.* 8
Mivart (St. George) Works by .. *Macmillan*.. 25
Mixing in Society .... *Routledge* .. 44
Mizpah; or, the Friends at Prayer. *Morgan* .. 2
Moabite Stone, Ginsburg...... *Reeves* .. 6
Moberly (Bp.) Works by ...... *Rivingtons*.. 13
Model Books, Eng. & For. Corres. *Asher* .. 7
Models and Instruments ...... *Chapman* .. 30
Model Manuals .... *Wayne* .. 35
—— Women .... *Hodder* .. 27
Modern Avernus (The) ...... *Hatchard* .. 15
—— Babylon, and other Poems. *Chatto* .. 28
—— Combat .... *Wilson* 1
—— Culture, its True Aims.... *Macmillan* .. 43
—— Doubt and Christian Belief.. *Clark* .. 34
—— Doubt in Christian Faith.. *Clark* .. 10
—— English, Hall .... *Williams* .. 6
—— European Celebrities .... *Ward & Lock* 7
—— Love, Meredith .... *Chapman* .. 22
—— Scepticism .... *Hodder* .. 4
—— Unbeliever .... *Wesleyan* .. 47
Modocs, Life among .... *Bentley* .. 10
Moeso-Gothic Glossary........ *Asher* .. 8
Mogul Empire................ *Allen* .. 15
Mohamedan Law of Inheritance.. *Allen* .. 8
Mohammed's Life, Syed Ameer Ali *Williams* .. 1
—— Life, Syed Ahmad........ *Trubner* .. 28
Molecular & Microscopic Science *Murray* .. 19
Molière's Plays, French ...... *Clar. Press.* 27
Mollusks, British, Tate........ *Hardwicke*.. 4
Molyneaux (Rev. Capel) Works by *Nisbet* .. 27
Mommsen's Rome............ *Bentley* .. 11
Monaco, History of .... *Tinsley Bros.* 7
Monarchs of the Main........ *Routledge* .. 31
Monastic Orders, Legends of .. *Longmans* .. 29
Money Market (The).......... *Trubner* .. 15
—— Market, Bagehot .... *King* .. 16
—— A Pop. Exp. in Rough Notes *Hodder* .. 16
—— Paper and Metallic ...... *Black* .. 14
—— Weights, and Measures .. *Stanford*.. 51
Monks, Montalembert .... *W. Blackw'd* 21
Monod's (Adolpe) Farewell .... *Nisbet* .. 27
Monographs, Personal and Social *Murray* .. 17
Monro (Rev. E.) Works by...... *Masters* .. 17

Monsell (Dr.) Works by .... Bell 36
Montagu (Mrs. E.) Doran ...... Bentley 6
Montalembert (De) Mems. ...... W. Blackw'd 21
Mont Blanc, Wanderings ...... Collins...... 3
Monteith's Languages, Ahn's S .. Allman 3
Montgomery's (Florence) Stories Bentley 11
Montrose, Marquis of .... Stevenson .. a
Monuments, &c. .... Hogger 13
Monuments .... J. R. Smith. 20
Monumental Brasses .... Parker...... 50
—— Designs .... Masters 10
—— Inscriptions .... Chatto 25
—— Memorials .... Masters 11
Moohummudan Law .... Smith & El. 2
Moon (The) Godfray .... Macmillan.. 13
—— Nasmyth .... Murray 24
—— Proctor .... Longmans .. 18
Moon's Disc, Telescopic View of .C. Smith.... 11
Moon (G. W.) Works by ...... Hatchard .. 15
Moonshine, Fairy Stories........ Macmillan.. 19
Moonstone .... Smith & El. 4
Moore (Daniel) Thoughts ...... Hatchard .. 15
—— Works by............ Rivingtons .. 0
Moore's Lalla Rookh, Illustrated Routledge .. 28
—— Melodies .... Longmans .. 6
—— Poetical Works ...... Nimmo 7
—— Poetical Works ...... Warne 18
Moorhouse (Rev. Jas.) Works by Macmillan.. 25
Moorland and Stream .... Tinsley Bros. 9
Mopsa the Fairy .... Isbister 22
Morag, A Tale of Highland Life Nisbet 27
Moral Difficulties with the Bible Soc. P. C. K. 18
—— Emblems, Illustrated ...... Longmans .. 28
—— Heroism .... Houlston .. 29
—— Laws, Dick .... Collins 3
—— and Metaphysical Philosophy Macmillan.. 24
—— Philosophy, Fleming ...... Murray 12
—— Philosophy, Fleming ...... Murray 30
—— Philosophy, Handbook...... Macmillan.. 5
—— Philosophy, Whewell ...... Bell 41
—— and Religious Truths ...... Jarrold 3
—— Sciences, First Principles .. Macmillan.. 3
—— Sentiments, Smith .... Bohn's Lib.. 9
—— Tales, Guizot .... Routledge .. 34
—— Teaching of New Testament Soc. P. C. K. 19
Morals, European .... Longmans .. 5
—— Foundation of.......... Murray 26
—— Mercantile .... J. Blackwood 10
—— and Mysteries .... Smith & El. 2
—— Four Phases of .... Edmonston .. 2
—— Principles, Wilson ...... Clar. Press.. 24
Morality, Christian .... Parker...... 3
—— Elements of.......... Bell 41
—— according to Lord's Supper.. Macmillan.. 9
—— Social, Maurice .... Macmillan.. 24
Moravians, History of .... Rel. Tr. Soc. 9
Moray, Social Life in.......... Edmonston .. 7
More than Conqueror .... Nisbet 38
—— Excellent Way .... Holder 25
—— Worlds than One ...... Chatto 6
Morgan (Lady) Memoirs ...... Allen 15
Morley (Henry) Works by ...... Chapman .. 22
Mormons, Lady's Life among .. Routledge .. 2
—— A Notice of Salt Lake and .. Chapman .. 25
—— and the Silver Mines...... Holder 20
Mormonism .... Isbister 38
Morning Dew Drops.......... Houlston .. 23
—— of Joy (The) .... Nisbet 7
—— on the Mountains ...... Nisbet 27
—— and Night Watches ...... Nisbet 21
Mornings of the Recess in 1861-4 Tinsley Bros. 8
Morocco, A Winter in ...... King 5
Mortality or Childbed .... Black 2
Norton, Farmer's Calendar .... Warne 11
Moscheles, Life of .... Hurst 2
Mosel, a Series of Etchings .... Murray 12
Moses, the Man of God........ Nisbet 16
—— and Modern Science...... Holder 24
Mosses, British .... Reeve 8
—— British .... Routledge .. 48
—— British, Tripp .... Bell 17
Moths and Butterflies .... Reeve 1
—— British .... Routledge .. 9
—— British, Morris .... Bell 17
Mother's Dictionary .... Lockwood .. 38

Mother's Last Words .... Jarrold 15
—— Legacie (The) .... W. Blackw'd 39
—— Pocket Guide .... MacPhun .. 15
—— Recompense .... Groombridge. 3
Mothers' Meetings, Bright Glimpses Nisbet 7
—— Meetings, Home Thoughts Nisbet 19
—— Meetings, Prayers for ...... Nisbet 30
—— Meetings, Thoughts for .... Hatchard .. 32
Mothers of Great Men .... Chatto 14
—— of Scripture .... Ward&Lock 28
Motion, Elementary Treatise .... Bell 20
Motley (J. L.) Works by ...... Murray 23
Mottoes, Handbook of .... Bell 14
—— Handbook of .... Routledge .. 44
—— for Monuments .... Murray 24
Moulder's and Founder's Guide.. Trubner .. 22
Moultrie (Rev. G.) Works by .. Masters 18
Mountain (The), by Michelet .... Nelson 1
—— Loch, and Glen .... Bell 5
—— Meadow, and Mere ...... King 32
—— Pastor, Lynch .... Nicholson .. 11
Mountains of Scripture .... Nisbet 5
Mount of Olives (The) .... Nisbet 17
Mourners, A Book for .... Morgan 3
Mourner's Letters to Sister .... Macmillan.. 11
Mourning Cards .... Haddon 6
Mouth, Deformities of .... Churchill .. 13
Mr. Fissistratus Brown in Highlds. Macmillan.. 26
Mr. Rutherford's Children ...... Warne 29
Mr. Sprout's Opinions .... Chatto 25
Mrs. Brown Series .... Routledge .. 55
Mrs. Jerningham's Journal .... Macmillan.. 26
My Beautiful Lady .... Macmillan.. 42
—— Box of Books .... Tract Society 32
—— Dog Match .... Warne 27
—— Indian Journal .... Edmonston ..
—— Market Table .... Warne 42
—— Schoolboy Friends ...... Nimmo 12
—— Schoolboy Friends, Sequel to. Nimmo .. 15
—— Schools and Schoolmasters .. Nimmo 4
—— Sunday Companion ...... Warne 39
—— Wife and I in Queensland .. Longmans .. 37
Myers (F. W. H.) Poems by .. Macmillan.. 26
Myology, Observations in...... Macmillan.. 17
Myra's Pink Dress .... S. S. Union. 10
Mysore, Experiences of a Planter. Chapman .. 17
Mystery of Iniquity (The) ...... Nisbet 22
Mysteries of Life, Death, Futurity. Lockwood .. 42
—— of Mount Calvary ...... Rivingtons .. 6
Mystery of Matter .... Macmillan.. 28
—— of Mr. E. Drood .... Chatto 25
—— of Pain .... Smith & El. 10
—— of the Good Old Cause .... Chatto 25
Mystifications .... Edmonston .. 4
Mythology (Fairy) .... Bohn's Lib.. 12
—— for Latin Versification ...... Macmillan.. 16
—— Murray .... Asher 5
—— of Aryan Nations .... Longmans .. 5
—— Scandinavian .... Macmillan.. 18
—— Stories from .... Masters 14
—— Tylor .... Murray 32
—— (Zoological) .... Trubner 14
Myths and Myth Makers ...... Trubner 12
—— Mediæval .... Rivingtons .. 25
Myttou's Life .... Routledge .. 72
Mughal Empire in India ...... Trubner 29
Muhammed, Life of .... Trubner 20
Mohammadanism in India ...... Macmillan.. 4
Mulgrave (Geo.) Lord's Dealings with Nisbet .. 28
—— (G.) Tracts .... Mack 5
—— (Max) Works by .... Longmans .. 0
—— Works by .... Trubner 20
Mulock's Domestic Stories ...... Smith & El. 5
—— Novels .... Hurst & B.. 13
—— Romantic Tales .... Smith & El. 17
Mulready's Pictures .... Virtue 10
Multiplication & Division Tables. Wilson 10
Multum in Parvo .... Williams 10
Munchausen (Baron) .... Trubner 21
Munich, Social Life in .... Allen 9
Murchison (Sir Roger) Works by . Murray 23
Murillo and Spanish Painting .. Routledge .. 3
Murray's Grammar and Exercises. Moxley 15
—— School Books .... Allman 11
Musa Burschicosa .... Edmonston ..

Musarum Deliciæ .... *Chatto* 26
Muses' Recreation (The) .... *Chatto* 26
Museum (British), Cowtan ...... *Bentley* 5
—— of Science and Art .... *Lockwood* 11
Mushroom Cultivation .... *Groombridge* 8
Mushrooms, How to Grow ...... *Bradbury* 11
—— and Toadstools .... *Hardwicke* 2
Music .... *Wesleyan* 39
Music of the most Ancient Nations *Murray* 11
—— H. C. Banister .... *Fell* 19
—— Books (Church) .... *Gall* 11
—— (Children's) .... *Warne* 35
—— Church .... *Masters* 0
—— Educational .... *Philip* 19
—— Elementary, Leslie .... *Cassell* 14
—— of the Future .... *Chapman* 4
—— for Home Circle .... *S. S. Union* 16
—— Manuscript Catalogue of .... *Pickering* 8
—— and Moonlight .... *Chatto* 26
—— and Morals .... *Ishister* 20
—— Primer for Schools.......... *Clar. Press.* 30
—— Sacred .... *Marr* 7
—— Sacred .... *Smith* 20
—— (School) Old & Sol-Fa Notatn. *Collins* 12
—— for Schools .... *Murby* 8
—— Tonic Sol-Fa .... *Marr* 6
—— Vocal, Pearson .... *J. Heywood* 29
Musical Instrument Instructors .. *Cameron* 8
—— Instrument Instructors...... *Marr* 2
—— Leaflets .... *Morgan* 23
—— Museum (Scot's) .... *W. Blackw'd* 16
—— Publications .... *Cocks* ..... a
—— Recollect. Last Half Century. *Tinsley Bros.* 3
—— Works .... *Cramer* ..... a
Musings in Many Moods........ *A. Heywood* 6
Mutineers of the Bounty .... *Murray* 3
Mutual Recognition of Saints .. *Hatchard* 14
Musketry Instruction at Hythe .. *Harrison* 19

Naaman the Syrian .... *Snow* 1
Nablus, Three Months' Residence *Murray* 22
Nágananda, a Buddhist Drama.. *Trubner* 5
Name of Jesus................. *Hatchard* 18
—— which is above Every Name *Nisbet* 31
Name System (Teutonic)....... *Williams* 5
Naomi, with Photos............ *Routledge* 27
Napier's Florentine History .... *Sotheran* 20
Napier (Sir Chas.) Life......... *Murray* 23
—— (Sir Wm.) Life and Letters. *Murray* 23
Napoleon Bonaparte's Life ..... *Routledge* 5
—— Bonaparte (Life of) .... *Warne* 27
—— Life of, Scott .... *Black* 29
—— History, Lanfrey .... *Macmillan* 26
—— at Fontainebleau .... *Murray* 7
Napoleon III., from Caricatures *Chatto* 27
—— Court and Social Life ..... *Tinsley Bros.* 3
—— Life, Jerrold.............. *Longmans* 1
—— Life .... *Marr* 15
—— Mother of................. *Hurst & B.* 9
—— Fallen .... *Ishister* 8
Narcotics, Hurley .... *Macmillan* 15
—— Seven Sisters of Sleep .... *J. Blackw'd.* 27
Nares' Glossary .... *J. R. Smith* 15
Natal, Colony of, Colenso ..... *Macmillan* 7
—— History of the Colony ..... *Wesleyan* 45
Nathan the Wise............... *Trubner* 18
Nations Around, Keary .... *Macmillan* 35
National Books .... *Warne* 37
—— Character and Christianity.. *Macmillan* 7
—— Debt, Baxter .... *Bush* ..... a
—— Gallery .... *Chatto* 1
—— Income, Baxter .... *Macmillan* 3
—— Manuscripts of England ... *Stanford* 64
—— Melodist, Keiser .... *Nimmo* 32
—— Subjects, Sermons, Kingsley *Macmillan* 18
—— Taxes, Stanford........... *Stanford* 70
Natural History .... *Groombridge* 12
—— History .... *Nelson* 20
—— History .... *Rel. Tr. Soc.* 14
—— History .... *Virtue* 18
—— History, Buckland .... *Bentley* 4
—— History, Huffon .... *Milner* 2
—— History, Buffon .... *Warne* 37
—— History, Cope............. *Milner* 2

Natural History, Darwin........ *Murray* 9
—— History, Knight .... *Songster* ..... o
—— History, Maunder .... *Longmans* 43
—— History, Richardson........ *Nicholson* 5
—— History, Wood .... *Routledge* 27
—— History, Works on .... *Routledge* 45
—— History, Anecdotes in ..... *Partridge* 4
—— History for Beginners ..... *L. Reeve* 1
—— History, Boy's Handy-Book *Ward& Lock* 15
—— History of British Isles ... *Van Voorst* ..... a
—— History, Dictionary of..... *Ward& Lock* 4
—— History, Elementary .... *Jarrold* 27
—— History, English Cyclop.... *Bradbury* 6
—— History, Essays on .... *Longmans* 23
—— History, Essays on .... *Warne* 7
—— History, Every Day Book .. *Mack* 12
—— History, Every Day Objects *Nimmo* 12
—— History, Gleanings in ..... *Murray* 19
—— History, Method of Study . *Trubner* 1
—— History (Picture) .... *Cassell* 9
—— History Picture Books ..... *Routledge* 30
—— History (Popular) .... *Cassell* 5
—— History Prints .... *Soc. P. C. K.* 19
—— History, Reason Why ...... *Houlston* 6
—— History, Romance of ...... *Nisbet* 15
—— History Sketches .... *Warne* 14
—— History, Waifs and Strays . *Bell* 19
—— History of the Year .... *Partridge* 8
Natural Philosophy .... *Chambers* 17
—— Philosophy .... *J. Heywood* 40
—— Philosophy, 1st Book ..... *Murray* 24
—— Philosophy, Camb. Elem.Crs. *Macmillan* 5
—— Philosophy, Elementary ... *Blackie* 6
—— Philosophy, Elementary ... *Cassell* 5
—— Philosophy, Elementary ... *Groombridge* 22
—— Philosophy, Notes on ..... *Churchill* 31
—— Philosophy for Gen. Readers *Longmans* 21
—— Philosophy, Lardner ...... *Lockwood* 14
—— Philosophy, Rud. Works .. *Lockwood* 23
—— Philosophy, Sir W. Thompson *Clar. Press.* 27
Natural Science & General Know. *Hardwicke* 5
—— Selections, Wallace .... *Macmillan* 39
Naturalist, Entertaining .... *Bell* 23
—— The Young .... *Routledge* 37
Naturalist's Collection Catalogue *Hardwicke* 5
Naturalists in Humble Life ..... *Hardwicke* 7
—— Notes for Young .... *Hardwicke* 7
Nature and Art, Sketches from . *Nisbet* 3
—— Forces of, Guillemin...... *Macmillan* 15
—— Gallery of .... *Chambers* 39
—— Pictures .... *Warne* ..... a
—— or the Poetry of the Earth . *Nelson* 1
—— Series .... *Macmillan* 26
—— and Unity of Creation ..... *Longmans* 23
Nature's Wonders .... *Nelson* 17
Nautical Astronomy, Evers. ... *Collins* 8
—— Surveying .... *Longmans* 20
—— Tables, Inman .... *Trubner* 17
—— Works .... *Griffin* ..... a
—— Works .... *Philip* 39
Naval Adventure, Tales of ..... *Routledge* 35
—— Architecture .... *Spon* 31
—— Architecture .... *Whittaker* 16
—— Architecture, Student's .... *Collins* 6
—— Daring (Deeds of)......... *Murray* 13
—— History, Great Britain, James *Bentley* 9
—— Hygiene and Scurvy ...... *Churchill* 7
—— and Military Heroes....... *Bohn's Lib.* 14
—— and Military Technical Trms. *Murray* 2
—— Reserve Drill Book .... *Harrison* 0
—— Tactics (French).......... *Harrison* 6
—— Trials.................... *Allen* 5
Navigation .... *Chambers* 17
—— Evers.................... *Collins* 8
—— Harbord .... *W. Blackw'd* 43
—— Harbord .... *W. Blackw'd* 2
—— and Naut. Astron., Inskip .. *Harrison* 1
—— Rudimentary Works....... *Lockwood* 22
Navy, Battles of British .... *Bohn's Lib.* 13
—— British, Yonge .... *Bentley* 15
—— Famous Ships of.......... *Ishister* 2
—— Mer.-Sea Officer's Manual. *Smith & El.* 1
—— Queen's Regulations for... *Harrison* 2
—— (Royal) Engnr. Officers' List *Spon* 17
Nazareth, its Life and Lessons .. *King* 27

Neale (Rev. J. M.) Works by .... *Masters* 18
—— Works by .... *Rivingtons* .. 8
Neander's Church History ...... *Bohn's Lib.* .. 8
—— Church History .... *Clark* 17
Near Home, or Europe Described *Hatchard* 9
Ned's Motto .... *Nelson* 14
Needlework Books................ *Ward & Lock* 25
—— Designs .... *Bosworth* .. 11
—— Patterns .... *Ward & Lock* 25
—— for Schools .... *Hardwick* .. 12
Negligence, Law of .... *Stevens* .. 13
Nehemiah the Tirshatha .... *Nisbet* 31
Neal's (Samuel) Works .... *Houlston* .. 46
Nelly Nowlan .... *Nelson* .. 16
Nelson's Life, by Southey ...... *Bell* 31
Nerves, Flower on the .... *Churchill* .. 10
—— of Human Body, Swan ...... *Bradbury* .. 12
—— Injuries of the............ *Smith & El.* 15
—— and Muscle, Dynamics of .. *Macmillan* .. 29
Nervous Affects., Brown-Séquard *Williams* 3
—— System, Works on .... *Churchill* 0
Nests and Eggs.................. *Groombridge* 13
Nestorians and their Ritual...... *Masters* 2
Netherlands (United) .... *Murray* 23
Net in the Bay .... *Hatchard* 2
Nettie's Mission .... *Nisbet* 28
Neuralgia, Anstie .... *Macmillan* 2
—— and Kindred Diseases........ *Churchill* .. 12
Never Caught .... *Chatto* 26
—— Forgotten .... *Burns* 22
—— Give up .... *Partridge* 9
New Brunswick, Adams .... *King* 4
Newcastle, First Duke & Duchess *Murray* .. 14
New Facts Upon All Subjects .. *Kilkenny* .. 12
—— Forest, Rambles in .... *Longmans* .. 37
—— Forest, Wise .... *Smith & El.* 27
—— Ground, Yonge .... *Mozley* 9
—— Homes for Old Country .... *Bentley* .. 11
—— Magdalen .... *Bentley* .. 16
Newland (Rev. H.) Works by .... *Masters* 19
Newman (F. W.) Works by ...... *Trubner* 21
—— (John Henry) Works by .... *Burns* 15
—— Works .... *Pickering* .. 29
—— Miscellanies .... *Lbister* 32
—— Sermons .... *Rivingtons* .. 15
—— Development, Answer to.... *Macmillan* 5
Newmarket and Arabia .... *King* 31
New Picture Book, Bohny .... *Edmonston* .. 3
Newspaper Press, its Origin, &c. *Tinsley Bros.* 4
—— Reader's Companion........ *Shaw* 7
—— Scrap Book .... *Letts* 2
New South Wales, Roa is in .... *Smith & El.* 4
Newth (Samuel) Works by ...... *Murray* .. 24
New Theories and the Old Faith *Williams* .. 11
Newton (Adelaide L.) Memoir of *Nisbet* 3
—— (A. L.) Works by .... *Nisbet* 28
—— (B. W.) Works by .... *Houlston* .. 37
—— (Rev. Dr.) Works by ...... *Partridge* .. 7
—— (J.) of Olney, Life and Letters *Rel. Tr. Soc.* 14
Newton's Principia, Evans ...... *Bell* 15
—— Principia, Frost .... *Macmillan* .. 12
—— Principia, Thomson & Blackw *Macmillan* .. 27
New Year's Bargain .... *Warne* .. 29
New Zealand .... *Smith & El.* 22
—— Zealand, Hochstetter ...... *Asher* 4
—— Zealand, Meade............ *Murray* .. 22
—— Zealand, Powell .... *Bentley* .. 11
—— Zealand, Trollope.......... *Chapman* 4
—— Zealand, Dictionary........ *Williams* .. 16
—— Zealand, Flora of .... *Reeve* 5
—— Zealand, Geography........ *Philip* 37
—— Zealand, Handbook .... *Stanford* .. 01
—— Zealand, Sheep Farmers .... *Stanford* .. 71
—— Zealand, Manners & Customs *Chapman* 4
—— Zealand, Pictorial Illusts. of *Stanford* .. 51
—— Zealand, Station Life ...... *Macmillan* 2
Nicaragua, Naturalist in ...... *Murray* 4
Nicene Creed, Explanation of .. *Parker* 3
Nichol's Lit. Hist. 18th Century *Sotheran* .. 20
Nicholson's P. J Carpenter's Gothic *Virtue* .. 20
Nick worth & his 3 Magic Wands *Nisbet* .. 28
Nigel Bartram's Ideal .... *Warne* .. 19
Nigel and Benaillah .... *Allen* .. 21
Nicholas, Juvenile Tales ...... *Edmonston* .. 16
Nigh Lamp (The) Macfarlane .. *Nisbet* 25

Night of Toil .... *Hatchard* .. 17
—— of Weeping (The) .... *Nisbet* 7
—— in the Woods .... *S. S. Union* 10
Nile and its Banks.............. *Murray* .. 23
—— Discovery .... *W. Blackw'd* 23
—— (The) Without a Dragoman *King* 5
—— Land of the................ *Nelson* .. 11
—— Sources of, Baker .... *Macmillan* 2
—— Tributaries of Abyssinia .. *Macmillan* 2
—— Valley, Naturalist in ...... *Edmonstone* 1
Nimrod's Chase, Turf and Road *Murray* 24
Ninety-Three, Story French Rev. *Bell* 25
Nineveh and Babylon, Layard .. *Murray* .. 20
—— and its Palaces .... *Bohn's Lib.* .. 13
—— and its Story .... *Nelson* .. 15
Nitrate Silver Treatment, Wounds *Churchill.* 20
Niven (W.) Works by .... *Hatchard* .. 17
Nizam (The) .... *Smith & El.* 8
No Cross no Crown .... *Nelson* 8
No Gains Without Pains .... *Partridge* 3
No such Word as Fail .... *J. Blackwood* 24
Noah and his Times .... *Collins* 3
Noaic Deluge .... *Hodder* .. 19
Nobility of Life .... *Warne* 3
—— of Life, its Graces, &c. .... *Sotheran* .. 22
Noble Deeds of Women .... *Bell* 25
Noblesse Oblige................ *Isbister* .. 45
Noctes Ambrosianæ .... *W. Blackw'd* 33
Noel (Baptist W.) Works by .... *Nisbet* 5
—— & Chapsal, French Ed. Wks. *Nutt* 26
Nolan's Hist. of Bh. Em. in India *Virtue* .. 21
—— Hist. of Liberators of Italy.. *Virtue* .. 21
—— Hist. of War against Russia *Virtue* .. 21
Nonsense, by Lear.............. *Bush* 0
Noontide at Sychar .... *Nisbet* .. 23
Norfolk Dialect, Specimen .... *A. Heywood* 10
—— Murford's................ *J. R. Smith* 15
Norica, Tales from the Olden Time *Trubner* .. 13
Norman Conquest .... *Bohn's Lib.* .. 9
—— Conquest .... *Clar. Press* .. 10
—— House, 300 Years of ...... *Tinsley Bros.* 8
Normandy, Architecture of .... *Blackie* 7
—— and England .... *Macmillan* .. 27
—— Life in .... *Edmonston* .. 14
Norse (Old), Thorpe .... *Trubner* .. 11
—— Popular Tales from the .... *Chapman* 4
—— Sea Kings, Tales of .... *Nisbet* 11
—— Tales, Dasent.............. *Edmonston* .. 6
Norseman in the West .... *Nisbet* 4
North (Brownlow), Tracts by .... *Morgan* 9
North's (Roger) Mems. of Musick *Sotheran* .. 20
North West Passage .... *Cassell* 5
Northampton, Archl. Notices.... *Parker* .. 53
Northamptonshr. Rector's Sermons *Macmillan* .. 33
Northern Circuit................ *Macmillan* .. 27
—— University Life .... *Marr* .. 16
Northesk (Countess of) Works by *Hatchard* .. 18
Norton (Mrs.) Works by ...... *Macmillan* .. 27
Norway, Doresfjeld.............. *King* 5
—— English Gipsies in .... *King* 5
—— and its Glaciers .... *Black* 12
—— How to See .... *Longmans* .. 37
—— Introduction of Christianity *Masters* .. 24
—— Love and Life in .... *Cassell* 11
—— Month in .... *Murray* .. 14
—— Naturalist in .... *Reeve* 4
—— A Pastoral of .... *Isbister* .. 43
—— its People, Produce, &c. .... *Chapman* 4
—— The Road and the Fell .... *Parker* .. 64
—— and its Scenery .... *Bohn's Lib.* .. 14
—— Summer and Winter in .... *Murray* 3
—— and the Voring-Fos ...... *MacGlashan* 3
Norwegian Grammar.......... *Rivingtons* .. 18
—— Peasant Life .... *Isbister* 3
—— Practical Introduction to.... *Williams* 6
Norwich, Bayne's History of .... *Jarrold* .. 12
—— Proceedings, &c............ *Parker* .. 53
Not Lost, but Gone Before .... *Nisbet* .. 29
Not Wisely, but Too Well ...... *Tinsley Bros.* 10
Notes of a Naturalist.......... *Edmonston* 1
—— of Thought .... *Murray* 6
Notices to Correspondents .... *Houlston* 5
Notitia Eucharistica .... *Rivingtons* 3
—— Venatica .... *Chatto* 9
Novelists (British) and their Styles *Macmillan* .. 30

Old Helmet (The) .... *Nisbet* 39
—— Humphrey, Books by ...... *Partridge* 6
—— Humphrey's Post Bag ..... *Rel. Tr. Soc.* 29
—— Humphrey, Works by ..... *Rel. Tr. Soc.* 14
—— Humphrey, Works by ..... *Houlston* 20
—— Jonathan .... *Mack* 7
—— Kensington .... *Smith & El.*
—— Man's Thoughts .... *Bell* 42
—— Margaret .... *Tinsley Bros.* .. 10
—— Masters, Choice, Gems from *Bemrose* ... 17
—— Merry's Travels, &c. ...... *Warne* 28
—— and New, Bonar .... *Nisbet* 6
—— Oak Farm .... *S. S. Union* 7
—— Prose Stories .... *Chatto* 25
—— Laws, new Set .... *Routledge* 33
—— Testament, Companion to .. *Rivingtons* .. 2
—— Test. History for the Young *J. Blackwood* 23
—— Testament in the New ..... *Williams* .. 15
—— Testament, Structure of ... *Hodder* .. 7
Oliphant (Mrs.) Novels by ..... *Hurst & B.* .. 14
—— Works by .... *W. Blackw'd* 23
—— Works by .... *Macmillan* .. 27
Olive Branch, &c. .... *Nelson* 19
Olivet, Memories of .... *Nisbet* 23
Ollendorff's Ger. Method, Dulcken *Nutt* 18
—— Method, Greek .... *Trubner* 17
—— Method of Languages ..... *Whittaker* .. 8
—— Spanish Method .... *Trubner* 22
On the Banks of the Amazon ... *Nelson* 6
On a Coral Reef .... *Cassell* 11
On Earth Above and Below .... *Warne* 28
On the Edge of the Storm ..... *Warne* 19
Once upon a Time .... *Routledge* 5
One by Herself .... *S. S. Union* 6
—— Hour a Week .... *Nelson* 12
—— Story by Two Authors .... *Masters* 19
—— Syllable Books .... *Cassell* 9
—— Syllable Books .... *Routledge* 16
—— of the Thirty .... *Chatto* 21
—— Thousand Gems .... *Nicholson* 2
—— Trip More .... *Cassell* 11
—— Year .... *Warne* 10
Only a Girl's Life .... *Warne* 28
Ontario for Working Men ..... *Marr* 16
Open-Air Sermons, Walker .... *Nisbet* 36
Opera, History of .... *Allen* 6
Operations of War .... *W. Blackw'd* 12
Ophthalmic Manual of Instruction *Harrison* .. 9
—— Test Types .... *Williams* .. 13
Ophthalmoscope in Nerv. Diseases *Macmillan* .. 2
Ophthalmology, Works on ..... *Churchill* .. 0
Opium-Eater, Confessions .... *Black* .. 11
Optics .... *Chambers* 17
—— Nugent .... *Isbister* 32
—— Elementary Treatise, Potter *Bell* 20
—— Treatise on, Parkinson .... *Macmillan* .. 28
—— Undulatory Theory of ... *Macmillan* .. 10
Oral Training Lessons in Science *Hardwicke.* .. 12
Orange River, Ten Years North.. *Edmonston* .. 15
Orator (British) .... *A. Heywood* 10
Oratorios .... *Cramer* .... a
Orbis Antiqus Descriptio ..... *Trubner* .. 19
Orbs Around Us .... *Longmans* 18
—— of Heaven (The) .... *Routledge* .. 35
Orchard Houses .... *Houlston* 10
Orchids (Cool) and How to Grow *Hardwicke.* .. 4
—— Fertilization of .... *Murray* 9
—— How to Grow .... *Reeve* 7
Ordination Addresses .... *Parker* 11
—— Questions .... *Hall* 3
—— Service .... *Parker* .. 11
—— Validity of .... *Parker* .. 5
Ordinum Sacrorum in Ecclesia,&c. *Parker* 5
Ordnance Survey Maps ...... *Smith* .. 8
—— Survey Maps .... *Stanford* .. 45
—— Survey Publications ...... *Stanford* 61
—— Trigonometrical, U. Kingdom *Stanford* .. 65
O'Reilly's (Miss) Books for Young *Bell* .. 10
Organ (The), Sutton .... *Rivingtons.* .. 10
Organs, Church .... *Rivingtons.* .. 10
—— Short Account of .... *Masters* 10
—— (Use of) Indefensible...... *MacP'lnn* .. 9
Organisms, Origin of Lowest ... *Macmillan* .. 3
—— Transformation of Lowest .. *Macmillan* .. 3
Oriental and American Books .... *Rivers* .... a

Oriental and American Literature *Trubner* 0
—— History, Lenormant .... *Asher* .. 5
—— History, Rawlinson .... *Longmans* .. 4
—— Religions .... *Trubner* .. 17
—— Works .... *Smith & El.* 28
Origin of Species, Darwin .... *J. Murray* .. 9
Original Poems for Infant Minds.. *Routledge* .. 25
Orissa, an Indian Province .... *Smith & El.* 11
Orkneyinga Saga .... *Edmonston* .. 1
Orley Farm .... *Chapman* .. 25
Orm, The Book of .... *Isbister* .. 10
Ornament and Style, Analysis of.. *Chapman* .. 21
Ornaments Discovered ...... *J. Blackw'd* 21
Ornamental Alphabets & Initials.. *Lockwood* .. 15
—— Drawing .... *Ward & Lock* 20
—— Penmanship .... *Johnston* .. 37
Orphan Bessie .... *S. S. Union* .. 10
—— Colony of Jews in China .. *Nisbet* .. 13
—— and the Foundling....... *S. S. Union* .. 6
—— Houses, Bristol .... *Mack* .. 9
—— Sisters .... *S. S. Union* .. 8
Orthodoxy, Scripture and Reason. *Williams* .. 8
Orval : or, The Fool of Time ... *Chapman* .. 20
Orville College Boys .... *Routledge* .. 31
Osborn (Sherard) Works by .... *W. Blackw'd* 23
O'Shaughnessy (Arthur) Poems .. *Chatto* .. 20
Ossian's Poems .... *W. Blackw'd.* 24
Osteology (Comparative) Atlas of.. *Williams* .. 7
—— Human .... *Churchill* .. 20
—— (Human), Humphry ...... *Macmillan* .. 13
—— of Mammalia .... *Macmillan* .. 11
—— for Students .... *Hardwicke.* .. 16
Other Countries, Bell .... *Chapman* .. 11
—— Folks' Lives .... *Isbister* .. 40
—— Men's Minds .... *Warne* .. 2
—— Shore (The) .... *Nisbet* .. 29
—— Worlds than Ours ...... *Longmans* .. 16
Otto's German Educational Works. *Nutt* .. 19
Ought We to Visit Her? ..... *Bentley* .. 10
Ouida, the Serf .... *Isbister* .. 50
Our Angel Companions ...... *Houlston* .. 34
—— Children's Pets .... *Partridge* .. 15
—— Dumb Companions ...... *Partridge* .. 14
—— Dumb Neighbours ...... *Partridge* .. 8
—— Exemplars, Poor and Rich .. *J. Blackwood* 14
—— Father in Heaven .... *Nisbet* .. 28
—— Forefathers .... *Nisbet* .. 20
—— Friends in Heaven ...... *Asher* .. 4
—— Life in the Highlands, Illust. *Bell* .. 3
—— Life, Illust. by Pen & Pencil *Rel. Tr. Soc.* 14
—— Lord, History of, Jameson .. *Longmans* .. 29
—— Lord, Temptation of ..... *Isbister* .. 22
—— Mother Church, Mercier ... *Rivingtons* .. 12
—— Nurseries and Schoolrooms.. *Hatchard* .. 12
—— New Masters .... *Isbister* .. 25
—— New Vicar .... *Bell* .. 48
—— Treasure of Light ...... *Mozley* .. 5
—— Work, by Grover (W. H.) .. *S. S. Union* 44
—— Year, Prose and Verse .... *Macmillan* .. 27
Ourselves, Our Food and Physic. *Chapman* .. 24
—— Essay on Women .... *Routledge* .. 44
Out of Doors .... *Longmans* .. 23
Outline Study of Man .... *Hender* .. 8
Outpost Duty, Military ...... *Chapman* .. 21
Ouvry (Miss) Tales by ...... *Bell* .. 24
Overland Expeditions .... *Isbister* .. 0
—— Southampton to Queensland.. *Stanford* .. 55
Over Turf and Stubble ...... *Bentley* .. 24
Ovid, Metamorphoses, King ... *W. Blackw'd.* 24
—— Oxford Classics .... *Parker* .. 55
Owen, Dr. John, Works by Goold *Clark* .. 29
—— (Rt.) Founder of Socialism .. *Trubner* .. 21
Owlglass (Tyll) Adventures of... *Trubner* .. 12
Ox (The) Diseases and Treatment. *Longmans* .. 42
Oxenden (Bishop) Works by ... *Hatchard* .. 18
Oxford & Cambridge Boat Races. *Bell* .. 2
—— and Cambridge Boat Races.. *Macmillan* .. 2
—— and Cambridge College .... *Rel. Tr. Soc.*
—— Geology of .... *Clar. Press* .. 18
—— Graduates, 1659-1850 .... *Clar. Press* .. 16
—— Handbook .... *Parker* .. 52
—— in 19th Century, Mansel ... *Murray* .. 22
—— Methodists .... *Hodder* .. 14
—— Museum, Pathological .... *Clar. Press* .. 15
—— Pocket Classics .... *Parker* .. 55

Oxford, Recollections of .... Macmillan .. 8
—— Reformers .... Longmans .. 3
—— Spectator (The) .... Macmillan .. 27
—— University Exam. Papers .. Parker 61
—— Univ. Student's Handbook .. Clar. Press .. 16
—— Youth and Years at ...... Wesleyan .. 51
Oxfordshire .... Parker 52
Oxfordshire .... J. R. Smith .. 16
Oxus (Source of the) .... Murray 32
Oxygen, its Action and Use ... Churchill .. 9
Oyster (The) Where & How to Find Trübner .. 23
Orme and Antoine .... Churchill .. 16

Pacific Islands .... Soc. P. C. K. .. 21
—— Islands, Buzacott .... Snow 3
—— Ocean, Lester .... Longmans .. 37
—— A Tale of the, Ballantyne ... Nisbet 4
Packing Case Maker .... Lockwood .. 9
Paget (Rev. F. E.) Works by ... Masters 20
Painted Glass, A Plea for ...... Parker 54
Painters, British Portrait .... Virtue 3
—— British Landscape .... Virtue 10
—— Dictionary of English ...... Longmans .. 28
—— Early Flemish .... Murray 7
—— Early Italian, Jameson .... Murray 19
—— of English School .... Smith & El. 17
—— and Engravers, Eng. Dic. .. Bell 39
—— Homely Scenes of Great ... Cassell 4
—— Lives of, Taubs .... Routley 2
—— Lives of, Vasari .... Bohn's Lib. .. 9
—— (Modern), Ruskin .... Smith & El. 13
—— (Old and Modern) .... Isbister 44
—— (Young) Handbook for .... Sosinson .. 7
Painter's Camp in the Highlands. Macmillan .. 15
Painting, Burnet on .... Murray 20
—— Epochs of, Wornum ...... Chapman .. 26
—— German, Dutch, Flemish .. Murray 19
—— History of, Heaton .... Bell 6
—— History of, Lanzi .... Bohn's Lib. 8
—— Italian Schools of .... Murray 19
—— in Italy .... Murray 7
—— in Italy, Burckhardt ...... Murray 6
—— (Landscape) Water Colours . Routledge .. 3
—— Lectures on, Wornum ..... Bohn's Lib. 19
—— in Oil and Fresco .... Whittaker .. 16
—— Popularly Explained ...... Lockwood .. 15
—— Spanish School of .... Routledge .. 13
—— Vere Foster's Course ..... M. Ward .. 18
—— Water Colour .... Cassell 15
Palace of Great King .... Collins 3
Palæontology, Owen .... Black 15
Palermo, A Tale of .... Macmillan .. 25
Palestine, Bonar .... Nisbet 6
—— Divon .... Chapman .. 14
—— Kitto .... Bohn's Lib. 13
—— Kitto's History .... Routledge .. 21
—— Vaughan .... King 4
—— Robinson .... Dickinson .. 10
—— Stanley .... Murray 28
—— Tristram .... Murray 32
—— Van de Velde .... W. Blackw'd 32
—— Works on, Macduff ...... Nisbet 23
—— Biblical Researches in .... Murray 27
—— Byways in .... Nisbet 13
—— Canoe Cruise in "Rob Roy" Murray 21
—— (The Christian in) .... Virtue 13
—— Domestic Life in .... Bell 12
—— Dresses of Lebanon ...... Murray 6
—— Exploration Survey ...... Bell 11
—— Exploration Fund, Photos . Stanford .. 66
—— Geography of, Meen ..... S. S. Union 42
—— Geography of, by Ritter ... Clark 21
—— Hand book to .... Murray 16
—— Hebrew Maps of .... Johnson .. 27
—— On Holy Ground .... Nimmo .. 31
—— Land and the Book ...... Nelson .. 5
—— Our Work in .... Bentley .. 12
—— Physical Geography ...... Murray 27
—— Rivers of .... Burns 33
—— Scenes in .... Soc. P. C. K. 23
—— Sketches of Travel ...... Isbister .. 32
—— (Through) on Horseback .. Soc. P. C. K. 20
—— Topography of .... Soc. P. C. K. 27
—— Traditions of .... Routledge .. 37
—— Travels in .... Snow 1

Palestine Travels in .... Harrison .. 4
—— Early Travels in .... Bohn's Lib. 12
—— Travels in, Tristram ..... Soc. P. C. K. 15
—— Walks in, Ashworth ..... Tubbs .. 2
—— Winter in the East ...... Masters .. 29
—— for the Young .... Rel. Tr. Soc. 15
Paley's Evidences, Fisk ...... Hall 3
—— Evidences of Christianity . Soc. P. C. K. 9
—— Natural Theology .... Soc. P. C. K. 20
Palgrave (F. T.) Works by .... Macmillan .. 27
—— (W. G.) Works by .... Macmillan .. 27
Pali-English Dictionary ...... Trübner .. 7
Palm Leaves, Genck .... Isbister .. 6
Palms and their Allies .... Routledge .. 48
Palmerston (Lord) Life ...... Bentley .. 12
Palmyra, Porter .... Murray .. 25
Palsy (Wasting), Roberts ..... Churchill .. 30
Pampas, Rapid Journey Across . Murray .. 14
Panama, Jottings on Roadside in Chapman .. 23
Pandurang Hari .... King 32
Pansies, for Thoughts .... Isbister .. 47
Pantheism, Essay on .... Isbister .. 22
—— Manning .... Dickinson .. 9
—— Modern, Essay on ...... Clark 21
Papa's Pretty Gift Book ...... Ward & Lock 19
Papacy, Growth of Temp. Power Macmillan .. 29
Papal Conclaves .... Edmonston .. 4
—— Power, Hussey .... Clar. Press. 11
Paper Rosette Work .... Bemrose .. 11
Papers for the People .... Chambers .. 35
Parable of the Sower, Stories on Nisbet .. 36
Parables for Children .... Macmillan .. 1
—— Maclachlan .... W. Blackw'd 40
—— from Nature .... Bell 19
—— of Our Lord, illus. in colours Macmillan .. 38
—— of Our Lord, French ..... Macmillan .. 37
—— of Our Saviour .... J. Blackwood 10
—— The Pearl of .... Nisbet .. 16
—— Pictures, Millais .... Routledge .. 27
—— Sermons on the .... Masters .. 19
—— Tales on .... Cassell .. 7
—— and Tales, Hake .... Chapman .. 19
Paradise of Birds .... W. Blackw'd 7
—— of Martyrs .... Hodder .. 9
Paradoxes (Budget of) ...... Longmans .. 16
—— and Puzzles .... W. Blackw'd 24
Paraguay, Mansfield .... Macmillan .. 23
Paraguayan War .... Stanford .. 54
Parallel Hist. of France and Engl. Macmillan .. 43
Parana (The) .... Stanford .. 56
Paris Commune, History of .. Chapman .. 26
—— Diary of a Besieged Resident Macmillan .. 19
—— and its Environs .... Bohn's Lib. 14
—— Exhibition, Notes, &c. ... Tinsley Bros. 7
—— At Home in .... Allen .. 3
—— (Member for), a Tale .... Smith & El. 15
—— Siege of .... Smith & El. 3
—— during the Siege .... Chapman .. 24
—— during the Siege (Inside) . Macmillan .. 17
—— after two Sieges .... Tinsley Bros. 7
—— Sunday Echoes from ..... Nisbet .. 33
—— after Waterloo .... W. Blackw'd 28
Parish Choir (The) .... Harrison .. 15
—— Law, Handy-Book of .... Routledge .. 42
—— Musings .... Rivingtons .. 7
—— Papers, Macleod .... Isbister .. 29
—— Priest : his Duties, &c. .. Murray .. 4
—— and the Priest .... Masters .. 20
—— Priest's Pocket-Book .... Masters .. 20
—— Registers in England .... J. R. Smith 6
—— Tune Book .... Warne .. 39
—— Work .... Parker .. 39
—— Work, Church .... Rivingtons .. 10
—— Work, Monsell .... Bell .. 48
Park's (Mungo) Life and Travels Nimmo .. 14
—— Travels .... Black .. 15
Parker (Jos.) Extracts from ... Dickinson .. 7
—— (Theodore) Works ...... Trübner .. 23
Parker's School Books .... Allman .. 1
Parliament (The) Long ...... Chatto .. 25
—— (The) Rump .... Chatto .. 31
Parliamentary Anecdote ..... Cassell .. 6
—— Buff Book .... Wilson .. 11
—— Government .... Longmans .. 4
—— Papers Classified .... Smith & El. 13

Parlour Pastimes............... *J. Blackwood* 27
Parochial Antiquities, Kennett ... *Clar. Press..* 16
—— Books .... *Masters* .. 0
—— Tracts .... *Parker* 0
—— Visiting, Hilton......... *Morley* .. 1
Parr (Mrs.) Novels by .... *Isbister* 33
Parrot Book .... *Ward&Lock* 11
Parsi Religion, Wilson .... *Stewart* .... a
Parsing Manual, Davidson ...... *J. Heywood* 23
Parsons (Mrs.) Works by ...... *Burns* 31
Pascal, Provincial Letters ..... *Collins* 3
—— Studies on .... *Clark* 11
Passing Bell (The), Poems .... *Bell* 36
Passion, History of Sacred, Palma *Burns* 14
—— Meditation, on the ...... *Masters* .. 3
—— of Our Lord, Durer ...... *Bell* 7
—— of Our Lord, Williams .... *Rivingtons..* 4
—— Reflections on the ...... *Masters* 4
—— Works on the .... *Burns* 32
—— Play (The) .... *MacGlashan* 3
—— Play, English Words ..... *Masters* 20
Past, Present, and the Future... *Trubner* 7
Pastimes of Merrie England .... *Cassell* 6
Pastor in his Closet .... *Parker..* .. 32
Pastor's Sketches .... *Nelson* 5
Pastoral Counsels, Robertson ... *Macmillan* .. 30
—— Epistles, Gk. Test. & Trans. *Clark* 36
—— Office, Burgon .... *Macmillan..* 4
—— Office, Oxenden .... *Hatchard* .. 19
—— Theology, Vinet .... *Clark* 20
—— Visitation .... *Bell* 53
—— Visitation .... *Parker* 39
—— Work, Exton .... *Rivingtons..* 11
—— Work, Practice of ...... *Rivingtons..* 10
Patagonians, At Home with .... *Murray* 9
Patents, Barlow .... *Marlborough* 9
—— Law of .... *Lockwood* .. 28
—— Law of .... *Stevens* 23
Patent Law, Dircks .... *Spon* 32
—— Laws, Newton .... *Trubner* 21
Path on Earth to Gate of Heaven *Ward* 28
—— to Heaven Prayer Book ... *Burns* 6
—— of Holiness .... *Rivingtons..* 6
Pathological Histology ...... *Trubner* 26
Pathologica Indica .... *Allen* 22
Pathway of Peace .... *Macintosh* .. a
—— of Safety (The) .... *Hatchard* .. 19
Patience of Hope .... *Isbister* 18
—— in Tribulation .... *Nisbet* 29
Patmos, Memories of .... *Nisbet* 23
—— to Paradise .... *W. Blackwd* 37
Patriarch and the Tsar........ *Trubner* 23
Patriarchs and Lawgivers....... *Macmillan..* 24
Patricius Walker, Rambles by .... *Longmans* .. 37
Patristic Theology, Catalogue of *Stewart* .... a
Patteson (Bishop) Sketch of Life *Soc. P. C. K.* 20
—— Life and Letters, Yonge .. *Macmillan..* 23
Pau, Climate of, Taylor .... *Churchill..* .. 35
Paul the Apostle .... *W. Blackwd* 8
—— the Pope, Trollope ..... *Smith & El.* 25
—— of Tarsus, by a Graduate .. *Macmillan..* 28
Pauline Epistles, Introduction to.. *Clark* 35
Paupers, Training of Juvenile ... *Macmillan..* 16
Pauperism, Cause and Remedies *Macmillan..* 11
Pawnbroking, Guide to .... *Routledge* .. 42
Payne (John) Poetical Works of.. *Pickering* .. 31
Peace (The) of God .... *Isbister* 23
Peach and Nectarine Culture... *Groombridge* 1
Peak and the Plain .... *Hamilton* .. 22
Pearl of the Antilles, Gallenga ... *Chapman* .. 4
Pears (S. A.) Works by .... *Hatchard* .. 6
Pearson on Creed, Chevallier ... *Cambridge..* 6
—— Theological Works ...... *Clar. Press..* 6
Pear Tree, Population of an Old *Macmillan..* 29
Peasant Boy Philosopher ...... *Routledge* .. 33
—— Life in the North ...... *Isbister* 34
—— Life, Romance of ...... *Cassell* 7
—— Preacher .... *Wesleyan* .. 41
—— Proprietors, Plea for.. *Macmillan..* 35
Peat Question, Meadows ...... *MacGlashan* 1
Peden the Prophet .... *Snow* 1
Pelita and Angelina .... *Parker..* .. 6
Peebles and its Neighbourhood .. *Chambers* .. 23
Peck's Prize Essays .... *Murray* 25
Peel's (Sir Robert) Memoirs .... *Murray* 25

Peep of Day Works .... *Hatchard* .. 21
Peeps at the Far East .... *Isbister* 29
—— at Foreign Countries .... *Isbister* 34
—— into the Human Hive .... *Chapman* .. 7
Peerage and Baronetage, Burke *Harrison* .. 1
—— Debrett .... *Dean* .... a
—— and Baronetage, Lodge ... *Hurst & B.* .. 12
—— (Historic) Nicholas ..... *Murray* 24
—— The Shilling .... *Hardwicke..* 13
—— &c., Walford .... *Hardwicke..* 12
Peerages (Extinct), Burke ..... *Harrison* .. 2
Peggy and other Tales .... *Cassell* 11
Pelargoniums .... *W. Blackwd* 49
Pelican Papers .... *King* 33
Peninsular Campaigns, Hamilton *W. Blackwd* 11
—— War, Battles and Sieges ... *Murray* 23
—— War, Burgoyne's Life .... *Bentley* .. 5
—— War, Story of .... *J. Blackwd* 11
Penman's Repository .... *J. Heywood* 19
Penmanship............... *Chambers* .. 10
Penn (W.) History of........ *Hurst & B.* .. 7
Pennsylvania.............. *Hurst & B.* .. 7
—— Dutch Dialect .... *Trubner* 15
—— Geology .... *W. Blackwd* 27
Penny Guides, Games, &c ..... *Milner* 12
—— Post .... *Parker..* .. 45
Pentateuch and its Anatomists .. *Hatchard* .. 3
—— Colenso on .... *Longmans* .. 34
—— Essays on the .... *Bell* 60
—— Inquiry into Genuineness . *Clark* 0
—— Trans. by Howard ..... *Macmillan..* 2
Pentateuchus Hebraeus ...... *Clar. Press..*
Pentecost, or Revival Work of God *Morgan* 3
People's Tune Book (The) ..... *Morgan* 3
Peoples of the World .... *Cassell* 11
Peopling, by a Pastor .... *Nisbet* 30
Pepper (Prof.) Bks. for the Young *Routledge* .. 29
Pepys' Diary .... *Warne* 22
—— Diary and Correspondence.. *Bohn's Lib.* .. 10
Percival (Rt. Hon. S.) Correspon. *Hurst & B.* .. 1
Percy Anecdotes .... *Warne* 22
Percy Raydon .... *S. S. Union* 24
Percy's (Bp.) Folio Manuscripts.. *Sotheran..* 22
—— Folio Manuscripts ...... *Trubner* 24
—— Reliques .... *Routledge* .. 61
—— (J.) Works on Metallurgy .. *Murray* 25
Perfect Life (The) .... *Williams* .. 4
—— Man, Jones .... *Rivingtons..* 14
Perils of the Polar Seas ...... *Murray* 7
Perimetritis and Parametritis ... *Black* 12
Periodicals to Complete Sets ... *Wheldon* .. a
Perkins's Tuscan Sculptors .... *Sotheran..* 22
Perowne (Canon) Works by .... *Isbister* 34
Perpetual Motion .... *Spon* 32
Perranzabuloe .... *Rivingtons..* 26
Perreyve (H.) by Gratry ...... *Rivingtons..* 15
Persia, Markham .... *Longmans* .. 3
—— Mounsey's .... *Smith & El.* 10
—— Watson .... *Smith & El.* 16
—— Ancient and Modern .... *King..* .. 3
—— during the Famine of 1872 .. *Pickering* .. 31
—— Sketches in .... *Murray* 31
—— Travels in .... *Allen* 4
—— Woman and Her Saviour in *Nisbet* 26
Persian Grammar .... *Smith & El.* 21
—— Language .... *Allen* 32
—— War, Cox .... *Longmans* .. 4
Personal Piety .... *Isbister* 34
—— Experience of Rom. Cathlcsm. *Morgan* 3
Persons who went to Aunt Piantas. *Chatto* 28
Perspective, Collins .... *Longmans* .. 31
—— and Drawing, Hayter .... *Bogue* 67
—— Easy Course .... *Philip* 41
—— (Linear), Burchett ...... *Chapman* .. 12
—— (Practical), Jewitt ...... *Cornish* .. 4
—— Principles of, Humphris ... *Chapman* .. 10
—— (School) .... *Isbister* 0
Peter the Apostle, Green ..... *S. S. Union* 43
—— Schlemihl, Trans. ...... *Hardwicke..* 14
Pet-land, Glimpses into ...... *Bell* 23
Petöfi's Poems .... *Trubner* 24
Petrarch's Sonnets, Trans. .... *Bell* 29
Petrifactions and their Teachings *Bohn's Lib.* .. 19
Perversion .... *Spon* 32
Pets, or Pastimes and Penalties.. *Isbister* 2

Place of the Physician, a Lecture *King* 31
Places and People .... *Tinsley Bros.* 9
Plague of the Village........... *S. S. Union.* 9
—— Year (The), 1665 .... *Soc. P. C. K.* 21
Plain Words on Christian Living *Isbister* 46
Plan of Redemption .... *Kellaway* 8
Planché (J. R.), Recollections .... *Tinsley Bros.* 3
Planetary and Stellar Worlds .... *Collins* 3
—— Theory .... *Macmillan*.. 6
Plantarum (Genera) .... *Williams* 3
—— (Icones) .... *Williams* 7
Planter, Cruikshank .... *W. Blackw'd* 49
Planter's Guide .... *W. Blackw'd* 53
Plant Hunters (The) .... *Routledge* .. 34
Plants, Beautiful Leaved ...... *Bell* 17
—— Encyclopædia of .... *Longmans* .. 24
—— Grasses, Pratt .... *Warne* 7
—— of Land and Water .... *Jarrold* 9
—— London Catalogue of British *Hardwicke* .. 3
—— their Natural Growth, &c. .. *M. Ward* ... 13
—— Natural History of .... *Reeve* 3
—— New and Rare, Hibberd.... *Bell* 16
—— Ornamental, &c .... *Sangster* 5
—— On Pop. Names of British. *Williams* 11
—— Profitable............... *Routledge* .. 48
—— of the World .... *Routledge* .. 48
Plasterer's, &c., Guide .... *Hagger* 13
Platelayer's Tables............ *Spon* 52
Plato, Christian Element of.... *Clark* 70
—— Grote .... *J. Murray*.. 13
—— Thompson .... *Whittaker* .. 2
—— by Various Editors ...... *Williams* 11
—— Translated .... *Bohn's Lib.*.. 17
—— Republic, Trans.......... *Macmillan*.. 14
Playing Cards, History of ..... *Chatto* 36
—— Card Tricks............. *Chatto* 32
Play-Book of Science .... *Routledge* .. 29
Play and Earnest .... *Masters* 29
Playfellow (The), Martineau .... *Routledge* .. 30
Play Hour Library .... *Laurie* 4
—— Hours and Half-Holidays .. *Routledge* .. 34
—— Hours in London .... *Mozley*...... 9
Playmate (Modern)............ *Warne* 3
Plays (Little) for Little People .. *Bell* 26
Pleading Saviour.............. *Nelson* 21
Pleas for the Faith............ *Parker*....... 4
Pleasant Fruits, Havergal ..... *Nisbet* 17
—— Pages .... *Houlston* .. 46
—— Paths for Little Feet ..... *Nisbet* 10
Pleasure and Instruction ...... *Warne* 5
Plon's Life of Thorwaldsen ..... *Bentley* 14
Plucky Fellows (Book for Boys).. *King* 17
Plumtre (Miss) Works by ...... *Nisbet* 30
—— (Professor) Works by ..... *Isbister* 9
Plunkett's (Lord) Life and Letters *Smith & El.* 16
Plurality of Worlds, Knight..... *Ragster* 70
Plutarch, Greek History from .. *Longmans* .. 8
—— his Life, Lives, and Morals. *Macmillan*.. 33
Plutarch's Lives, Selections from *Nimmo* 15
Plymouth Brethren, Heresies of.. *Houlston*..... 33
Pneumonia, Bennett .... *Black* 2
Poacher's Sons .... *S. S. Union.* 8
Pocket Miscellany .... *Chambers* ... 36
—— Prayer Book (The) .... *Nisbet*....... 30
Poe (E. A.) Poetical Works..... *Nimmo* 11
—— Tales of Mystery .... *Ward&Lock* 28
—— Works .... *Chatto* 13
Poems, Browning (R.) .... *Smith & El.* 1
—— by Delta .... *W. Blackw'd* 21
—— from Eastern Sources ..... *Macmillan*.. 38
—— English and Latin .... *Masters* 2
—— of the English Roadside ... *Chapman* .. 22
—— for Infant Minds, Taylor... *Routledge* .. 16
—— Longer English .... *Macmillan*.. 15
—— of Natural History ...... *Nelson* 2
—— by a Painter, Paton (J. N.) *W. Blackw'd.* 25
—— and Pictures .... *Cassell* 6
—— Religious .... *Nisbet* 32
—— Sacred (Book of) .... *Cassell* 7
—— Written for a Child ..... *Nisbet* 35
—— for the Young, Wordsworth. *Isbister* 48
—— for the Young and Old .... *Soc. P. C. K.* 8
Poetical Gift Book .... *Houlston* ... 16
—— Gift Book .... *Milner*...... 10
—— Illustrations............. *Houlston*.... 16

Poetical Series .... *Gall* 7
Poetic Wit and Legends in Verse *J. Blackwood* 7
Poets, British .... *Routledge* .. 61
—— Aldine Edition .... *Bell* 30
—— Cabinet Edition .... *Bohn's Lib.* .. 9
—— Oracles from .... *Isbister* 32
—— of the 19th Century ..... *Warne* 13
—— Chandos .... *Warne* 18
—— Children's Garland from Best *Macmillan* .. 7
—— Contemporary .... *Houlston* ... 15
—— Corner .... *Routledge* .. 10
—— English .... *J. Blackwood* 6
—— English .... *Cassell* 0
—— English .... *Milner* 1
—— Globe Editions .... *Macmillan* .. 13
—— Homes and Haunts of Brit. *Routledge* .. 5
—— Half Hours with Sacred .. *J. Blackwood* 12
—— (Lansdowne) .... *Warne* 23
—— (Old) .... *Routledge* .. 62
—— Our Living, an Essay .... *Tinsley Bros.* 7
—— Passages from the ...... *Mozley*...... 9
—— Pen and Pencil Pictures from *Nimmo* 10
—— People's Edition .... *Cameron* 9
—— Popular Edition .... *Nimmo* 7
—— Selections from British .. *Bell* 9
—— Theology in the English .. *King* 10
—— Words from the .... *Macmillan* .. 42
Poet Hero (A) .... *Cassell* 6
Poetry .... *Rivingtons* .. 26
—— Amusing .... *Chatto* 33
—— Book .... *Ward&Lock* 12
—— Books of Easy .... *Routledge* .. 16
—— for Children .... *Lockwood* .. 40
—— for Children, Lamb ..... *Pickering* .. 25
—— Church .... *Mozley* 9
—— Church .... *Parker* 0
—— Class Book .... *Black* 16
—— De Vere's Selection .... *Burns* 32
—— English Sacred .... *Rel. Tr. Soc.* 7
—— Essay on English .... *Murray* 7
—— The Fleshly School of ... *Isbister* 9
—— Garland of Sacred ..... *Nicholson* .. 5
—— 1001 Gems of English ... *Routledge* .. 1
—— Gems of National ...... *Warne* 21
—— (Greek & Latin Trans. Eng.) *Nutt* 9
—— Household Book, English. *Macmillan* .. 38
—— Lectures on, Doyle ..... *Macmillan* .. 5
—— from Life, by C. M. K. .. *Smith & El.* 16
—— (Mother's Book of), Gatty *Bell* 20
—— and Poets of Great Britain *Black* 15
—— (Recent) .... *Bell* 31
—— (Recent) .... *Bemrose* 8
—— (Recent) .... *King* 30
—— (Recent) Selections from. *Isbister* 26
—— Religious .... *Masters* 0
—— Sacred .... *Parker* 26
—— Sacred, for the Young ... *Macmillan* .. 14
—— Standard .... *J. Heywood* . 25
—— of Science, Hunt ...... *Bohn's Lib.* . 19
—— Studies in .... *Lockwood* .. 40
—— (Eng.)Trans. Latin, Newman *Trübner* 21
—— from best Authors ..... *Warne* 28
Poisons, Taylor on .... *Churchill* 35
Polar World (The) .... *Longmans* .. 23
Polarity (Diamagnetic) ...... *Longmans* .. 22
Pole to Pole (From) .... *Nisbet* 17
Police Guide............... *Stevens* 2
Policeman G. .... *Chatto* 29
Polish Insurrection.......... *Macmillan* .. 4
Polish Jew................. *Ward&Lock* 23
Political & Agricultural Fallacies *Stanford* ... 55
—— Economy .... *Chambers* ... 17
—— Economy for Beginners .. *Macmillan* .. 11
—— Economy, Elementary ... *J. Heywood* . 32
—— Economy, Fawcett ..... *Macmillan* .. 11
—— Economy, Jevons ...... *Macmillan* .. 17
—— Economy, M'Culloch ... *Black* 14
—— Economy, Manual ..... *Clar. Press* .. 24
—— Economy, Mill .... *Longmans* .. 10
—— Economy, Newman .... *Trübner* 21
—— Economy, Recent ..... *Williams* 12
—— Economy, Ricardo .... *Murray* 24
—— Economy, Ruskin ..... *Smith & El.* 18
—— Economy Survey ...... *Edmonston.* . 15
—— Economy, Theo. & Practical *Macmillan* .. 5

Political Cyclopædia .... *Bohn's Lib...* 10
—— Essays, Cairnes .... *Macmillan* .. 5
—— Portraits .... *Isbister* 35
—— Problems .... *Trubner* 14
—— Series .... *Gall* 7
—— Sketches of Europe ...... *Edmonston..* 16
—— Survey, G. Duff. .... *Edmonston..* 7
—— Women .... *King* 1
Politics, Comparative .... *Macmillan* .. 12
Pollock (Sir Geo.) Life .... *Allen* 23
Pollok (R.) Poems .... *W. Blackw'd* 26
Polychromatic Ornament ...... *Sotheran..* 23
Polynesia, Mission to, Williams . *Snow* 13
—— Physical Features, &c. ...... *Soc. P. C. K.* 21
—— Ten Years in South Central, *Wesleyan* 51
—— Nineteen Years in, Turner . *Snow* 16
Polynia (Gateway to the) ...... *King* 5
Pompeii, History of, Dyer ...... *Bell* 11
—— Ruins of, Dyer .... *Bell* 9
Poole (Joshua) Life of .... *Morgan* 5
Poor Jack, Marryat .... *Bell* 22
—— Law Books and Forms.... *Knight* ...... a
—— Laws, English, Irish, Scotch *Murray* 74
—— Man's Cry (The)........ *Nisbet* 30
Poore (J. L.) Memoir of ...... *Hodder* 21
Popery, Anatomy of .... *Wesleyan* .. 46
—— Ancient and Modern...... *Snow* 3
—— Dissuasive from .... *Clar. Press..* 13
—— the Man of Sin .... *MacPhun* .. 14
—— Text Book of .... *Houlston* .. 34
—— Tracts against.......... *Clar. Press..* 13
Pope's Works, Elwin .... *Murray* 25
—— Works .... *Bohn's Lib...* 14
—— Works, by Pattison ...... *Clar. Press..* 32
Pope and the Council .... *Rivingtons..* 12
Pope, Supremacy of, Barrow .. *Clar. Press..* 13
Pope's (The) Supremacy ...... *Cambridge* .. 5
—— Supremacy, Barrow .... *Soc. P. C. K.* 3
Popes of Rome, Ranke........ *Murray* 26
—— History of, Ranke........ *Bohn's Lib...* 8
—— Last Four, Wiseman .. *Hurst* 14
—— of Middle Ages, Fables of . *Rivingtons..* 25
Popish Transubstantiation .... *Parker* ...... a
Popoff (Basil) Works by ...... *Masters* 21
Poppies in the Corn .... *Tinsley Bros.* 9
Popular Educator .... *Cassell* 6
—— Objections to Revealed Truth *Hodder* 5
—— Recreator .... *Cassell* 7
—— Sacred Harmonies........ *Tubbs* 7
Porter (Noah) Works by ...... *Isbister* 35
Port of Refuge (The), Hopkins . *King* 31
—— Royal, Beard .... *Williams* 2
Portrait and Landscape Gallery . *Allman* 12
Portraits, Webster .... *Macmillan* .. 42
Portsmouth, Story of "Domus Dei" *Parker* 53
Portuary (A) .... *Parker* 33
Portugal, History of .... *Masters* 13
—— (Carnarvon's) .... *Murray* 6
—— Dunbar .... *W. Blackw'd* 7
—— and Spain, Wars of Succession *Stanford* .. 50
Portuguese, Colloquial ...... *Trubner* 10
—— English Dictionary, Lacerda *Nutt* 31
—— English Dictionary, Vieyra.. *Nutt* 32
—— Testament and Com. Prayer *Bagster* 20
Positive Philosophy, Comte.... *Trubner* 8
—— Religion, Catechism of.... *Trubner* 8
Positivism (English), Taine.... *Williams* 14
Possession and Profession .... *Nisbet* 9
Post and Paddock .... *Warne* 11
Post Office Directory, French.... *Asher* 11
—— Office Gazetteer .... *Longmans* .. 20
Poste (Rev. B.) Works ...... *J. R. Smith* 17
Postman's Bag (The) .... *Isbister* 33
Potato, Cultivation of........ *Groombridge* 8
Potter (T. J.) Works .... *MacGlashan* 4
—— Works .... *Washbourne* 15
Pottery (Ancient) Birch........ *Murray* 4
—— and Porcelain .... *Bohn's Lib..* 15
—— and Porcelain, Marryat .... *Chapman* .. 20
—— and Porcelain, Marryat .... *Murray* 22
Poultry Account Book .... *Letts* 1
—— as a Meat Supply ...... *Kissime* 27
—— Book, Tegetmeier ...... *Routledge* .. 27
—— Dickson and Mowbray...... *Bohn's Lib..* 9
—— and Domestic Animals .... *Ward & Lock* 12

Poultry (Illustrated) Wright .... *Cassell* 6
—— Keeper's Manual ...... *Houlston...* 24
—— and Pigeons .... *Ward & Lock* 11
—— Practical Guide ...... *Groombridge* 21
Pounceford Hall .... *S. S. Union..* 5
Powder Monkey .... *J. Blackwood* 5
Power of the Keys .... *Macmillan..* 7
—— in Motion, J. Armour .... *Lockwood* .. 10
—— in Weakness .... *Hodder* 22
—— of Zeal (The) .... *Nisbet* 20
Powers of the World to Come .. *Collins* 3
Practical Christian's Library .. *Masters* 22
—— Christian's Library ...... *Parker* 34
—— Manuals .... *Groombridge* 19
Praise Book (The), with Tunes . *Nisbet* 32
Prakrit Grammar............ *Trubner* 9
Prayer, Aids to .... *Isbister* 3
—— Aids to .... *Rivingtons..* 8
—— Answered, Shipton........ *Morgan* 3
—— Book and Church Service .. *Suttaby* .... a
—— Book for Hospitals ...... *Churchill* .. 36
—— for the Departed........ *Isbister* 24
—— Domestic Altar .... *Cassell* 2
—— (Form of) for Ceremonies.. *Masters* 10
—— (The) Gates of.......... *Nisbet* 23
—— Help to.............. *Parker* 32
—— Power of .... *Collins* 3
—— Remarkable Answers to .. *Nisbet* 30
Prayers for the Closet ...... *Mozley* 9
—— for the Dead .... *Bell* 60
—— for Divers Occasions...... *Parker* 32
—— for English Sisters........ *Rivingtons..* 8
—— Family .... *Hagger* 6
—— Family and Private ...... *Hatchard* .. 23
—— for Married Persons ...... *Parker* 30
—— and Med. for Holy Commun. *Rivingtons..* 7
—— Private .... *Masters* 0
—— for Private Use .... *Hodder* 22
—— for Schools .... *Remrote* 12
—— for Schools .... *Masters* 0
—— (School and College).... *Parker* 33
—— for the Sick, Slade........ *Rivingtons..* 31
—— for the Sick and Dying.... *Rivingtons..* 8
—— for Travellers .... *Hatchard* .. 31
Praying and Working .... *Isbister* 41
Pre-Adamite Man .... *Nisbet* 12
Preacher (Local), Own Book .. *Walker* 5
—— (Model) The .... *Wesleyan..* 50
Preacher's Assistant (The) .... *Nicholson* .. 9
—— Lantern .... *Hodder* 16
—— Portfolio .... *Marlborough* 4
—— Treasury .... *Dickinson* .. 19
—— (Extempore) Sermon Sketches *Masters* .. 2
Preachers, Post-Mediæval .... *Rivingtons..* 11
—— and Teachers .... *Nisbet* 7
Preaching (Apostolic) Considered *Hatchard* .. 27
—— Broadus on .... *Nisbet* 8
—— Beecher on .... *Dickinson* .. 2
—— Lectures on .... *Nelson* 8
—— Papers on .... *Bell* 52
—— for the People .... *Isbister* 23
—— (Street) .... *Wesleyan..* 50
—— Texts and Thoughts........ *Longmans* .. 35
—— Theory of .... *Clark* 20
—— Thoughts on .... *Hatchard* .. 15
Precious Things of God........ *Nisbet* 38
Preces Paulinæ .... *Nisbet* 30
—— Privata .... *Parker* 30
Predestination, Mozley........ *Murray* 23
—— (Scriptural) .... *Bagster* 20
Predictions Realized .... *Lockwood* .. 42
Premiums Paid to Experience.. *Isbister* 16
Preparation for Death ...... *Rivingtons..* 6
Presbyterianism .... *W. Blackw'd* 37
—— in Ireland............ *Mullan* .... a
Presbytery, Annals of English . *Nisbet* 23
Prescott's Historical Works...... *Routledge* .. 20
Presence of God in His Temple.. *Isbister* 45
Present Day Papers .... *Isbister* 36
Pressensé (Mad.) Works, French *Nutt* 27
Pressensé's (Dr. De) Works...... *Hodder* 15
Pretenders, History of, Jesse .... *Bohn's Lib..* 10
Price's Calculus .... *Clar. Press..* 18
Prichard (Dr. J. C.) Works by .. *Houlston...* 25
Pride and his Prisoners........ *Nelson* 9

Pridham's Notes on the Epistles *Yapp* 3
Priest to the Altar .... *Rivingtons* .. 4
—— and Parish .... *Rivingtons* .. 10
Priest's Prayer Book .... *Masters* 23
Priests and Philosophers .... *Masters* 11
Priesthood, Doctrine of the ..... *Masters* 4
—— Power of .... *Parker* 3
—— St. Chrysostom on the ..... *Williams* 4
Primer, Old Humphrey's........ *Partridge* .. 11
Primers .... *Nickolson* .. 15
Primeval Man, Argyll .... *Ishister* 5
—— World .... *Clark* 22
—— World .... *Nelson* 11
Primitive Culture .... *Murray* 32
Prince (J. C.) Poetical Works .. *A. Heywood* 6
—— Hohenstiel-Schwangau .... *Smith & El.* 3
—— of the House of David...... *Routledge* .. 65
—— of Peace .... *Jarrold* 13
—— Perrypets, A Fairy Tale ... *Macmillan* .. 19
—— of Wales's Visit to the East.. *Smith & El.* 9
Princess of Thule .... *Macmillan* .. 3
Principia Hebraica .... *Mack* 9
Principles and Art of Teaching.. *S. S. Union* 44
—— at Stake .... *Murray* 25
Printing, Ottley's Inquiry ...... *Sotheran* .. 22
Prints (Script) for Parochial Use *Parker* ... 45
Priority (Law of) .... *Stevens* 13
Prison Chaplain (The) .... *Macmillan* .. 7
Private Account Books .... *Letts* 1
—— Devotions................ *Parker* 32
—— Devotion, Macduff .... *Nisbet* 23
Privy Council Tracts .... *Pickering* .. 32
Prize Library of History & Travel *Nelson* ... 4
Probabilities (Theory of), Quetelet *Layton* 9
Probate & Succession Duty Acts *Stevens* 7
Problem of Evil, Naville ...... *Clark* 11
Problems of Life and Mind .... *Trubner* 18
Procrastination, a Tale for Girls.. *Snow* 12
Procter (A.) Legends and Lyrics *Bell* 36
—— (R. A.) Borderland of Science *Smith & El.* 17
—— (R. A.) Works on Astronomy *Longmans* .. 9
Professor (The) .... *Smith & El.* 2
Projectiles, Text-book .... *Allen* 20
—— Text-book on Motion of ... *Harrison* ... 10
Prometheus Bound .... *Macmillan* .. 49
Promessi Sposi, Trans. .... *Burns* 32
Promise (The) and the Promiser *Morgan* 3
Proper Lessons, Book of ...... *Rivingtons* .. 2
—— Lessons, Commentary on... *Macmillan* .. 3
—— Lessons, Wogan's Essay on *Mozley* 13
—— Names of the Bible ...... *Wesleyan* ... 37
—— Names of the Old Test., Jones *Bagster* ... 33
—— Names of the Old Testament *Williams* ... 5
Property Law, Handy-Book on.. *W. Blackw'd* 27
Prophecy .... *Clark* 18
Prophecy .... *Marlborough* 10
—— Cumming................ *Bentley* 5
—— Cumming on .... *Hurst & B.* 9
—— Discourses on .... *Parker* 8
—— Goodhart .... *Shaw* 8
—— (Tracts on) .... *Yapp* 12
—— (Fulfilled), Goode .... *Hatchard* .. 9
—— Smith's Book of .... *Wesleyan* .. 49
—— The Sure Word of .... *Nisbet* 12
—— Vision of, and other Poems *Nisbet* 8
Prophet of Fire (The) .... *Nisbet* 23
Prophet's Mantle .... *W. Blackw'd* 40
Prophets (The)............... *Parker* 9
—— (The) and Kings .... *Macmillan* .. 24
Prophetic Enquiry, Aids to.... *Houlston* ... 37
—— Spirit in Christian Era ... *Rivingtons* .. 12
Prophetical Landmarks........ *Nisbet* 6
—— History.................. *J. Heywood* 37
Prose & Prose-Writers of Britain *Black* 16
—— Specimens, Demaus ...... *Black* 11
Proctor (Mrs.) Tales by....... *Rel. Tr. Soc.* 16
Prosecution Considered ...... *Churchill* .. 6
Protection to Native Industry.. *Stanford* ... 70
Protestant Religion .... *Clar. Press.* 14
Protestants in Cevennes, Revolt of *Murray* .. 5
Protestantism and Catholicity .. *Burns* 21
Protoplasm, Beale .... *Churchill* .. 8
Proverbs (Acting) .... *Routledge* .. 7
—— Birthday Book of .... *Nimmo* 32
—— and Comediettas .... *Ishister* 15

Proverbs, Commentary on, Miller *Nisbet* 27
—— English and Foreign ..... *Bohn's Lib.* 12
—— Foreign................. *Bohn's Lib.* 12
—— Hand-Book of........... *Routledge* .. 44
—— Herbert's Collection ..... *Rivingtons* .. 7
—— N. Jerrold .... *Marlborough* 9
—— Stories on .... *Mozley* 12
Providence of God Displayed .. *Houlston* ... 33
—— Record of .... *Houlston* ... 33
Provincial Dialect, Works on .. *Asher* 9
—— Dialects of England ..... *J. R. Smith* 18
Prussia, History of .... *Whittaker* .. 9
Prusso-Danish War, Hozier ... *Macmillan* .. 16
Pryme (G.) Autob. Reminiscences *Bell* 40
Prynne (Rev. G. R.) Works by .. *Masters* ... 23
P's and Q's; or Question, &c .. *Macmillan* .. 42
Psalm 119th, Illustration of ... *Snow* 13
Psalms (The) .... *Nelson* 3
—— Analysis of .... *Whittaker* .. 15
—— Book of, with Expo., Wilson *Nisbet* 38
—— Book of, New Translation .. *Bell* 43
—— Commen., for Heb. Students *Williams* .. 13
—— Commentary on, Neale ... *Masters* 18
—— of David, Chron. Arranged.. *Macmillan* .. 29
—— in English Verse .... *Snow* 3
—— Horne's Commentary on .. *Soc. P. C. K.* 13
—— and Hymns, Baptist ..... *Haddon* 1
—— and Hymns, Hall .... *Rivingtons* .. 5
—— and Hymns for Public Wor.. *Soc. P. C. K.* 3
—— and Hymns, Walker...... *Nisbet* 36
—— of Life .... *Houlston* ... 16
—— and Litanies for Devout Per. *Williams* .. 16
—— Notes & Reflec. on, Pridham *Nisbet* 31
—— Plain Commentary .... *Parker* 9
—— Parochial Lectures on .... *Parker* 9
—— Readings on .... *Masters* 12
—— Slade's Explanation of ... *Soc. P. C. K.* 25
—— Study and Use .... *Macmillan* .. 36
—— Trans. from Hebrew, Kay .. *Rivingtons* .. 9
—— Voice of God in the ..... *Macmillan* .. 11
Psalmist, Novello .... *Haddon* 3
Psalmody, Hallelujah (The) ... *Haddon* 2
Psalter .... *Parker* 26
—— Bentley .... *A. Heywood* 37
—— James .... *Mozley* 5
—— Troutbeck .... *Heywood* .. 13
—— and Canticles .... *Soc. P. C. K.* 34
—— and Canticles, Pullen .... *Macmillan* .. 29
—— (The Choral), Hopkins ... *Nisbet* 8
—— Golden Treasury .... *Macmillan* .. 14
—— and the Gospels .... *Parker* 5
—— and Hymns, Mercer ..... *Nisbet* 40
—— (The), Pointed .... *Rivingtons* .. 5
—— Scottish .... *Macl'hun* .. 16
Psalters, Various Languages ... *Bagster* 54
Psychology, Elements of ..... *Longmans* .. 14
—— Elements of .... *Parker* 62
—— Elements of .... *Trubner* 8
—— (English) .... *King* 6
—— Principles of, Spencer ... *Williams* ... 9
—— Works on .... *Churchill* .. 0
Public Health Manual .... *Smith & El.* 4
—— Meetings, Handy Guide to.. *Houlston* ... 46
—— and Private Readings .... *Castell* 4
—— Records .... *Pickering* .. 14
—— Schools .... *W. Blackw'd* 26
—— School Series .... *Ishister* 36
—— Speaking, Papers on .... *Bell* 52
—— Worship .... *Hodder* 24
—— Worship .... *Parker* 9
—— Worship, Plain Help to .. *Mozley* 9
Puck on Pegasus............ *Chatto* 28
Puerperal Diseases.......... *Churchill* .. 7
Pukklito Dictionary .... *Trubner* 4
Pulmonary Disease, Works on .. *Churchill* .. 0
Pulpit, Curiosities of .... *Virtue* 15
—— Discourses, Willis .... *Nisbet* 37
—— Eccentricities .... *Chatto* 8
—— Eloquence .... *Hodder* 21
—— Helps for the .... *Nicholson* .. 1
—— Notes, Parker........... *Ishister* 23
—— (Plain) Talk .... *Hodder* 23
—— Studies for the .... *Shaw* 9
—— Theories .... *Nicholson* .. 2
Pump-Fitter's Guide......... *Spon* 33

Pumping Engine, Cornish ..... Spon 13
"Punch," Pencillings from ..... Bradbury 2
—— Re-issue ..... Bradbury 12
"Punch's" Letters to His Son ..... Bradbury 8
Punctuality, Importance of ..... Wilton 7
Punctuation Reduced to a System Harrison 14
Punsana, Rowley (H.) ..... Chatto 29
Punjaub, Agricl. Resources of... Smith & El. 19
—— and Delhi ..... W. Blackw'd 6
——Gazetteer of ..... Allen 8
—— History of ..... Allen 10
—— Rajas of the ..... Trubner 14
Pupils of St. John the Divine ..... Macmillan 34
Puritans, History of, Marsden ..... Hatchard 14
Puritanism, Leaders ..... W. Blackw'd 41
Pursuit of Holiness ..... Rivingtons 9
Pursuivant of Arms ..... Chatto 29
Pusey's Minor Prophets ..... Rivingtons 3
—— Works and Translations ..... Parker 0
Put Yourself in his Place ..... Smith & El. 17
Pyramid (Inheritance in the Gt.) Isbister 40
Pyramids ..... Edmonston 6
Pyrenees, Excursions in ..... King 7
—— — Guide to, Packe ..... Longmans 38
—— — Watering Places of ..... Churchill 35
Pyrotechny ..... Ward&Lock 9

Quadroon (The) ..... Routledge 34
Quakerism, Past and Present ..... Smith & El. 18
Quale' Self-Checking Acct. Bks. ..... Letts 8
Qualitative Analysis ..... Longmans 21
Quarles's Emb., Bennitt & Rogers Nisbet 31
Quartetts & other Games of Cards Hamilton 28
Quaternions, Kelland and Tait ..... Macmillan 13
—— Tait ..... Clar. Press. 25
Quedah ..... W. Blackw'd 23
Queechy ..... Nisbet 31
Queechy ..... Ward&Lock 26
Queen of the Adriatic ..... Nelson 11
—— of Palmyra ..... Warne 20
Queen's English (The) ..... Isbister 4
—— Isle (The) ..... Masters 23
—— Jester ..... Penrose 18
Queens of Society ..... Routledge 4
Queensland, Four Years in ..... Stanford 57
—— My Wife and I in ..... Longmans 37
Queer Folk, Seven Stories ..... Macmillan 19
Quest of the Chief Good ..... Isbister 11
Questions of the Day, Hall ..... Nisbet 15
—— of the Day ..... Wesleyan 48
Quichua Gram. and Dictionary ..... Trubner 19
Quiet Resting Places ..... Black 16
Quirinus, Letters from Rome ..... Rivingtons 12
Quotations, English Familiar ..... Murray 17
—— Familiar ..... Routledge 43
—— Index to Familiar ..... Hamilton 72
—— New Dictionary of ..... Shaw 7
—— Taylor (T.) ..... Chatto 17
—— Treasury of Choice ..... Isbister 43

Rabelais, Works of ..... Chatto 30
Rabies and Hydrophobia ..... Chapman 8
Races of Mankind ..... Cassell 7
Rachel, or Little Faults ..... Partridge 19
Racine's Plays, French ..... Clar. Press 29
Raffaele of Urbino ..... Macmillan 30
—— Original Studies ..... Bell 7
—— Gallery ..... Bell 5
Ragged Homes, How to Mend ..... Nisbet 5
—— School Work ..... Snow 16
Railway Anecdotes ..... Lockwood 45
—— Companies, Law of ..... Stevens 10
—— Crossings ..... Spon 33
—— Curves ..... Spon 33
—— Library ..... Routledge 43
—— Mechanism, Colburn ..... Collins 2
—— Reading ..... J. Blackwood 30
—— Reading ..... Murray 33
—— Stations (Examples of) ..... Spon 34
—— Tale : Life on ..... Nisbet 5
Railways ..... Chambers 35
—— About ..... Chambers 28
—— Narrow Gauge ..... Spon 31
—— or No Railways ..... Wilson 12
—— Rambles on ..... Wilson 9

Rain, How, When, &c ..... Stanford 70
—— and Rivers, Tyndall ..... King 8
—— upon Mown Grass ..... Holder 11
—— Cloud and Snow Storm ..... Soc. P. C. K. 21
Rainfall, British, 1872 ..... Stanford 70
Rainy Days, How to Meet Them Partridge 0
Raleigh (Sir Walter) Life of ..... Chapman 23
—— Life ..... Sotheran 23
—— (Dr.) Works by ..... Isbister 37
Ralph Darnell ..... W. Blackw'd 31
Ramayana. Scenes from the ..... Trubner 14
Rambler, Recollections of a ..... Chapman 25
Rambles in the Four Seasons ..... Soc. P. C. K. 21
—— of an Archæologist ..... Virtue 9
—— of a Rat ..... Nelson 9
Ramsay's Tea Table Miscellany ..... Sotheran 23
Ran away to Sea ..... Routledge 34
Raphael's Royal Book of Fate ..... Cornish 4
Rat (The), with Anecdotes ..... Routledge 11
Ratepayers of London ..... Isbister 11
Rational Godliness ..... Bell 61
Rationalism, History of ..... Trubner 16
—— in Europe ..... Longmans 16
Rawes (Father) Works by ..... Burns 16
Rawlinson's (Canon) Herodotus... Murray 26
Rawnsley (R. D. B.) Works by ..... Hatchard 24
Rays of Sunlight for Dark Days ..... Macmillan 30
Read Me a Story ..... Mozley 16
Reade (Compton) Take Care, &c. Smith & El. 17
—— (Ch.) Put Yourself, &c. ..... Smith & El. 17
—— (Wm.) Savage Africa ..... Smith & El. 17
—— African Sketch Book ..... Smith & El. 17
Reader, Adv. Prose and Poetical Black 9
Readers, Hist., Science, Scripture J. Heywood 27
—— New Code Standard ..... J. Heywood 26
—— Northrop and Miller ..... Allman 15
—— Catholic ..... Burns 17
—— Adapted to Standards ..... Cassell 14
—— Adapted to Standards ..... Chambers 19
—— National ..... Chambers 3
—— Scientific ..... Chambers 17
—— Academic Progressive ..... Collins 9
—— Adapted to Standards ..... Collins 8
—— Scottish Sch. Book Ass. Ser. Collins 13
—— Extra ..... Collins 10
—— Adapted to Standards, Man. J. Heywood 25
—— Adapted to Standards ..... Isbister 36
—— Adapted to Standards ..... Jarrold 13
—— Kensington Series ..... Laurie 1
—— "School Manger's" Series ..... Lockwood 29
—— Adapted to Standards, Snow Milner 16
—— Adapted to do., "Excelsior" Murby 4
—— Consecutive Narrative ..... Murby 2
—— Standards, Cromwell ..... Philip 35
—— Juvenile ..... Routledge 17
—— Adapted to Standards ..... Soc. P. C. K. 22
Reading, A Short Cut to ..... Trubner 30
—— Choice ..... J. Blackwood 8
—— Disentangled ..... Stanford 68
—— Made Easy ..... Mozley 16
—— Made Easy ..... Nicholson 15
—— without Tears ..... Hatchard 25
—— Books, Special for Girls ..... Mozley 3
Readings, Cottage ..... Mozley 3
—— on First Lessons for Sundays Soc. P. C. K. 22
—— for the Christian Year ..... Mozley 11
—— for Evening Schools ..... Mozley 13
—— for Sundays ..... Warne 29
—— Illustrated ..... Cassell 3
—— Penny ..... Warne 47
—— for Winter Gatherings ..... Rel. Tr. Soc. 16
—— and Recitations ..... A. Heywood 11
—— and Recitations ..... J. Heywood 44
—— and Recitations ..... Marr 3
—— and Recitations ..... Milner 3
—— and Recitations ..... Nicholson 3
—— and Recitations ..... Routledge 61
Ready Reckoner ..... J. Blackw'd .....
—— Bijou ..... Warne 40
—— Correct ..... Walker 5
—— for Farmers and Auctioneers Virtue 26
—— Fractional ..... Mozley 2
—— Earnshaw ..... Mozley 12
—— Henderson ..... Collins 4
—— Instant ..... Lockwood 43

Ready Reckoner, Large Type ... *Nicholson* .. 10
—— Masters .... *Routledge* .. 63
—— Miniature .... *Houlston* .. 9
—— Sixpenny .... *Chambers* .. 32
—— Sixpenny .... *Ward & Lock* 11
—— for Tons, Cwts., Qrs., Lbs. *Cornish* .. 4
—— Tradesman's .... *Milner* .. 3
—— and Trade Tables ...... *Cassell* .. 7
—— Universal .... *MacPhun* .. 10
—— Universal .... *Wilson* .. 5
Ready for Work, by Grosser (W.H.) *S. S. Union*. 44
Realm of Truth .... *King* .. 28
Reason, Descartes......... *W. Blackw'd* 7
—— and Revelation ...... *Black* .. 10
Reason Why, Series ...... *Houlston* .. 5
Reasoning, True Principle, Jevons *Macmillan* .. 17
Receipt Book, Family ...... *Murray* .. 11
Receipts for Everything ... *Milner* .. 3
Reciter, The Beautiful... *Nicholson* .. 4
—— The Excelsior ...... *Nicholson* .. 4
Recitations and Readings ... *Routledge* .. 63
Reclus (E.) Works by ...... *Chapman* .. 6
Recognition of Friends in Heaven *Nisbet* 31
Recommended to Mercy ...... *Tinsley Bros.* 10
Records of the Past ...... *Bagster* .. 76
—— of the Rocks ...... *Murray* .. 31
Recreations of a Country Parson *Longmans* .. 15
Recreator, Popular ...... *Cassell* .. 7
Rector and His Friends ...... *Bell* .. 48
Rectory of Valehead ...... *Smith & El.* 7
Redeemer (The) Present ...... *Clark* .. 20
Redemption, Discourses on .. *Clark* .. 20
—— Lectures on ...... *Houlston* .. 35
—— Unfolded ...... *Nisbet* .. 14
—— Works on ...... *Kellaway* .. 8
Redgrave (R.) Century Painters *Smith & El.* 10
Red Cotton Night-Cap Country.. *Smith & El.* 3
—— Flag and other Poems .. *Isbister* .. 32
—— River Expedition, Huyshe .. *Macmillan* .. 17
—— River, Flood at ...... *Hatchard* .. 2
—— Shirt (The), Mario ...... *Smith & El.* 17
Reed (Andrew) Memoirs of.... *Isbister* .. 38
—— (Mrs.) Works by ...... *Jarrold* .. 14
Reed's (Prof.) Lectures...... *Shaw* .. 7
Reeve (Rev. J. W.) Works by.. *Nisbet* .. 31
Reeve's History of English Law.. *Reeves* .. a
Reference Books......... *Ward & Lock* 7
Reflections in a Lent Reading.... *Parker* .. 9
Reform, Parliamentary...... *Murray* .. 13
Reformation (The), Fisher .. *Hodder* .. 13
—— Burnet ...... *Clar. Press.* 11
—— Champions of ...... *Nimmo* .. 6
—— D'Aubigné ...... *Collins* .. 2
—— D'Aubigné ...... *Rel. Tr. Soc.* 6
—— D'Aubigné, Young Persons. *Jarrold* .. 7
—— of Ch. of England, Heylyn. *Harrison* .. 16
—— of English Church ...... *Rivingtons* .. 25
—— History for the Young .. *Nisbet* .. 28
—— Leaders of ...... *W. Blackw'd* 44
—— Men and Women of ...... *Washbourne* 5
—— Period of, Hausser ...... *Isbister* .. 20
—— Records of ...... *Clar. Press.* 12
—— Reformers and Theology of.. *Clark* .. 15
—— Story of, D'Aubigné ...... *Routledge* .. 21
—— Stories of ...... *Jarrold* .. 18
—— Studies of the ...... *Blackie* .. 20
—— Seebohm ...... *Longmans* .. 3
—— in Switzerland ...... *Clark* .. 21
Reformers, British, Writings of.. *Rel. Tr. Soc.* 4
—— before the Reformation .. *Clark* .. 17
Registers for Baptisms ...... *Marr* .. 19
—— Burials ...... *Marly* .. 19
Rehearsals, a Book of Verses .... *Isbister* .. 46
Reid (Mayne) Juvenile Books, by *Routledge* .. 34
—— Novels ...... *Chapman* .. 24
—— (Rev. Wm.) Works by .. *Nisbet* .. 31
Reign of Law, Argyll...... *Isbister* .. 5
—— of Law, Sermons ...... *Macmillan* .. 31
—— of Terror, Recollections of .. *Washbourne* 7
Rejected Addresses ...... *Murray* .. 26
Relations of Kingdom to World.. *Nisbet* .. 12
Religio Chemici, Wilson ...... *Macmillan* .. 41
Religion and Chemistry ...... *Collins* .. 3
—— (Every-Day) ...... *Nisbet* .. 21
—— (Christian) Evidences, Keith *Longmans* .. 34

Religion of Geology ...... *Collins* .. 3
—— of Geology ...... *J. Blackwood* 19
—— of the Heart ...... *Trubner* .. 16
—— of Israel ...... *Williams* .. 8
—— of Mankind ...... *Snow* .. 14
—— Passing Thoughts on .. *Longmans* .. 36
—— Philosophy of ...... *Collins* .. 5
—— Pleasures of ...... *Tubbs* .. 5
—— Principles of ...... *Mozley* .. 10
—— Science of ...... *Longmans* .. 5
—— Supernatural ...... *Longmans* .. 34
—— of the Universe ...... *Williams* .. 6
Religions of the World ...... *Macmillan* .. 25
—— before Christ ...... *Clark* .. 17
Religious Beliefs, Gould ...... *Rivingtons* .. 12
—— Cheap Series ...... *Collins* .. 3
—— Duty, Cobbe ...... *Williams* .. 4
—— Education ...... *Rivingtons* .. 16
—— Gift Books ...... *Warne* .. 38
—— Instruction, Books on .. *Masters* .. 0
—— Instruction, Early ...... *Hatchard* .. 2
—— Progress ...... *Collins* .. 3
—— Questions of the Day .. *Murray* .. 13
—— Reading ...... *Nelson* .. 21
—— Teaching by Example .. *Collins* .. 3
—— Thought in England ..... *Isbister* .. 21
—— Truth Illustrated from Science *Collins* .. 3
Remarkable Charctrs., Lamartine *Bentley* .. 5
—— Men ...... *Soc. P. C. K.* 22
—— Places, Visits to ...... *Longmans* .. 38
—— Trials, &c. ...... *Chatto* .. 30
Rembrandt Gallery ...... *Bell* .. 5
Reminiscences of a Septuagenarian *Murray* .. 5
Renaissance, Studies in Hist. .. *Macmillan* .. 28
Renan (Ernest) Works by ...... *Trubner* .. 25
Renan's Life of Christ, Crit. Exam. *Kellaway* .. 10
—— Jesus, Lectures on ...... *Macmillan* .. 38
Rents and Tillages, Valuing .. *Longmans* .. 33
Reporting, Editing, Authorship.. *Snow* .. 8
Reptiles, British ...... *Hardwicke* .. 4
—— and Birds, Figuier ...... *Cassell* .. 7
Republic of Fools ...... *Allen* .. 24
Republican Institutions ...... *King* .. 32
Rescued from Egypt ...... *Nelson* .. 9
Reserve Force, Circulars, &c... *Harrison* .. 11
Reservoirs, Catch-Water ...... *Spon* .. 34
Rest in Jesus ...... *W. Blackw'd* 40
Restoration ...... *Parker* .. 54
—— of Belief ...... *Macmillan* .. 35
—— of Paths to Dwell In.... *Isbister* .. 42
Resurrection (The), Cox ...... *Isbister* .. 11
—— of Christ ...... *W. Blackw'd* 40
—— of Dead ...... *W. Blackw'd* 36
—— Gospel of the ...... *Macmillan* .. 40
—— (The) and the Life ...... *Nisbet* .. 11
Retributive Justice of God .. *Hatchard* .. 13
Retrospect (The), Marks ...... *Nisbet* .. 25
Reuben Davidger ...... *Ward & Lock* 8
—— Inch ...... *Wilson* .. 17
Re-Union of Christian Churches. *Rivingtons* .. 12
Revelation (Book of) at One View *Kellaway* .. 13
—— Notes on Book of ...... *Nisbet* .. 29
—— Lectures on Book of ...... *Masters* .. 10
—— of St. John, Lec. on, Vaughan *Macmillan* .. 38
—— Considered as a Light .. *Isbister* .. 14
—— What is ...... *Macmillan* .. 24
Revival of the Work of God.... *Morgan* .. 3
—— Tune Book ...... *Morgan* .. 3
Revolt of the Field ...... *Hodder* .. 7
Revue Analytique des Ouvrages.. *Trubner* .. 10
Reward Books............... *Masters* .. 44
—— Books ...... *Nisbet* .. 47
—— Books ...... *Parker* .. 43
—— Books ...... *S. S. Union* 10
—— Books (Catholic)...... *Burns* .. 6
—— Books, Coloured ...... *Routledge* .. 32
—— Books and Picture Packets.. *Routledge* .. 60
—— Books, Packets ...... *Morgan* .. 13
—— Books, Sunday School.... *Mozley* .. 2
—— Cards...... *Wesleyan* .. 38
—— Picture Cards ...... *Tract Society* 34
—— Ticket ...... *Wesleyan* .. 38
—— of Piety ...... *Wesleyan* .. 48
Reynard the Fox............... *Trubner* .. 25
—— the Fox in South Africa .. *Trubner* .. 5

Reynolds (Sir J.) Life and Works *Murray* 29
—— Literary Works .... *Bohn's Lib.* .. 8
—— as Portrait Painter........ *Macmillan* .. 30
Rhetoric, Whately .... *Longmans* .. 11
—— Christian System of .... *Houlston* ... 35
Rheumatic Gout .... *Churchill* .. 6
Rheumatism, Fuller on.......... *Churchill* 16
Rhymes and Reasons .... *Masters* 24
—— for Mothers and Children .. *Macmillan* .. 15
Rhyming Dictionary, English.... *Trübner* 19
Ribblesdale, by Shuttleworth .... *Smith & El.* .. 19
Ribbon Stories, Barker .... *Macmillan* .. 3
Ricardo's Political Works ...... *Murray* 20
Richard Owen .... *S. S. Union* .. 9
Richard II., True Stories Times of *J. Blackwood* 20
Richardson (Mr. C.) Memoirs .... *Wesleyan* 43
Richter (J. Paul F.) Works by .... *Trübner* 25
Riddles in Rhyme .... *Lockwood* 45
—— and Jokes .... *Routledge* .. 7
Ridicula Rediviva .... *Macmillan* .. 31
Ridley (Rev. W. H.) Works by .... *Mozley* 11
Ridpath's Border History of Eng. *Sotheran* .. 23
Rifle Exercises & Musk. Instruc. *Harrison* .. 7
—— and its Projectiles........ *Smith & El.* .. 7
Rifles, Modern Breach-Loader .. *Cassell* 5
Rifled Ordnance, Construction of *Harrison* .. 11
Rigg's Works .... *Wesleyan* 48
Rigger's Guide .... *Griffin* .. 4
Right Lines in their Right Places *Cassell* 14
Rights and Wrongs .... *Nisbet* 15
Rig-Veda, Hymns of the .... *Trübner* 21
—— Sanhita, Wilson .... *Trübner* 26
Rills from the Fountain of Life .. *Partridge* 19
Ring (The) and the Book .... *Smith & El.* .. 3
Rippon's Collection of Tunes.... *Haddon* .. 3
—— Selection of Hymns ...... *Isbister* 38
—— and Watts's Hymn-Books .. *Houlston* 41
Rise of Great Families, Burke.... *Longmans* .. 9
Ritter (Carl) Life .... *W. Blackw'd* 26
Ritual of Church of England .... *Masters* .. 12
Ritualism .... *Hodder* 35
—— Errors of .... *Tubbs* .. 4
—— Hand-Book on .... *Hodder* 16
—— and its Related Dogmas .... *Snow* 11
—— Refutation of .... *Snow* .. 4
Riviera, Pen and Pencil Sketches *Bell* 5
Rizpah, G. Beresford .... *Nisbet* 5
Road (The), Whistling Commercial *Walker* 6
Roads, Steam Rolling of .... *Spon* .. 34
Roba di Roma .... *Chapman* .. 25
Roberts (Rev. Arthur) Sermons .. *Nisbet* 32
Robertson (Rev. F. W.) Life, &c. *King* .. 2
—— Works .... *King* 30
—— (Rev. J.) Life .... *W. Blackw'd* 41
—— (Dr. John) Sermons ...... *Isbister* 38
—— (T.) French Ed. Works .... *Nutt* 8
Robin Hood .... *Routledge* .. 30
—— Hood, Life of .... *Nicholson* .. 14
—— Hood, Story of .... *Cassell* 11
Robinson (H. C.) Diary & Corr. *Macmillan* .. 30
—— (Matthew) Autobiography .. *Macmillan* .. 25
—— (Rev. Dr.) Works by ...... *Murray* 27
Robinson's Romans .... *Dickinson* .. 15
Robinson Playfellow .... *Routledge* .. 29
—— Crusoe .... *Bell* 21
—— Crusoe .... *J. Blackwood* 3
—— Crusoe .... *Cassell* 11
—— Crusoe .... *Milner* .. 4
—— Crusoe .... *Nelson* .. 2
—— Crusoe .... *Ward & Lock* 8
—— Crusoe .... *Warne* .. 37
—— Crusoe, Globe Edition .... *Macmillan* .. 13
—— Crusoe, Illust. by Doyle .. *Black* 16
—— Crusoe, Watson's Illust. .. *Routledge* .. 27
—— Crusoe (The True) .... *Cassell* 11
Rob Roy, Grant .... *Routledge* .. 33
Rob Roy on the Jordan .... *Murray* .. 21
Roby Family .... *Nelson* .. 9
Roche (A.) French Works by .... *Nutt* 4
Rochefoucauld's Reflections .... *Chatto* .. 30
Rock Ahead .... *Tinsley Bros.* 10
—— Light .... *Warne* .. 28
—— Names, Handy-Book of .... *Hardwicke.* .. 8
Rocks, British Palæozoic .... *Cambridge* .. 4
—— Classified and Described .... *Longmans* . 24

Rockstro (W. S.) Works by .... *Masters* 24
Rocky Mountains .... *Blackie* .. 16
—— Mountains .... *Smith & El.* 15
Rod, History of .... *Chatto* .. 15
Rogers's Agricultural Prices .... *Clar. Press.* 16
Rogers (Henry) Essays.......... *Longmans* .. 9
—— Essays, "Good Words"...... *Isbister* 38
—— (Samuel) Poetical Works.... *Routledge* .. 27
Rogers's Superhum. Origin of Bible *Hodder* .. 2
Rolando's Travels .... *Routledge* .. 79
Romance and Reality .... *J. Blackwood* 3
—— of History................ *Warne* 21
—— Languages, Dictionary of .. *Williams* .. 5
—— Languages, Grammar of .... *Williams* .. 5
—— of the Streets .... *Hodder* .. 3
—— without Fiction .... *Wesleyan* .. 42
Romances (Pop.) of Middle Ages.. *Longmans* .. 39
Romanism (Letters on) Butler .. *Macmillan* .. 5
Romanoff (H. C.) Works by .... *Rivingtons* .. 25
Romantic Tales .... *Smith & El.* 17
Rome, Antiquities of .... *Lockwood* .. 7
—— and the Early Christians .. *Warne* 20
—— The Seven Kings of ...... *Macmillan* .. 42
—— The Kings of, Dyer ...... *Bell* 38
—— History of................ *Lockwood* .. 3
—— History of, Keightley .... *Whittaker* .. 9
—— History of, Mommsen .... *Bentley* .. 11
—— Emperors of, Gray........ *Hatchard* .. 10
—— (Imperial), Page from History *Masters* .. 21
—— Fall of, Sheppard .... *Routledge* .. 21
—— By Story .... *Chapman* .. 25
—— Walks in .... *Isbister* 19
—— and the Campagna .... *Bell* 11
—— and its Ruins .... *Soc. P. C. K.* 23
—— Illustrated, by Wey ...... *Chapman* .. 6
—— Temples and Tombs of.... *Nelson* 11
—— (Old) Pictures of.......... *Chapman* .. 18
—— (Old) and New Italy...... *Tinsley Bros.* 2
—— and Venice .... *Tinsley Bros.* 7
—— A Winter Journey to ...... *Stanford.* .. 54
—— Letters from .... *Murray* .. 5
—— Letters from, on Council .. *Rivingtons.* .. 12
—— Letters to and from ...... *Williams* .. 8
—— and Back .... *Smith & El.* 3
—— Church of................ *Parker.* .. 6
—— and the Council in 19th Cen. *Clark* 16
—— Folk-Lore of, Busk ...... *Longmans* .. 39
—— Hall's Forum and Vatican.. *Nisbet* 16
Roman Archæology .... *Parker.* 49
—— Antiquities, Rich .... *Longmans* .; 12
—— Catholicism, Personal Experi. *Morgan* .. 3
—— Civil Law................ *Bell* 31
—— Classical Literature ...... *Bentley* .. 4
—— Empire, Gibbon .... *Virtue* 19
—— Empire Gibbon (Bohn's).... *Bohn's Lib.* .. 11
—— Empire, Gibbon (Smith's) .. *Murray* .. 12
—— Empire of the West ...... *Trübner* .. 8
—— Empire (Holy) .... *Macmillan* .. 4
—— History, Bullock .... *J. Heywood* 34
—— History, Ihne .... *Longmans* .. 5
—— History, Merivale .... *Longmans* .. 4
—— Husbandry .... *Parker* 62
—— Law .... *W. Blackw'd* 20
—— Law, Early .... *Macmillan* .. 7
—— Private Law .... *Macmillan* .. 28
—— Literature, Wagner ...... *Bell* 14
—— Republic, Michelet ...... *Bohn's Lib.* .. 8
—— Republic, Decline of...... *Bell* 38
—— and Teuton, Kingsley .... *Macmillan* .. 18
Romola, George Eliot .... *Smith & El.* 17
Roots : A Plea for Tolerance .... *Bentley* 12
Ropemaking, Treatise on........ *Spon* 34
Rosa : or, The Two Castles .... *Partridge* .. 10
Rosa's Wish .... *Warne* 26
Roscoe (H. E.) Works by ...... *Macmillan* .. 31
Rose, Amateur's Guide .... *Longmans* .. 24
—— Book, Culture............ *Groombridge.* .. 7
—— Garden (The) .... *Smith & El.* 17
Roses, Hole .... *W. Blackw'd* 49
—— and Holly .... *Nimmo* .. 10
Rosicrucians : Rites & Mysteries.. *Chatto* 21
Ross (C. H.) Tales .... *Chatto* .. 31
Rossel's Posthumous Papers .... *Chapman* 24
Rosteri's Italian Ed. Course .... *Nutt* 32
Roumania, Songs and Legends of. *Smith & El.* 16

Round the Fire Stories.......... *Warne*...... 28
—— the Globe Library .... *Warne*...... 30
—— about the Islands .... *Timely Bros.*.. 2
Roundheads, Army List of the .. *Chatto*...... 4
Rousseau, by Morley............ *Chapman*.... 7
Roxburghe Library .... *Reeves & T.* 2
Roxobel .... *Houlston*.... 38
Roy (George) Works of .... *Marr*....... 16
Royal Captives................ *Hatchard* .. 27
—— Gems, Galleries of Europe .. *Virtue*..... 11
—— Holiday & Student's Book.. *J. Blackwood* 5
—— Mint .... *Wilson*..... 12
—— Preacher (The) .... *Nisbet*..... 17
—— Princesses, Hall.......... *Routledge* .. 4
—— Rosebuds .... *Mozley*..... 10
—— Supremacy .... *Parker*..... 6
—— Truths, Beecher .... *Isbister* 6
Royle (J. F.) Works on India .. *Smith & El.* 13
Rubric (The) .... *Hall*....... 3
Rude Stone Monuments ...... *Murray* 12
Rule (Rev. W. H.) Works by.. *Wesleyan* .. 19
Ruling Eldership.............. *W. Blackw'd.* 35
Rump Parliament (The) ...... *Chatto*..... 31
Runaway (The), A Story ...... *Macmillan* .. 31
Run to Earth .... *Ward&Lock* 16
Runnymede and Lincoln Fair.. *Ward&Lock* 8
Ruptures, Holthouse on ...... *Churchill* .. 21
—— Lawrence on .... *Churchill*... 23
Rural Affairs, Sketches of...... *Soc. P. C. K.* 23
—— Architecture, &c. .... *Hagger* 23
—— Economy .... *W. Blackw'd* 18
—— Life of England .... *Longmans* .. 38
Ruskin's (John) Works .... *Smith & El.* 18
—— Lectures on Art .... *Clar. Press*. 17
Russia, Ancient and Modern .. *Rel. Tr. Soc.* 16
—— Armed Strength of .... *Harrison* .. 19
—— Behind the Scenes in .... *Bell* 12
—— and Germany (War in 1812). *Murray* 7
—— History of, Kelly .... *Bohn's Lib.* . 9
—— History of the War ...... *Virtue* 21
—— in Europe, Murchison .... *Murray* 23
—— Late Empress .... *Edmonston*.. 1
—— Modern.................. *Smith & El.* 6
—— Oliphant .... *W.Blackw'd.* 22
—— Progress of Science, &c., in.. *J. Blackw'd.* 27
—— Through .... *Hurst & B..* 1
—— Travels in Northern ...... *Macmillan* .. 27
Russians at Home .... *Allen* 6
—— in Central Asia .... *King*....... 3
—— on the Amur .... *Trubner* ... 25
Russian Church, Works on ...... *Masters* ... 2
—— Church, Palmer .... *Trubner* ... 23
—— Church, Neale .... *Masters* ... 18
—— Church, Romanoff........ *Rivingtons*.. 25
—— Clergy (The) .... *Burns* 33
—— Conspirators in Siberia.... *Smith & El.* 18
—— Court in Mid. of Last Century *Isbister* 22
—— Fables .... *Isbister* 24
—— Folk Tales .... *Smith & El.* 17
—— Historical Narratives .... *Rivingtons*.. 25
—— Metallurgical Works........ *Wilson*..... 9
—— Sermons, Philaret........ *Masters* ... 21
—— Society .... *Smith & El.* 5
Russo-Indian Question, Trench .. *Macmillan*.. 38
Ruth, Book of, in Hebrew ..... *Williams* ... 16
—— Lectures on Book of, Price.. *Hatchard* .. 24
Rutter's Works .... *Wilson*..... 6

Sabbath Chimes, Punshon ...... *Nisbet* 31
—— Day (The), Maurice ...... *Macmillan* .. 25
—— Facts, Illustrated .... *Partridge* .. 8
—— School Index .... *Nisbet* 29
Sacra Privata, Wilson ...... *Mozley* 13
Sacred Annals .... *Wesleyan* .. 49
—— Anthology .... *Trubner* ... 8
—— Garland .... *Milner* 4
—— History, Intrody. Sketch of *Parker*..... 8
—— Latin Poetry .... *Macmillan* .. 38
—— Music, Works on .... *Houlston* .. 47
—— Poetry .... *Parker* 26
—— Poets, Half Hours with .. *J. Blackwood* 12
—— and Profane History...... *Clar. Press*.. 11
—— Readings for Young Children *Ward&Lock* 20
—— Trichords................ *Hatchard* .. 25
Sacrifice, Doctrine of.......... *Macmillan*.. 24

Sacrifice and Divine Service .. *Parker*..... 8
Saddle and Sirloin .... *Warne*...... 9
Saddles, Dwyer .... *W. Blackw'd.* 8
Sadler's English Language .... *Nutt*....... 27
Sadler (Rev. M. F.) Works by . *Bell* 50
Safe Compass (The) .... *Nisbet* 28
Sahara, Horses of .... *Allen* 10
—— and Lapland .... *Asher* 6
Sailor Hero .... *Ward&Lock* 28
Sailors (Songs for), Bennett...... *King*....... 21
Sailor's Horn-Book, Piddington.. *Williams* ... 11
—— Life, Two Years Before Mast *Black* 10
—— Prayer-Book .... *Snow* 14
—— Text-Book, Macduff...... *Nisbet* 24
Saints and Martyrs, Legends of.. *Longmans* .. 29
Saint (The) and his Saviour .... *Isbister* 41
—— Abe and his Seven Wives .. *Isbister* 38
St. Albans, Abbey of .... *Bell* 14
St. Aldhelm .... *Parker*..... 7
St. Anslem, Church .... *Macmillan*.. 35
St. Augustine, Life of .... *Washbourne* 3
—— Works by, Latin .... *Nutt*....... 3
—— Writings of .... *Clark* 5
St. Augustinus.............. *Parker*..... 7
St. Bartholomew (Eve of) .... *Shaw* 3
—— Massacre of .... *Murray* 32
St. Bernard's Life, Morison.... *Macmillan*.. 3
St. Chrysostom, Life and Times.. *Murray* 30
—— on the Priesthood........ *Williams* ... 4
St. Clement, Pope and Martyr .. *Nutt* 5
St. Columba in Ireland........ *Parker*..... 13
St. Cyril, The Three Epistles .... *Parker*..... 7
St. Francis of Assisi .... *Macmillan*.. 35
—— de Sales .... *Rivingtons*.. 0
—— de Sales, Consoling Thoughts *MacGlashan* 1
St. George's Key .... *Warne*...... 28
St. George & the Dragon, Ballad *Isbister* 15
St. Gregory the Great, Dialogues *Burns* 14
—— Pastoral Rule of.......... *Parker* 7
St. Helena, Description of .... *Reeve* 15
St. Mark, Last Twelve Verses .. *Parker*..... 10
St. Paul, by a Graduate ...... *Macmillan*.. 28
—— the Apostle .... *S. S. Union* 43
—— the Apostle .... *Snow* 6
—— the Apostle of Jesus Christ.. *Williams* ... 9
—— at Athens .... *Black* 1
—— Character of .... *Isbister* 21
—— Companions of .... *Isbister* 4
—— The Devotions of .... *Nisbet* 39
—— Footsteps of .... *Nisbet* 23
—— in Britain .... *Parker*..... 13
—— in Rome, Macduff........ *Nisbet* 23
—— Voyage and Shipwreck .... *Longmans* .. 34
—— his Life & Ministry, Blaney *Nisbet* 5
—— and Protestantism........ *Smith & El.* 1
—— Stories about .... *Hatchard* .. 17
—— Life, Lewin .... *Bell* 47
—— Life and Epistles .... *Longmans* .. 34
St. Paul's Epistles .... *Parker*..... 9
—— Epistles, Davies.......... *Macmillan*.. 9
—— Commentary on.......... *Longmans* .. 35
—— Commentary on, Hodge .... *Nisbet* 18
—— Explained, G.B. .... *Nisbet* 14
—— Introduction to .... *Clark* 35
—— Notes on, Pridham ...... *Nisbet* 39
—— Pridham's Notes .... *Yapp*....... 3
SS. Paul & John, Private Letters *Isbister* 11
St. Paul's Cathedral, Longman .. *Longmans* .. 30
—— Milman .... *Murray* 22
St. Peter, Apostle, never at Rome *Parker*..... 13
—— his Name and Office........ *Washbourne* 3
—— 1st Epistle, Leighton .... *Soc. P. C. K.* 15
St. Petersburg................ *Hurst & B* 1
—— and Moscow .... *Smith & El.* 1
St. Stephen's, a Poem .... *W. Blackw'd.* 7
St. Vincent de Paul, Life of.... *Burns* 35
St. Winifred's ; a Boy's Book.... *Black* 8
Sales, Leading Cases on ...... *Stevens* 22
Salmonia, Davy, Sir H........ *Murray* 9
Salon in last Days French Empire *Bentley* 13
Salt (Common), Nat. Hist. & Man.. *Soc. P. C. K.* 23
Salts, A Theory of, Mansfield.... *Macmillan*.. 23
Salvage, Law of .... *Stevens* 11
Salvation, Biblical Doctrine of .. *Williams* ... 7
Samarang (H.M.S.) Voyage .... *Reeve* 14

V 2

Samaritan Grammar .... *Bagster* 41
Samaritans (Modern), Mills..... *Murray* 22
Sam Slick, Works by .... *Hurst & B.* 13
Samson, Biography of .... *Edmonston* .. 4
Sanderson's Works .... *Clar. Press.* 14
Sandford and Merton .... *Nimmo* 19
—— and Merton .... *Warne* 26
—— New History of .... *Bradbury* .. 4
Sandwich Islands Mission ..... *Hodder* 31
Sanitary Instructions, Lancaster *Hardwicke* .. 15
—— Engineering .... *Spon* 34
—— Association Tracts .... *Jarrold* 10
Sanscriti (Auctores) .... *Trubner* 3
Sanskrit Dictionary, Benfey .... *Longmans* .. 17
—— Dictionary .... *Trubner* 13
—— English Dictionary .... *Clar. Press.* 4
— - Grammar .... *Trubner* 5
— - Grammar .... *Clar. Press.* 4
— - Ballantyne .... *Trubner* 3
—— Idylls from .... *Smith & El.* 9
— - Language .... *Allen* 30
—— Literature, Hand-Book of .. *Williams* .. 13
—— Prosody .... *Trubner* 6
—— Texts, Muir .... *Trubner* 20
Saphir (Rev. Adolph) Works by.. *Nisbet* 33
Sapper's Manual .... *Allen* 19
Saracens, History of .... *Bohn's Lib.* 8
Sargant (W. L.) Works by ..... *Williams* .. 12
Sargent (G. E.) Works by ..... *Rel. Tr. Soc.* 16
Sartorius (A.) Works by .... *Smith & El.* 18
Sarum Missal, Sequences from .. *Bell* 56
—— Psalter .... *Masters* 23
Sassanian Coins .... *Trubner* 29
—— Inscriptions .... *Trubner* 29
Satan's Invisible World Displayed *T. Stevenson* 2
Saturday Journal .... *Strahan* 3
—— Review, Essays from ..... *Smith & El.* 6
—— Review, Essays from ..... *W. Blackw'd.* 28
Saturn and its System .... *Longmans* .. 18
Saunders the Cricketer, Life of .. *Morgan* 5
Savage Habits................ *Ward &Lock* 8
— — Life, Scenes and Studies of *Smith & El.* 21
Saving Knowledge .... *Isbister* 38
Saxon Chronicles .... *Clar. Press.* 14
Sayings ascribed to Our Lord... *J. Parker* .. 10
Scalæ Novæ, Thompson .... *Williams* .. 15
Scandinavian Churches, Letters on *Masters* .. 22
—— Mythology, Keary .... *Macmillan* .. 18
—— Sketches .... *King* 4
— — Tales .... *Bohn's Lib.* 12
Scarborough, Round About, &c... *Tinsley Bros.* 2
Scarlet Fever, Hood on .... *Churchill* .. 21
Scenes and Characters .... *Mozley* 11
— — of Scottish Story .... *Edmonston* .. 2
— in the East, Tristram ...... *Soc. P. C. K.* 23
Scenici Poetæ Græci .... *Nutt* 9
Schiller's Saemmtliche Werke.... *Sotheran* .. 25
—— Works, in German........ *Nutt* 19
—— Works .... *Bohn's Lib.* 9
—— Plays .... *Whittaker* .. 8
— — Plays, Text and Notes.... *Williams* .. 12
—— William Tell, German .... *Clar. Press.* 30
—— Piccolomini .... *Smith & El.* 16
—— Maid of Orleans, translation *Smith & El.* 19
Schlegel's Works.............. *Bohn's Lib.* 9
Schleswig-Holstein War .... *Tinsley Bros.* 8
Schmid's Contes pour les Enfants *Nutt*........ 27
—— Tales for Children, in German *Nutt* 20
"Schonberg-Cotta" Series .... *Nelson* 7
School Books .... *Gall* 16
—— Books of Christian Brothers *MacGlashan* 1
—— Books, Irish National .... *Collins* 11
—— Books used at Eton ...... *Williams* .. 4
—— Books (Scottish) Assoc. Series *Collins* ... 11
—— Boy Heroes .... *Nelson* 13
—— Boy's Letters for Copying .. *Stanford*... 68
—— Boy Tales, Adams........ *Routledge* .. 33
—— Days at Saxonhurst ...... *Black* 16
—— Diagrams .... *C. Smith*... 6
—— Large Diagrams......... *Chapman* .. 31
—— (Infant) Management .... *MacGlashan.* 1
—— Life, Pictures of........ *Cassell* 11
—— Life, Brief Words on...... *Bell* 52
—— Life, Stories of, Hope .... *Nimmo* 13
—— Life at Winchester College.. *Chatto* 31
School Management .... *J. Heywood* 42
—— Management, Currie ..... *Lawrie* 3
—— Management, Harding.... *Lawrie* 3
—— Management, Joyce ..... *MacGlashan* 1
—— Management, Menet ..... *Bell* 37
—— Manual of Health........ *Hardwicke.* 15
—— Models, in Boxes .... *Chapman* .. 30
—— Music .... *Murby* 8
—— (Night) Help for the..... *Mozley* 13
—— Prayers .... *Masters* ... 0
—— Prayers .... *Mozley*.... 10
—— Picture Books........... *Bell* 39
—— Punishment Register ..... *Stanford*... 68
— — Registers .... *J. Heywood* 47
—— Registers .... *Jarrold* 16
—— Registers .... *Lawrie* 4
—— Registers .... *Murby* 8
—— Registers .... *Philip* 44
—— Registers, Conduct ...... *Whittaker* .. 15
—— Registers, Conduct ...... *Allman* 6
—— Register, Durham........ *Stanford*... 68
—— Registers, Sherratt ..... *A. Heywood* 13
—— Series of Illustrations .... *Johnston*... 10
—— Sermons, Faber .... *Macmillan* .. 10
—— Songs, with Music, Thring... *Macmillan* .. 36
—— (Catholic) Songs and Music *Burns* 20
—— (Village) Songs .... *Cassell* 15
—— and College English Classics *Collins* 10
—— and College Prayers ..... *Parker* 33
Schoolcraft's Indian Tribes .... *Sotheran* .. 25
Schoolmaster's Drill Assistant.... *Bemrose* .. 12
Schools for the People, Building of *Murray* .. 26
—— (Great) of England ..... *Isbister* 41
—— Health for .... *Isbister* 40
—— (Industrial) Manuals..... *Masters* ... 16
—— (Public) .... *W. Blackw'd* 26
Schooling of Life (The) ...... *Macmillan*... 38
Schubert (Franz) Biography .... *Allen* 8
Sciatica, Treatment of .... *Hardwicke.* 16
Science, Borderland of .... *Smith & El.* 17
—— and Art, Educational Series *Murby* 8
—— Class Books .... *J. Heywood* 38
—— and Commerce .... *Hardwicke..* 10
—— Dictionary of, Brande ... *Longmans* .. 24
—— Dictionary, Rodwell ..... *Ward&Lock* 32
—— Elucidative of Scripture .. *Lockwood* .. 13
—— Fragments of .... *Longmans* .. 22
—— and History........... *Nelson* 11
—— and Humanity......... *Hodder* 22
—— for the Household....... *Jarrold* 17
—— Lectures for the People .. *J. Heywood.* 5
—— Manuals .... *Groombridge* 22
—— Martyrs of .... *Chatto* 6
—— Play-book of .... *Routledge* .. 29
—— Primers .... *Macmillan* .. 30
—— Principles of, Jevons..... *Macmillan* .. 17
—— of Religion .... *Longmans* .. 5
—— Series, Advanced .... *Collins* 7
—— Series, Elementary ...... *Collins* 6
—— Simplified .... *Warne* 44
—— Text Book .... *Longmans* .. 21
—— Stray Leaves of .... *Tinsley Bros.* 8
—— Wonders of, Mayhew .... *Routledge* .. 33
Sciences .... *Chambers* .. 17
—— and Arts, English Cyclop... *Bradbury* .. 6
—— Classification of the ..... *Williams* .. 14
Scientific Amateurs, Receipts for *Spon* 46
—— Amusement .... *Routledge* .. 37
—— Class Books .... *Chambers* .. 17
—— Class Books .... *Macmillan* .. 22
——— Conclusions and Religion *Isbister* 43
—— Education, Youmans .... *Macmillan* .. 43
—— Manuals .... *Cassell* 13
—— Men, Corres. of 17th Century *Clar. Press..* 18
—— Pol. & Spec. Essays, Spencer *Williams* .. 14
—— Reader .... *Chambers* .. 17
—— Subjects, Herschell ..... *Isbister* 21
—— Subjects, Lectures....... *Longmans* .. 21
—— Subjects, Letters on ..... *J. R. Smith* 9
—— Studies, Pract., in Contrast *Spon* 34
—— Terms .... *Smith & El.* 3
—— Terms, Nuttall .... *Isbister* 32
—— Treasury, Maunder ..... *Longmans* .. 43
Scilly Islands, White .... *Chapman* .. 26
Scinde..................... *W. Blackw'd* 24

Sciography, Puckett .... Chapman .. 23
Scoti-Monasticon .... Virtue 4
Scotland, Angler and Tourist in .. Black 32
—— Ancient Churches of .... Virtue 4
— — Ancient Pillar Stones ...... Edmonston .. 16
—— Annals of .... Chambers .. 27
—— Archaeology .... W. Blackw'd 32
—— Ballads of.................. W. Blackw'd 3
—— by W. Beattie............... Virtue 12
—— Book of Common Prayer.... Masters ... 3
—— Church of .... Edmonston .. 6
—— Church of, Lee .... W. Blackw'd 39
—— County Maps .... W. Blackw'd 4
—— Church of, Lee .... W. Blackw'd 18
—— Clans of .... Sotheran.... 19
— -- Clans, Geography of ...... Johnston.... 21
—— Court of Session, Galland .. Sotheran.... 25
—— Descriptive Notices .... Parker 53
—— Ecclesiastical History ...... Edmonston .. 11
—— Fourteen Days in .... A. Heywood. 6
—— Gilderoy, the Hero of ...... Routledge .. 35
—— Guide to .... Black 6
—— Handbook to .... Murray ... 17
—— Historians of .... Edmonston .. 12
—— History of................ Chambers .. 27
—— Burton .... W. Blackw'd 6
—— History, Macarthur .... Macmillan .. 21
—— School History .... Edmonston .. 14
—— Pictorial History of .... Virtue 21
—— History of, Tytler .... Black 32
—— Tytler's History of........ Nimmo 27
—— Highland Scenery .... Bell 5
—— Industries of .... Black 8
—— Lays of the Kirk .... Nisbet 27
—— Laws of Railways .... Edmonston.. 6
—— Maps of................. Johnston.... 6
—— Memorable Wars of .... Nimmo 16
—— Old Church Architecture... Edmonston .. 5
—— Peasant Life in .... Isbister 24
—— Popular Rhymes of .... Chambers .. 27
—— Queens of................ W. Blackw'd 30
—— Reform of Church .... Edmonston.. 14
—— Scenery and Phys.Geograph. Macmillan .. 12
—— Scenes and Legends of North Nimmo 4
—— and the Scottish Church .. Parker 13
—— Songs of .... W. Blackw'd 16
—— Songs, prior to Burns ..... Chambers .. 37
—— Songstresses of .... Isbister 44
—— Sporting in .... Routledge .. 72
—— Statutes (Public) .... W. Blackw'd 26
—— Tales of West Highlands... Edmonston.. 4
—— Wild Sports of Highlands .. Murray 30
Scoto-Oxonian Philosophy, Bolton Chapman .. 12
Scots Worthies, Historical Account MacPhun .. 16
Scotsmen, Eminent .... Blackie 14
Scott (Rev. John) Addresses ... Wesleyan.... 48
Scott (Sir W.) Life, Lockhart .. Black 29
—— Epitome of Lockhart's Life of Black 13
—— Life, by Gleig .... Black 13
—— Life, by Carruthers .... Chambers .. 27
—— Reminiscences of, Gibson .. Black 13
—— Works .... Black 27
—— Poetical Works .... Collins 2
—— Poetical Works .... Warne 18
—— and Abbotsford .... Virtue..... 20
Scott and Sebright .... Warne 9
Scottish Anecdote .... Routledge .. 3
—— Ballads .... Chambers .. 27
—— Ballads and Poetry .... Stevenson .. 2
—— Ballads and Songs........ Blackie 15
—— Banks, Somers .... Black 31
—— Chiefs, Porter .... Milner 4
—— Church (Early) .... Clark 17
—— Covenanters, Brown ...... Snow 3
—— Covenanters, Tales of .... MacPhun .. 3
—— Covenanters, 50 Years Strug. Houlston.. 22
—— Dictionary, Jamieson ..... Nimmo 30
—— Evangelist (The), Mathison.. Morgan .. 2
—— Highlands .... Smith & El. 13
—— History, Sketches of Early.. Edmonston.. 12
—— Highlands, Lays of .... Isbister 7
—— Highlands, Painter's Camp in Macmillan .. 15
—— Highland Parish .... Isbister 29
—— Highlands, Western ...... Chapman .. 24
—— Legal Antiquities .... Edmonston .. 12

Scottish Legends.............. Edmonston.. 11
—— Life, Familiar Illustrations of Houlston.. 25
—— Minstrel, Rogers .... Nimmo 7
—— People, Traits & Stories of .. Houlston.. 25
—— Poetry .... Edmonston.. 13
—— Protestant (The)......... MacPhun .. 16
—— Record Publications ...... Black 10
—— Reformation Catechisms.. Nisbet 6
—— Royal Academy........... Edmonston.. 11
—— Saints, Forbes .... Edmonston.. 9
—— Songs, Mackay .... Houlston.. 16
—— Songs, Ancient and Modern Sotheran.. 13
—— Surnames............... Edmonston.. 12
—— Worthies, Last Words of ... MacPhun .. 16
Scouring of the White Horse .. Macmillan .. 32
Scratchley (A.) Works by..... Layton 14
Screw Propulsion, Burgh ..... Spon.... 35
Scriptures Arranged (The), Linton Bagster .. 73
Scripture Characters, Candlish .. Black 10
—— Class Book .... Black 11
—— Coincidences, Craig ...... Bagster 61
—— Continuity of .... Murray 14
—— Figurative Language in .. Parker.... 8
—— Geography, Outlines ..... S. S. Union 43
— —— History .... J. Blackwood 15
—— History .... J. Heywood . 36
—— History .... Virtue 19
—— History, Brewer .... Jarrold 5
—— History, Pinnock .... Hall 3
— —— History for the Young ... Masters 4
—— History, Old Testament .. Soc. P. C. K. 10
—— Illustrations .... Stanford.... 41
—— Itself the Illustrator ...... Nisbet 7
—— Knowledge, Green .... S. S. Union. 41
—— Lands, Drew .... King 29
—— Manners and Customs .... Soc. P. C. K. 23
—— Manual .... Hodder 11
—— Manuals .... Murby 5
—— Manuals .... Philip 38
—— Misread Passages .... Hodder 18
—— Names, Dictionary of .... S. S. Union 43
—— Names of Persons and Places Clark 20
—— Names, Student's Manual of Parker.... 8
—— and Nature .... Hodder 12
—— Natural History .... Soc. P. C. K. 24
—— Object Lessons .... Shaw 8
— —— Obscure .... Hodder 11
—— Plea for a New Version .. Macmillan.. 29
—— Portraits .... Isbister 41
—— Prints .... Parker.... 45
—— Proper Names in .... Parker 8
—— Questions............... Jarrold 12
—— Reader's Guide .... Nisbet 14
—— Readings, Yonge .... Macmillan.. 43
—— and Science not at Variance Hatchard .. 22
—— Student's Assistant ...... Blackie 14
—— Symbolical Numbers of ... Clark 18
—— Texts, Secular Annotations. Hodder 10
—— Topography (Gentile World) Soc. P. C. K. 24
—— Typology................ Clark 14
Scriptural Coincidences, Craig .. Bagster 61
Sculpture, Ancient Greek & Rom. Pickering .. 1
—— British School of .... Virtue 22
—— History of, Lübke .... Smith & El. 14
—— Italian .... Chapman .. 24
—— Lectures on, Flaxman .... Bohn's Lib.. 13
—— Schools of, Westmacott ... Black 32
—— Tuscan .... Sotheran.... 1
Sea (The) and its Living Wonders Longmans .. 23
—— Bathing and Sea Air...... Churchill .. 19
—— Conquest of the .... Chatto 7
—— Countries, Cooper........ King.... 4
—— Depth of the .... Macmillan .. 35
—— Drift .... J. Blackw'd. 29
—— and her Famous Sailors ... Virtue 14
—— Fights, &c. .... Warne 27
—— Fights and Land Battles... Warne 30
—— Fisherman .... Longmans .. 42
—— Kings (Norse)........... Nisbet 4
— —— Margins, Ancient .... Chambers .. 27
—— Officer's Manual .... Smith & El. 16
—— Rule of Road at .... Stanford.... 53
—— Sermons .... Rel. Tr. Soc. 17
— —— Stories .... Ward & Lock 15
— —— Tales of Adventures on the .. Nisbet 4

Sea, Wonders of the Deep ...... *J. Blackw'd.* 16
Seaman's Friend (The) .... *Philip* 39
—— Medicine Chest .... *Churchill* .. 38
—— Wages Tables .... *Wilton* 8
—— (Young) Manual .... *Trubner* 6
Seamanship, by Capt. Nares .... *Griffin* 8
—— (The Boy's Manual) .... *Trubner* 6
Seamen (Our) .... *Virtue* 12
Sea-Shore, Gosse .... *Isbister* 17
—— Common Objects of .... *Routledge* .. 9
—— Wonders of, Kingsley ...... *Macmillan* .. 19
Sea-Side Book .... *Rel. Tr. Soc.* 17
—— Half-Hours at the.......... *Hardwicke* .. 9
—— Naturalist .... *Isbister* 15
—— Walks .... *Groombridge.* 12
Seaweeds, British .... *Reeve* 8
—— British .... *Routledge* .. 48
—— British, Gatty............. *Bell* 16
—— Nature Printed .... *Bradbury* .. 11
Search after Sunshine .... *Bentley*..... 13
Seasons of the Year .... *Nimmo* 13
—— of the Year, Natural History. *Partridge* .. 8
—— The Four, Chemistry of .... *Churchill* .. 18
—— Short Devotions for .... *Masters* 25
—— of the Church, Sermons .... *Masters* 9
—— of the Church, Newland .... *Mozley* 12
—— Pictorial Calendar of...... *Bohn's Lib..* 13
—— (Four) Rambles in......... *Soc. P. C. K.* 21
Seatonian Poems............... *Masters* 19
Seats and Saddles .... *W. Blackw'd* 8
Sebastopol, Scamper to........ *Bentley* 13
Second (The) Adam & New Birth *Bell* 50
Secret Drawer................. *S. S. Union.* 7
—— of a Long Life .... *King* 33
—— of the Lord (The) .... *Morgan* 3
—— Out .... *Chatto* 32
—— Trials of the Christian Life. *Mozley* 10
Secular Annotations Scrip. Texts. *Hodder* ... 5
Securities, American & Canadian. *Wilton* 8
Sedan, Plan of the Battle of..... *Stanford* ... 54
Seed for Spring-Time.......... *Nisbet* 21
—— Time and Harvest......... *Nelson* 13
—— Truths, by Church........ *Clark* 13
Seekers after God .... *Macmillan..* 34
Seeley (J. R.) Lects. & Essays.. *Macmillan..* 32
Selborne (White's) .... *Bell* 73
—— Natural History of .... *Routledge* .. 45
—— White's Natural History... *Soc. P. C. K.* 24
Selenographia .... *C. Smith* ... 11
Self Culture, Beard........... *A. Heywood* 17
—— Culture, Blackie.......... *Edmonston..* 2
—— Help, Smiles .... *Murray* 27
—— Made Men .... *Snow* 1
—— Renunciation .... *Rivingtons* .. 7
—— and Self Sacrifice .... *Groombridge* 2
Sempill Ballads .... *Stevenson* .. a
Sen (Chunder) Lectures and Tracts *Isbister* ... 39
Senators (British) .... *Tinsley Bros.* 8
Senses and the Intellect....... *Longmans* .. 17
Sepoy War, Grant .... *W. Blackw'd* 11
Sepulchral Crosses .... *Parker*...... 11
Sepulchre in the Garden ...... *Nisbet* 20
Septuagint (The)............. *Bagster* 32
Serious Subjects (Small Books). *Rel. Tr. Soc.* 23
Serjeants at Law, Lives of .... *Allen* 29
Sermon, Claude on Composition.. *Cornish* ... 4
—— Framework .... *Dickinson* .. 11
—— on the Mount .... *Macmillan* .. 11
—— Plans, Methodist .... *Dickinson* .. 11
Sermons .... *Bell* 57
Sermons .... *Parker*...... 20
Sermons .... *Rivingtons* .. 13
—— to Children .... *Dickinson* .. 16
—— for Children .... *Bell* 27
—— for the Christian Seasons... *Parker* 36
—— for Christian Year .... *Dickinson* .. 8
—— on Church Seasons....... *Rivingtons* .. 14
—— for my Curates .... *Isbister* 27
—— by Foreign Preachers .... *Dickinson* .. 5
—— at Lincoln's Inn .... *Murray* 8
—— (Open-Air), Notes on..... *Nisbet* 36
—— in Plain Language........ *Mozley* 11
—— for very Plain People ..... *Dickinson* .. 9
—— Plans of................. *Nicholson* .. 0
—— on Prep. and Delivery of.... *Nisbet* 8

Sermons Preached at Ramsgate .. *Snow* 2
—— Simple, Ranken .... *Rivingtons..* 15
—— (Single) .... *Masters* 35
—— Sketches, Burns.......... *Dickinson* .. 3
—— 15 Short for People ...... *Dickinson* .. 9
—— for Sick Seamen .... *W. Blackw'd* 13
—— to Soldiers .... *Smith & El.* 27
—— on Subjects of the Day.... *Rivingtons..* 15
—— for Sundays, &c. .... *Soc. P. C. K.* 24
—— in Stones .... *Bentley* 10
—— for the Times .... *Longmans* .. 36
Servants, Hints to .... *Bell* 63
—— How Should we Treat .... *Mozley* 5
—— Letters to Young .... *Mozley*...... 6
Service for the Poor .... *Macmillan* .. 34
—— Book of the Ch. of England *Parker*...... 37
Setter, How to Breed and Rear.. *Longmans* .. 42
Seven Champions of Christendom *J. Blackw'd.* 21
—— Common Faults .... *Rivingtons* .. 17
—— May-Days .... *Nisbet* 20
—— Sisters of Sleep .... *J. Blackw'd.* 27
—— Sayings of Christ on the Cross *Hatchard* .. 8
—— to Seventeen .... *Warne* 25
—— Weeks' War, Horner....... *Macmillan* .. 16
Sewage, Preparation of Plans, &c. *Harrison* ... 13
—— Utilization of .... *Macmillan..* 8
—— Works on .... *Spon* 35
Sewer Gas, Reynolds .... *Macmillan* .. 37
Sewell (Miss) Works by........ *Longmans* .. 0
—— Sentences from Works of... *Masters* 25
—— (Mrs.) Homely Ballads .... *Jarrold* 15
Shadows of the Great Sacrifice . *Nisbet* 37
Shaftesbury (First Earl of) .... *Macmillan..* 32
—— (Earl) Speeches .... *Chapman* ... 25
Shakspeare, ed. H. Glasford Bell *Collins* 2
—— Campbell .... *Routledge* .. 62
—— Clarke and Wright........ *Macmillan..* 32
—— Mary Cowden Clarke .... *Nimmo* 6
—— Collier .... *Whittaker* .. 16
—— Dyce .... *Chapman* ... 17
—— Handy Volume .... *Bradbury* .. 7
—— Hazlitt .... *Routledge* .. 70
—— Illustrated .... *Cassell* 7
—— Knight .... *Bell* 29
—— Phelp's Standard Edition .. *MacPhun* .. 11
—— Pocket Volume Edition ... *Bell* 20
—— Staunton .... *Routledge* .. 27
—— Valpy's Cabinet Edition .. *Bell* 29
—— Bowdler's Family .... *Longmans* .. 41
—— Cabinet Edition .... *Chambers* .. 37
—— Family Edition .... *Gall* 4
—— Rugby Edition .... *Rivingtons..* 27
—— for Schools .... *Chambers* .. 9
—— Works .... *Milner* 2
—— Works .... *Routledge* .. 70
—— Works .... *Sotheran..* 26
—— Works .... *Virtue* 21
—— Works .... *Warne*..... 28
—— for Schools .... *Washbourne* 4
—— Kean's Selections from .... *Bradbury* .. 11
—— Readings, Kemble........ *Bell* 29
—— Select Plays, W. G. Clarke. *Clar. Press..* 31
—— Hamlet, Dissertations on .. *Williams.* .. 8
—— Beauties .... *Warne* 2
—— Gems .... *Routledge* .. 28
—— Pearls of .... *J. Blackwood* 21
—— Songs .... *Virtue*...... 16
—— Sonnets and Songs........ *Macmillan..* 28
—— Commentaries .... *Smith & El.* 8
—— and the Emblem Writers... *Trubner* 11
—— Birthplace of .... *Smith & El.* 19
—— English of .... *Chapman* ... 14
—— Female Characters .... *Routledge* .. 43
—— in Germany............. *Asher* 3
—— Home and Rural Life .... *Longmans* .. 7
—— Lamb's Tales from....... *Routledge* .. 33
—— Legal Acquirements of.... *Murray* 7
—— Mad Folk of .... *Macmillan..* 4
—— Philosophy of .... *Lockwood* .. 41
—— Studies of............... *Routledge* .. 70
—— and Topography......... *Trubner* 5
Shakesperian Grammar .... *Macmillan..* 1
—— Parallels and Bible Truths. *Hodder* 12
Shakspeariana .... *J. R. Smith* 27
Shaksperianum (Sertum) .... *Macmillan..* 19

Share and Stock Tables.......... Wilson 4
Sharpe (Samuel) Works .... J. R. Smith 21
Shaving them .... Chatto 31
— of Shagpat .... Chapman .. 22
She Spake of Him .... Mack 10
Sheep .... W. Blackw'd. 28
— Farming, Brown on .... Black 9
Sheepshanks Gallery .... Bell 9
Shelley's Early Life .... Chatto 32
— Poetical Works .... Chatto 32
Shells .... Reeve 9
Shells, Catalogue, Brit. Museum Pickering .. 33
— Sowerby .... Routledge .. 46
— their Nature, Uses, &c. .... Groombridge 13
Shelmerdine's Chants........... Isbister ... 39
Sheltering Vine (The) .... Hatchard .. 18
Shepheard (Rev. H.) Works by . Nisbet 33
Shepherd and His Flock .... Nisbet 83
— and His Lambs .... Tubbs 5
— of Grove Hall .... Snow 14
— of Hermas .... Rivington... 17
Sheridan (R. B.) Works .... Chatto 33
— Works .... Sotheran .. 12
— Dramatic Works........... Bohn's Lib. 9
Sherwood Forest, Birds of ..... Reeve 14
— (Mrs) Works by........... Hatchard .. 25
— Works by .... Houlston .. 18
— Popular Tales .... Allman 13
— Tales .... Milner 10
Shetland and Orkney Dialect .. Asher 8
Shifting Winds, A Tough Yarn . Nisbet 4
Shilling, Passages in History of a Partridge .. 9
— Bible Illustration Books .... Nelson 20
— Instructive Books .... Nelson 17
Shining Light, Marsh .... Nisbet 96
Ship-Boy's Life Aboard .... Ward 27
Shipbuilding in Iron and Wood . Black 15
— Iron and Steel .... Murray 26
— and Masting .... Whittaker .. 16
— Rudimentary Works .... Lockwood .. 22
Shipley (Rev. O.) Works by .... Masters ... 25
— Works Edited by .... Rivingtons . 6
Shipmasters, Counsel and Aid to King 31
Shipping Dues and Charges .... Philip 39
— Lee's Works on .... Philip 48
Ships (Famous), Adams .... Isbister ... 3
— Ironclad, Reed .... Murray 26
— (Unseaworthy) Analyt. Index Virtue 12
Shipton (Anna) Works by ...... Morgan ... 3
— Works by .... Yapp 3
Shipwrecks, Kingston .... Routledge .. 29
— Notable .... Cassell ... 11
— of Faith, Trench .... Macmillan . 38
Shirley .... Smith & El. 2
— Hall Asylum .... Isbister ... 17
Shooter's Diary .... W. Blackw'd 51
Shorthand, Short Hints on ..... Houlston .. 19
— Parliamentary :........... Bell 63
— Self Taught .... Stanford .. 71
Short Sermons for Family Reading Parker 36
Short Studies on Great Subjects. Longmans .. 15
Shut Your Mouth and Save, &c.. Trubner ... 7
Shuttlecock Papers............ Tinsley Bros. 5
Siam, Travels and Discoveries . Murray 23
Siberia, Christian Mission to .... Snow...... 15
— Russian Conspirators in .... Smith & El. 25
— Tronson .... Smith & El. 25
Siberian Overland Route ...... Murray 22
Siborne's War in France ...... Sotheran .. 26
Sicily, Forbes .... W. Blackw'd 9
— (History of) to Athenian War Murray 27
Sick and Afflicted, Books for ... Masters ... 0
— Bed Vows, How to Keep.... Nisbet 33
— and Lonely, Poems for..... Hatchard .. 18
— Persons, Lectures for ...... Hatchard .. 2
— Room Attendant .... Nisbet 33
— Room, Readings for .... Morgan ... 4
— Room, Shadows of a .... Murray 27
— and Wounded Troops, ... Harrison.... 6
Sickness and Affliction .... Parker 33
— Consoling Thoughts in..... Rivingtons . 8
— Kennaway's Consolatio .... Rivingtons . 8
— Sunshine in .... Mozley.... 12
— its Trials and Blessings .... Rivingtons . 7
Sieges (Great) of History ..... Routledge .. 22

Sierra Leone, by a Lady .... Murray 20
— Seddall................... Hatchard .. 25
Sign Boards, History of .... Chatto 33
Signs of the Times, Hastings ... Kellaway .. 9
Sikhim, by Col. Gawler .... Stanford .. 54
Silas the Conjuror .... Ward&Lock 8
Silence and Voices of God ..... Macmillan . 10
Silk Exchange Tables .... Smith & El. 4
— and Scarlet .... Warne 9
— and Tea Tables .... Wilson 9
Silkworms.................... Ward&Lock 11
Siluria, Murchison............ Murray 23
Silver Casket .... Nelson 9
— Cup (The) .... Warne 28
— Lake (The) .... Warne 28
Silverland, Author of "Guy Liv." Chapman .. 25
Simple Truth to Working People Isbister ... 29
Simpson (Sir J. Y.) Works of... Black 31
Sin, its Causes and Consequences Allen 25
— Forms of, Whitemarsh..... Bell 53
— (Human) The Burden of.... Macmillan . 30
— Short Treatise on, Glover .. Bell 60
Sins (Small), Grosart .... Nisbet 15
Sinai and Jerusalem, Scenes from Soc. P. C. K. 24
— Ordnance Survey .... Stanford .. 65
— and Palestine .... Murray 28
— Rock Inscriptions .... Bentley ... 22
— and Syene, To .... Smith & El. 5
Sinclair (Sir Geo.) Memoirs ... Tinsley Bros. 7
Singing made Easy .... Groombridge 19
Sinlessness of Jesus .... Clark 11
Sinner's Friend (The) .... Nisbet 16
— Author's Autobiography .... Nisbet 16
Sinner's Guide (The) .... Rivingtons . 6
Sister of Mercy, Tales from Diary Burns 35
Sister's (A) Bye Hours .... Isbister ... 22
Sisters of Charity .... Masters ... 26
— (English) Prayers for, Neale Rivingtons . 8
— of Mercy, Devotions for ... Masters ... 5
— of Mercy at Home .... Nisbet 35
Sisterhoods .... Smith & El. 9
— (Anglican) Whately .... Harrison... 3
— Inquiry into .... Macmillan . 34
Sisterhood, Tales in a .... Masters ... 12
Six Cushions (The)........... Mozley.... 11
— of Spades................ W. Blackw'd 50
— by Two................... Virtue 8
— Weeks in the Saddle....... Macmillan . 39
Sixtus the Fifth, Life and Times Longmans .. 8
Skelton's Poetical Works ...... Sotheran .. 26
Sketches of the Bar and Press... King 33
— at Home and Abroad ...... Chapman .. 4
— of Irish Character .... Chatto 18
— of Young Couples .... Chatto 33
Sketching from Nature, Delamotte Bell 5
Skilled Labour applied to Produc. Virtue 22
Skin Diseases, Anderson ...... Churchill .. 7
— Diseases, Anderson .... Macmillan . 2
— Diseases of, Cauty......... Churchill .. 12
— Disease, Milton .... Hardwicke . 16
— Diseases, Nayler .... Churchill .. 27
— (Healthy), Wilson......... Churchill... 39
Skye, A Summer in .... Isbister ... 40
Slang Dictionary .... Chatto 34
Slave Catching, Indian Ocean.... Longmans .. 37
Sleep, Philosophy of .... MacPhun .. 6
Slezer's Theatrum Scotiæ...... Sotheran .. 27
Slide-Valve, Burgh............ Spon 37
Sling and the Stone .... Trubner ... 30
Ship in the Fens (A) .... Macmillan . 33
Slip History Papers .... Cornish ... 11
Slugs and Snails, Tate .... Hardwicke . 4
Small Beginnings .... Virtue 14
Smedley (M. B.) Works by .... Isbister ... 40
Smiles (Samuel) Works by ..... Murray 27
— Huguenots in France ...... Isbister ... 40
Smith (Alex.) Works .... Isbister ... 40
— (Barnard) Works .... Macmillan . 33
— (Cath. B.) Poems .... Macmillan . 33
— (Goldwin) Works .... Macmillan . 33
— (Rev. James) Works....... Milner 12
— Works .... Nelson 21
— (J. H.) Mathematical Works. Rivingtons . 24
— (R. Pearsall) Small bks. by . Morgan ... 16
— (Sid.) Life and Letters ..... Longmans .. 8

Smith (Sydney) Works .... Longmans .. 0
— (T. A.) Memoirs .... Chatto ... 36
— (Dr. W.) Works .... Murray ... 38
Smith's Wealth of Nations ..... Clar. Press.. 17
— Wesleyan Methodism ...... Wesleyan .. 47
Smoker's Text Book .... Chatto ... 31
Smollett's (T.) Works .... Sotheran .. 12
— Works .... Bell 34
— Works, with Life .... Nimmo 7
Smyth (Prof.) Lectures on History Bohn's Lib... 9
Soaps, Manufacture of .... Trubner .. 20
Social Circle, Books for .... Lockwood .. 45
— Deposits, Gilbert .... Isbister ... 16
— Duties on Christm. Principles Hatchard .. 7
— Duties Considered .... Macmillan .. 33
— Economy .... Cassell 14
— Economy, About .... Isbister ... 3
— Economy, Ellis .... Smith & El. 6
— Evil, Great .... Hodder 21
— Morality .... Macmillan .. 24
— Reform, Ten Chapters on .. Stanford... 69
— Science, Ellis .... Smith & El. 6
— Statics, Spencer .... Williams .. 14
— Subjects, Essays on .... Macmillan .. 11
Socialism in England.......... Trubner .. 23
Society, Abominations of Modern Nicholson .. 2
— — Improvement of .... Collins ... 3
— — Queens, Wits, and Beaux of Routledge .. 4
Sociology, Descriptive English . Williams .. 13
— — Study of, Spencer ...... King 8
Socrates and Soc. Schools ..... Longmans .. 5
So Great Love, Brightwell ..... Snow..... 2
Solar Physics, Lockyer......... Macmillan .. 20
— Spectrum, Kirchhoff........ Macmillan .. 19
Soldier of the Cross........... Collins..... 3
— and Patriot .... Cassell 11
— Reminiscences of a........ Hurst 1
Soldier's Pocket Book .... Allen 21
— Pocket Book for Field Service Macmillan.. 41
— Testimony (A)............. Nisbet ... 25
— Text Book, Macduff........ Nisbet ... 24
Soldiers' Biographies .... W. Blackw'd 21
Soldiers, Brave British .... Ward & Lock 8
— Sermons for .... Masters ... 29
— and Servants of Christ ..... Nisbet ... 21
— Work Among .... Hatchard .. 2
Soldiering, Maurice .... Cassell 5
— and Scribbling .... King..... 33
Solomon's Song, Newton ...... Nisbet ... 28
— Song, Reville .... Williams .. 11
— Song, Beauty in the Word .. Nisbet ... 5
— Song, Exposition of, Stuart.. Nisbet ... 34
— Song, Meditations on ...... Yapp 5
— Song, Commentary .... Masters ... 15
— Song, Thrupp .... Macmillan .. 36
— Song, Trans. from Hebrew .. Williams .. 13
Soltan's (The) Tabernacle....... Yapp ... 3
Some Influences of Christianity .. Macmillan.. 7
Somerville (Mary) Works........ Murray 31
Song Book for Children.......... Bell 21
— Books.................. Cameron .. 7
— Books.................. Routledge .. 71
— Books, Cheap .... Marr 9
— Book, Irish .... MacGlashan 2
— Books, Sacred .... Routledge .. 26
— Book, Words and Music .... Macmillan.. 14
— of the New Creation ...... Nisbet ... 6
— of a Pilgrim (The) .... Nisbet ... 19
Songs, Book of .... Ward ... 11
— for Children, Illustrated .. Nelson ... 20
— Christy Minstrels'......... Marr 3
— of the Cross and the Crown.. Isbister .. 41
— of Eminent Wits, 1639 ..... Chatto .. 31
— Fishing .... W. Blackw'd 7
— of Grace and Glory .... Nisbet ... 46
— of Ireland.............. Cameron .. 2
— of Innocence .... Pickering .. 5
— of Lancashire............ A. Heywood 7
— of Life and Death........ King 22
— for Little Folks .... Cassell ... 9
— Military .... Chapman .. 2
— The Nat. Melodist & Music Nimmo ... 32
— — One Hundred, and Music .. Marr 5
— of the People .... Houlston .. 16
— and Recitations .... Milner ... 3

Songs of Roumania .... Smith & El. 16
— for Sailors .... King 21
— of Scotland, subs. to Burns Nimmo 7
— Sea, Dibdin.............. Bell 22
— of the Soul.............. Lockwood .. 43
— for Students............. Edmonston.. 2
— and Verses .... W. Blackw'd. 29
— for the Weary .... Hodder ... 21
— Young Folk's, Sacred ..... Marr 3
— Young Folk's, Secular.... Marr 3
— English............... Macmillan .. 13
— French............... Macmillan .. 14
— German............... Ward 24
— German War .... Edmonston.. 2
— Scotch, with Music ...... W. Blackw'd 16
— Scottish............... Blackie .. 15
— Scottish.............. Marr 3
Songsters, Our Native .... Soc. P.C.K. 25
Sonnenschein, Teaching to Read Macmillan .. 34
Sons of God.............. Hodder ... 13
Sonship and Brotherhood, &c. .. Black ... 9
Sophocles, Blaydes........... Whittaker .. 2
— Greek Text, rev. by Blaydes Williams .. 13
— Notes by Wunder .... Williams .. 13
— Oxford Editions......... Parker ... 0
— Tragedies, Wunder ...... Nutt.... 9
Sorrow and Consolation....... Nisbet ... 15
Soul, Existence of, after Death . Parker..... 4
— Gatherer (The) .... Nisbet ... 4
— (The) and Money .... Tinsley Bros. 9
— (The) Her Sorrow, &c. ... Trubner ... 31
Soul's Exodus .... Smith & El. 3
— (The) Inquiries .... Hatchard .. 16
— Renewal (The) .... Hodder ... 17
Sound .... Chambers .. 17
— and Atmospheric Vibrations Macmillan .. 1
— Lectures on, Tyndall ..... Longmans .. 20
— and Light.............. Longmans .. 21
— and Music .... Macmillan .. 35
— Phenomena of.......... Jarrold ... 5
— Wonders of .... Cassell ... 8
South Pole (At the).......... Cassell ... 11
— Sea Bubbles .... Bentley .. 13
— Sea Islands .... Murray ... 82
— Sea Islands, Brenchley .. Longmans .. 37
— Seas, &c .... Chatto ... 34
South's Sermons .... Clar. Press.. 14
Southern Seas, Flying from Shadow Smith & El. 15
Southey (C. B.) Poems ...... W. Blackw'd. 29
Sowerby's English Botany .... Bell 15
Sowing and Reaping .... Nisbet ... 35
Spa, Notes on .... Churchill .. 14
Spain, Age Philip 3rd and 4th.... Murray ... 7
— Bible in.............. Murray ... 5
— under Charles the Second .. Murray ... 31
— Daybreak in .... Cassell ... 2
— Gatherings from....... Murray ... 12
— Geology of, Sullivan..... Williams .. 14
— Gothic Architecture in..... Murray ... 31
— Handbook to .... Murray ... 15
— History of .... Masters ... 13
— Martyrs of .... Nelson ... 7
— Medicine in.......... Churchill .. 17
— and its People .... Nelson ... 4
— and Portugal .... W. Blackw'd 7
— and Portugal, O'Shea ... Black ... 6
— Reformation in .... W. Blackw'd 19
— and the Spaniards ..... Hurst & B. 1
— Summer in .... Tinsley Bros. 7
— Through by Rail ...... Wilson ... 7
— The Troubadors ...... Smith & El. 18
— Wanderings in........ Isbister ... 19
Spanish Ballads, Lockhart ... Murray ... 24
— Barber (The) .... Nisbet ... 33
— Brothers .... Nelson ... 8
— Inquisition .... Nimmo ... 14
— Literature, History of ... Trubner ... 29
— Pictures .... Rel. Tr. Soc. 17
— School of Painting...... Routledge .. 3
— Stories, with Notes ..... Asher ... 2
— Testament and Com. Prayer Bagster .. 19
— Dialogues........... Hachette .. 5
— Dictionary .... Trubner ... 30
— Dictionary, Elwes....... Lockwood .. 30
— Dictionary, Wessely....... Routledge .. 14

Spanish Educational Works ..... *Whittaker* .. 6
—— English Conversation ...... *Trubner* ... 11
—— English Conv., Rowbotham *Nutt* 32
—— English Dictionary .... *Nutt* 30
—— Grammar, Del Mar .... *Nutt* 30
—— Grammar, McHenry........ *Lockwood* .. 35
—— Method, Velasquez .... *Trubner* ... 30
—— Teacher, Butler .... *Trubner* ... 6
Sparkling Diamonds .... *J. Blackwood* 24
Speaker and Reader .... *Warne* 26
Speaker's Bible Com. Crit. Ead. *Longmans* .. 30
Speaking Voice, Cultivation of .. *Clar. Press.* 30
—— to the Heart .... *Isbister* ... 19
—— to the Life .... *Wesleyan* .. 42
Specifier, Comprehensive ...... *Longmans* .. 45
Specifications, Blenkarn ...... *Spon* 37
—— Donaldson .... *Lockwood* .. 8
Specimens of Early English .... *Clar. Press.* 28
—— of English Literature ...... *Clar. Press.* 28
Spectator (The), Addison ...... *Routledge* .. 1
Spectroscope and its Application. *Macmillan* .. 80
—— and its Applications ...... *Macmillan* .. 19
Spectrum Analysis .... *Longmans* .. 19
—— Analysis, Roscoe .... *Macmillan* .. 31
Speculative Philosophy .... *Clark* 21
Speculum Gregis .... *Rivingtons* .. 11
—— Humanæ Salvationis...... *Stewart* .... a
—— Treatise on .... *Churchill* .. 24
Speech, Families of .... *Longmans* .. 12
—— Impediment of .... *Churchill* .. 10
—— in Season .... *King* 29
Spelling .... *W. Blackw'd* 43
—— Derivative .... *Lockwood* .. 29
—— English-Welsh .... *J. Heywood* 23
—— Guide to .... *Murby* 3
—— Books .... *Chambers* .. 8
—— Books .... *A. Heywood.* 17
—— Books .... *Marlborough* 15
—— Books .... *Milner* 15
—— Books .... *Mozley* 16
—— Books .... *Nicholson* .. 15
—— Books .... *Routledge* .. 18
—— Books .... *Ward&Lock* 10
—— Books .... *Warne* 36
Spellings .... *J. Blackwood* 30
Spencer and Cawdray, Illustrated *Dickinson* .. 11
Spenser's F. Queene, Kitchen .. *Clar. Press.* 11
Sphere and Spheroid .... *Stanford* ... 66
Spider Spinnings............ *Routledge* .. 46
Spiders, British .... *Reeve* 2
Spine, Curvature of .... *Macmillan* .. 3
—— Curvature of the .... *Churchill* .. 3
Spinoza's Life and Letters .... *Trubner* ... 27
Spirit and Mind Polarity ...... *Houlston* .. 26
—— Controversy (The)........ *Williams* .. 3
—— of Praise .... *Warne* 18
Spiritual Combat............ *Burns* 34
—— Garland (The).......... *Nicholson* .. 9
—— Garland .... *Dickinson* .. 11
—— Guidance .... *Rivingtons* .. 7
—— Life, Griffith .... *Hatchard* .. 10
—— Philosophy .... *Macmillan* .. 14
—— Sacrifices and Holy Com... *Macmillan* .. 18
—— Songs .... *Isbister* ... 16
—— Songs, Monsell .... *Longmans* ..
Spiritualism, Works on ...... *J. Burns.* .. a
—— Oriental .... *Trubner* ... 6
Spitta and Tersteegen, Imitns. from *King* 21
Spitzbergen, Yacht Voyage..... *Murray* 10
—— Wells. .... *King* 5
Spontaneous Combust., Notes on *Layton* 13
Sport and Adventures .... *Chapman* .. 5
—— at Home and Abroad .... *Hurst & B.* 9
—— Chase, Turf, and Road .. *Murray* 34
—— Hunting Grounds Old World *Routledge* .. 31
—— Moorland and Stream .... *Tinsley Bros.* 9
—— St. John's Wild .... *Murray* 30
—— Scenery and Adventure .. *King* 32
—— Over Turf and Stubble... *Bentley* 12
Sporting Advens. in Many Lands *Routledge* .. 71
—— Adventures in Prairies.... *Routledge* .. 72
—— Library, Druid .... *Warne* ..... a
—— Rifle .... *Smith & El.* 7
—— Sketches, Home and Abroad *Warne* 0
—— Works .... *Routledge* .. 72

Sporting Works, Colquhoun...... *W. Blackw'd* 7
—— Works, Illustrated........ *Bradbury* .. 3
Sports .... *Virtue* 16
—— British Rural .... *Warne* 9
—— for Boys and Girls...... *J. Blackwood* 23
—— Encyclopædia of Rural .. *Longmans* .. 41
—— (Wild) in the Far West .. *Routledge* .. 34
—— and Pastimes (British) .. *Isbister* ... 8
—— and Pastimes for Boys .. *Routledge* .. 18
Sportsman, Life of a .... *Routledge* .. 72
Sportsman's Complete Guide .. *Longmans* .. 43
—— (Young) Manual........ *Bell* 24
Sportsmen, Hints to .... *Chatto* 17
—— Knapsack Guide for .... *Bradbury* .. 11
Spring Comedies............ *Macmillan* .. 2
Spurgeon's "Saint and Saviour" *Isbister* ... 41
Stable Economy .... *W. Blackw'd* 30
—— Expenses Book .... *Letts* 2
Stage, English Annals of .... *Allen* 6
Staircasing and Handrailing .. *Hagger* 14
Stamp Albums.............. *Marlborough* 10
Standard English, Sources of .. *Macmillan* .. 19
—— Library, Modern ...... *Hurst & B.* 12
—— of Cross in Champ de Mars *Nisbet* 34
Standing Orders .... *Waterlow* .. a
Stanfield's Pictures .... *Virtue* 3
Stanford (C.) Works by...... *Hodder* 21
Stanhope (Dean) Epistles and Gos. *Soc. P. C. K.* 25
—— (Earl) Works by........ *Murray* 31
Stanley (Dean) Works by .... *Isbister* ... 41
—— Works .... *Macmillan* .. 34
—— Works .... *Murray* 28
Star Atlas, Proctor.......... *Longmans* .. 18
—— Chamber .... *J. R. Smith* 6
—— Library (The) .... *Nicholson* .. 3
—— of Hope Books .... *Warne* 32
—— out of Jacob (The)...... *Nisbet* 34
Stars: The Radcliffe Catalogue.. *Parker* 62
—— Half-hours with the .... *Hardwicke* .. 10
—— Occultations of, Penrose .. *Macmillan* .. 28
Starling (The), Macleod .... *Isbister* ... 30
Statesman's Year-Book...... *Macmillan* .. 23
Statesmen of the Day........ *King* 2
—— Three English .... *Macmillan* .. 33
Statics, Elementary .... *Bell* 15
Staton (J. T.) Works by .... *A. Heywood* 8
Statutes, Bigg's Edition of .. *Waterlow* .. a
Steam, Elementary Treatise on .. *Macmillan* .. 28
—— and its Uses .... *Lockwood* .. 13
—— Boilers, Wilson .... *Lockwood* .. 10
—— in the Engine .... *Blackie* ... 10
—— Engine (The) .... *Ward&Lock* 26
—— Engine, Bourne .... *Longmans* .. 31
—— Engine, Catechism of .. *Longmans* .. 31
—— Engine, Goodeve........ *Longmans* .. 21
—— Engine, Model .... *Houlston* .. 24
—— Engine, Tredgold ...... *Virtue* 21
—— Engine and Boilers .... *Spon* 37
—— Engine and Steam ...... *J. Heywood* 38
—— Engine (High-Pres.) Inv. of *Spon* 43
—— Engine (High-Pressure) .. *Lockwood* .. 10
—— Engine, Land, Mar. & Loc. *Collins* 8
Steel, Manufacture of .... *Trubner* ... 32
Steinmetz's, German Ed. Books .. *Nutt* 20
Stella and other Poems........ *W. Blackw'd* 30
Stems and Twigs............ *Dickinson* .. 11
Stephen (J. Fitzjames) Works by *Smith & El.* 21
Stephenson (G. and R.) Lives.. *Murray* 27
Stepping Heavenward .... *Nisbet* 34
—— Heavenward .... *Nelson* 16
Steps to the Altar .... *Masters* ... 26
Sterne's (Laurence) Works .... *Sotheran* .. 12
—— Works .... *Nimmo* 7
—— Works .... *Routledge* .. 43
Stethoscope, Cotton on the .... *Churchill* .. 14
Stevenson (Rev. John) Works by *Bagster* ... 77
Stevens, Methodism .... *Wesleyan* .. 34
Steward (George) Memoir of .. *Nisbet* 34
Stewardship of Life .... *Hodder* 17
Stewart (Balfour) Works by.... *Macmillan* .. 34
Stier (Dr.) Works by........ *Clark* 0
Stilling (Heinrich) Life of .. *Houlston* .. 43
Stock Exchange .... *Ward&Lock* 7
—— Exchange Arbitrageur.... *Wilson* 42
Stockmar's (Baron) Memoir .... *Longmans* .. 9

Stockton and Neighbourhood....	*Marlborough*	16
Stoics, Epicureans, and Sceptics	*Longmans*	5
Stokes (Wm.) Works	*Houlston*	45
Stollberg (Anna, Countess of) ...	*Isbister*	41
Stomach, Diseases of............	*Churchill*	10
—— Diseases of, Fox.............	*Macmillan*	11
—— Diseases of, Habershon ...	*Hardwicke*	15
—— (Morbid State of the)	*Churchill*	10
Stone in the Bladder............	*Churchill*	14
—— Witnesses.................	*Morgan*	5
Stones of the Temple...........	*Rivingtons*	10
Stonehenge, Turusachan, &c. ...	*Stanford*	66
Stoppage in Transitu...........	*Stevens*	13
Storehouse of Stories...........	*Macmillan*	34
Stories About, Barker	*Macmillan*	2
—— about Boys	*Nimmo*	15
—— for all Readers	*J. Blackwood*	21
—— for Children...............	*Bell*	25
—— for Children, Candy	*Mosley*	2
—— for Darlings..............	*Murray*	30
—— for My Children...........	*Macmillan*	19
—— for Reading to Children ...	*Mosley*	10
—— Books for the Young.......	*Nelson*	17
—— for Summer Days, &c......	*Groombridge*	26
—— from Famous Ballads......	*Warne*	29
—— from over the Sea	*Nimmo*	15
—— of Eng., Ireland & Scotland	*Jarrold*	7
—— of the Kings.............	*Warne*	23
—— of Old	*Warne*	25
—— of Old	*Warne*	29
—— of the Olden Time.........	*Cassell*	11
—— of the Prophets	*Warne*	28
—— of Success...............	*Soc. P. C. K.*	25
—— of the Wars	*Ward&Lock*	8
—— of Youth and Childhood ...	*Mosley*	12
—— in Precious Stones.........	*King*	18
—— Told to a Child	*Isbister*	22
—— Told to a Child	*King*	17
—— with a Purpose	*Nelson*	18
—— and Mis. Read. Evg. Schools	*Mosley*	12
Storm Warriors	*Macmillan*	12
Storms, Handbook of..........	*Philip*	37
—— in Indian Ocean, Thom. ...	*Smith & El.*	25
—— Law of, Dove............	*Longmans*	20
—— Sailors' Horn Book, Law of	*Williams*	11
Story of Burnt Njal...........	*Edmonston*	6
—— of Our Doll..............	*Nelson*	20
—— of Earth and Man	*Hodder*	22
—— of Elizabeth.............	*Smith & El.*	23
—— of Harecourt (The)........	*Isbister*	30
—— of a Honeymoon..........	*Chatto*	31
—— of his Love..............	*Bentley*	13
—— of Little Alfred	*Partridge*	11
—— of Miss Dollikins	*Nelson*	20
—— of My Mission in S. Africa.	*Wesleyan*	49
—— of a Needle..............	*Nelson*	9
—— of Pauline	*Macmillan*	7
—— of a Pin.................	*Nelson*	17
Stothard's (Thos.) Life	*Murray*	30
Stoughton (Dr. J.) Works by ...	*Rel. Tr. Soc.*	18
—— Eccles. Hist. England	*Hodder*	17
Stow (David) Life	*Nisbet*	34
Stowe (H. B.) Agnes of Sorrento	*Smith & El.*	22
—— (Mrs.) Works by	*Bell*	26
Stowell (Canon) Model, &c....	*Hatchard*	26
Strafford Thos. (Earl) Life	*Tinsley Bros.*	2
Straightforward	*Mosley*	12
Strains on Girders, Young	*Macmillan*	43
—— in Girders, Humber.......	*Lockwood*	1
—— in Trusses	*Longmans*	32
Straits of Magellan, Masters ...	*Murray*	33
Strange (Sir R.) Masterpieces ..	*Bentley*	13
—— Adventures of a Phaeton ..	*Macmillan*	3
—— Dwellings...............	*Longmans*	23
—— Footsteps...............	*Bemrose*	5
—— Tales, Ashworth	*Tubbs*	2
Stranger Here (A)	*Nisbet*	7
—— of Screplus	*Macmillan*	4
Strangers and Pilgrims	*Ward&Lock*	16
Strasbourg, Siege of	*Smith & El.*	14
Strauss and Renan	*Trubner*	32
Strawberry, its Culture	*Groombridge.*	8
Stray Leaves, Mudie	*Macmillan*	26
Streams from Hidden Sources....	*King*	32
—— from Lebanon	*Nisbet*	32
Stream (The) of Time	*C. Smith*	10
Streets and Lanes of a City	*Macmillan*	34
Street Preaching.............	*Wesleyan*	30
—— Literature	*Sotheran*	9
Strength of Iron (Cast)........	*Lockwood*	7
—— of Iron and Timber	*Spon*	41
—— of Materials, Anderson	*Longmans*	21
—— of Materials.............	*Lockwood*	3
Stretton (Rev. H.) Works by ...	*Masters*	27
—— (Hesba) Works by	*King*	16
Strickland's Queens of England.	*Bell*	25
—— Queens of England	*Bohn's Lib.*	10
—— Lives of Queens of Scotland	*W. Blackie'd*	30
Struggles of a Neutral Volunteer.	*Chapman*	16
Strype's Works..............	*Clar. Press.*	12
Stuarts, Reign of the, Jesse	*Bohn's Lib.*	10
Stuart, Last Four Princesses ...	*Bell*	38
Students, Counsels for Young...	*Macmillan*	39
Student's Guide to Measuring...	*Lockwood*	8
—— Historical Manuals	*Murray*	30
Studies from the Antique	*Isbister*	29
—— in Animal Life	*Smith & El.*	11
—— in English	*Trubner*	26
—— in Divine Things	*Houlston*	30
—— in English Prose.........	*Lockwood*	41
—— of Man	*Trubner*	27
—— and Romances...........	*King*	33
—— for Sunday Evenings......	*Edmonston*	53
—— for Stories..............	*Isbister*	22
Study of Nature	*Nelson*	20
—— (The) Preacher's Serial ...	*Dickinson*	12
Style, &c., De Quincey	*Black*	31
Subterranean World (The)	*Longmans*	23
Substitution of Similars	*Macmillan*	17
Suburban Life, Scenes of	*Masters*	20
Success in Life.............	*Nelson*	17
Successful Student...........	*Wesleyan*	50
Suckling (Rev. R. A.) Works by.	*Masters*	27
Suez Canal, Badger	*Smith & El.*	1
—— Canal, Map of	*Johnston*	34
Suffering Saviour (The)	*Clark*	19
Sugar-Growing and Manufacture.	*Spon*	41
Sulphuric Acid..............	*Spon*	42
Summer Cruising in South Seas.	*Chatto*	34
—— Drinks	*Routledge*	8
—— Scenes, Birket Foster	*Bell*	9
Sumner (Archbishop) Works by..	*Hatchard*	27
Sun (The)	*Bentley*	7
—— (The) Procter	*Longmans*	18
—— Under the, by Sala	*Tinsley Bros.*	7
Sunbeam Stories............	*Lockwood*	47
—— Susette	*S. S. Union.*	6
Sunbeam's (A) Influence	*Nisbet*	19
Sunbeams for all Seasons	*Houlston*	29
Sunday: Its Origin, History, &c.	*Murray*	14
—— Afternoon, 52 Sermons ...	*Hodder*	18
—— Afternoon, Pictures & Poems	*Bagster*	61
—— Album	*Routledge*	31
—— Book	*Virtue*	5
—— Book (Pictorial), Kitto ...	*Sangster*	6
—— Book of Poetry	*Macmillan*	14
—— Evening Book	*Isbister*	42
—— Evenings at Brockleigh Hall	*Hatchard*	27
—— Half-Hours	*Sangster*	7
—— Lessons (Aunt Charlotte's)..	*M. Ward*	3
—— Library	*Macmillan*	34
—— Picture Books...........	*Soc. P. C. K.*	20
—— Picture Puzzles	*Shaw*	2
—— Readings...............	*Warne*	29
—— Readings (Family Use)....	*Hatchard*	20
—— Readings for Farm Boys...	*Nisbet*	34
—— Reading for the Home Circle	*Nelson*	12
—— Readings (Pictorial)	*Sangster*	5
—— School Reward Books	*Mosley*	2
—— School Reward Bks. & Cards	*Soc. P. C. K.*	37
—— School Reward Books	*Gall*	18
—— School Reward Books	*Nimmo*	18
—— School Reward Tickets ...	*Walker*	6
—— School Rewd. Tickets & Cards	*Gall*	9
—— Scholar's Spelling Books ..	*Wesleyan*	34
—— Schools	*Nelson*	5
—— School, by Davids	*S. S. Union.*	45
—— School History and Progress	*Nisbet*	29
—— School Addresses	*Wesleyan*	38
—— School Art of Teaching ...	*S. S. Union.*	44

Sunday School Books........ *Wesleyan* .. 5
—— School Class Papers ...... *Wesleyan* .. 36
—— School Lessons, Collects, &c. *Nisbet* ... 15
—— Scholar's Daily Text Book ...*S. S. Union* ... 2
—— School Dialogues .... *Walker* 15
—— School Exercises .... *S. S. Union* .. 4
—— School Handbook .... *S. S. Union* .. 2
—— School Hymn Books .... *Gall* 2
—— School Hymn Book ...... *Haldon* 6
—— School Hymn and Tune Books *Tubbs* 2
—— School Hymns .... *Hodder* 51
—— School Hymns .... *J. Heywood* .. 2
—— School Hymns .... *Jarrold* 2
—— School Illustrations ...... *Partridge* .. 2
— S. School Management .... *S. S. Union* .. 4
—— School Notes and Lessons .. *Gall* 35
—— School Reciter .... *Routledge* .. 63
—— School Registers ...... *S. S. Union* .. 2
—— School Roll Book ...... *Wesleyan* .. 38
—— School Speaker and Reciter *Nicholson* .. 4
—— School Teachers, Counsels to *S. S. Union* .. 4
—— School Teachers, Manual for *J. Heywood* .. 25
—— School Teachers, Memoirs of *Snow* 12
—— School Teachers, Lessons .. *Laurie* 3
—— School Teaching : Object, &c. *Nisbet* 33
—— School World .... *Stock* 0
—— Service of the Methodists .. *Wesleyan* .. 2
—— Services, Companion to .... *Masters* .. 2
—— Stories .... *Routledge* .. 36
—— Teaching, Monthly Paper of *Mosley* 1
—— Thoughts, Geldart ...... *Tubbs* 4
Sundays Abroad .... *Isbister* .. 14
—— at Encombe .... *Warne* 12
Sun-Dials, Book of .... *Bell* 10
Sunny Sabbaths .... *Hogger* 4
Sunsets on Hebrew Mountains .. *Nisbet* 2
Sunshine and Showers .... *Keeve* 2
—— in Sickness .... *Mosley* 2
—— in the Workhouse ...... *Nisbet* 33
Sun-spots, Observation of .... *Williams* .. 2
Supernatural in Relation, &c. .. *Macmillan* .. 3
—— Religion .... *Longmans* .. 34
Superstition, Warnings against .. *Macmillan* .. 1
Surgeon's Vade-Mecum ...... *Churchill* .. 15
Surgery, Works on .... *Churchill* .. 0
—— System of, Gross ...... *Smith & El.* .. 9
—— System of, Holmes ...... *Longmans* .. 2
—— A System of, Miller .... *Black* 15
—— Lectures on, Spence .... *Black* 31
—— Science and Art, Erichson *Longmans* .. 1
Surgical Pathology, Paget .... *Longmans* .. 1
Surnames .... *Chatto* 21
Surnames .... *J. R. Smith* .. 9
Sursum Corda .... *Masters* .. 20
Surtees (R.) Sporting Works by *Bradbury* .. 0
Surveying .... *W. Blackw'd* 4
—— Land and Marine ...... *Lockwood* .. 2
—— Land and Marine ...... *Spon* 4
—— and Levelling .... *W. Blackw'd* 12
—— Marine .... *Black* 31
—— Military .... *Trubner* .. 34
—— Military .... *Allen* 10
—— Nautical .... *Longmans* .. 20
—— Practical .... *Murray* 2
—— Trigonometrical ...... *Lockwood* .. 4
Sussex (Works on) .... *J. R. Smith* 30
Suzy's Flowers .... *Nelson* .. 18
Swainson (Dean) Works by .. *Macmillan* .. 35
Sweden and Finland, Travels in .. *Macmillan* .. 27
Sweet Violet .... *Hatchard* .. 32
Swift's Works .... *Bell* 34
—— Works, Carefully Selected *Nimmo* .. 1
Swim, How to .... *Bradbury* .. 11
Swimming, Manual of ...... *Lockwood* .. 4°
Swinburne (A. C.) Works .... *Chatto* .. 35
Swiss Family Robinson ...... *Nelson* .. 2
—— Family Robinson ...... *Warne* .. 20
—— Family Robinson ...... *Warne* .. 31
—— Round (Regular) ...... *Isbister* .. 23
Switzerland, Illustrated ...... *Virtue* .. 13
—— Month in .... *Smith & El.* 27
—— Mountains and Lakes of *Bell* 2
—— Scientific Guide to ...... *Smith & El.* 15
Swizzers (The), Dixon ...... *Hurst & B.* 5
Sword and Keys, Joyce........ *Kevington* .. 12

Sybil's Book, Barker........ *Macmillan* .. 3
Sydney (Algernon) Life & Times *Tinsley Bros.* 4
—— (E. S. B.) Works by .... *Masters* ..27
—— Stuart .... *Warne* .. 27
Sydonie's Dowry............ *Bell* 24
Sylvan Holt's Daughter .... *Smith & El.* 13
Sylvester Sound .... *Warne* .. 46
Sylvia & Janet .... *Warne* .. 25
Symbols of Christ .... *Hodder* .. 22
Symbolism, Essays on, Barlow .. *Williams* .. 2
—— Haig .... *W. Blackw'd* 2
—— A Lecture on .... *Masters* .. 3
Sympathy of Christ with Man .. *Nisbet* .. 38
Synchronistical Annals ...... *Parker* .. 8
Synonyms and Antonyms...... *Bell* 63
—— Dictionary of .... *Collins* .. 5
—— Dictionary of .... *Whittaker* .. 11
—— Dictionary of .... *Stanford* .. 67
—— of the Old Testament .... *Longmans* .. 34
—— Whately .... *Longmans* .. 11
Synopsis Evangelica .... *Nutt* 7
Synoptical Lectures on Holy Scrip *Nisbet* .. 13
Syntax's Three Tours ...... *Chatto* .. 30
Syphilis & Local Contagious Dis. *Smith & El.* 10
—— Works on .... *Churchill* .. 0
Syria, Medical Hints for Travellers *Churchill* .. 37
—— and Palestine .... *W. Blackw'd* 32
—— Unexplored .... *Tinsley Bros.* 2
Syriac Apocryphal Literature .. *Williams* .. 10
—— Chrestomathy and Lexicon.. *Williams* .. 3
—— Documents, Cureton .... *Williams* .. 5
—— Grammar, Cowper ...... *Williams* .. 5
—— Grammar, Phillips...... *Bell* 27
—— Orthography .... *Williams* .. 9
—— Reading Lessons ...... *Bagster* .. 42
Syrian Deserts, Rambles in...... *Murray* .. 26

Tabernacle, Holy Vessels of. .... *Yapp* 1
—— and the Priesthood........ *Morgan* .. 2
Table for Arches.......... *Spon* 2
—— (Arithmetical) Books .... *Mosley* .. 15
—— Book, The Universal .... *Cornish* .. 4
—— of Products, by Factors 1 to 9 *Layton* .. 12
—— of Quarter-squares...... *Layton* .. 12
—— of Reciprocals of Numbers .. *Layton* .. 13
—— Talk, Book of.......... *Routledge* .. 43
—— Talk, Coleridge ...... *Murray* .. 8
—— Talk, Hazlitt .... *Bohn's Lib.* .. 8
—— Talk, L. Hunt........ *Smith & El.* 11
—— Talk, Luther .... *Bohn's Lib.* .. 8
—— Traits, Doran .... *Bentley* .. 6
Tables for Actuaries ...... *Layton* .. 15
—— of Annuities .... *Layton* .. 6
—— for Bricklayers .... *Spon* 5
—— of Curves, Beazeley .... *Lockwood* .. 5
—— of Decimal System...... *Layton* .. 10.
—— of Discount, Evans .... *Mosley* .. 3
—— for Earthwork Cuttings .. *Spon* 10
—— for the Use of Engineers .. *Stanford* .. 50
—— of Eng. Prices for Fr. Goods *Houlston* .. 2
—— (Exchange) India ...... *Smith & El* .. 19
—— of Interest .... *Letts* 2
—— for Land Valuers ...... *Lockwood* .. 16
—— of Latitude and Declination *Isbister* .. 39
—— of Life Assurance ...... *Layton* .. 3
—— for Lifeholds, Leaseholds, &c. *Longmans* .. 45
—— Linen Yarn Trade ...... *Wilson* .. 8
—— Loans and Debentures .... *Layton* .. 13
—— of Logarithms .... *Spon* 42
—— Lunar and Horary ...... *Allen* 2
—— for Marine Engineers .... *Lockwood* .. 4
—— Mechanical .... *Whittaker* .. 15
—— of Metric System ...... *Lockwood* .. 11
—— Multiplication and Division *Wilson* .. 10
—— for Packing-Case Makers .. *Lockwood* .. 9
—— for Planting Underwood, &c. *Lockwood* .. 9
—— for Platelayers .... *Spon* 32
—— for Purchasing Estates .... *Lockwood* .. 11
—— for Screw-Cutting ...... *Spon* 35
—— for Seamen's Wages .... *Wilson* .. 8
—— Share and Stock........ *Wilson* .. 4
—— of Simple Interest ...... *Wilson* .. 2
—— of Squares and Cubes .... *Spon* 42
—— for Tea and Silks ...... *Smith & El.* 4
—— for Telegraph Operators .... *Spon* 16

Tables, for Timber Merchants .. *Lockwood* .. 9
—— Time and Money .... *Wilson* 8
—— for Travellers .... *W. Blackw'd* 3
—— Traverse .... *W. Blackw'd* 28
—— Universal .... *Wilson* 12
—— Weight of Iron, &c. ...... *Hagger* 15
—— for Weight of Iron .... *Spon* 48
—— for Workmen's Wages ...... *Spon* 45
Tacitus, Frost .... *Whittaker* .. 2
—— Translated by Church .. *Macmillan* .. 35
—— Orelli .... *Nutt* 10
..aine (H.) Notes on England .. *Isbister* .. 42
—— Selections, Van Laun .... *Rivingtons* .. 18
—— Works by.............. *Williams* .. 14
Take Care whom you Trust..... *Smith & El.* 17
—— my Advice .... *J. Blackwood* 25
Tale for a Chimney Corner .... *Chatto* ...21
—— (A) of Two Old Songs.... *Nisbet* .. 9
Tales of Adventure on the Sea .. *Nisbet* .. 4
—— of Adventure by Flood, &c. *Nisbet* .. 4
—— and Allegories.......... *Masters* ... 0
—— and Allegories, &c. ...... *Parker* .. 43
—— and Allegories, "Penny Post" *Parker* .. 44
—— Ballantyne .... *Nisbet* .. 4
—— for Boys and Girls........ *Warne* ... 27
—— from the Fjeld .... *Chapman* .. 4
—— of a Grandfather........ *Black* .. 28
—— of the Great and Brave.... *Hatchard* .. 30
—— of Many Lands .... *Isbister* .. 44
—— for me to Read to Myself .. *Masters* ... 27
—— Old and New .... *Bell* ... 25
—— of Old Travel, Kingsley .. *Macmillan* .. 19
—— and Stories .... *Chambers* .. 38
—— and Stories .... *Warne* ... 29
—— and Stories, Mitford .... *Warne* ... 25
—— for Travellers .... *Chambers* .. 38
—— Various Authors........ *Burns* .. 35
—— of Wonder .... *Burns* .. 34
—— for the Young .... *Warne* ... 29
—— for Young Men and Women *Burns* .. 31
—— for Young Men and Women *Parker* .. 44
Talking to the Children ...... *Hodder* ... 27
Talmage (Dr.) Works ...... *Dickenson* .. 13
—— (Dr.) Works .... *Hodder* ... 19
Talmud, Deutsch .... *Murray* .. 10
Tamil Language .... *Allen* .. 33
Tangled Talk .... *Isbister* .. 42
Tanglewood Tales .... *Routledge* .. 36
Tappy's Chicks .... *Isbister* .. 11
Tara, Taylor (M.) ...... *W. Blackw'd.* 31
Tariff and Customs' Duties .. *Wilson* .. 9
Tartary (High) Visit to........ *Murray* .. 27
Tasmania, Flora of.......... *Reeve* .. 6
—— and Victoria, 13 Years in.. *Houlston* .. 9
Tasmanian Lily (The) ...... *King.* .. 18
Tasso's Jerusalem.......... *Bohn's Lib.*.. 15
—— Delivered.............. *Routledge* .. 61
Tauchnitz Classics.......... *Nutt*...... 94
Tautphœus (Baroness) Novels.. *Bentley* .. 16
Taxation, History, Tayler .... *Stanford* ... 70
—— Local, Goschen .... *Macmillan* .. 14
—— Local, Palgrave .... *Murray* .. 24
—— Past, Present, and Future .. *Williams*.... 12
Tayler (Rev. C. B.) Works .... *Rel. Tr. Soc.* 18
—— (Rev. J. James) Letters, Life *Williams* .. 15
Taylor (Bayard) Works by .... *Isbister* .. 43
—— Family (Ongar) Wks. of .. *Houlston* .. 27
—— (Sir H.) Poems .... *Smith & El.* 22
—— (Isaac) Works .... *Bell* ... 61
—— (Isaac) Works........ *Macmillan* .. 35
—— (Jeremy) Holy Living, &c... *Rivingtons* .. 7
—— Holy Living and Dying .. *Bohn's Lib.*.. 9
—— Works by.............. *Pickering* .. 7
Tea Exchange Tables ...... *Smith & El.* 4
Teacher and His Books, by Groser *S. S. Union* 44
—— Taught (The) .... *Nisbet* .. 7
Teacher's Cabinet (The) ...... *S. S. Union* 46
—— Companion, by Collins .. *S. S. Union* 44
—— List (The) .... *Stanford* .. 58
Teachers, Topics for]......... *Stock* 2
Teaching, Practical Hints on .. *Bell* 37
—— Principles .... *S. S. Union* 44
Technical Analysis, Bolley .. *Bohn's Lib.* .. 18
—— Arithmetic .... *Longmans* .. 21
—— Dictionary, Fr. and English *Spon* 21

Technical Education, Russell .. *Bradbury* .. 12
—— Educator .... *Cassell* 7
—— Manuals .... *Cassell* 15
—— Series of School Readings .. *Jarrold* .. 31
—— Vocabularies in 8 Languages *Stanford* .. 55
—— Works .... *A. Heywood* .. 15
Technological Dict., 3 Languages *Nutt*...... 20
—— Dictionary .... *Trubner* .. 28
—— Military Dic., Fr. Ger. Eng. *Williams* .. 5
Technology, Chemical ...... *Churchill* .. 37
Teeth, Pathology of .... *Trubner* .. 31
—— Surgical Diseases of .... *Longmans* .. 27
—— Works on the .... *Churchill* .. 0
Teheran across Turkoman Desert *Murray* .. 32
Telegraph Cable .... *Spon* 42
Telegraph, The Progress of the .. *Macmillan.* 41
Telegraphic Code .... *Wilson* 6
Telescope, Half-hours with the .. *Hardwicke.* 10
Tell Mamma .... *Routledge* .. 34
—— Jesus, Shipton .... *Morgan* 4
Teloogoo Language .... *Allen* 33
Temperance, The Four Pillars of *Partridge* .. 9
—— Library .... *Milner* .. 6
—— Manual .... *Partridge* .. 9
—— Physiology of .... *Bohn's Lib.* .. 19
—— Prize Tales .... *Nelson* .. 13
—— Publications .... *A. Heywood* .. 13
—— Publications .... *Tubbs* ... 8
—— Publications .... *Walker* .. 6
—— Tale, Westons of Riversdale *J. Heywood* 44
—— Tales .... *Marr* 8
—— Tracts .... *Jarrold* ... 19
—— Speaker and Reciter .... *Nicholson* .. 2
Temple Anecdotes .... *Groombridge.* 25
—— Church, Half Hours in.. *Isbister* .. 45
—— (Dr.) Sermons .... *Macmillan.* 35
Temptations, The Two Great .. *Macmillan* 39
Ten Commandments, Dale .. *Hodder* .. 4
Ten Virgins, Parable of the.... *Nisbet* 14
Tennyson (Alfred) Works by .. *King.*...... 19
—— Doré, Series of Illustrated .. *Ward&Lock* 31
—— Latin Selections from .... *Macmillan.* .. 7
—— May Queen .... *Warne.* ... 2
—— A Study of the Works of ... *Chapman* .. 25
Terence, Parry .... *Whittaker.* .. 2
Teresina Perigrina .... *Bentley* .. 14
Testament, Alford .... *Isbister* 3
—— Tyndale's, 1526 .... *Bagster* .. 76
—— with Wesley's Notes .. *Nicholson* .. 5
—— Authority of New ...... *Macmillan* .. 35
—— On Authorized Version .. *Macmillan* .. 37
—— for Children .... *Parker* .. 36
—— Chronology of .... *Parker* .. 8
—— Concordance .... *Houlston* .. 35
—— Critical .... *Isbister* .. 11
—— Criticism of, Scrivener .... *Bell* .. 44
—— Divine Authority of .... *Bell* .. 62
—— Ecclesiastical Polity of...... *Isbister* .. 23
—— for English Readers, Alford *Rivingtons* .. 1
—— English and Greek Lexion .. *Kellaway* .. 1
—— On a Fresh Revision...... *Macmillan.* .. 20
—— Historic Evidence of...... *Bagster* .. 43
—— How to Study .... *Isbister* .. 4
—— Illustrated .... *Longmans* .. 28
—— Illustrated .... *Murray* .. 7
—— Improvements, &c....... *Bell* .. 45
—— Introduction to New, Bleek *Clark* 22
—— Large Print............ *Bagster* .. 47
—— Origin and History .... *Hodder* .. 25
—— Plea for Authorized Version *Hatchard* .. 14
—— Progress of Doctrine in .... *Macmillan* .. 3
—— Study of, Davidson ...... *Longmans* .. 35
—— Synonymes, Trench ...... *Macmillan* .. 37
—— The New .... *Pickering* .. 37
—— New, Textual Crit........ *Clar. Press.* 30
—— New, View of the Old,..... *Hodder* 16
—— New, Words altered .... *Clark* 36
—— Commentary .... *Hodder* .. 6
—— Commentary, Dalton .. *Nisbet* .. 45
—— Commentary on New, Meyer *Clark* .. 33
—— Commentaries .... *Soc. P. C. K.* 7
—— Greek, Alford .... *Rivingtons* .. 1
—— Greek, Griesbach ...... *Bell* 45
—— Greek, Macmichael ...... *Whittaker* .. 5
—— Greek, Scrivener .... *Bell* 43

Testament, Greek, Valpy........ *Whittaker* .. 6
—— Greek, Wordsworth ...... *Rivingtons* .. 2
—— Greek Companion to ...... *Bell* 45
—— Greek, Grammar of ...... *Trubner* 6
—— Greek, Grammar of New .. *Clark* 12
—— Greek-English Lexicon to.. *Bell* 45
—— Greek, Syntax of .... *Rivingtons* .. 4
—— Greek-English .... *Cambridge* .. 5
—— Greek-English .... *Clar. Press.* . 8
—— Greek and Eng. Concordance *Kelloway* .. 11
—— Polyglot .... *Bagster* 7
Testamenta XII. Patriarcharum *Bell* 43
Testaments .... *Rel. Tr. Soc.* 20
—— Greek and Latin .... *Nutt* 6
—— Polyglot .... *Bagster* 47
Teubner's Grk. and Latin Classics *Nutt* 17
—— School Classics .... *Nutt* 39
Teutonic Lands, Tales of ...... *Longmans* .. 39
—— Languages, Comparative .. *Macmillan* .. 15
—— Name-System .... *Williams* .. 6
Text Books .... *Bagster* 58
—— Books .... *Mack* 1
—— Books .... *Routledge* .. 66
—— Books .... *Warne* 38
—— Books, Bijou .... *Warne* 35
—— Books (Daily) .... *Milner* 10
—— Books, New Series ...... *Nelson* 21
—— Books, Sacred Trichords .. *Hatchard* .. 25
—— Books and Scripture Prints.. *S. S. Union* 13
Texts, Illuminated .... *Rel. Tr. Soc* 34
—— on Rollers .... *Rel. Tr. Soc.* 35
—— Scripture .... *Morgan* .. 20
—— Scripture, Finding of .... *Hodder* .. 11
—— Scripture, for Walls .... *Yapp* 8
—— Simple, for Infant Children . *Nisbet* 13
—— Tales upon .... *Routledge* .. 31
—— and Thoughts, &c........ *Longmans* .. 35
—— Wall .... *Jarrold* 12
Textile Fabrics, Rock ...... *Chapman* .. 24
Textual Criticism, New Test. .. *Clar. Press.* 23
Thackerayana .... *Chatto* 37
Thackeray's (Miss) Works .... *Smith & El.* 23
—— (W. M.) Works .... *Smith & El.* 23
Thames, Book of the .... *Isbister* .. 19
—— (From the) to the Humber .. *Chapman* .. 26
—— Valley of, Geology ...... *Clar. Press.* 18
That's It .... *Houlston* .. 47
Theatre-Français, Moderne...... *Trubner* .. 28
Theatrical Anecdotes .... *Routledge* .. 3
Their Majestie's Servants...... *Allen* 25
Theism, Doctrinal and Practical.. *Trubner* .. 21
—— Tulloch .... *W. Blackw'd* 41
Them Also, Story Dublin Mission *Nisbet* 34
Theocritus, Trans. Eng. Verse .. *Bell* 35
Theologia Germanica .... *Macmillan* .. 14
Theological Essays, Maurice .. *Macmillan* .. 24
—— (Foreign) Library ...... *Clark* 2
—— and Literary Essays ...... *Isbister* .. 22
—— Student's Bible .... *Freud* .. a
—— Translation Fund ...... *Williams* .. 15
—— Works .... *Dickinson* .. 0
—— Works .... *Masters* .. 0
—— Works .... *Parker* .. 3
Theology .... *Nelson* .. 3
—— Blunt's Dictionary of .... *Rivingtons* .. 11
—— Pirie .... *W. Blackw'd* 41
—— Tulloch .... *W. Blackw'd* 41
—— Works on .... *Bell* 43
—— Catechism of .... *Masters* ..
—— Christian, Payne .... *Snow* .. 12
—— of Church of England .... *Longmans* .. 33
—— of the Church of Rome.... *Mosley* .. 6
—— Dogmatic .... *Masters* .. 20
—— in the English Poets .... *King* .. 10
—— Hand-Book of .... *Hall* 4
—— Homiletical and Pastoral... *Isbister* .. 7
—— Historical .... *Clark* .. 15
—— Household .... *Rivingtons* .. 18
—— Lectures on, Randolph.... *Rivingtons* .. 11
—— and Life .... *Isbister* .. 35
—— of New Testament...... *Hodder* .. 2
—— Outlines of .... *Isbister* .. 46
—— Practical .... *Clark* .. 19
—— Protestant .... *Clark* .. 31
—— in Science............ *Jarrold* 5

Theology. Science of .... *Nisbet* 15
—— System of, Dwight........ *Houlston* .. 34
—— Systematic .... *Clark* .. 12
—— Thoughts in .... *Hodder* .. 21
—— Lectures on the Study of.... *Parker* .. 4
Theophrastus .... *Macmillan* .. 35
Therapeutics, Garrod ...... *Longmans* .. 27
—— Rogers .... *Churchill* .. 31
Theresa's Journal .... *Nisbet* 34
Thesaurus of English Words .. *Longmans* .. 11
Thessalonica, or the Model Church *Kelloway* .. 9
Thibet, Large Game Shooting in *Harrison* .. 3
—— by Prinseps .... *Allen* 23
Thiers' History of the Consulate.. *Sotheran* .. 27
Things Above, Trench ...... *Nisbet* .. 35
—— in the Forest .... *Nelson* .. 17
—— New and Old .... *Dickinson* .. 11
—— Not Generally Known .... *Lockwood* .. 46
Thinking for Oneself .... *Masters* .. 27
Thirty-nine Articles .... *Parker* .. 5
—— Articles .... *Rivingtons* .. 16
—— Articles, Boultbee ...... *Longmans* .. 33
—— Articles, Browne ...... *Longmans* .. 34
—— Articles, Hardwick .... *Bell* .. 48
—— Articles, Jelf .... *Rivingtons* .. 5
—— Articles, Welchman .... *Bell* .. 48
—— Articles, Welchman .... *Soc. P. C. K.* 29
Thirty Years' War, Gardiner .. *Longmans* .. 6
—— Years' War, Motley ...... *Murray* .. 23
This Present World, Arnot .... *Nisbet* .. 3
Thomas (John) Memoir...... *Macmillan* .. 35
Thomas's (Dr.) Works ...... *Dickinson* .. 14
Thompson (Rev. H.) Works by .. *Masters* .. 27
Thomson's Seasons, Illust. .... *Nisbet* .. 35
Thornbury (W.) Criss-Cross Jnys. *Hurst & B.* 2
Thorndale, Smith .... *W. Blackw'd* 28
Thornton (Hatchard) Works by *Hatchard* .. 27
—— (W. T.) Works by ...... *Macmillan* .. 36
Thorold (Rev. A. W.) Works of.. *Isbister* .. 43
Thorough Business Man ...... *Isbister* .. 18
Thorvaldsen, Life and Work .. *Bentley* .. 14
Thought, Elements of ...... *Bell* .. 41
—— Laws of, Boole .... *Macmillan* .. 4
—— Laws of .... *Longmans* .. 11
—— Laws of Discursive .... *Macmillan* .. 23
Thoughts for the Age........ *Longmans* .. 36
—— for the Day .... *Nisbet* .. 35
—— for the Devout .... *Snow* .. 8
—— Golden .... *Macmillan* .. 14
—— (Passing) in Religion .... *Longmans* .. 36
—— in Solitude .... *Masters* .. 27
—— for the Times .... *King* .. 29
—— Wise and Otherwise .... *Chatto* .. 29
—— for Young Thinkers .... *Partridge* .. 11
Three Crosses of Calvary .... *Snow* .. 10
—— English Statesmen ...... *Macmillan* .. 33
—— Great Teachers of Our Time *Smith & El.* 12
—— Homes .... *Cassell* .. 7
—— Kingdoms, Book for Young . *Snow* .. 15
—— Kingdoms of Nature...... *Cassell* .. 15
—— Little Spades (The) ...... *Nisbet* .. 35
—— Marys (The), Stuart .... *Nisbet* .. 34
—— Paths in Life .... *Nisbet* .. 4
Threefold Cord (The)........ *Macmillan* .. 29
Threescore Years and Ten .... *Masters* .. 29
Thring (Edward) Works ...... *Macmillan* .. 36
Throat Hospital Pharmacopœia . *Churchill* .. 25
—— and Larynx, Affections of . *Hardwicke* .. 16
—— (Sore), James .... *Churchill* .. 22
Throne of Grace (The) ...... *Isbister* .. 43
Through the Looking Glass.... *Macmillan* .. 6
—— the Mist .... *Virtue* .. 6
Thrupp (Rev. J.) Works ...... *Macmillan* .. 36
Thucydides, Books 6 and 7, Frost *Macmillan* .. 36
—— Peloponnesian War, English *Longmans* .. 4
Thugs, &c. of India .... *Allen* .. 27
Thunder Storm (The), Tomlinson *Soc. P. C. K.* 27
Tiarks's German Ed. Works .... *Nutt* .. 20
Tibet, Tartary, and Mongolia.. *Allen* .. 27
Tides and Currents.......... *Cassell* .. 13
Tiger Prince (The) .... *Isbister* .. 11
Tilly Trickett .... *Warne* .. 30
Tim Bobbin .... *J. Heywood* .. 44
Tim's Troubles .... *Nelson* .. 13
Timbs's Anecdotical Works .... *Bentley* .. 15

Timbs's (Jno.) Popular Works .. *Lockwood* .. 44
—— Wonderful Inventions ...... *Routledge* .. 31
Timber Merchant's Com.,Dowsing *Lockwood* .. 9
—— Merchant's Freight Book .. *Lockwood* .. 9
—— Merchant's Guide .... *Lockwood* .. 9
—— Merchant's Tables.......... *A. Heywood* .. 15
—— Value.................... *W. Blackw'd.* 51
Time Books .... *Wesleyan* .. 39
—— Egypt's Record of.......... *Rivingtons* .. 26
—— Improvement of.......... *Haddon* .. 21
—— and Money Tables.......... *Wilson* 8
—— and Space.............. *Longmans* .. 17
—— Tables .... *Chambers* .. 38
Times of the Gentiles, Baylee .. *Nisbet* 5
"Times" (The) Literary Essays.. *Murray* .. 25
Titan, by Richter .... *Trubner* .. 25
Tithes, Ch. of Eng., Orig. & His. *Soc. P. C. K.* 27
Titian Portraits .... *Bell* 3
Titled People, How to Address .. *Hardwicke* .. 13
To Esther .... *Smith & El.* 23
Tobacco, History and Cultivation *Chapman* .. 14
Todd's Lectures to Children .... *MacPhun* .. 8
Todhunter (Isaac) Works....... *Macmillan* .. 36
Toilers and Spinsters.......... *Smith & El.* 23
Toiling in Rowing .... *Nisbet* 35
Told by the Waves .... *Virtue* 5
Tolerance, Roots ; a Plea for .. *Bentley* 12
Tom, History of a very Little Boy *M. Ward* 8
Tom Brown's School Days ...... *Macmillan* .. 37
Tom Cringle's Log .... *W. Blackw'd* 31
Tombs, &c., Designs .... *Hagger* 13
Tomlins (Rev. R.) Works....... *Masters* .. 27
Tomlinson's Cyclo. of Useful Arts *Virtue* 21
Tommiebeg Shootings .... *Routledge* .. 78
Tommy Try, A Book for Boys.. *Chapman* .. 23
Tommy's Marbles .... *S. S. Union* 9
Tonbridge School, History of .. *Rivingtons* .. 25
Tongue not Essential to Speech .. *Murray* .. 32
Too Strange not to be True..... *Bentley* 16
Toplady (Aug.) Whole Works of.. *Cornish* 2
Topographer and Genealogist .. *J. R. Smith* 24
Topographical Plan Drawing .. *Murray* .. 26
—— Works .... *Parker* 52
Topography, English Counties .. *Pickering* .. 37
Torn Bible (The).............. *Warne* .. 29
Torpedo Warfare .... *Spon.* 43
Torquay, its Medical Aspect .. *Churchill* .. 18
Tortoises, Terrapins & Turtles .. *Sotheran* .. 18
Tottie's Trial .... *Isbister* 41
Totty Testudo .... *Nimmo* 31
Touches of Nature .... *Isbister* 43
Tourist's Flora................ *Reeve* 4
—— French Pronouncing Hd.-Bk. *Routledge* .. 44
—— Guide Books .... *Bemrose* .. 14
—— Guide Books .... *Black* 5
—— Guide Books .... *A. Heywood* .. 4
—— Guide for Plain & Mountain *Hardwicke* .. 7
—— Handbooks, Eng. & Foreign *Murray* .. 15
—— Maps and Plans............ *A. Heywood* .. 4
—— Maps and Plans............ *Johnston* 5
Tournier's French Educatnl. Wks. *Nutt* 28
Town (The) .... *Smith & El.* 11
—— Geology .... *Isbister* 24
Toy Books.................... *Routledge* .. 73
—— Books.................... *Tract Society* 24
—— Books.................... *Walker* .. 16
—— Books.................... *Ward&Lock* 17
—— Books, Japanese & Illuminat. *M. Ward* .. 14
—— Books, Aunt Louisa ...... *Warne* 33
Tractatus De Veritate .... *Parker* 4
—— Theologico Politicus....... *Trubner* .. 27
Tract 90...................... *Parker* 5
Tracts .... *Houlston* .. 40
Tracts .... *Kellaway* .. 10
Tracts .... *Masters* .. 38
Tracts .... *Mosley* 9
Tracts .... *Wesleyan* .. 52
—— and Addresses .... *Mack* 0
—— and Addresses .... *S. S. Union.* 46
—— and Addresses .... *Yapp* 10
—— Barham and Pluckley ...... *Hatchard* .. 27
—— Blackdown .... *Morgan* 9
—— Brownlow North .... *Morgan* 9
—— Catholic .... *Burns* 7
—— for Children.............. *Rel. Tr. Soc.* 31

Tracts on Christian Doctrine .... *Mosley* 12
—— for the Christian Seasons .. *Parker* .. 36
—— Gosse's Gospel Narraive .. *Morgan* .. 18
——— Household .... *Jarrold* .. 8
—— on Health .... *Jarrold* .. 10
—— Herald of Mercy .... *Morgan* .. 10
——— Kelso .... *Nisbet* .. 7
——— Kinsale.............. *Nisbet* .. 10
—— in Large Type .... *Nisbet* .. 27
—— (" Missing Link ") in 1 Vol. *Nisbet* .. 14
—— for Parochial Use .... *Parker* .. 46
—— Rare and Curious .... *Sotheran* .. 24
Trade, Growth of .... *Virtue* .. 22
—— Marks .... *Stevens* .. 23
—— Marks, Law of .... *Bell* .. 41
—— Products, Dictionary of .... *Routledge* .. 12
—— Romance of.............. *Cassell* .. 7
—— Sullivan on .... *Stanford* .. 70
—— Unions, England & Scotland *Edmoniston* .. 11
—— Unions, Paris on .... *Smith & El.* 16
Trades, The Book of .... *Routledge* .. 9
—— Illustrations of .... *Soc. P. C. K.* 27
—— (Playing) .... *Cassell* 9
Trader's Check-Book .... *Cornish* 4
Trading, and the House in Town *Nisbet* .. 35
Tradition with Reference to Myth *Burns* .. 35
Traditions of Eden............ *Nisbet* .. 33
Training, On, Lee .... *Smith & El.* 13
—— in Theory and Practice .... *Macmillan.* .. 21
—— of the Twelve .... *Clark* .. 19
Traits of Character in Bible Story *Hodder* .. 10
Translating into French, Materials *Trubner* .. 18
Translations into Eng. and Latin *Bell* .. 35
—— for School Prizes .... *Bell* .. 9
Trap to Catch, Juv. Bks. by Author *Routledge* .. 33
—— to Catch Series .... *Lockwood* .. 47
Trapp's Commentary .... *Dickinson* .. 15
Travancore and its People ...... *Snow* .. 10
Traverse Tables .... *Allen* 4
—— Tables .... *W. Blackw'd* 28
Travel and Adventure .... *Nelson* .. 15
—— and Adventure for Boys .. *Nelson* .. 6
—— Amusements of .... *Burns* .. 3
—— Art of .... *Murray* .. 22
—— Books of .... *Bell* .. 11
—— Consolations .... *Murray* .. 9
—— Pictures of, Heine ...... *Trubner* .. 15
—— and Research in Bible Lands *Nelson* .. 5
—— Talk, Eng., Fr., Ger., Italian *Murray* .. 15
Travels in the Air .... *Bentley* .. 15
—— Illustrated .... *Cassell* 4
—— by Sea and Land .... *Soc. P. C. K.* 27
Traveller's Aid in Unciv. Regions *Hardwicke.* .. 6
—— Manual of Conversation .... *Nutt* .. 11
—— Remembrancer .... *Houlston* .. 9
—— Scientific Manual .... *Murray* .. 12
—— Tables .... *W. Blackw'd* 3
Travelling About .... *Routledge* .. 29
—— Atlas, English .... *Chapman* .. 19
—— Maps.................. *Black* .. 7
—— Sketches .... *Chapman* .. 25
Treasures of the Earth .... *Warne* .. 20
Treasury of Devotion .... *Rivingtons* .. 6
—— of Literature and Art .... *Nimmo* .. 11
Tredgold on the Steam Engine .. *Virtue* .. 21
Tree of Life (The) .... *Nisbet* .. 33
—— and Serpent Worship...... *Allen* .. 9
Trees, Chapters on .... *Cassell* 7
—— Firs and Pines .... *Hatchard* .. 6
—— Forest, Brown .... *W. Blackw'd* 43
—— Planting of .... *W. Blackw'd* 53
—— On Planting............ *Bradbury* .. 9
—— Raising and Managing.... *Edmoniston* .. 11
—— and Shrubs of the Ancients *Parker* .. 62
—— and Shrubs, Hardy ...... *Longmans* .. 25
—— and Shrubs, Loudon ...... *Warne* .. 23
—— and Shrubs, Mongredien.. *Murray* .. 23
Trench (Archbishop) Works by .. *Macmillan* .. 27
Trevithick's (R.) Life.......... *Spon.* .. 43
Trevor (Canon) Works by...... *Mosley* .. 13
Trials, Naval and Military .... *Allen* 5
Triangle (Plane) .... *Parker* .. 60
Triangles, Properties of ...... *Rivingtons* .. 5
Tricks with Cards .... *Chatto* .. 32
Tried in the Furnace.......... *Burns* .. 35

Trigonometrical Surveying ...... *Lockwood* .. 5
Trigonometry, Elementary ...... *Bell* .. 18
—— Hall ...... *Allen* .. 3
—— for Naval Students ...... *Houlston* .. 6
—— (Plane) Elementary ...... *Macmillan* .. 3
—— Snowball ...... *Macmillan* .. 33
Trimmer's Abridgmt.,O. & N.Test .*Rivingtons* .. 17
—— (Mrs.) Fabulous Histories .. *Routledge* .. 37
—— Story of the Robins ...... *Warne* .. 27
Tripartite Nature of Man ...... *Clark* .. 14
Triumphs of Invention ...... *Nelson* .. 11
Trollope (A.) Novels by ...... *Smith & El.* 25
—— Three Clerks ...... *Bentley* .. 16
—— Vicar of Bullhampton ...... *Bradbury* .. 12
—— Works by ...... *Chapman* .. 25
—— (W.) Works ...... *Hall* .. 4
Tropical Climates, Martin ...... *Churchill* .. 26
—— World (The) ...... *Longmans* .. 23
Tropics, Health in the ...... *Churchill* .. 26
Troubadors, their Loves & Lyrics *Smith & El.* 18
Trower (Bishop) Works...... *Soc. P. C. K.* 27
Troy (Plain of) Described ...... *Black* .. 14
True (The), Beautiful, and Good.. *Clark* .. 21
True to the End ...... *Shaw* .. 1
—— and False Riches ...... *Warne* .. 21
—— of Heart ...... *Isbister* .. 41
—— Hero ...... *S. S. Union.* 6
—— to Life, Stanley's...... *Macmillan* .. 34
—— Manhood, Landels ...... *Nisbet* .. 21
—— Reformer ...... *W. Blackw'd* 31
—— Riches ...... *Nelson* .. 14
—— Sanctuary (The) ...... *Morgan* .. 9
Truly Noble ...... *Cassell* .. 11
Truth, by Duc de Saldanha...... *Burns* .. 35
—— in Christ, Whitfield ...... *Nisbet* .. 37
—— and Error...... *Macmillan* .. 15
—— Guesses at...... *Macmillan* .. 14
—— and Life, Sermons...... *Hatchard* .. 13
—— without Novelty ...... *Hatchard* .. 19
—— will Out ...... *Cassell* .. 11
Truths Illustrated by Gt. Authors *Lockwood* .. 43
Try Again, &c....... *Nelson* .. 19
Tübingen School, Mackay ...... *Williams* .. 9
Tucker (H. St. G.) Life...... *Allen* .. 15
Tunnelling, Practical...... *Lockwood* .. 3
Tupper's Proverbial Philosophy.. *Routledge* .. 28
—— Proverbial Philosophy ...*Ward & Lock* 33
Turkey (Highlands of), Tozer.. *Murray* .. 31
—— Life in ...... *Chapman* .. 19
—— Ottoman Empire ...... *Rel. Tr. Soc.* 14
—— Resources and Admin. of... *Murray* .. 20
—— Three Years in ...... *Snow* .. 10
—— in Asia, Handbook to ...... *Murray* .. 16
—— in Europe, Broughton ...... *Murray* .. 5
—— in Europe, Travels in ...... *Isbister* .. 29
Turkish Bath, Wilson ...... *Churchill* .. 39
—— Cookery ...... *Allen* .. 28
—— Grammar ...... *Allen* .. 34
—— Harems ...... *Hurst & B.* 9
Turner (C. Tennyson) Poems ... *Macmillan* .. 38
Turner's England and Wales ... *Bell* .. 4
—— Landscapes ...... *Bell* .. 4
Turning, Geometric ...... *Longmans* .. 30
—— Lathe ...... *Trubner* .. 18
—— and Lathes ...... *Longmans* .. 31
—— Patterns for...... *Murray* .. 11
—— Points in Life ...... *Bentley* .. 15
Twain (Mark) Works...... *Chatto* .. 24
—— Works ...... *Routledge* .. 1
Twenty-five Years of My Life... *Bentley* .. 9
Twickenham, Memorials of..... *Smith & El.* 4
Twilight and Dawn ...... *Bell* .. 25
—— Hours ...... *Isbister* .. 47
Twin Records of Creation...... *Lockwood* .. 42
Two Brothers (The) ...... *Rivingtons* .. 26
—— Queens, History of...... *Hurst & B.* 1
Vocations (The) ...... *Nisbet* .. 35
—— Watches, &c ...... *Nisbet* .. 13
—— Years Before the Mast...... *Black* .. 10
—— Years of School Life...... *Warne* .. 27
Tyas (Rev. R.) Gift Books ...... *Houlston* .. 14
Tyborne, and Who went Thither *Burns* .. 35
Tyerman (L.) Works by ...... *Hodder* .. 14
Tylor (E. B.) Works by ...... *Murray* .. 32
Tyndale, Life of...... *Rel. Tr. Soc.* 6

Tyndall (Prof.) Works by........ *Longmans* .. 0
Types and Antitype ...... *Mozley* .. 12
Typical Selections from Eng. Aut. *Clar. Press.* 23
Typology of Scripture ...... *Clark* .. 14
Tyrol, Tales and Legends of the *Chapman* .. 4
—— War Patriots in the ...... *Burns* .. 35
Tytler (C. C.) Works by ...... *Isbister* .. 43
—— (The Misses) Works by ... *Hatchard* .. 39
—— (S.) Sisters and Wives...... *Smith & El.* 26

Ueberweg's History of Philosophy *Hodder* .. 1
Ulcers, Pathology & Treatment of. *Churchill* .. 31
—— Treatment of ...... *Churchill* .. 12
Ullathorne (Bishop) Works by ... *Burns* .. 35
Ultramontanism ...... *Hatchard* .. 31
Una; or, Early Marriage...... *Hodder* .. 24
Uncle Jack ...... *Warne* .. 21
—— John's Library ...... *Tract Soc.* 25
—— Tom's Cabin ...... *Bohn's Lib.* 10
—— Tom's Cabin ...... *Routledge* .. 33
Under His Banner ...... *Soc. P. C. K.* 25
—— Grey Walls ...... *S. S. Union .* 7
—— the Microscope ...... *Nelson* .. 19
—— the Shadow, Duncan ...... *Nisbet* .. 12
—— the Surface, Poems ...... *Nisbet* .. 17
Uniforms of H.M.,Civil Servants *Harrison* .. 3
Union Tune Book ...... *S. S. Union.* 15
Unity in Variety ...... *Isbister* .. 13
Universe (The), Pouchet ...... *Blackie* .. 12
—— and Coming Transits ...... *Longmans* .. 18
Universal Lib. of Stand. Authors. *J. Blackwood* 9
—— Simple Interest Tables ... *Wilson* .. 9
Universities and the Poor...... *Macmillan* .. 31
—— Religious Office of the ... *Macmillan* .. 41
University Enactments in Parlmnt. *Clar. Press.* 12
—— Oars ...... *Macmillan* .. 26
Unlikely Tales...... *Chatto* .. 31
Until Seventy Times Seven ... *S. S. Union* 12
Untrodden Peaks ...... *Longmans* .. 37
Uphill Work...... *Houlston* .. 29
Up in the North, Shairp ...... *Chapman* .. 15
Upliftings of the Soul to God ... *Nisbet* .. 32
Upwards and Downwards...... *Nelson* .. 13
Urinary Analysis for Students... *Smith & El.* 16
—— Diseases, Works on ...... *Churchill* .. 0
Urquhart (J.) Memoir & Remains *Nisbet* .. 35
Useful Arts, Cyclopædia of ...... *Virtue* .. 21
—— Arts, Tomlinson ...... *Soc. P. C. K.* 28
—— Handbooks ...... *Chambers* .. 23
—— Useful Knowledge, Dicty. of *Houlston* .. 3
—— Knowledge Handy Books *Nimmo* .. 27
—— Manuals ...... *Warne* .. 41
—— Plants ...... *Nelson* .. 18
—— Works ...... *J. Blackwood* 25
Utilitarian Philosophy ...... *Bell* .. 41
Utilitarianism, Mill...... *Longmans* .. 10

Valiant Women ...... *Burns* .. 35
Valley of the Nile ...... *Nelson* .. 15
Valuation of Estates, Biden...... *Layton* .. 7
Valve-Gears, Zenner ...... *Spon* .. 44
Vancouver Island ...... *Murray* .. 22
Vandeleur (Arthur) Life of ...... *Nisbet* .. 21
Van Diemen's Land, Bushranger of *King* .. 18
Van Doren's Commentary ...... *Dickinson* .. 15
Van Laun's French Ed. Course.. *Isbister* .. 37
—— Selections, French Authors. *Rivingtons* .. 18
Van Oosterzee's Christ. Dogmatics *Hodder* .. 2
—— Theology of New Testament *Hodder* .. 2
Varicose Disease, Gay ...... *Churchill* .. 17
—— Veins...... *Churchill* .. 12
Various Forces of Nature...... *Chatto* .. 14
Varty's Series of Lesson Sheets. *Stanford* .. 43
Vatican, Mysteries of...... *Allen* .. 21
Vaudois Church History ...... *Rel. Tr. Soc.* 13
—— of Piedmont ...... *Shaw* .. 1
—— The, Books of, Todd ...... *Macmillan* .. 36
Vaughan (Rev. C.) Works by... *King* .. 23
—— Works by ...... *Isbister* .. 4
—— Works by ...... *Macmillan* .. 35
—— (Rev. David J.) Works by .. *Macmillan* .. 33
—— (Jas.) Sermons ...... *Dickinson* .. 16
Vegetable Anatomy & Physiology *Collins* .. 8
—— Kingdom, Dresser ...... *Isbister* .. 13
—— Kingdom, Lindley...... *Bradbury* .. 9

Vegetable Kingdom, Rhind .... *Blackie* 12
—— Kingdom, Illustrations of .. *Chapman* .. 31
—— Narcotics .... *Macmillan* .. 15
— — Physiology .... *Bohn's Lib* .. 18
—— Physiology .... *Chambers* .. 17
—— World, Figuier (L.) .... *Cassell* 8
Veil Lifted (The)................ *Morgan* 3
Velasquez, Works of .... *Bell* 4
Venice, Architecture of, Ruskin .. *Smith & El.* 18
—— Past and Present .... *Nelson* 11
—— Stones of, Ruskin .... *Smith & El.* 18
—— Stories of .... *Isbister* 31
Venus, Transit of .... *Longmans* .. 18
—— and Psyche................. *W. Blackw'd.* 7
Ventilation, Burn (R. S.) .... *W. Blackw'd.* 49
—— Hood .... *Whittaker* .. 16
—— of Buildings............... *Spon* 44
Vera, Essays by Author of,' ...... *Smith & El.* 7
Vere Foster's Writing Copy Books *M. Ward* .. 20
—— Foster's Course, Water Colour *M. Ward* .. 1
Verena .... *J. F. Shaw* .. 1
Verney (Lady) Novels by........ *Smith & El.* 36
Vernon Gallery .... *Virtue* 11
Vers de Société .... *Chatto* 38
Verses for Sundays & Holidays .. *Masters* .. 28
Very Young Couple .... *M. Ward* .. 10
Vespers Book for the Laity ...... *Burns* 35
Vessels and Voyages .... *J. Blackwood* 23
Vestiges of Nat. History Creation *Churchill* .. 36
Vesuvius, Mount .... *Clar. Press.* 18
—— in 1872 .... *Asher* 5
—— Mount, a Descriptive Account *Stanford* 58
Veterinary Art, by Blaine........ *Houlston.* .. 7
—— Medicine, Dick .... *Black* 11
—— Medicine, Dun .... *Edmonston.* .. 7
—— Medicine, Works on .... *Churchill* .. 0
—— Pharmacopœia .... *Churchill* .. 36
—— Tablet .... *Philip* 43
Vicar of Wakefield .... *Cassell* 8
—— of Wakefield .... *Nimmo* 19
—— of Wakefield .... *Warne* 21
Vicarious Sacrifice (The) .... *Isbister* 9
Vicars (Hedley), Life of .... *Nisbet* 26
Victoria, its Principal Cities...... *Smith & El.* 22
—— the British Eldorado .... *Stanford* .. 70
—— Glimpses in .... *Edmonston.* .. 10
—— Life and Homes in.......... *Isbister* 7
—— Educational Series......... *Warne* 37
—— Gift Books .... *Warne* 19
—— Tales .... *Warne* 36
—— & Her Contemporary Sovgns. *Masters* .. 28
Victories and Defeats........... *King* 12
Victory and Service .... *Tubb* 4
—— of the Spirit .... *Masters* 1
—— of the Vanquished.......... *Nelson* 7
—— Won (The) .... *Nisbet* 26
Vidal (Mrs.) Tales by .... *Masters* .. 28
Viga Glums Saga .... *Williams* .. 15
Vignettes in Rhyme .... *King* 21
Villa Architecture, Wickes ..... *Lockwood* .. 7
Villas and Cottages, Young...... *Spon* 13
—— &c., Designs .... *Hagger* 14
Village Communities, East &West *Murray* .. 21
—— Dialogues, Crowdy .... *Nisbet* 10
—— Observer (The) .... *Nisbet* 25
—— on the Cliff .... *Smith & El.* 23
—— Sketches .... *Routledge* .. 36
Villager's (Christian) Guide Book *Nisbet* 10
Villette .... *Smith & El.* 2
Villiers (Bishop) Works by ...... *Nisbet* 35
Viol (On) and Flute, Poems...... *King* 21
Vinci (Leonardo da) & his Works *Macmillan* .. 20
Vine Culture under Glass........ *Houlston.* .. 13
Vinegar Hill, by A. Golden Ladder *Nisbet* 36
—— Manufacture of .... *Trubner* .. 31
Vinet (Alex.) Works by......... *Isbister* .. 46
Vinet's Studies on Pascal .... *Clark* 11
Virgil's Works, Trans. Globe Ed. *Macmillan.* .. 13
—— Conington .... *Whittaker* .. 2
—— Ravensworth .... *W. Blackw'd* 32
Virgin's Lamp .... *Rivingtons..* 8
Vital Causes, Treatise on .... *Churchill* .. 19
— — Statistics, Neison .... *Layton.* 13
Vitis Mystica .... *Washbourne* 5
Vivid, A Story................. *Warne.* 19

Vlieland's Fr., It. & Ger. Sch. Bks. *Yarrold* 19
Vocabularies, A Volume of ...... *Trubner* 32
Voice, Speaking .... *Clar. Press.* 30
—— of Christian Life in Song.... *Nelson* 7
—— of Christian Life in Song ... *Nisbet* 36
—— of Church on the Coming, &c. *Kellaway* .. 8
—— of Jubilee................. *Snow* 16
Voices of Comfort .... *Rivingtons..* 7
—— of Many Waters............ *Snow* 1
—— from the Willow and Palm .. *Isbister* .. 46
—— of Nature, Cheever .... *Collins* 3
—— of the Soul Answered in God *Nisbet* 31
—— from the Valley .... *Nisbet* 37
Volcanoes (Extinct) of France.... *Murray* 27
—— Lobley .... *Stanford...* 58
—— Palmieri .... *Asher* 5
—— and Earthquakes .... *Blackie* .. 18
— — Vesuvius .... *Clar. Press..* 18
Voltaire, by Morley .... *Chapman* .. 7
Voltaire's Charles XII.......... *Williams* .. 15
—— Pierre le Grand .... *Williams* .. 15
Volunteer's Field Pocket Book .. *Macmillan* .. 41
Voyage of H.M.S. Curaçoa ..... *Longmans* .. 37
—— of H.M.S. Galatea .... *Allen* 5
—— of H.M.S. Herald .... *Sotheran* .. 28
—— and Venture.............. *Routledge* .. 34
Voyages, Famous .... *Ward* 12
—— and Travels............... *J. Blackwood* 4
Vovsey Judgment, Sermons on .. *King.* 30
Vulgar Tongue, Dictionary of.... *Chatto* .. 17

Wadsworth's Sermons .... *Dickinson* .. 16
Wages Calculator, Cameron .... *MacPhun* .. 18
— — Tables .... *Spon.* 45
Wagner (Rev. Geo.) Works by .. *Nisbet* .. 36
—— and the Music of the Future. *Chapman* .. 4
Waiting Hours................. *Morgan* 3
Waldenses, Sufferings of ...... *Nisbet* 24
Wales, Giraldus Cambrensis .... *Bohn's Lib.* 12
—— Guide to .... *Black* 7
—— Handbooks to .... *Murray* .. 16
—— History of .... *Virtue* 21
—— (North), Geology of .... *Stanford* .. 67
—— Picturesque Scenery .... *Allman* .. 12
—— Rocks of, Symonds .... *Murray* .. 31
—— Subjects Relating to .... *Snow* 13
—— Tourist's Companion to .... *Philip* 4
—— (Wild). Its People, &c..... *Murray* 5
Walford's Works on Insurance .. *Layton* .. 16
Walk in the Light .... *Morgan* 3
Walks from Eden .... *Nisbet* .. 36
Walker (E.) Works by .... *Nisbet* .. 36
—— (S. A.) Tracts .... *Mack* 6
Walking, Swimming, and Flying *King* 8
Wallace (Alf. R.) Works by .... *Macmillan.* .. 39
—— the Hero of Scotland....... *Nimmo* .. 14
Walter at the Seaside.......... *Nelson* .. 18
Walter's Escape .... *Warne* 27
Waltham .... *Parker.* 53
Walton's Lives................ *Clar. Press.* 12
—— Lives.................... *Soc. P. C. K.* 38
—— Lives, Pocket Edition ..... *Bell* 32
Wandering Homes, &c. .... *Nisbet* .. 36
—— Jew, Legend of .... *Cassell* 3
—— Willie .... *Macmillan* .. 49
Wanderings over Bible Lands ... *Nelson* 5
—— of a Naturalist .... *Edmonston..* 1
—— in Scripture Lands .... *Dickinson* .. 10
War .... *Ward&Lock* 23
—— of 1870-71 .... *Bumpus* .... a
—— Art of, Jomini .... *Trubner* .. 17
— —(On), Clausewitz .... *Trubner* .. 7
—— Franco-German .... *Hagger* .. 10
—— Game, Rules for the ...... *Harrison* .. 12
—— Laws of, Commerce, Shipping *Smith & El.* 25
—— Modern, Roberts .... *Chapman* .. 24
— —— Office List .... *Harrison* .. 3
—— Operations of .... *Allen* 20
—— Weapons of, Demmin ...... *Bell* 12
Wars, Annals of, 18th & 19th Cent. *Murray* 14
Wars of the Roses .... *Warne* .. 27
Warburton (Eliot) Works by ... *Hurst* 13
Warfare (Modern), Macdougall *Murray* 21
Warming and Ventilation.. ..... *Whittaker* .. 16
Warnings and Consolations ..... *Mozley* 13

Warnings of the Holy Week .... *Rivingtons* .. 13
Warp and Woof .... *Smith & El.* 13
Warrant of Faith .... *Bagster* 61
Warren (J. L.) Poetry by........ *Isbister* 46
Warren (S.) Works.............. *W. Blackw'd.* 32
Warriors of 17th Century .... *J. Murray* .. 9
Warrior Judges, Macduff........ *Nisbet* 23
—— Priest and Statesman ..... *Nimmo* 12
Warton's English Poetry .... *Reeve* ...... a
Washed Ashore .... *Warne*...... 28
Washing Book .... *Ward & Lock* 8
Washington (G.) Story of........ *Cassell* 11
Waste Not, Want Not .... *Partridge* .. 5
Waste Products, &c. .... *Hardwicke* .. 11
Watching Servants of Christ .... *Bemrose* 4
Watchwork (Coutts' Prize Essay) .*Spon* 6
—— Nelthropp .... *Spon* 45
Water, Analysis of .... *Trubner* 31
—— Babies (The) .... *Macmillan* .. 18
—— (Forms of) in Rain and Rivers *King* 8
—— Impurities of .... *Hardwicke* .. 16
—— Supply of Towns, Humber . *Lockwood* .. 1
—— Wonders of .... *Cassell* 8
Watering Places, Guide to English *Black* 7
Waterland's Works.............. *Clar. Press* .. 14
Waterloo .... *Ward & Lock* 23
—— Battle of .... *MacPhun* .. 19
—— Lectures, Chesney .... *Longmans* .. 3
—— Mercer .... *W. Blackw'd.* 21
—— (from) to the Peninsular .. *Tinsley Bros.* 7
—— Political & Military History .. *Trubner* .. 17
—— Simpson .... *W. Blackw'd.* 28
—— Story of .... *Murray* 13
Waters (A. T. H.) Medical Wks. by *Churchill* .. 38
Waterworks for Towns.......... *Lockwood* .. 4
Waterworth (Rev. W.) Works .. *Burns* 36
Watson (Rev. A.) Works by .... *Masters* 29
—— (Rev. R.) Works.......... *Wesleyan* .. 22
Watson's Apology for the Bible .. *Soc. P. C. K.* 28
—— Comic & Serious Scots Poems *Sotheran* 28
Watts's Divine and Moral Songs.. *Haddon* 4
—— Improvement of the Mind .. *Nimmo* 15
—— Songs.................... *Partridge* .. 11
—— Songs and Catechisms ...... *Mozley* 13
—— Songs, Illust. .... *Routledge* .. 28
Waugh (Edwin) Works by ...... *A. Heywood.* 6
Wave and the Battle Field ...... *Isbister* 41
—— upon Wave .... *S. S. Union.* 5
Waverley Manual (The) .... *Black* 10
—— Novels .... *Black* 17
—— Stories from.............. *Black* 32
Way of Faith (The) .... *Bagster* 68
—— Home (The) .... *Isbister* 9
—— Home (The) .... *Nisbet* 4
—— of Life .... *Rivingtons* .. 32
—— the Lord hath Led Me .... *Yapp* 1
Wayside Service .... *Morgan* 3
Weale's Rudimentary Series .... *Lockwood* .. 18
Wealth of Nations .... *Black* 31
—— and Welfare.............. *Isbister* 17
Wearyfoot Common .... *Warne*...... 27
Weather Folk Lore .... *W. Blackw'd* 30
—— Glass .... *Bemrose* 17
—— Method of Mapping ...... *Macmillan* .. 12
Weathercasts, Manual of ...... *Routledge* .. 67
Webb (Caleb) Works .... *Houlston.* .. 39
—— (Mrs.) Works by .... *Hatchard* .. 31
Webster (Augusta) Works by .... *Macmillan* .. 49
Webster's Dictionaries .... *Bell* 23
Wedding Gift .... *Morgan* 3
—— Gift (The) .... *Masters* 11
—— Prayers (The) .... *Nisbet* 11
Wedgwood (Catalogue of) Manuf. *Bell* 6
—— and his Works............ *Bell* 3
—— (H.) Works by .... *Trubner* 31
Weights and Money (Ancient) .. *Parker* 64
Weitbrecht (Rev. J. J.) Memoir .. *Nisbet* 36
Well is Deep (The) .... *Nisbet* 37
Well-Timed Series .... *Ward* 27
Wells, Architectural Antiquities *Parker*...... 53
—— Cathedral Church .... *Macmillan*.. 11
—— of Salvation .... *Yapp* 3
Wellington (Duke) Character, &c. *Murray* 22
—— Despatches .... *Murray* 32
—— Life .... *Routledge* .. 5

Wellington, Life of .... *J. Blackwood* 4
—— Life, Gleig .... *Longmans* .. 8
—— in India................ *Allen* 28
—— Military Life .... *Allen* 31
—— Victories of .... *Bohn's Lib.* .. 14
Wellington Coll. French Primer. *Nutt.*...... 24
Welsh Calvinistic Methodism .. *Nisbet* 37
—— Hymn and Tune Books .. *Haddon* 5
—— S. S. Lesson Books ...... *S. S. Union* .. 35
Wensderholme .... *W. Blackw'd* 11
Wentworth (Earl Stafford) Life . *Tinsley Bros.* 2
Wesley, Fireside Convrns. about *Tubbs* 5
—— (John) by Julia Wedgwood *Macmillan* .. 40
Wesley's Hymns.............. *Wesleyan* .. 37
—— Hymns, Companion to..... *Wesleyan* .. 10
—— Life .... *Wesleyan* .. 51
—— Life, by Southey .... *Bohn's Lib.*.. 9
—— Life and Times .... *Hodder* 14
—— Place in Church History .. *Rivingtons*.. 26
—— Works .... *Wesleyan* .. 23
Wesleys, Anecdotes of .... *Hodder* 14
—— (Mother of the) .... *Jarrold* 9
Wesleyan Hymnology .... *Snow* 3
—— Methodist Tune Books..... *Wesleyan* .. 39
—— Preacher's Manual........ *Wesleyan* .. 49
West Indian Life, Story of .... *King* 32
West Indies, Christmas in ...... *Macmillan* .. 18
—— Residence in .... *Murray* 30
West (J. R.) Works by .... *Masters* 29
Westbourne Grove Sermons. .... *Marlborough* 11
Westbury (Lord) on Arbitration.. *Stevens*.... 12
Westcott (Dr.) Works by ...... *Macmillan* .. 40
Western World Revisited ...... *Parker*...... 13
Westminster Abbey, Gleanings fr. *Parker*...... 52
—— Abbey, Stanley .... *Murray* 28
—— Confession of Faith ...... *Blackie*..... 24
—— Confession of Faith ...... *Williams* ... 7
—— Plays .... *Macmillan* .. 40
Westward Ho! Kingsley........ *Macmillan* .. 15
Weymouth, Geology of .... *Stanford*.... 53
Whaler, Life in a .... *Ward* 27
What Katy Did .... *Warne*...... 25
—— to Observe .... *Houlston*.... 9
—— Shall I Be? .... *Nelson*..... 14
—— She Could, and Opportunities *Nisbet* 37
—— is Truth? .... *Hodder* 31
Whately (Archbishop) Works by *Longmans* .. 0
Wheatly on Common Prayer .... *Cambridge* .. 6
Whedon's Commentary New Test. *Hodder* 7
Wheel of the Law .... *Trubner* 31
Wheels, Teeth of .... *Spon* 43
Wheeler (J. T.) Scripture Hists. *Isbister* 42
When I was a Little Girl ...... *Macmillan*.. 43
—— I was Young .... *Isbister* 9
Where Shall We Go?.......... *Black* 7
—— there's a Will there's a Way *Hardwicke*.. 7
Where's the Harm .... *Bumpus* 2
Whims and Oddities .... *Chatto* 29
Whisper to a Newly Married Pair *Houlston*.... 29
Whispers in the Palms .... *Morgan* 2
Whist, Cavendish's Law of ...... *De La Rue*.. 1
—— Game of .... *Longmans* .. 44
—— Player, Blyth .... *Chapman* .. 12
—— (Short) Laws of .... *Harrison* ... 5
—— Studies, A.C. and B.D. .... *Smith & El.* 27
White (J.) 18 Christian Centuries *W. Blackw'd* 47
—— (Geo.) Works .... *Houlston*.... 48
—— (Walter) Books of Travel.. *Chapman* .. 26
—— Doe of Rylstone .... *Bell* 29
—— Rose and Red .... *Isbister* 47
Whitefield, Anecdotes of ...... *Hodder* 14
—— (George) Life of........ *Morgan* 2
Whitfield (Rev. F.) Works by .. *Nisbet* 37
Whittier's Complete Poetical Wks. *Macmillan* .. 41
Whittington (The Story of).... *Isbister*..... 2
Whole Duty of Man .... *Soc. P. C. K.* 29
Wholesome Fare.............. *Lockwood* .. 48
—— Words of Jesus Christ .... *Macmillan* .. 19
Wickets in the West .... *Tinsley Bros.* 7
Wide, Wide World .... *Bohn's Lib.*.. 10
—— Wide World .... *Nisbet* 37
—— Wide World, Coloured.... *Routledge* .. 32
—— Wide World Library ...... *Milner*...... 5
Widow of East Anglia .... *Morgan* 2
—— Green and her Three Nieces *Partridge*... 5

Widow's Portion (The).......... *Nisbet* 37
Wife's (The) Trials .... *Isbister* 48
Wightman (Mrs. C.) Works by .. *Nisbet* 37
Wigtown Martyrs .... *Edmonston*.. 16
Wilberforce's (Bp.) Essays ..... *Murray* 32
—— Sermons before the Queen .. *Hatchard* .. 31
—— (Rev. R. J.) Works by...... *Mozley*..... 13
Wild Flowers, Pratt .... *Soc. P. C. K.* 29
—— Garden, Robinson .... *Murray* 27
—— Men and Wild Beasts ...... *Edmonston*.. 5
—— Sports in Zulu Land ...... *Warne*...... 24
—— Times .... *Burns* 22
Wilford (Florence) Works by .... *Masters* 29
Wilkes, Sheridan, Fox .... *Isbister* 37
Wilkie Gallery................. *Virtue* 11
Wilkinson's Analysis of Butler .. *Parker* 4
William the Conqueror .... *Tinsley Bros.* 2
—— Henry's School Days ...... *Warne* 29
—— with the Ring... .... *Tinsley Bros.* 5
Williams (Rev. Isaac) The Altar *Masters* 29
—— (Isaac) Poetical Works .... *Parker* 27
—— (Isaac) Works by .... *Rivingtons* .. 9
—— (Rowland) Works by........ *Bell* 61
—— (Rowland) Works by .... *Williams* 15
Willie Herbert .... *Warne* 30
Willie's Home Exercises ...... *J. Heywood*.. 25
Willich's Popular Tables .... *Longmans* .. 45
Willing to be Useful .... *Nelson* 13
Willis the Pilot .... *Warne*...... 28
Willow Brook .... *Nisbet* 37
Wilson (Bishop) on Lord's Supper *Soc. P. C. K.* 29
—— Lord's Supper.............. *Rivingtons*.. 9
—— "Christopher North," Mem. *Edmonston*.. 10
—— (George) Works by .... *Macmillan*.. 41
—— (Horace H.) Works by...... *Trubner* 32
—— (Prof.) Works .... *W. Blackw'd* 33
—— (Erasmus) Works by........ *Churchill* ... 39
Wilson's Glossary of Judicial Terms *Allen* 34
—— Legal Handy-Books........ *Wilson*..... 3
—— Tales of the Borders....... *Nimmo* 30
Winchester College, School Life at *Chatto* 31
—— Archaeological Inst. at ...... *Parker*...... 53
Wind, Laws of the, West Europe *Stanford* .. 58
Windings of the River, &c. .... *Collins*..... 3
Windwafted Seed .... *Isbister* 47
Wine Cellar Book .... *Letts* 1
—— Chemistry of .... *Churchill* .. 27
—— Defence of its Use.......... *Wilson*..... 11
—— Origin, Nature & Varieties.. *Macmillan* .. 36
—— Practical Notes on .... *Smith & El.* 8
—— Ancient and Modern....... *Bohn's Lib.* .. 15
Wines, Home Made .... *Groombridge* 18
Wingate (D.) Poems .... *W. Blackw'd.* 34
Wings and Stings .... *Nelson* 9
Winifred Bertram .... *Nelson* 7
Winter Cough, Dobell .... *Churchill* .. 15
—— Evenings .... *Isbister* 19
Winslow (Rev. Octavius) Works *Nisbet* 38
—— (O.) Works .... *Shaw* 6
Wisdom, Wit, and Allegory..... *Nimmo* 14
Wise Counsels, Binney .... *Houlston*... 17
—— Men (The), Upham .... *Hodder* 2
Wit, Doran's Table Traits ...... *Bentley* 2
—— and Humour .... *Lockwood* .. 45
—— and Humour .... *Smith & El.* 11
—— and Humour, World of...... *Cassell*..... 8
—— and Mirth................. *Chatto* 13
—— and Wisdom from W. Africa *Tinsley Bros.* 6
Wits' Recreations .... *Chatto* 26
Wits and Beaux of Society ..... *Routledge* .. 4
—— and Humourists, Lives of .. *Bentley* 2
Without and Within .... *Nisbet* 38
Witness of History to Christ..... *Macmillan*.. 10
Wittich's German Ed. Works ... *Nutt*........ 21
Wives and Daughters .... *Smith & El.* 8
Wolf's Life of Wild Animals ... *Macmillan* .. 41
Wolseley (Sir Garnet) Works by *Macmillan* .. 41
Woman, Mental and Moral .... *Snow* 12
—— Noble Deeds of .... *Bell* 25
—— her Position and Power .... *Cassell* 8
—— (A) Sold, and other Poems .. *Macmillan*.. 40
—— and the Times we Live in .. *Tubbs* 5
—— What Men have said about *Routledge* .. 43
—— in White .... *Smith & El.* 4
Womankind in West Europe .... *Sotheran* .. 28

Woman's Friendship .... *Groombridge.* 3
—— Sphere and Work .... *Nisbet* 21
—— Work in the Church .... *Isbister* 26
—— Work, Essays on .... *Isbister*..... 23
Women, Biographies of Good .... *Mozley*..... 1
—— Book of Fair .... *Cassell*...... 3
—— Change of Life in .... *Churchill* .. 36
—— Characteristics of .... *Routledge* .. 41
—— Celebrated .... *Routledge* .. 5
—— Celebrated .... *Ward* 27
—— An Epic of .... *Chatto* 26
—— Essays on .... *Routledge* .. 41
—— Essay in Defence .... *Tinsley Bros.* 9
—— Extraordinary.............. *Routledge* .. 4
—— Higher Education of........ *Isbister* 12
—— of History .... *Nimmo* 15
—— Illustrious .... *J. Blackwood* 9
—— of Last Days of Old France *Warne*...... 10
—— Memorable .... *J. Blackwood* 15
—— Political .... *King*........ 1
—— of Scripture............... *Houlston*... 20
—— of Scripture .... *Shaw* 3
—— Studious .... *Isbister* 13
—— Subjection of .... *Longmans* .. 10
—— Tales of Celebrated .... *Burns* 35
—— Works on Diseases of ...... *Churchill* .. 9
Won at Last .... *Wesleyan* .. 50
Wonder Seeker .... *W. Blackw'd* 31
Wonderful Characters.......... *Chatto* 31
—— Escapes.................. *Cassell*..... 6
Wonderful Things, 10,000...... *Routledge* .. 72
—— Things of all Nations ...... *Houlston*... 6
Wonders, World of .... *Cassell*..... 8
—— of the Deep............... *J. Blackwood* 16
Wood (Mrs. H.) Orville Coll Boys *Routledge* .. 31
—— Novels .... *Bentley* 15
—— (J. G.) Juvenile Books by .. *Routledge* .. 33
—— Works on Natural History .. *Longmans* .. 9
—— Index Entomologicus ...... *Sotheran*.... 28
—— Index Testaceologicus ..... *Sotheran*.... 28
Wood-Cart (The), and other Tales *Mozley*..... 13
Wood Carving .... *Bemrose* 10
—— Carving.................. *Lockwood*.. 13
—— Carving, Rogers........... *Virtue* 21
Woodcuts from Fairy Hazel Bush *Hatchard* .. 7
Wood Engraving.............. *J. R. Smith* 7
—— Working Machines .... *Spon*....... 48
Wooden Walls of Old England .. *Hatchard* .. 30
Woodford's (Bishop) Sermons.. *Masters* 30
Woodleigh Stories .... *Warne* 25
Woodrooffe (Mrs.) Works by .... *Bell* 25
Woodward's History of Wales... *Virtue* 21
Woollen and Worsted Manufacture *Smith & El.* 3
Worboise (E. J.) Juvenile Books *Marlborough* 3
—— Works by .... *Isbister* 47
Worcester, Ancient............ *Parker*...... 53
Worcestershire................ *J. R. Smith* 2
Word Formation, Morris .... *Macmillan* .. 26
Word of God (The), Villiers..... *Nisbet* 35
Word of Life (The)............. *Nisbet* 8
Word Series (The) .... *Nisbet* 39
Word-Sketches in Sweet South .. *Bentley* 15
Word to My Wife .... *Wilson*..... 4
—— of Cheer .... *Nelson*..... 14
Words of the Angels .... *Isbister* 41
—— of Comfort to Parents .... *Nisbet* 22
—— (Difficult) Lexicon of...... *Routledge* .. 13
—— of Hearty Friendship ...... *Nisbet* 26
—— of Peace, Oxenden........ *Hatchard* .. 19
—— and Phrases, Roget .... *Longmans* .. 11
—— and Places .... *Macmillan* .. 35
—— Reduplicated English ...... *Asher* 8
—— on the Study of, Trench .... *Macmillan* .. 37
—— to Take with Us.......... *Rivingtons* .. 8
—— and Their Uses .... *Chatto* 17
—— of Wisdom .... *Murray* 32
—— for the Wise............. *Nelson* 14
Wordsworth (Bp.) Works by .... *Rivingtons*.. 0
Wordsworth's (Wm.) Life....... *Routledge* .. 5
—— Poems, Illustrated......... *Routledge* .. 27
—— Poetical Works .... *Warne* 8
Work Among the Lost .... *Hatchard* .. 32
—— and Play .... *Mozley*..... 13
—— and Play, Hours of........ *Williams*.... 4
—— Position of British Labourer *Macmillan* .. 11

Work and Wages, Brassey ...... *Bell* 41
Worker's A.B.C. About .... *Isbister* ... 3
Working Class, Agricultural ...... *Chapman* .. 14
—— Claims & Interests of ...... *Chapman* 25
Working Classes, Habits, &c. .... *Tinsley Bros.* 9
—— Progress of .... *Isbister*..... 27
Working (Learning and) .... *Macmillan*.. 25
—— People, Better Days for .... *Isbister* 7
—— Simple Truth Spoken to .. *Isbister* 29
—— Man and the Franchise .... *Isbister* 31
—— Men, Lectures to, Mursell .. *Tubbs* 5
—— to Win .... *Cassell* 11
Workmanship (Art)............... *Asher* 1
Workshop (The) .... *Hogger* 12
—— Amateur Mechanics .... *Trubner* 2
—— Appliances .... *Longmans* ... 21
—— Heroes of the .... *Routledge* 5
—— Receipts .... *Spon* 46
World, All Round the, Doré's Ill. *Collins* 2
—— All Round, Simpson ...... *Longmans* ... 37
—— Boy's Voyage Round the.... *Murray* 27
—— before the Deluge ...... *Cassell* 8
—— Dissertation on the Age of .. *Smith & El.* 26
—— Great Wonders of the ...... *Routledge* .. 35
—— at Home .... *Nelson* 2
—— of Ice .... *Nelson* 6
—— we Live in .... *Allen* 3
—— (Our), its Cities, &c........ *Jarrold* 12
—— Peoples of the .... *Cassell* 11
—— Religions of the .... *Macmillan*.. 25
—— Round the, 1870, Carlisle .. *King*....... 5
—— Round the, Darwin ...... *Murray* 9
—— Round the, Tyerman ...... *Snow* 16
—— of the Sea................ *Cassell* 8
—— Seven Wonders of .... *Routledge* .. 34
—— Tour Round the............ *Routledge* .. 79
—— Travels Round the .... *Hatchard* .. 5
—— (Use and Abuse), Sermons .. *Soc. P. C. K.* 30
—— Voyage Round of Galatea .. *Allen* 5
—— of Wit and Humour .... *Cassell*..... 6
—— of Wonders .... *Cassell* 8
—— Wonders of .... *Ward* 27
World's Birthday.............. *Nelson* 12
—— Explorers .... *Ward & Lock* 8
—— (The) Pictures............ *Bell* 9
Wormell's Mathematical Works .. *Marby* 6
Worms, Cobbold's Lectures on .. *Churchill* .. 13
Wornum (R. N.) Works........ *Chapman* .. 26
Worship of God & Fellowship, &c. *Macmillan*.. 42
—— (Public)................ *Parker*...... 40
—— from the Word .... *MacPhun* .. 13
—— Plain Help to Public........ *Mozley*...... 9
Worthies, Book of .... *Macmillan*.. 14
Wright (H. E.) Works .... *Hatchard* .. 32
—— (Ned) Story of Life ...... *Hodder* 13
—— (Thos.) Works............ *J. R. Smith* 25
Wrinkles .... *Chatto* 17
Writing-Desk, Guide to the...... *Hardwicke*.. 13
Written Word (The), Green...... *S. S. Union.* 43
Wuthering Heights............ *Smith & El.* 2
Wyclif's Works................. *Clar. Press.* 14
Wynford Grange .... *J. Blackwood* 23

Xavier's Life, by Coleridge...... *Burns* 14

Yachts and Yacht Building ...... *Spon*........ 48
Yankee Drolleries .... *Chatto* 40

Yarkand and Kashgar .... *Murray* 27
Year 1800 .... *Stanford*.... 66
—— Book of Facts, Science & Art *Lockwood* ... 13
—— (A) with the Everards ...... *Nisbet* 9
Yeast, Kingsley .... *Macmillan* .. 18
Yelverton's 50,000 Miles ...... *Bentley* 14
Yesterday, To-day, and For Ever *Rivingtons*.. 26
Yonge (C. M.) Key Notes, &c. .. *Soc. P. C. K.* 14
—— Stories, English History .. *M. Ward* .. 2
—— Works .... *Macmillan*.. 44
—— Works .... *Mozley*...... 13
—— Henrietta's Wish .... *Masters* 11
Yonge (Professor) Works........ *Bentley* 15
—— (Prof.) Works by .. .. *Longmans* .. 0
York, Memoirs of .... *Parker*...... 53
Yorke (J. C.) Works by ...... *Hatchard* .. 32
Yorkshire Cattle Doctor ...... *Walker* 5
—— Congregat. Churches ...... *Snow* 17
—— Dialect, Specimen........ *A. Heywood.* 10
—— Ditties .... *Nicholson* 4
—— Geology of .... *Murray* 25
—— Home Scenes in............ *Marlborough* 16
—— Month in .... *Chapman* .. 26
—— Rivers, Climate, Scenery .. *Murray* 25
—— Roman Catholics in .. .. *Chatto* 31
—— Tales of, North Riding .... *Smith & El.* 22
—— Works on .... *J. R. Smith* 26
Young (C. M.), Tragedian ...... *Macmillan*.. 43
—— (John, LL.D.) Works by .... *Isbister* 48
Young Fur Traders.............. *Nelson*...... 6
—— Housekeeper's Pocket Guide *MacPhun* .. 15
—— Lady's Book of Amusement.. *Nicholson* .. 11
—— Life Equipping Itself, &c. .. *King* 29
—— Man Setting Out in Life .. *Hodder* 28
—— Man's Companion .... *Virtue* 20
—— Marooners (The) .... *Routledge* .. 33
—— Men, A Book for .... *Isbister* 43
—— Men, Lessons for .... *Hodder* 28
—— Men, Saving Knowledge .. *Isbister* 39
—— Men's Christ. Asso. Lectures *Nisbet* 13
—— Men's Class in Sun. Schools *S. S. Union* 45
—— Pilgrim .... *Nelson* 9
—— Prince Marigold.......... *Macmillan*.. 23
—— Squire .... *Warne* 20
—— Troublesome .... *Bradbury* .. 2
—— Woman's Companion ...... *Virtue* 20
Youth's Companion and Counsellor *Chambers* .. 28
Yule-Tide Stories .... *Bohn's Lib.* 17
Yu-Pe-Ya's Lute .... *Macmillan*.. 40

Zanzibar, by Captain Burton .... *Tinsley Bros.* 6
Zenobia, Queen of Palmyra...... *Warne* 20
Zoological Diagrams .... *Chapman* .. 31
—— Gardens, Visit to .... *Routledge* .. 35
—— Mythology .... *Trubner* 14
—— Recreations .... *Ward & Lock* 8
—— Works .... *Mullan* .... a
Zoology .... *Chambers* .. 17
—— Carpenter.............. *Bohn's Lib.* 18
—— Nicholson .... *W. Blackw'd* 44
—— for Schools .... *Black* 32
—— for Students, Lancaster .. *Collins* 8
—— of Voyage of H.M.S. Herald *Sotheran* 28
Zoophytes, British .... *Routledge* .. 48
Zulus, Nursery Tales, &c., of.... *Trubner* 7
Zululand, Wild Sports, &c...... *Warne* 28
Zwingle, Life of .... *Clark* 21

www.ingramcontent.com/pod-product-compliance
Lightning Source LLC
Chambersburg PA
CBHW031443270326

41930CB00007B/847